EL MUNDO ZURDO 3

SELECTED WORKS FROM THE 2012 MEETING OF THE SOCIETY FOR THE STUDY OF GLORIA ANZALDÚA

EDITED BY
LARISSA M. MERCADO-LÓPEZ,
SONIA SALDÍVAR-HULL,
AND ANTONIA CASTAÑEDA

aunt lute books

San Francisco

Aunt Lute Books
P.O. Box 410687
San Francisco, CA 94141
www.auntlute.com

Cover design: Amy Woloszyn, Amymade Graphic Design
Cover art: © 2012 "Liminal Incubation" by Adriana M. García
Text design: Amy Woloszyn, Amymade Graphic Design
Senior Editor: Joan Pinkvoss
Managing Editor: Shay Brawn
Production: Laura Chin, Learkana Chong, Ellen French, Lisa Hastings, Taylor Hodges, Kara Owens, Erin Peterson, Allison Power

Library of Congress Cataloging-in-Publication Data
El Mundo Zurdo 3 : Selected Works from the 2012 Meeting of the Society for the Study of Gloria Anzaldúa / edited by Larissa Mercado-López, Sonia Saldivar-Hull, and Antonia Castañeda.
pages cm
ISBN 978-1-879960-89-3 (acid-free paper)
1. Anzaldúa, Gloria--Criticism and interpretation. 2. Mexican Americans in literature. I. Mercado-López, Larissa, editor of compilation. II. Saldívar-Hull, Sonia, 1951- editor of compilation. III. Castañeda, Antonia, editor of compilation.
PS3551.N95Z794 2013
818'.5409--dc23
2013038532

Printed in the U.S.A. on acid-free paper

10 9 8 7 6 5 4 3 2 1

CONTENTS

ANZALDÚAN THEORY AND PHILOSOPHY ACROSS TIME, SPACE, AND THE ACADEMY

INNER WORK, CREATIVE EXPRESSIONS

INTRODUCTION

"CHANGE IS INEVITABLE, NO BRIDGE LASTS FOREVER": CONOCIMIENTO AS AN EPISTEMOLOGY OF TRANSFORMATION

LARISSA M. MERCADO-LÓPEZ

The theme for El Mundo Zurdo 2012, "Transformations," was proposed in the summer of 2011, in anticipation of the Mayan prediction of a global transformation that was expected to occur as the Mayan calendar cycle came to a close that following December. While apocalypse watchers searched for signs of a cataclysmic event, others looked forward to a global change of consciousness and spiritual renewal—the possibility of a world that would more closely resemble Gloria Anzaldúa's vision of "el Mundo Zurdo."[1] The organizing committee, hoping to draw papers that documented the transformative effects of Anzaldúan theory within academia, social movements, and creative expression, agreed that "Transformations" would effectively bring together a cadre of artists, scholars, and community activists whose works were invested in the project of realizing el Mundo Zurdo and fostering conocimiento in their respective classrooms and communities. While the ongoing political debates surrounding immigration and ethnic studies reminded those of us in the areas of Chicana/o and Latina/o

1 For a tracing of el Mundo Zurdo in Anzaldúa's work, see Sonia Saldívar-Hull's introduction to *El Mundo Zurdo 2*, "Before Borderlands and Beyond: 'Making the Word Luminous and Active'."

studies that we were and continue to be in times of great opposition, Anzaldúa's work shows us that it is within oppressive contexts that conocimiento—*knowledge*—unfolds and transformation begins (*Reader* 320).

Knowledge is, and has always been, political and a site of struggle. Who can create knowledge? Who gets to decide which knowledge "counts"? These questions are worthy of being asked, Rusty Barceló declares in her keynote address, but, she continues, "[I]t is we—who were barred for so long from access to knowledge and its creation in the academy—who have been struggling for decades to *change the answers*. We have brought our own ways of knowing and being to our institutions; we have transformed our institutions; and yet the transformation is incomplete." Colonial projects have long focused their attacks on the intellectual traditions, methods of transmitting histories, and spiritual practices of indigenous peoples to delegitimize indigenous thought. From the beginning pages of *Borderlands/La Frontera: The New Mestiza* to "now let us shift," Anzaldúa insists that we recognize the long neo/colonial history of epistemicide in the Americas that was and continues to be deployed through military invasion, historical erasure, and academic imperialism. However, as Anzaldúa has made evident, it is through this attempted erasure from which an epistemology of la mestiza has emerged, what she calls "conocimiento."

Even more profound than its literal translation to "knowledge," Anzaldúa's conocimiento in its fullest form is an "ethical, compassionate strategy with which to negotiate conflict and difference within self and between others" ("now let us shift" 545). She states,

> A form of spiritual inquiry, conocimiento is reached via creative acts—writing, art-making, dancing, healing, teaching, meditation, and spiritual activism… Breaking out of your mental and emotional prison and deepening the range of perception enables you to link inner reflection and vision—the mental, emotional, instinctive, spiritual, and subtle bodily awareness—with social, political action and lived experiences to generate subversive knowledges. (541-542)

In the introduction to *Bridging: How Gloria Anzaldúa's Work and Life Transformed Our Own*, AnaLouise Keating elaborates on the "inner reflection and vision" and public acts of conocimiento, explaining that "Anzaldúa's intense focus on the personal always leads outward, enabling her to develop new insights and make connections with others; with this new knowledge and these connections with others, she facilitates social change" (2). Kelli Zaytoun's concept of the "self-in-coalition" describes this movement outward as this coalitional self requires that we "explore our own and each other's specific journeys and situations and the inextricable connections between them." Likewise, Kandace Creel Falcón writes of the pedagogical applications of Anzaldúa's imperative to focus on the personal to forge connections with others. Recounting her experiences as an assistant professor, Falcón "articulate[s] the value in exploring our own experiences and positions within writing, creative and scholarly endeavors for transformative work," especially within the Women's and Gender Studies classroom.

For Anzaldúa and many academics committed to social justice scholarship, the classroom has always been a site of conflict over knowledge. The most evident proof is the battle over Mexican American Studies in Arizona (and throughout the country), namely the concerted efforts to systemically suppress the conocimientos of Chicana/o youth that emerge from and are validated through the consciousness-raising curricula of ethnic studies courses. Recognizing the transformational potential of these conocimientos, lawmakers have eliminated teachers and banned books in their efforts to subdue the growing consciousness of an enlightened youth. Indeed, Anzaldúa would agree that epistemicide is being wielded once again as a weapon of neo-colonization.

However, as those in Chicana/o studies and other social justice-centered area studies experience and even lead counterattacks on the opposition to ethnic studies in their communities and universities, many have found that the spaces previously perceived as "safe" and welcoming of alternative knowledges are oftentimes harbors of institutional violence; in fact, Anzaldúa's own works were largely produced in and in response to such spaces. In their essay Stephanie Alvarez, et al, describe the hostile reaction to the Gloria Anzaldúa exhibit they created at Anzaldúa's alma mater, the University of Texas, Pan American, to bring her work into a space where she had been institutionally invisible. Citing Anzaldúa's assertion that "Conocimiento pushes us into engaging the spirit in confronting our social sickness with new tools and practices whose goal is to effect a shift" (*Reader* 311), the authors explain that "The new tools and practice for us were the creation of the exhibit in the hopes to create a shift in us and the public"; further, they hoped to subvert and re-work "borders between 'academia' and community" in order to "introduce Anzaldúa's mestiza consciousness to a public that has not had access to it." Clearly, conocimiento has the power to mobilize people toward spiritual activism.

However, it is not only institutional space where conocimientos are created, but in the public spaces of the everyday. Anzaldúa describes the experiences of walking across bridges, surviving violence, and re-membering personal histories, as epistemically rich moments in which mestizas/os can begin to construct critical knowledges about power and oppression. But, as Megan Sibbett cogently explains, it is not only violence that characterizes the mestiza/o's experience in the borderlands, but "the incessant *threat of violence* and the accompanying terror." In her nuanced reading of Anzaldúa's articulation of "intimate terrorism," Sibbett emphasizes the significance of the mundane, the "terrorizing threat of constant, daily violence," arguing that through Anzaldúa's theorization of the mundane "we gain a larger more complex understanding of 'terrorism' and violence in U.S. imperializing patterns and projects." Here, Anzaldúa's theory indicates the possibility of an epistemology of the terrorized, a knowledge paradigm that emerges from and is shaped by the more subtle forms and effects of violence, and reconstitutes borderlands subjects as agents of knowledge production. Here, she asks us to consider, "Can the subaltern know?" Indeed, I believe she would argue they can.

Testimonios and theories of terror and the systemic suppression of conocimientos have remained consistent Mundo Zurdo conference themes, and over its five years, the conference has evolved into a co-constructed space of healing. Through the program itself, Chicana/o scholars, artists, and community activists have challenged the traditionally hegemonic concept of "the" academic conference by integrating music performances, poetry readings, healing workshops, and indigenous blessing ceremonies, thereby centering their identities within the site of the conference.[2]

The dynamic panel on music and Chicana identity during the 2012 conference profoundly embodied this shift, wherein academics became performers and music was the site of theory production. For example, in her essay on "artivistas," panelist Martha Gonzalez documents the transformative potential of creative expression for neighborhoods in East Los Angeles whose residents use music to "de-construct power, challenge multiple patriarchal systems, and build community." The power of music is further illustrated by fellow panelists Brenda Romero and Rusty Barceló, whose essays on being an academic and musician (Barceló) and an ethnomusicologist (Romero) recast the performance and study of music as processes through which Chicanas can reclaim suppressed indigenous histories and reconcile the tensions of mestizaje. As Barceló explains in her section on writing music, "It [writing] bridges divides, bears witness, and moves us toward wholeness and authenticity—and transformation... And so the song I write is, to borrow again from Gloria, 'the dialogue between my Self and el espiritu del mundo. I change myself, I change the world'" (Anzaldúa qtd. in Barceló).

Earlier this year, as conference organizers sifted through the conference proposals for El Mundo Zurdo 2014, it became evident that there was a thematic shift from the previous conference: whereas in 2012 the "Borders"

---

2 Because the Society for the Study of Gloria Anzaldúa is housed in the University of Texas at San Antonio Women's Studies Institute (UTSA WSI), the past four conferences have been held at the UTSA Downtown Campus. A special thank you to WSI student assistant, Meagan Longoria, for her help in the preparation of this manuscript.

track received the most submissions, this time around the "Spirituality" track, the once least popular category, dominated. In her discussion of Nepantleras, Norma Alarcón asks, "Are these politico-spiritual activists to be the leaders of a 'new tribalism' that Anzaldúa invokes?" I ask this question as community and academic nepantleras continue to gather at this meeting, in the words of Alarcón, to "pursu[e] another line of inquiry in an effort to free themselves from colonial structures of experience and knowledge" in the service of "generat[ing] alternative spaces for new forms of political thought and action."

It is fitting, then, that the conference is titled "El Mundo Zurdo," for Anzaldúa's Mundo Zurdo is a space of epistemological rupture, where "los atravesados"—the queer, mestizas, and those who, according to Anzaldúa "do not fit" and therefore are a "threat"—co-habitate and form alliances to dismantle the binaries that render la mestiza and "las otras" invisible. El Mundo Zurdo, both the conference and the vision, for Chicana/o academics and their allies, is a space of visibility, possibility, and transformation—where the creative, spiritual, and academic minds, violently pulled apart by the academy, are sutured into wholeness once again. The essays in this collection reflect a wide range of "inner work" and "public acts," as well as their resultant critical knowledges that are honed through experiences of institutional oppression, articulated in scholarship, and expressed through pedagogy and performance. As the authors of the essays in this collection reveal, it is through the personal and public path of conocimiento that we can transform our world into one that is more inclusive and just.

BEYOND BORDERLANDS: A NEW CONSCIOUSNESS FOR INSTITUTIONAL TRANSFORMATION

KEYNOTE ADDRESS

RUSTY BARCELÓ

At the end of a long day, I often sit down with Gloria Anzaldúa and reread poems and essays that I've read maybe a hundred times. When I read her words, I feel the power of her presence, and I am reminded of how often those words have given me the courage and strength to persevere. As I join friends and colleagues at El Mundo Zurdo 2012, Gloria's presence once again renews the sense of wholeness and belonging that I experience in few places in my life as a college president.

Ever since I first met Gloria, both on the page and in person, her words have been my inspiration and guide. In applying the spirit of those words to my work, first as a diversity officer and now as a college president, I have dedicated myself to the cause of institutional transformation—a full-throttle, full-blown, full-scale reimagining of our institutions as places driven by the core values of equity and inclusion toward "multiplicity that is transformational" (*this bridge we call home* 4).

When I was nominated for the presidency I now hold, I saw an opportunity. I saw Northern New Mexico College as a capstone place where I could fully apply all that I had learned at the predominantly white research universities where I had spent so many years of my professional life; and where, quite frankly, I had too often been disappointed by our lack of progress in the struggle to move diversity to the center of both discourse and practice. It seemed that every time a barrier came crashing down, another was erected in its place. And commitments to equity and inclusion in mission statements rarely translated into sustained action leading to sustainable institutional—i.e., infrastructural—change. Resources were often contingent and "soft," or non-recurring, responsibilities for the work were compartmentalized and viewed as tangential to the core academic mission, and the success and survival of programs were subject to the vagaries of the fiscal and political climate, as well as changes in leadership.

Over the years, many of my colleagues supported diversity in theory. It was even being written into policy. It was being taught in classrooms. It was even part of strategic planning processes. It's just that for the majority culture, it wasn't really a priority. It wasn't as important as, say, the next round of rankings or tenure reviews or budget talks. And fundamentally changing the structure of our institutions to reflect a new consciousness that made diversity a core value was just too hard. The message to me was, "You do your job, and we'll do ours"—even while my message to them from the beginning was this: "This work is *everyone's* work. Diversity needs to be reimagined as a central priority and a driving force. It needs to be embedded in every policy and practice, every reward system, every curriculum, every syllabus, every strategic plan, every job description. It needs to be infrastructural."

This, I said, was how we would prepare, and help our students prepare, for this new Century of Diversity.

I saw my new post at Northern as an opportunity to do just that, at an institution and in a region whose history is defined by issues of equity and inclusion, and whose economy and culture had been shaped in powerful ways by the people my new college was constituted to serve. So as president of a Hispano and Native-serving college, I believed I would be at home in my work, in a way. In a sense, I am. And yet, as a Chicana lesbian, I continue to inhabit the institutional borderlands even as I do my work from a position of formal institutional leadership. In fact, from the very beginning, just by walking through the door, I collided with business-as-usual and transgressed the prevailing institutional and cultural borders.

I realized very quickly that the vision I had in my head was more than a little out of sync with the institutional realities. As "diverse" as the college was, with a predominantly Hispano and Native student population, the faculty was not. Moreover, I found little evidence when I arrived that diversity was a priority in the curriculum, in teaching, in strategic planning, in reward systems, or in the social, cultural, and intellectual life of the college.

In fact, no one talked about it—until I brought it up. I got little sense of a pervasive *multicultural consciousness*. Everyone seemed to believe that diversity was just a given. It was all around us, they said. It just *was*. There was no need to study it or critique it, or even to reflect on our own biases, our own identities, or our own place in this microcosm of New Mexico. And certainly there was no need to talk about the kind of multifaceted, intersectional diversity of cultures and knowledge systems that is so important to the cultural and intellectual life of any higher education institution.

In short, even in this place that in so many ways felt like home, I encountered walls of resistance. I discovered very quickly that I had my work cut out for me. I saw that only a major systemic restructuring would realign the college's academic and student life, and its overall culture, with the values of equity and inclusion that I had been advocating for more than forty years. I vowed that we would do this together—faculty, administrators, staff, students, and members of the regional communities. We would build a culture of inclusion that fundamentally affirms diversity as a catalyst for excellence—not as a line on a spreadsheet or strategic plan but as integral to the educational mission.

As I settled into my new presidential role, I found myself struggling with many of the same challenges I'd been addressing since the beginning of my career. Once again, diversity was a hard sell. And even as president I could not just pull rank and make it happen. If it was transformation I was after, I would need to focus on community building both within and beyond campus, as well as between internal and external communities. Delicate diplomacy would be required. All identities would be welcome, all perspectives given a hearing.

And so I have spent much of my time as president in focused but searching conversations. I have brought to those conversations the community building strategies that I have learned over the years as an activist administrator in the academic borderlands, working to bridge the differences around the table and build support networks one person at a time, one group at a time. And I have done all of this from the tenuous middle ground that I occupy as a Chicana lesbian who only *happens to be* a president—balancing my formal role as chief executive officer with my multiple roles and identities as a member of multiple cultural communities. It's a painstaking process, requiring advanced negotiating skills. And that's not easy for someone whose life and career have been driven by a deep and fierce personal passion for social justice that is fueled by a growing sense of urgency, especially as political backlash and gridlock play out in such destructive ways on the social and economic terrain of our communities of color.

I have said many times in the past few years that this is a defining moment in our history and in our nation's history. And I say that for four fairly obvious reasons:

First, the lingering economic recession, which disproportionately affects communities of color and is widening opportunity and achievement gaps and further polarizing our country.

Second, dramatically changing demographics, which, as we all know, are transforming the U.S. social, economic, cultural, and educational landscape.

Third, the continuing revolution in communication technologies, making it easier for us to tell our stories but harder than ever for our voices to rise above and be heard through the collective noise, especially the noise of the backlash.

And fourth, rising new generations of young people who are globally connected and also grew up with heightened expectations of and acceptance of equity and inclusion in education and in our communities.

Even as these new generations bring a more open and inclusive consciousness to bear, with all of these powerful forces at play our work has special urgency—especially as the rifts in the political landscape widen. If we don't seize this moment, someone else will. That means continuing to confront and engage those who would seek to silence us. If we are to move forward, we must do our work as a labor of love, finding spaces of liberatory connection and healing in solidarity with each other. As Chela Sandoval said in *Methodology of the Oppressed,* "It is love that can access and guide our theoretical and political 'movidas'—revolutionary maneuvers toward decolonized being" (141).

It is against this backdrop that I have found myself calling upon Gloria again and again for wisdom and guidance. As I have struggled to resolve the binaries that persistently get in the way of social and institutional transformation, I've especially been thinking a lot about *nepantla*, a concept all of us know so well, but one little understood beyond our community. It has a special resonance for us as Chicanas. We've lived it, and we're living it now—in this "in-between space, an unstable, unpredictable, precarious, always-in-transition space lacking clear boundaries" ("[Un]natural bridges, [Un]safe Spaces" 243).

"Nepantla is the only place where change happens," Gloria said ("now let us shift" 574). It's where we come together, both affirming and bridging our differences, to work in common cause, embracing the multiple identities, hyphenated identities, all of the complex realities of people's lives as cultural beings.

And this, said Gloria, "is a mark of inclusivity, increased consciousness, and dialogue... [reflecting] the hybrid quality of our lives and identities—*todas somos nos/otras*" (*this bridge we call home* 3). It is also, in my view, a perfect metaphor for the transformed institutions that we have been struggling to build in the emerging multicultural spaces of the 21st-century academy.

In *La Frontera*, which many of us first read so many years ago and have reread multiple times since, Gloria said that all of us who were born on the margins began our journey of resistance and struggle locked in a "counterstance"—"stand[ing] on the opposite river bank, shouting questions, challenging patriarchal, white conventions" (*Borderlands* 100). But she also reminded us that we need to move beyond that stance, or we become, in our opposition, in our us-vs.-them stance, complicit with and defined by those who seek to dominate us: "A counterstance locks one into a duel of oppressor and oppressed," she said. "All reaction is limited by, and dependent on, what it is reacting against... [This is] a step towards liberation from cultural domination. *But it is not a way of life*" (*Borderlands* 100, emphasis added). "At some point," she says, "on our way to a *new consciousness*, we will have to leave the opposite bank...so that we are on both shores at once and, at once, we see through serpent and eagle eyes" (100-01, emphasis added).

Many of us here have spent our lives developing this special sight and practicing the intellectual and cultural calisthenics that allow us to straddle and mediate worlds, with one foot firmly planted in our own histories, heritage, and identities, and the other on the inside, toes poised at the edge of the dominant culture. The robust "new consciousness" we have developed has been a powerful survival mechanism. And as the hate-fueled resistance to our efforts has built across the nation and put our work at risk, it enables us to see through the constructed political and media smokescreens and *really see* what's happening.

We do this by occupying that shifting and unsteady middle ground where we struggle to unite across our own differences without losing ourselves. In *nepantla*, and in that new consciousness, lies transformation. That we know this, and are able to act upon it, is perhaps Gloria's greatest legacy. She taught us not only how to fight back, but how to embrace the struggle. She taught us about the New Tribalism. She taught us about joining hands in solidarity across differences. She taught us how to negotiate without acquiescing, without compromising our core values, without negating our selves.

In a way, the New Tribalism is a very pragmatic idea: "a social identity that could motivate subordinated communities to work together in coalition," Gloria said in her published interview with AnaLouise Keating (283). It moves us beyond binaries, and what she calls the "multiply colonized geographies of the borderlands" (*Borderlands*) toward a *multiplicity that is transformational*. It's a multiplicity that never demands assimilation, that never attenuates into a bland, identity-crushing sameness, that keeps us (and our differences) intact and whole even as we find common ground across our multiple identities.

Gloria knew that we must build a critical mass of advocacy and activism; that we must widen our circles of inclusion to make them ever more power*ful*, ever more empower*ing*, and ever more invincible. She knew that if we build a fortress, it must have permeable walls, for both access and egress. That's how we'll survive. That's how we'll make our work sustainable.

In the same interview, Gloria says that "issues of conocimiento" are at the core of the work we do: How do we know? How do we perceive? Who produces knowledge and is kept from producing it? Who has access to it and who doesn't? (*Interviews/Entrevistas* 178). These are clearly central questions for the academy. And it is we—who were barred for so long from access to knowledge and its creation in the academy—who have been struggling for decades to *change the answers*. We have brought our own ways of knowing and being to our institutions; we have transformed our institutions; and yet the transformation is incomplete.

How does the academy-with-a-capital-'A' answer those questions? As much as things have changed, the answers aren't so very different than they were twenty-five years ago. There has been a lot of rhetoric about change. There has even been some real change. But the new normal still looks a lot like the old normal, even when people like us are in faculty, staff, and leadership positions. That's because the structures of our institutions have not changed *fundamentally*.

The academy is more diverse than it was even twenty years ago. But the real gains are more in numbers than in institutional culture. As I have said many times, the programs, structures, and methodologies that we pioneered have become models for the kinds of interdisciplinary and robust civic engagement that are now staples of academic life at universities throughout the country. And yet: our contributions have not been recognized. Many of the changes we have brought to the academy—new interdisciplinary programs and curricula, new knowledge traditions, new pedagogies, new methodologies, and new scholarly perspectives—have been sidelined, assimilated, or appropriated.

Traditional hierarchies of power and privilege persist, including many of the reward systems. We may be at some tables, but continuing biases keep us from having a real voice at *The* Table. (Believe it or not, that's even true when you're the president.) We remain in that middle ground, *in* the academy, consigned *to* it, but not considered *integral* to it. And too often, the parts of us that remain on the outside, rooted in our heritage and communities—those parts that *make us who we are*—have not been fully integrated into the selves that we bring to the academy, so we continue to feel *dis*-integrated.

We explore issues of race, gender, and sexuality in society through an integrative lens, but we don't always live the truths that we theorize about. And there are far too few of us in leadership positions—in part, of course, because we're so busy just trying to establish our legitimacy as scholars and colleagues and administrators. We have not positioned ourselves in the academy to be central players in the institutional narrative, doing work that embodies and affirms who we are but also creates the change that would minimize the challenges to our full participation in higher education.

Our knowledge and perspectives aren't strictly outlawed, at least not in most states, at least not for now. But do we have the kind of legitimacy we have sought? When budgets get slashed, what programs are at the top of the list for downsizing or elimination? Have the numbers of faculty of color changed in any significant way? Has the *climate* changed? Can we even *imagine* trying to launch or expand an ethnic studies program in this climate? Gloria said:

> I use the idea of outlawed knowledge to encourage Chicanas and other women and people of color to...originate our own theories for how the world works. I think those who produce *conocimientos* have to shift the frame of reference, reframe the issue or situation being looked at, connect the disparate parts of information in new ways or form a perspective that's new.
>
> I see conocimiento as a consciousness-raising tool, one that promotes self-awareness and self-reflection. It encourages folks to empathize and sympathize with others, to walk in the other's shoes, whether the other is a member of the same group or belongs to a different culture. It means to place oneself in a state of resonance with the other's feelings and situations, and to give the other an opportunity to express their needs and points of view. To relate to others by recognizing commonalities... Receptivity is the stance here, not the adversarial mode, not the armed camp. (*Interviews/Entrevistas* 178)

What we are up against in this country—the backlash, the retrograde legislation, the draconian court decisions, the hate rhetoric— is what Gloria calls *desconocimientos*: "A not-knowing, a refusal to know, an ignorance that damages, miscommunications with irreversible harmful effects, that betray trust, that destroy. *Desconocimientos* are the evils of modern life" (*Interviews/Entrevistas* 178).

And when this country's legislatures and school boards compel ignorance by writing it into public policy—as they have in Arizona—we're really in trouble. Champions of not-knowing have even been so audacious as to claim that they're "defending" democracy against subversion and race hatred by outlawing ethnic studies programs.

Wherever we look, we see *not-knowing* being institutionalized:

In the entrenchment and mainstreaming of radical right ideologies that are turning back the clock on issues of social and economic justice. In the increasingly toxic anti-immigration fever that has infected our schools and public spaces, resulting in censorship, book seizures, English-only policies, and attacks on the curriculum.

In the continuing conservative attempts to establish an Academic Bill of Rights and overturn all vestiges of affirmative action—with a pivotal Supreme Court decision pending. In the attacks on and erosion of public programs that promote access to higher education and health care for people of low income and people of color. In the renewed public challenges across the country to the legitimacy of our work around race, gender, and sexuality. Gloria encouraged us to face these evils with courage and in a positive spirit, to move from victimhood to active resistance, from reflective inner work to public acts. And that brings us back to *nepantla*, the place where different perspectives come into conflict, where ideas and identities are questioned and challenged, and where *the tension that's created can lead to transformation.*

The question is: Can the academy meet the challenges of this defining historical moment—this time of economic uncertainty coupled with destructive political movements—as an opportunity to go beyond fixes, even beyond reforms, to true transformation? If we look at best practices in diversity work and multicultural education in higher education, we already have models for doing this.

At the University of Minnesota, where I was Vice President and Vice Provost for Equity and Diversity, we said, "Diversity is everybody's everyday work." And isn't that, after all, what higher education is all about in the 21st century? Aren't teaching, research, and discovery all about throwing diverse perspectives, ideas, cultures, and identities into a multicultural and multidisciplinary pot without a recipe, and mixing it up to see what kind of wonderful alchemy results?

I've already said that Gloria's concept of transformation through multiplicity directly informs my vision for advancing institutional transformation in higher education. But let me say what I mean when I use the term "transformation." I mean institutional change that moves us beyond questions of access, beyond boundaries, beyond restrictive definitions, beyond traditional structures and conceptual frameworks to create new ways of being, acting, teaching, learning, and knowing.

In a way, what that means is a systemic restructuring whose *center of gravity* is nepantla.

Gloria said, "It is in living and giving voice to our differences, and also bridging those differences, that we form truly inclusive multicultural communities" (*this bridge we call home* 3). I believe that it's only from within such communities that we can preserve what we have built and move forward against the formidable challenges we face in the current climate of fear and loathing.

And our adversaries aren't just the usual suspects, whose hate-filled rhetoric fills the pages of blogs and commentaries and fouls the air in our halls of state. No less pernicious are the views of "nice people" who just want to put race and gender wars behind us, who say we live in a post-race, post-feminist society. I'm afraid these people just haven't been paying attention, or they don't want to face any facts that challenge what they want to believe. It's also clear that the society they wish for—culturally homogenous and utterly conformist—is not free and open and egalitarian, but repressive and totalitarian. It is the antithesis of democracy.

"Our goal," Gloria said, "is not to use differences to separate us from others, but neither is it to gloss over those differences… Though most people self-define by what they exclude, we define who we are by what we include—what I call the new tribalism" (*this bridge we call home* 3).

"Today," she said, "the division between the majority of 'us' and 'them' is still intact. This country does not want to acknowledge its walls or limits… [But] the future belongs to those who *cultivate cultural sensitivities to differences* and who *use these abilities* to forge a hybrid consciousness that transcends the 'us' vs. 'them' mentality" (*Interviews/Entrevistas* 254).

And so we must aspire not to "get past" differences but to recognize and acknowledge them. "Post-race" is not only a myth; it's an idea that runs counter to what we are trying to do—to build consensus and community that does not ignore differences, but embraces them. In a true democracy, and in the 21st century academy that we aspire to create, we have no choice but to choose the messiness and noise of discord over the inertia of assimilation and coerced agreement. That means we must *recommit* ourselves to the difficult, ongoing work of understanding, bridging, and deploying differences *in the service of* institutional transformation—not pretending that those differences don't exist.

If we need to "get past" anything, it's the pervasive binary thinking that's threatening us and our democratic institutions. It's that kind of thinking that pushes us toward assimilation. It's that kind of thinking that asks us to choose between diversity and excellence—as if they are antithetical. Or to choose between economic prosperity and economic justice. Or to choose between American history and Native and Chicana/o history. Or between so-called "legal" and "illegal" immigrants.

Binary thinking draws lines and foments hate, fear, and oppression. Nepantla is our bulwark against tyranny—and also against institutional inertia and atrophy.

Gloria said a borderland is a place of transformation, "where the Third World grates against the first and bleeds. And before a scab forms it hemorrhages again, the lifeblood of two worlds merging to form a third country—a border culture" (*Borderlands* 25). I think of that border culture as a prototype for the academy we are still working to create—a place where disparate ideas, cultures and identities, and knowledge systems collide and are reborn. It's a breeding ground for the "multiplicity that is transformational." And it all begins with each and every one of us. As Gloria said in "Toward a Mestiza Rhetoric," an interview with Andrea Lunsford:

> I am the dialogue between my Self and el espíritu del mundo, the spirit of the world. I change myself, I change the world... Now there's no such thing as the 'other.' I can't disown the white tradition, the Euro-American tradition, any more than I can the Mexican, the Latino, or the Native, because they're all in me. (*Borderlands* 70)

I know that this kind of integrative, truly multicultural, self-reflective work is about the hardest work we can do. It means that we have to work through our own biases, our own personal ambitions, our desire to "belong" and be "accepted." It's so very tempting in the academy to become complicit, and be seduced by the very system that has marginalized us—so we can get tenure, be invited to lunch with colleagues and deans, be recognized for our work, and advance our careers.

We're justifiably hungry for legitimacy and acceptance. We want our piece of the action, our share of the rewards. But since reward systems haven't changed very much over the years, we're still often on the outside looking in. So yes, it's very tempting to play the game by the old rules—but at what cost? Gloria would tell us, of course, that we *must not* compromise our identities, that we *must not* give up the struggle. But that's easier said than done. Not all of us have Gloria's courage.

As for me, I may be an insider on the organizational chart, but I've never given up my outsider status. That has been my *choice*—because I knew that compromising my identity would be a kind of death—and it would certainly make me ineffective as a change agent. My identity is the ground of my being. And the tension between my own identity and culture, and the institutional culture of the academy, has given me my critical and creative edge and made me, *I hope*, an agent of change. My challenge has always been to maintain that edge, to keep from being so seduced by positional authority that I simply validate and replicate existing institutional structures.

As a college president at a Hispano and Native-serving institution, I am challenged more than ever to maintain that edge of critique—and that requires constant self-reflection. I've always said that this work begins at the most personal level, and this is my true test, my hardest test. I know that the only way to create the kind of change we need is to continue challenging the status quo and the borders that keep us on the margins of the academy. We can never let up. But that doesn't mean taking the system down; it means transforming it, and reimagining our role in the transformation. It means aligning our identities and interests with those of our institutions without losing our selves or our ways of knowing, and then continuing to bring about change from within—taking care to maintain the sharp edge of critique that we have always brought to this work, and taking care not to be co-opted by the systems that we depend on for our rewards and advancement.

When I look back, I know that I didn't get here by being an insider playing an insider's game. I've always known that we couldn't work with integrity or advance our agenda by squeezing ourselves into the old institutional boxes. We've had to shake the very foundations of our institutions to make them better. And that's what we must continue to do. Our work has always been about struggle and disruption, and even pain. And I've said many times that it's by embracing the struggle that we reaffirm who we are and find points of connection.

Struggle hurts. And yet I also find much comfort in the idea of struggle as passion and also as a catalyst for connection and liberation—and, in the end, joy. That's because the struggle is one we share and one whose liberatory goals we cherish.

What I think is especially important for all of us is that we be able to bridge the dualities and contradictions within ourselves, between the movement and the academy, between the activist and the scholar or administrator, between the outsider and the institutional insider. We must be both—activist scholars and activist administrators whose social justice commitment and practice aren't add-ons to our roles as scholars and administrators, but integral to those roles.

I know I've said this before, and I'll say it again, because it comes from my heart: My journey to this day has been long and sometimes grueling. Ask anyone who knew me back when, and they'll tell you: I didn't get here by keeping my mouth shut or staying out of trouble. But I've never really been alone. Gloria has been with me ever since she first spoke to me from the pages of *La Frontera.*

Many of you, too, have been with me from the beginning. We've spent our lives and careers challenging the status quo, dismantling systems of exclusion and bias, and building something new. We put ourselves on the line. And if we learned anything, it's that activist leadership is hard work, and it's risky. And for every step forward, we may be pushed a few steps back by those who oppose us.

Now, as the opposition gathers strength and ferocity, we and our young Chicana heirs are challenged as never before to find new ways to sustain our work and our gains over the long term. The stakes are high. And many of us are tired of fighting the same old battles. But having risked everything, we have also gained unimaginable worlds. Working together with renewed passion for our work and with new generations, we are a powerful and invincible force for change.

If we can embrace our multiple identities, take the conversations in new directions, and form new alliances across institutional barriers, we can forge a new agenda. We can begin our work anew, and move toward a new *national consciousness* that embraces the richness of our culture, history, and our contributions to the academy and society.

We know we can do it, because we already have.

WORKS CITED

Anzaldúa, Gloria. *Borderlands/La Frontera: The New Mestiza.* 2nd ed. San Francisco: Aunt Lute, 1999.

Anzaldúa, Gloria, and AnaLouise Keating, eds. *this bridge we call home: radical visions for transformation.* New York: Routledge, 2002.

Anzaldúa, Gloria E. *Interviews/Entrevistas.* Ed. AnaLouise Keating. New York and London: Routledge, 2000.

Moraga, Cherríe, and Gloria Anzaldúa, eds. *This Bridge Called My Back: Writings by Radical Women of Color.* New York: Kitchen Table/Women of Color Press, 1981.

Sandoval, Chela. *Methodology of the Oppressed.* Minneapolis: U of Minnesota P, 2000.

Special thanks to Eugenia Smith, who collaborated with me in the editing and research for this piece, and helped me take my thinking further. Together, we have come to know Gloria even better.

RE-VISIONING LITERARY ARCHIVES AND GENEALOGIES

AN ALTERNATIVE LITERARY GENEALOGY? JOHN RECHY, GLORIA ANZALDÚA, AND GREGG BARRIOS[1]

BETH HERNANDEZ-JASON

There are multiple ways to determine the significance of an author and her work to particular literary traditions and communities. The more traditional methods include arguments for the literary quality of a text, its continued relevance over time (the ability to "stand the test of time"), and the amount of scholarly attention that a text or author has received. Thus, the tastes of literary critics and their choices of texts to study play an important role in canon formation. However, reception theory provides us with multiple alternative ways to measure the significance of an author's work by considering scholarly, popular, and literary/artistic response of readers. Manuel M. Martín-Rodríguez has pioneered the use of this theory in the field of Chicano/a Literature, and my work further extends his approach by considering how the work of Chicano/a LGBTQ writers has been received by different readerships.[2] In my dissertation, I examine how the reader responses shed light on the significance of John Rechy's work for different literary traditions and communities, and here I argue that the literary and extra-literary responses of two early LGBTQ Chicano/a readers-turned-writers illustrate the significance of Rechy's earliest work for Chicano/a literature and literary history. This essay discusses the intertextual responses of Gloria Anzaldúa and Gregg Barrios, both Texas Chicano/a writers, while drawing on archival findings and interviews. I begin by examining the references Anzaldúa makes to Rechy in her groundbreaking book *Borderlands/La Frontera: The New Mestiza* and in her archived private writings. I also explore what her initial responses to Rechy's first published novel, *City of Night* (1963), might tell us about how she and other non-heterosexual female readers might have responded to Rechy's first novel in the 1960s. Finally, I analyze the references to Rechy and his early novels by Gregg Barrios in several of his books of poems. My findings are significant for Chicano/a Studies and LGBTQ Studies because they illustrate the important role that John Rechy's work played in the development of two LGBTQ Chicano/a writers.

For reasons that are too complex to fully address here, John Rechy's work continues to be viewed as peripheral to Chicano/a literature. Compared with the scholarly attention to authors such as Rolando Hinojosa, Tomás Rivera, and even José Antonio Villarreal, Rechy was understudied or ignored by many Chicano/a scholars prior to the 1990s.[3] Nevertheless, Chicano/a readers and future authors read his novels as early as the 1960s, and as a result, from a reader-oriented perspective, his work is an integral part of early Chicano/a literary history. Furthermore, *City of Night* (1963) in particular provides an alternative literary genealogy for Chicano/a literature. Manuel de Jesús Hernández-G has referred to Rechy and the work of other writers such as Anzaldúa as contributing to "U.S. Latina/o lesbigay cultural production," which broadens their impact to include multiple disciplines outside of literature, but this seems to diminish the actual connections between these writers, almost implying that they each wrote in a vacuum, unaware of the work of earlier writers (297). Thus, I prefer to refer to this as an alternative literary genealogy, based on the evidence of intertextual connections. Also, it is worth mentioning that in her 2011 dissertation, "Schooling La Raza: A Chicana/o Cultural History of Education, 1968-2008," Melissa Martha Hidalgo writes about a "genealogy of queer Chicano educational formation," drawing on *Pocho*, two novels by Arturo Islas, and the play *Sissies* by Ricardo Bracho (86-7). Again, in Hidalgo's approach, there is no documentation that any of the later authors actually read the earlier texts, and she does not examine Rechy's work.

This alternative genealogy is non-heteronormative and depicts sexuality as a central component in life, even if it is neither rooted in the reproductive cycle nor openly embraced by one's relatives or community. When I first began studying the connection between Rechy and Anzaldúa (and later, Barrios), I didn't know how to define it—was it simply an intertextual reference, a literary affiliation, or evidence of a literary genealogy? At first I avoided the terms "genealogy," "forebear," and "filiation" because they can evoke paternalistic, hierarchical approaches. Yet genealogy can also mean family, and the lines can be horizontal, vertical or diagonal. In "La Prieta," Anzaldúa writes that in *El Mundo Zurdo* (the left-handed world), "I with my own affinities and my people with theirs can live together and transform the planet" (209). She defines "my people" as "a network of kindred spirits, a kind of family. We are the queer groups, the people who don't belong anywhere, not in the dominant world nor completely within our own respective cultures" (209). Thus, to argue that Rechy's *City of Night* is one of Anzaldúa's and Barrios' literary forebears, and that they are part of the same literary genealogy is not to say that their work is derived from or even primarily influenced by Rechy's work. This does not create an instant alliance between gay and lesbian Chicanos/as, but it does indicate an important shared root that includes other non-LGBTQ Chicano/a authors as well, which I further discuss in my dissertation.

City of Night and the following texts I discuss explore sexuality and desire through the act of reading and writing, and, as we will see, authors Gloria Anzaldúa and Gregg Barrios both appeared to learn a great deal about sexuality through the act of reading across ethnic, national, and gender boundaries.

GLORIA ANZALDÚA

Gloria Anzaldúa, co-editor of *This Bridge Called My Back: Writings by Radical Women of Color* (1981) and author of *Borderlands/La Frontera: The New Mestiza* (1987), is considered a pioneer of Chicana feminist and lesbian literature and theory in the 1980s. In one of her earliest published pieces, she writes about the impact of reading:

> One day when I was about seven or eight, my father dropped on my lap a 25¢ pocket western, the only type of book he could pick up at a drugstore. The act of reading forever changed me. In the westerns I read, the house servants, the villains, and the cantineras (prostitutes) were all Mexicans [...] The racism I would later recognize in my school teachers and never be able to ignore again I found in that first western I read. (Anzaldúa, "La Prieta," 222)

Borderlands/La Frontera is now a seminal text in Chicano/a and feminist courses, and in this collection of essays, theory, and poetry, Anzaldúa traces her literary roots:

> In the 1960s, I read my first Chicano novel. It was *City of Night* by John Rechy, a gay Texan, son of a Scottish father and a Mexican mother. For days I walked around in stunned amazement that a Chicano could write and get published. (81)

It is worth noting that up to this point, few, if any, Chicano/a scholars have mentioned the passage above when discussing the work of Anzaldúa, and when they do, it is quoted with little analysis of its significance. Some scholars have hinted at the thematic connections between these two works (and other later Chicano/a texts) without necessarily making the case that these later authors read *City of Night* or any of Rechy's other work, or were potentially influenced by his work. For example, Ramón Gutiérrez writes:

> Rechy's novels were intellectual forerunners to postmodernism among Mexican Americans. The themes of marginality, of fractured identities, of suspension betwixt and between worlds, were themes he first articulated, but which would not emerge again until 1987 [with the appearance of *Borderlands/La Frontera*]. (371)

Yet the passages Gutiérrez briefly analyzes from *Borderlands/La Frontera* do not include Anzaldúa's mention of *City of Night*, nor does he discuss Anzaldúa's assertion that it was the first Chicano novel she had read.[4]

It is striking that instead of beginning with Américo Paredes or other well-known authors, Anzaldúa's first Chicano book is by John Rechy. The 1958 folklore study *With His Pistol in His Hand* by Américo Paredes is often credited with inspiring many Chicano/a authors, such as Rolando Hinojosa and Tomás Rivera (Saldívar 26, Limón 86). In Sandra K. Soto's 2010 *Reading Chican@ Like a Queer: The De-Mastery of Desire*, she describes Américo Paredes as "the most commanding figure in Chican@ Studies" and suggests that as early as 1953, he was "challenging, if not himself queering, tejano patriarchal and heteronormative systems" (89). Her work focuses on "what is not said and what is under-described" in Paredes' early work and reaffirms his important role within Chicano/a literature. Soto laudably refutes Chicano/a literature's "traditional periodization, which marks the appearance of explicitly sexual work in the early 1980s as a distinctly new chapter in Chican@ literary history" (14). However, she never mentions Rechy, a surprising oversight that, inadvertently or not, replicates a common approach to Rechy that sees his early work as gay but not Chicano, with the 1991 novel *The Miraculous Day of Amalia Gómez* seen as his "breakthrough" into the realm of Chicano literature. *City of Night*, *Numbers*, *This Day's Death*, *The Vampires*, *The Fourth Angel*, *The Sexual Outlaw*, and *Rushes* all pre-date the 1980s.[5]

After reading Anzaldúa's comments about *City of Night* in *Borderlands/La Frontera*, I hoped to find a more detailed description of her reaction to *City of Night* in her archives at the University of Texas at Austin.[6] I began looking at the draft of what later became *Borderlands/La Frontera*, labeled "Autobiography" from 1985. There, I found a short piece in Spanish titled "Y no se nos olvide los hombres" ("and let's not forget the men"): "Asombra pensar que hemos, / como feministas y lesbianas, / cerrado nuestros corazones a los / hombres, / a nuestros hermanos jotos, / desheredados y marginales como / nosotras" ("Autobiography").[7]

In the final published version, the poem appears in a prose-like format. I wondered if she was thinking about Rechy when she wrote this, or perhaps some gay male friends she knew personally. Then, in a folder that had no official date, I found a collection of Anzaldúa's small spiral-bound notebooks, which contained lists of books that she wanted to read and their library call numbers. The authors include Rimbaud, Dostoevsky, Kerouac, Steinbeck, and there are lists of nonfiction self-help books, as well as books on writing and publishing (see figures 1 and 2).

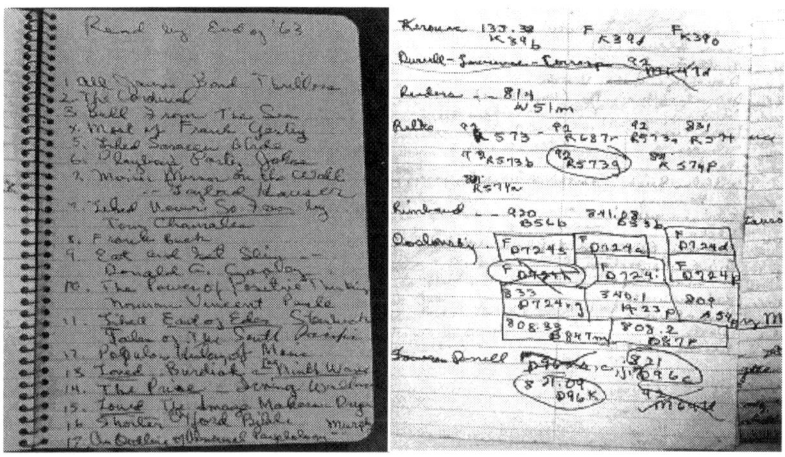

["Read by End of '63," Figure 1] ["Call Numbers," Figure 2] Anzaldúa's words and images © Gloria E. Anzaldúa; used by permission of the Gloria E. Anzaldúa Literary Trust.

Finally, under the heading "Dirty Book??" *City of Night* appeared, circled with a checkmark, alongside Terry Southern's *Candy*, Jean Genet's *Our Lady of the Flowers*, *Fanny Hill*, and William Burrough's *Naked Lunch* (see figure 3). It is not clear how Anzaldúa came up with this list (perhaps she had read a newspaper article about these books), but Grove Press had incidentally published many of the books. Finally, in a sheaf of loose papers within this collection, I found a piece of paper with the title "Three Memories." In this diary-like undated piece, Anzaldúa describes in further detail her experience reading *City of Night*, and the memories it triggered:

> I finished one [of] John Rechy's chapters from his first novel. I am interested in the way he turned inward because his father led a hopeless life. Somehow the story reminds me of my own dead father.

> He died in '55 in January, or February? Funny how I don't remember and it wasn't too long ago. (n.p.)[8]

It is important to note that when she wrote this, Anzaldúa had not yet read the entire book. Interestingly, the connection she makes to her own life focuses on the protagonist's father, not on sexuality or Chicano identity. In terms of dating this document, given that her father died in 1955 and the 1963 publication date, this might have been written in the mid- to late 1960s, which she stated in *Borderlands/La Frontera* as being the decade in which she read the book. Also, given the fact that *City of Night* was published in 1963, I assume that this was written sometime before 1966 because other pieces in that box are dated from 1965. This means that at least one Chicana was reading Rechy's work in the 1960s, before it was being explicitly marketed to a Chicano/a readership. This documented response also demonstrates that Anzaldúa was able to identify with this novel, so much so that she felt compelled to write about her experience reading it. Given Anzaldúa's early reading habits, it is not surprising that she read this best-selling novel written by a fellow Texan.

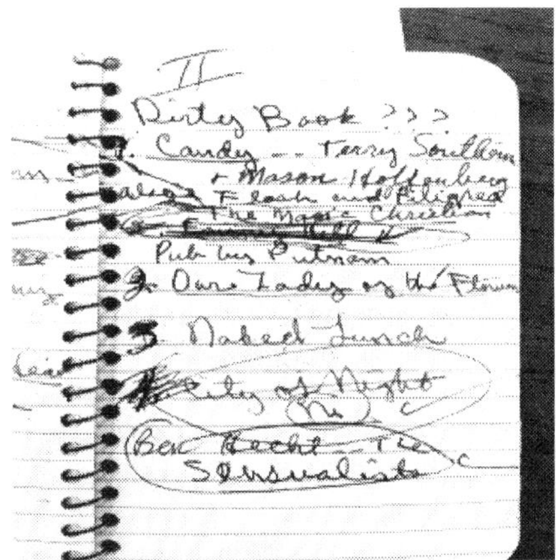

["Dirty Book," Figure 3]

Anzaldúa's words and images © Gloria E. Anzaldúa; used by permission of the Gloria E. Anzaldúa Literary Trust.

While this is a significant finding in and of itself, it is interesting to note that Anzaldúa does not talk more about Rechy's work in her published writings; I cannot help but wonder what she thought of his depiction of non-heteronormative sexuality, and in particular, lesbians. I assume that as a woman and as a lesbian (though I am not sure when she first openly identified as a lesbian), she might have felt excluded by *City of Night* and Rechy's other early novels, or might have read them with a resistant stance.[9] Rechy's novels, and the work of many Grove Press authors, did not explicitly market to female readers in terms of publication venues, cover design or advertising materials, and the portrayal of women in Rechy's early novels—particularly lesbians—was at times one-dimensional and demeaning. Using Anzaldúa as a sort of case study, I would like to consider how she and other queer female readers might have responded to *City of Night* in the 1960s.

Anzaldúa writes about the politics of writing and reading as a lesbian woman in "To(o) Queer the Writer—Loca, escritora y chicana." Anzaldúa notes the dynamics of identification, particularly around sexual orientation and gender:

> Identity formation is a component in reading and writing whether through empathy and identification or through disidentification. If it's a lesbian who's reading, she will have more incentive to keep reading when she reaches a dyke-concerns-laden passage in my writing. There will be more doors and windows through which she can access the text than if she's a non-lesbian. (272)

At the same time, she describes her own ability to read in multiple ways, seeming to fit the role of the "resisting reader" that Judith Fetterly writes about:

> ...as a reader, I usually have more in common with the Chicana dyke than I do with the white, middle-class feminist. I am in possession of both ways of reading—Chicana working-class, dyke ways of reading, and white middle-class heterosexual and male ways of reading. I have had more training in reading as a white, middle-class academic than I do reading as a Chicana. Just like we have more training reading as men. (Anzaldúa, "To(o) Queer the Writer," 273)

When Anzaldúa first read *City of Night*, after reading about the protagonist's experience of El Paso and his loneliness (which she talked about in the unpublished "Three Memories"), she likely read the "Miss Destiny" section (if she read *City of Nights* from front to back, in order), which features the well-educated but lonely drag queen who bonds with the protagonist over their shared knowledge of Shakespeare.

Then, assuming she read the entire book, she read the chapter where the protagonist meets Barbara, one of the few female characters. In this chapter, the male protagonist identifies with Barbara's "toughmasked lonesomeness" and finds her attractive (*City of Night* 144). Barbara knows he's a hustler and gives him a hard time about it, eventually unmasking the truth for him: "All of you keep telling yourselves you're straight—and you make it with chicks to prove it—and when you make it with other guys, you say it's only for the bread... Why don't you split the scene, man—if you really want to!" (146). The narrator implies that they have sex, but a few days later their budding relationship ends when he shows up at her apartment and discovers she's with a "tall, slender girl... dressed in black slacks" who looks at him "with almost-hatred" and "roughly" tells him to "split—Barbara don't need you guys any more [...] She's got me" (147). The protagonist acknowledges "a feeling of loss which had to do with Barbara—but also with something unrecognized which extended beyond her—" and moves on to San Francisco (147). What is this loss that is implied, and how might Gloria Anzaldúa have responded to this scene? It appears that the butch lesbian here is in direct opposition to the protagonist, challenging him and keeping him from Barbara—a heterosexual relationship. Yet he also kept himself from it, choosing to remain a hustler. This is one of two references to lesbians in the entire novel. The other two are one-line descriptions of people he sees in bars, one of whom is actually a drag queen. I cannot help but wonder if these portrayals might have cooled Anzaldúa's interest in Rechy's other works, which incidentally, later established a sort of kinship with women.[10]

In thinking about these tensions, and this imagined response, I am reminded of Rechy's reaction to *Pocho*, the 1959 novel by José Antonio Villarreal. In 1960, when Rechy had already published several short excerpts of his developing novel, Donald Allen sent Rechy a copy of *Pocho* in the hope that Rechy would review it. Allen also sent Rechy copies of several books, including works by Jean Genet and the novel *Pedro Páramo* (1955), so this was not out of the ordinary. Allen initially wrote to Rechy:

> There's a new novel coming out: *Pocho* by José Antonio Villarreal. He's a young Mexican-American from California, and this his first novel is about the El Paso scene mostly. It's not too exciting, probably, but would you be interested in reading it and if you want to write a short review of it for *ER*? They'd like to have it. (Letter from Allen to Rechy, January 20, 1960)

Rechy's response was short: "im returning 'pocho' and i hope very much youll give it to someone else to review. i wish i could have done a review of pedro paramo—could i, still?" (Letter from Rechy to Allen, n.d.). When asked in an interview what he thought of Chicano literature, he didn't have much to say—he only commented that the quality didn't seem very good.[11] At the time I was surprised, but considering his response in its context, the time in which he really came into his own as a writer, it is not that remarkable that for a gay Chicano writer in 1960 reading *Pocho* might have been painful, given the hyper-masculine and homophobic attitudes in the first half of the novel.

I am not sure if Anzaldúa took issue with parts of *City of Night* or if she read any of his other books, nor do we know how much Rechy's sexual identity and subject matter in *City of Night* might have inspired Anzaldúa to write about the body or about non-heteronormative sexuality. Perhaps when her journals are open to researchers this will become clearer. However, we do know that she read *City of Night* early on, as she herself acknowledged in her published and unpublished writings. Therefore, the connections between the work of Rechy and Anzaldúa (and the work of other LGBTQ-identified U.S. Latino/a authors) deserve further study and acknowledgement. Thus, I will now turn to another Chicano author who can be considered part of this alternative genealogy, and whose work is much more intimately connected to the subject matter of Rechy's early novels.

GREGG BARRIOS

Gregg Barrios (1945-) is another Texas Chicano writer who read Rechy's work early on. Based in San Antonio, Barrios has worked as a journalist and newspaper editor, and continues to publish pieces on books and music. He has also published several books of poetry, has had several of his plays staged, and continues to write plays.[12] In an interview, he explained that he was inspired to write by Françoise Sagan's 1954 novel *Bonjour Tristesse* because "it was written by an eighteen-year old whose first language was not English, yet it spent eighteen weeks on the best-seller list."[13] Barrios also stated that although the first Chicano book he read was *Pocho*, reading Rechy's early depiction of gay subculture appealed to him and helped him come to terms with his own sexuality. Barrios and Rechy both had to negotiate mainstream culture, and in Barrios' words, "Rechy did it sexually, while I did it intellectually." According to a self-interview posted on the website "Latinopia: Latino arts, history and culture," Barrios first encountered Rechy's work while stationed at the Bergstrom Air Force base in the 1960s:

> About this time, I read a book in which I saw myself as a Mexican American. It was *City of Night* by John Rechy. And in the first two chapters its [sic] about a little Mexican boy living on the border who loses his dog and cries. And he describes his loneliness and how he cannot find a place under heaven where he can find solace. Later he becomes a street person. He says, at one point, instead of going to Columbia University, I went to Times Square. And I said, "Wow! He didn't believe that he had barriers or boundaries, neither do I!" ("Gregg Barrios - In His Own Words" n.p.)

Barrios' poetry is infused with references to Rechy's early novels, with dedications to Rechy and references to his work appearing in *The Air-Conditioned Apollo* (1979), *Puro Rollo* (1982), and *La Causa* (2010). This essay focuses on *The Air-Conditioned Apollo* and *La Causa*, which have the most interesting references to Rechy.

The Air-Conditioned Apollo, which appears to be self-published, features an introduction by Rechy, yet rather than praising the poems, Rechy unequivocally states why he dislikes them at the very beginning: "I don't like this book of poems by Gregg Barrios—for a very personal reason. It's about male hustling [...] and it supplied unwanted judgments" (6). Yet the introduction turns ambiguous, like a backhanded compliment:

> Romance? Hell, no! [...] Well, fleetingly. Sometimes. But don't look into that, forget it, flee from it. But Barrios doesn't. He dredges up from the loveless cum-spattered encounters in crushed rooms and cars—he dredges up romance. And that fantasy-romance recalls, in judgment-ridden memories, all the lovelessness in my own life. (6)

Rechy's introduction ends with a plaintive question: "[...] if what Barrios says is true—if there is romance (and therefore the mangled, avoided word [...] 'love')—and is there? *is there?*—then, goddamnit, why the war?" The war he refers to is between the hustler and the "score": "The score adores/desires the hustler—and hates him for that (every hustler knows that), just as the hustler hates the score—but needs him, oh, how much" (6). This connects to themes that are prevalent in *City of Night*, *Numbers*, *The Sexual Outlaw* and *Rushes*—the concept of desire and hatred being commingled, particularly for those who are perceived as being unattainable because of their attractiveness.

While many of the poems in *The Air-Conditioned Apollo* are about non-heterosexual sexuality, one poem in particular seems to point to scenes from *City of Night*. Titled "Get a Job," the poem describes the hustling scene:

> Loitering is a passion
> credit card honored anywhere
> as all leads to darkness
> and F*A*S*C*I*N*A*T*I*O*N
> begins the beguine. (13)

In *City of Night*, the same sign is described: "And a great hungry sign groping luridly at the darkness screams: F * A * S * C * I * N * A * T * I * O * N" (30). The sexual scenes in this book of poems are very explicit, and while some are about hustlers who call the paying men "faggots," others are about mutual desire and affection. In "Shake Up," the narrator picks up a hustler named Larry and his friend, and in a motel room, it is not clear if the narrator asks Larry (or vice versa) " 'do you / like me?' strange / words coming at you: / 'yeah!' 'i want you / to be my date tonite / at the pearl street / ware house'" (50). However, it appears that it won't work out: "and home / less nomads driving on / back to the station / dropping names and them / off making excuses / not wanting to look / back as you see / your reflection / on the window pane / in the rear/view

/ mirror" (50). Again, it's not clear who is "making excuses" and who doesn't want to "look back"—the hustler and his friend, or the narrator. It seems that it is this exploration of the desire for a mutual relationship that Rechy is referring to in his introduction. However, unlike Rechy's early novels, Barrios' narrator is the paying "john" rather than the hustler, and his narrators observe the hyper-masculine pose but do not necessarily embrace it themselves.

Finally, in his latest collection of poems, *La Causa* (2010), the poem "Boulevard of Broken Noses" is dedicated to Rechy as well, and seems to be a mash-up of references to Rechy and different characters from his books. The protagonist of the poem is named "Romeo" and is described as being on a "mission improbable / to be a Latino James Dean," a description that fits images of the young John Rechy, who often wore white T-shirts with black leather jackets (60). Romeo has a United Farmworker eagle tattoo on his chest, and sells fruit "on the exit ramp" (perhaps a coy reference to Rechy's hustling), and each stanza provides a snapshot of his life after a day, week, month, and six months have passed (61). In one scene, he sits on a patio with a "needle-damaged arm," and "kisses his glow-in-the-dark / rosary to hex this day's death" (62), a likely reference to the title of Rechy's 1969 novel *This Day's Death*. In the "Notes" of the book, Barrios writes that "Boulevard of Broken Noses" is "for John Rechy aka Johnny Rio" (82). Barrios' poems intertwine Rechy's books and sexuality with classic Chicano Movement imagery (the UFW tattoo), suggesting that it is an ongoing literary project for Barrios to reconcile Rechy and the Chicano culture that still only half-heartedly embraces Rechy and what he represents.

In fact, recent plays by Barrios illustrate a larger effort to reconcile homosexuality and Chicano identity. Ben Olguín summarizes the storyline of the 2005 production of *I-DJ Mofomixmaster*:

> A young gay Chicano wants to proclaim his existence by joining the Chicano Civil Rights Movement of the 1960s and 70s—el Movimiento—but his fellow Chicano activists respond by paraphrasing Eldridge Cleaver's outrageous party line, that the only position for a woman or a fag in our movement is the lateral position. ("Queering the Movimiento")

To a certain extent, the reception of the poetry and plays of Gregg Barrios mirrors that of Rechy's later work, which Barrios explains in an interview titled "Queering the Movimiento," published in the *San Antonio Current:*

> Because it [my message] doesn't fit neatly into any pre-established categories, few people want to stage my work. It's too Chicano for the white venues, not Chicano enough for the Chicano venues, too queer for straight ones, not queer enough for the queer spaces, and just too much of this and not enough of that for everyone else. (Barrios, "Queering the Movimiento")

There are no major scholarly articles on the work of Barrios, and they are rarely anthologized in Chicano/a or LGBTQ collections. While Rechy is more well known, there is still a dearth of in-depth analysis of his work (which this study hopes to help address), suggesting that in the important push to "recover" the texts of U.S. Latinos/as, we must not overlook this generation of authors who wrote shortly before, during, and just after the Chicano Movement, when homosexuality and Chicano identity were often seen as incompatible.[14]

There is still more work to be done. For example, while Gil Cuadros' published poems, short stories, and his papers (housed at the University of California, Los Angeles) do not show any explicit references to Rechy or provide evidence that Cuadros read his work, it is hard to imagine that he was not aware of Rechy's early novels. While Rechy pioneered an open depiction of working-class, non-normative Chicano sexuality, Cuadros was one of the first openly gay and HIV positive writers, and he also openly wrote about sexuality. Similarly, in a critical biography of Arturo Islas, Frederick Luis Aldama writes that the "political and racial awareness" of Islas

> was deepened, too, by the discovery of writers John Rechy and James Baldwin. Islas was struck by John Rechy's chronicling of a queer Mexican-Scottish American character from El Paso in his best-selling *City of Night*, and he became an avid reader of all of James Baldwin's novels and journalistic essays. (Aldama 135-6)

This is another connection that can be further explored, in addition to interviewing or looking through the archives of other Chicano Movement-era writers. Rechy was a pioneer for Chicano/a readers who were looking for models of Chicano/a authors, and for LGBTQ readers (Chicano/a and non-Chicano/a readers, as I discuss in my dissertation), because he openly wrote about non-heterosexual sexuality. His work features protagonists of Mexican descent, and his work was read and continues to be read by Chicano/a authors, including Gloria Anzaldúa, Gregg Barrios, as well as contemporary authors such as Dagoberto Gilb and others. Rechy, Barrios and Anzaldúa are an example of a literary "El Mundo Zurdo," sharing an outsider status within different cultures and literary canons, although at this point Anzaldúa's work has been given a great deal of critical attention, in part due to work of the Society for the Study of Gloria Anzaldúa, while Rechy and Barrios still remain on the periphery of Chicano/a scholarship. Nevertheless, all three can in some way relate to Anzaldúa's characterization of herself as Shiva:

> Shiva, a many-armed and legged body with one foot on brown soil, one on white, one in straight society, one in the gay world, the man's world, the women's, one limb in the literary world, another in the working class, the socialist, and the occult worlds... Who, me confused? Ambivalent? Not so. Only your labels split me. ("La Prieta" 205)

ENDNOTES

1 The author would like to thank Professor Manuel M. Martín-Rodríguez and the editors and reviewers of *El Mundo Zurdo 3* for their candid and helpful feedback, as well as the Benson Latin American Collection staff at the University of Texas at Austin, the staff at the Mandeville Special Collection Library at UC San Diego, Gregg Barrios, and last but not least John Rechy, for their generous assistance.

2 I have also contributed to the Chicano/a Literature Intertextual Database, a research project started by Martín-Rodríguez. This focus on intertextual references in Chicano/a literature piqued my interest in intertextual references within Rechy's work as well as references to Rechy in different literary traditions.

3 Prior to the 1990s, eight scholars in the fields of Chicano/a Studies and Chicano/a Literature published articles on Rechy's work (Bruce-Novoa wrote four articles, for a total of twelve), and there was one dissertation written in the field of U.S. literature in 1976. On the other hand, Chicano scholars prior to the 1990s discussed José Antonio Villarreal's novel *Pocho* in at least two dissertations, and there are at least eight articles by different scholars, while Chicano/a scholars prior to the 1990s analyzed Rolando Hinojosa's work in at least thirty-seven articles and interviews. While Juan Bruce-Novoa was a major scholar in Chicano/a literary studies, very few other scholars wrote about Rechy prior to the 1990s, and when they did, it was sometimes a side note. In contrast, at least seventeen articles or chapters were published about Rechy's work in the 1990s.

4 Similarly, Shelley Fisher Fishkin does note that Anzaldúa cites *City of Night* in *Borderlands/ La Frontera*, but she only analyzes or points out the influence of poets, nonfiction writers, and female authors that Anzaldúa never cited in the book ("The Borderlands of Culture: Writing by W.E.B. Du Bois, James Agee, Tillie Olsen, and Gloria Anzaldúa," in *Literary Journalism in the Twentieth Century*, 161).

5 This article has a complementary aim to that of Soto's work, and my overall project continues and expands the work first begun by Juan Bruce-Novoa, tracing the reception and significance of Rechy's work across ethnic, national and sexual readerships.

6 Anzaldúa's journals are closed for the next twenty years, but when they become available, scholars might be able to find more information about her response to John Rechy's work.

7 "It's amazing to think that we have, as feminists and lesbians, closed our hearts to men, / to our joto brothers, / disinherited and marginal like / us" (my translation). Anzaldúa's words and images © Gloria E. Anzaldúa; used by permission of the Gloria E. Anzaldúa Literary Trust.

8 Anzaldúa's words and images © Gloria E. Anzaldúa; used by permission of the Gloria E. Anzaldúa Literary Trust.

9 See Judith Fetterly who, in *The Resisting Reader: A Feminist Approach to American Fiction*, exhorts female readers to "become a resisting rather than an assenting reader," rejecting the often-simplistic or negative portrayals of women in fiction (xxii).

10 However, Rechy's work never features a positive portrayal of a lesbian—Rechy's novels often reference glamorous movie stars like Marilyn Monroe and Maria Felix.

11 John Rechy, interview by Beth Hernandez-Jason, April 1, 2011.

12 In 2009 Barrios received a Ford Foundation grant to develop and write *Rancho Pancho*, a play about the relationship between Tennessee Williams and his lover, Pancho Rodríguez. Conducting his own research, Barrios discovered that Williams' relationship with Rodríguez, not Frank Merlo, was the inspiration behind *A Streetcar Named Desire* ("Afterword," *Rancho Pancho*, 51-4). In 2008 Rancho Pancho was performed at the Provincetown Tennessee Williams Theater Festival, and was the only piece performed that was not originally written by Williams.

13 Gregg Barrios, interview by Beth Hernandez-Jason, May 19, 2012 in San Antonio, Texas.

14 The Recovering the U.S. Hispanic Literary Heritage Project, begun at the University of Houston, has done important work in the area of "recovery," and continues to do so.

WORKS CITED

Aldama, Frederick Luis. *Dancing with Ghosts: A Critical Biography of Arturo Islas*. Berkeley: U of California P, 2005.

Allen, Donald. Letter to John Rechy. 20 January 1960. TS. Donald Allen Collection. Mandeville Special Collection Lib., University of California, San Diego.

Anzaldúa, Gloria. *Borderlands/La Frontera: The New Mestiza*. 1987. San Francisco, CA: Aunt Lute Books, 1999. Print.

---. "La Prieta." *This Bridge Called My Back*. 1981. Eds. Cherríe L. Moraga and Glorı́a E. Anzaldúa. New York: Kitchen Table: Women of Color Press, 1983. 198-209.

---. "Three Memories." MS. Gloria Evangelina Anzaldúa Papers, Benson Latin American Collection, University of Texas Libraries, the University of Texas at Austin.

---. "To(o) Queer the Writer—Loca, escritora y chicana" in *Living Chicana Theory*. Ed. Carla Trujillo. Berkeley: Third Woman Press, 1998. 263-276. Print.

Barrios, Gregg. *The Air-Conditioned Apollo*. Austin: Harbinger Press, 1979. Print.

---. "Gregg Barrios - In His Own Words." Latinopia.com 21 June 2010. Web. 20 September 2012. Online.

---. *Healthy Self.* Austin: Harbinger Press, 1979. Print.

---. *La Causa*. East Brunswick, NJ: Hansen Publishing Group, 2010. Print.

---. *Puro Rollo*. Los Angeles, CA: Posada Press/Quetzalcoatl Publications, 1982. Print.

---. "Queering the Movimiento: Gregg Barrios's Theater of the Repressed, Recovered, and Revolutionized" by B.V. Olguín. *San Antonio Current* 8 October 2008. Web www2.sacurrent.com. 2 November 2012. Online.

Fetterly, Judith. *The Resisting Reader: A Feminist Approach to American Fiction*. Bloomington: Indiana UP, 1978. Print.

Gutiérrez, Ramón. "Community, Patriarchy and Individualism: The Politics of Chicano History and the Dream of Equality." 1993. Rpt. in *Locating American Studies: The Evolution of a Discipline*. Ed. Lucy Maddox. Baltimore: John Hopkins UP, 1999: 353-81. Print.

Hernández-G., Manuel de Jesús. "Building a Research Agenda on U.S. Latino Lesbigay Literature and Cultural Production: Texts, Writers, Performance, and Critics." *Chicano/Latino Homoerotic Identities*. Ed. David William Foster. New York: Garland Publishing, 1999. 287-304. Print.

Hidalgo, Melissa Martha. *Schooling La Raza: A Chicana/o Cultural History of Education, 1968-2008*. Diss. University of California, San Diego, 2011. UC San Diego Electronic Theses and Dissertations: b7069243. Retrieved from: http://escholarship.org/uc/item/8t69s3wd

Limón, José E. *Mexican Ballads, Chicano Poems: History and Influence in Mexican-American Social Poetry*. Berkeley and Los Angeles: U of California P, 1992. Print.

---. Letter to Donald Allen. N.d. TS. Donald Allen Collection. Mandeville Special Collection Lib., University of California, San Diego.

Rechy, John. *City of Night*. New York: Grove Press, 1963. Print.

Saldívar, Ramón. *Chicano Narrative: The Dialectics of Difference*. Madison: The U of Wisconsin P, 1990. Print.

Soto, Sandra K. *Reading Chican@ Like a Queer: The De-Mastery of Desire*. Austin: U of Texas Press, 2010. Print.

FROM GENEALOGIES TO GYNEALOGIES: COMPARING *BORDERLANDS* TO ITS FIRST ALL-POETRY MANUSCRIPT

CAROLINA NÚÑEZ-PUENTE

INTRODUCTION: APPROACHING THE GENEALOGY OF BOTH *BORDERLANDS* AND THIS ARTICLE

It is 12:50 p.m. on a Saturday in July 2011 in Austin, Texas. I am walking in the street. The weather is 93 degrees Fahrenheit with a humidity index of 85%. Coming from Northwest Spain, I find the Texas summer almost unbearable. I wear a cap, an umbrella, sunglasses, and 50-SPF moisturizer. There are very few people walking in the street, which makes me feel even more bizarre... Gloria Evangelina Anzaldúa's papers are archived in the Benson Library at the University of Texas, Austin. In the summer of 2011, I travelled from Spain to work on the earliest manuscript of *Borderlands*. I first came into contact with the book during a graduate course at Rutgers University in 2001. Since then, I have presented papers at conferences and written articles on Anzaldúa (see Nuñez-Puente 2003); still, I keep feeling the need to return to *Borderlands*. How can a book have such an impact on a person's life that she voluntarily sacrifices her summer? I often wondered this during my research at the archive. Now I know the answer has to do with the experience of reading Anzaldúa.

Apart from being demanding and uplifting, reading *Borderlands* was an educational experience, which helped me not only to understand Chicano/a culture, but also to understand myself. Anzaldúa pushed me to revisit the so-called Spanish conquest of America. This was a tough moment since, like many Spaniards, I abhor that part of our history. Anzaldúa also taught me about the flexibility and porosity of the boundaries between sexual identities. Furthermore, with Anzaldúa I learnt the crucial importance of the body and spirituality in the formation of identity. Briefly put, Anzaldúa's concept of identity goes beyond the "I think, therefore I am," and comprehends the other (e.g., body, spirit) as well as the others (e.g., relationships with other people).[1] Thanks to Anzaldúa, I gained a more holistic comprehension of feminism, which led me to promote and practice solidarity among feminists. I could go on naming other lessons I took from Anzaldúa, but to summarize, I can say that reading *Borderlands* changed my way of looking at the world, which actually means, it changed my life. Considering all this, I believe my gratitude and love for mi maestra were the reasons for me to fly away from home and suffer the Texas summer. Regarding this sacrifice, I remember a litany which went on in my brain while working at the archive: "Scholars' work? Archival dust." This article deals with Anzaldúa's very first manuscript of her most famous book, and with how the dust of the archive turned out to be poetry.

One day at the archive, I decided to check box 32, folder 1. In a letter dated July 30 1985, Anzaldúa says: "I'm in the midst of writing a book of poems called Borderlands...it grew out of one of the poems I read at Common Differences ...it's a monster now and the extended preface/process essay is part of [the] 'Atravesando Fronteras' essay. It's all coming together but it takes its own sweet time." Eureka! I thought to myself, I found it! The genealogy of *Borderlands* is right in front of me: it started out as an all-poetry book. It was not until later that it transformed into a multigenre text, divided into two parts. Part one, titled "*Atravesando Fronteras*/Crossing Borders," is comprised mainly of prose and some scattered poems. Part two bears the name "*Un Agitado Viento*/Ehécatl, the Wind" and consists only of poems. Coming back to Anzaldúa's letter in her archive, we learn that part one of *Borderlands* was originally intended to be the introduction to the book. However, as Anzaldúa wrote, it grew longer and longer and ended up being half of the book, as both parts are each roughly a hundred pages.

Knowing about the curious genealogy of *Borderlands* is surprising and somehow humorous from both a Foucaultian and a non-Foucaultian point of view. To start with the latter, there is something ironic in the fact that an introduction can turn into half a book. Apparently Anzaldúa not only wanted to introduce her poetry, which is already too complex to be introduced briefly, she also wanted to introduce herself. In his article "Nietzsche, Genealogy, History," Michel Foucault argued that even "historical beginnings are lowly...derisive and ironic" (79); thus, Foucault urged us to pursue genealogical studies that "cultivate the details and accidents that accompany every beginning" (80). In this respect, the genealogy of Anzaldúa's aforementioned book is probably as sinuous as any other. Following Foucault, it seems urgent to examine Anzaldúa's earliest all-poetry manuscript, which is just titled *Borderlands*, while delving into other unexpected traces.

In the following pages, I do a comparative reading of the aforementioned original manuscript, comprised solely of poetry, and the poetry of *Borderlands*, the book which was ultimately published. Hereafter my use of "manuscript" refers to the original all-poetry manuscript of *Borderlands*; by saying "book" or "*Borderlands*" I refer to the published poetry-and-prose book, whose full title is *Borderlands/La Frontera: The New Mestiza*.[2] My ultimate goal is to show that comparing the original manuscript to the final version of the book offers a different, suggestive, and enlightening reading of the latter.

The paper is organized into three more sections and a coda. In the next section, I classify and discuss the poems' inclusions, transformations, and additions by comparing the earliest manuscript to the published book. Anzaldúa made both minor and major changes in her poems before publishing them. By "minor" changes I mean: changing a word, a short phrase or even the title; respelling or (re)accenting certain words; going from regular font to italics; breaking a verse or stanza into more units; and so forth. By "major" changes I imply Anzaldúa did a full rewriting of at least some parts of the poems which I classify together.[3]

Section three is intended to comment upon the poems in the original manuscript which were not included in the published version, and upon the possible reasons for Anzaldúa's decision to put them aside. Among these reasons, I hypothesize upon her shyness, her misunderstandings with her family, her criticism of certain myths (e.g., mother-daughter bond), her aunts' and grand-mother's secrets, her problems as a graduate student, and her attempt to soften some of the lesboerotic features of her writing. Reading Anzaldúa's archived poems is a really exciting experience. For now I can only say that, as Foucault wrote, the findings I reflect upon in the paper will be "surprising" for many of my readers.

Section four reads some of Anzaldúa's most addictive, recurring, goddess-like poems, mainly to assess the stages they underwent during the creative process. My use of the words "addictive" and "recurring" refer to the fact that Anzaldúa was somehow haunted by some poems, which led her to rewrite them several times. There are also poems which are "goddess-like," though not only because they revise myths about certain goddesses. Given the mysteriously empowering force of poetry, Anzaldúa seems to turn into a goddess by writing these poems.

The coda comments upon Anzaldúa's initial decision to write a poetry book by discussing the Aztec poetry festivals called *flor y canto* (flower and song); the coda continues exploring the concept of gynealogy. Being my own concept, gynealogy pays tribute to Norma Alarcón's widely acclaimed article on *Borderlands*' gynetics (1996). A gynealogy can be defined as a kind of genealogy intended to acknowledge past women's lives and works and, therein, to cherish how women have contributed to our current practices and ideas. A gynealogical reading of literature strives to rescue the women writers of the past, and to show the connections between their works. In the case of Anzaldúa, I compare her to two women poets of the Spanish peninsula: first, to nineteenth-century Galician poet, Rosalía de Castro—which might be a "surprising" connection; second, to a twenty-first-century Basque poet, Itxaro Borda—as readers might know, part of Anzaldúa's genealogy is in the Basque Country. Finally, the coda celebrates the new gynealogies, for example, in the shape of female trinities (e.g., Anzaldúa, de Castro, and Borda), which can emerge thanks to the transformative energies of poetry.

As for the poems Anzaldúa wrote before the publication of *Borderlands*, I prove that all of them—including those in the manuscript that are not in the book—should be read alongside the prose fragments of *Borderlands*. In other words, the article is comparative on three levels: linking the all-poetry manuscript with the poetry of *Borderlands*; joining the poetry (of the manuscript and the book) with the prose fragments of *Borderlands*; and connecting Anzaldúa, de Castro, and Borda in what I call a gynealogical Trinity. Finally, I hope my article encourages others to also pursue archival research in the G.E.A. papers.

FROM THE ORIGINAL MANUSCRIPT TO THE BOOK: INCLUSIONS, TRANSFORMATIONS, ADDITIONS

Let me start with an overview of the main structural differences between the original manuscript and the *Borderlands* book. On the one hand, the first manuscript (1985) is organized into five sections and has a total of thirty-four poems. On the other, the poetry part of the book has thirty-eight poems arranged into six sections, none of whose titles coincide with those in the manuscript. Anzaldúa used just one of the all-poetry manuscript titles, "Entering into the Serpent," to entitle a section in the prose part of her book. Another difference between the two texts is the order in which the poems are presented. Next I classify the poems under different headings, depending on the changes they underwent in the passage from manuscript to book:

2.1. Manuscript poems included in *Borderlands*' poetry section with minor or no changes: "horse," "Holy Relics," "En el Nombre de Todas las Madres que Han Perdido Hijos en la Guerra," "Cervicide," "el entierro" (retitled as "Cultures"), "Nopalitos," "Antigua, Mi Diosa," "I Had to Go Down," "Creature of Darkness," "the Border" (retitled as "Interface"), and "Cancion de la Diosa de la Noche."

2.2. Manuscript poems included in *Borderlands'* poetry section with major transformations: "A Sea of Cabbages," "Un Mar de Repollos," "Como Ella: Immaculate, Inviolate" (retitled as "Immaculate, Inviolate: Como Ella"), "My Black Angelos," "Poets Have Strange Eating Habits," and "Cagado abismo, quiero saber."

2.3. Manuscript poems added to *Borderlands'* prose fragments without changes: "Poets," "protean being."

2.4. Manuscript poems excluded from *Borderlands*: "In the Name of All the Mothers Who Have Lost Sons in the War," "Tihueque," "Entering into the Serpent," "Del Otro Lado," "Never Momma," "Tejas, why do you call me? Una cancion," "Cowardly Abyss, I Want to Know," "The Dark Muse," "Enemy of the State," "Ancient, My Goddess," "Encountering the Medusa," "Despierto en un monte oscuro," "Wolf," "The Dance of Death," and "Serpent Woman."

As can be inferred from my classification, Anzaldúa did not include all the poems of the manuscript in the final version of *Borderlands*. Instead, she added twenty-one new poems to the poetry section of the book, and many others to the prose one, which proves her prolific although quite overlooked gift as a poet.[4] We must not forget that the so-called prose part of the book has a circular structure, which begins and ends in verse: opening with a song by a band called "Los Tigres del Norte" and closing with the stanza "This land was Mexican once / was Indian always / and is. / And will be again" (Anzaldúa 1999, 113). As we will see, the circular pattern is characteristic of Anzaldúa's life and work. Circular structures deconstruct the traditional idea of teleology, which was also widely criticized by philosophers like Foucault. Teleology is inherent to official accounts both of history and genealogy, whose implications of progress are beloved by Western capitalist ideology. Anzaldúa's circular writing format privileges the indigenous cultures of the Americas, for whom life (besides history and genealogy) is a circle. Furthermore, Anzaldúa included two manuscript poems together with new poems in the prose section of *Borderlands*, a fact which underscores that she did not consider the poetry and prose parts of the book as isolated from each other. Moreover, when examining some fragments of the prose, it is hard to distinguish whether they are lyrical prose or poetry.[5] Two conclusions can be drawn in reference to these genre issues: first, Anzaldúa's mixing of genres is intended both to celebrate *mestizaje* and to escape classifications of all kinds—such as those of races, sexualities, genders, or nationalities; second, people must carefully read *Borderlands'* poetry while connecting it to the prose, since they are intimately related.

The manuscript starts with a poem titled "A Sea of Cabbages," followed by "Un Mar de Repollos," both of which honor the humble people *que trabaja en las labores*. The poetry section of *Borderlands* opens with "White-Wing Season," in which a woman who "wrings the *sábanas*" needs to let the "*gringos*" kill her doves so that she can afford to "reshingle her roof" (Anzaldúa 1999, 124). It must be noticed that, both in the manuscript and in the book, Anzaldúa chose to introduce herself to the readers by returning to her farmworker (or *campesina*) origins. Not only the poetry but also the prose part of *Borderlands* has several fragments that identify Chicanos and Chicanas according to economic class: e.g. "As working class people our chief activity is to put food in our mouths" (39). In fact, the prose part opens and closes with such reflections; in the early pages of the book, Anzaldúa denounces the *"herida abierta"* (25), or the border that divides the first world from the third, which many Mexicans desperately need to cross in order to survive. In the last pages of the prose section, Anzaldúa assesses "the 1982 peso devaluation in Mexico" while she quotes her brother complaining "It's been a bad year for corn" (112). From here we can argue that Anzaldúa's denunciation of Mexican and Chicano/a socioeconomic problems frames part one of *Borderlands*.

The same circular reading can be made of the poetry part of the book, which, after opening with "White-wing Season," closes with "Don't Give In, *Chicanita*." In these poems, Anzaldúa not only pursues a socioeconomic critique, but also dignifies different female figures: a working-class woman in the first case, and her niece in the second one. It appears that the spirit to criticize any form of socioeconomic injustice is not lost in the passage from manuscript to book; second, I agree with Sonia Saldívar-Hull that, by writing about *mestizas'* experiences, Anzaldúa was able to fill a gendered gap that male historians were unable to recount (2000, 75). To continue with Anzaldúa's family, one of the most exciting transformations when going from manuscript to book happened to the poem about her grandmother. Originally, "Como Ella: Immaculate, Inviolate" has fifteen more verses than its retitled published version. In these fifteen verses which close the poem, Anzaldúa identifies herself very much with her *Mamagrande* and says: "Like her / I have never grown attached to palos. / Dicen que soy orgullosa como ella / ... / I too have gotten burned, / ... / Like her I have never learned / to live with it. / But unlike her and las tias / I talk about it."[6] This closing section reveals two aspects of Anzaldúa's genealogy and gynealogy: one, her grandmother's dislike of penises was inherited by the author (although the literal meaning of *palos* is sticks); two, her aunts felt secretly unsatisfied with heterosexuality. As suggested above, Foucault taught us that it is vital to question why certain ideas, customs, or texts are abandoned in the course of a work. The quoted verses disclose a couple of family secrets, which is perhaps the reason why Anzaldúa decided to omit them and publish a shorter version of the poem. This would not be the only time that Anzaldúa either obviated or softened the lesbian character of her poems before publishing them (see also below). This seems to have been a major reason for her to exclude certain manuscript poems from the *Borderlands* book, and to transform others before publication. It must be mentioned that some of the manuscript poems that were not included in the book are the author's own translations of her poetry. What about the manuscript poems, which were momentarily put aside?[7]

POEMS OF THE FIRST MANUSCRIPT WHICH ARE NOT IN THE *BORDERLANDS* BOOK

Here I discuss four manuscript poems excluded from the published version of *Borderlands*—"Del Otro Lado," "Never, Momma," "Tejas, why do you call me? Una cancion," and "Serpent Woman." The first three of these poems have a circular structure, which means they end by repeating the words stated in the titles.

Returning to her genealogical tree, "Del Otro Lado" and "Never, Momma" appear to be autobiographical poems in which Anzaldúa portrays her family's rejection of her lesbianism. In both poems, the use of a conversation format satirizes the lack of a real, ethical, and respectful dialog. Perhaps due to shyness, in "Del Otro Lado" Anzaldúa does not use the pronoun "I" and refers to herself in the third person ("She"). Moreover, the mother's and the sister's voices have a particularly bitter tone: "She remembers / the horror in her sister's voice / 'Eres una de las otras,' / the look in her mother's face / as she says 'I'm so ashamed' [...]" The lyrical voice also remembers how her mother kicks her out of the home by saying "Don[']t bring your queer friends / into my house, my land, the planet. / Get away, don't contaminate us. / Vete a la chingada de aqui." Undoubtedly, being rejected and even insulted by one's genealogical family must be unspeakably painful. As sung by the lyrical voice: "Away, she went away. / But every place she went to / they'd push her to the other side." This "other side"—which reappears three times in English and one in Spanish, "al otro lado"—seems to be an all-comprehensive *frontera* that can shelter those who feel like outcasts from collectives such as family, ethnicity, race, sex, gender, and nationality, among others.

Despite the gravity of the family situation in "Del Otro Lado," when looked at from a cooler perspective, the mother's reaction is so blown out of proportion that it can actually make us laugh. The mother adds: "You should be ashamed of yourself. / People are starving ... / ... / while you talk about gay rights and orgasms." On the one hand, I believe that using one's sense of humor always helps in these kinds of situations, since trying to have a serious dialog with a close-minded person is actually impossible. That is why I think feminists should use humor more often; humor is something I miss when reading Anzaldúa's work, although she might have included a comic wink in this poem. On the other hand, it is well known that Anzaldúa acted in solidarity with those who suffered, either from lack of food or lack of rights. In fact, Anzaldúa's idea of the "Otro Lado," which titles this poem, is close to that of "*El Mundo Zurdo*," a left-handed world which shelters both "the queer groups [and] the people that don't belong anywhere" (Anzaldúa 1983, 209). In later years Anzaldúa might have transformed her concept of *El Mundo Zurdo* into her "new tribalism" (see "(Un)Natural bridges, (Un)safe spaces"). As Anzaldúa theorized through both concepts, she believed that the efforts born from the union among different peoples can provoke changes in the status quo leading to a radical democracy; hence the latent claim for solidarity in the aforementioned poem.

"Never, Momma" describes a mother who "never had much schooling," and who did all sorts of jobs only to be overworked and exploited. The stanzas in the middle of the poem reproduce part of a telephone call: "When are you coming home, Prieta? / I got fired. / I need you to help out." It is only in the last stanza that the call is answered: "Never, Momma. / I'm never coming home." After reading "Del Otro Lado," in which the mother kicks the daughter out of the home, the reader is not very surprised by the daughter's reaction in this poem. Still, it is brave on Anzaldúa's part to demystify the traditional belief in the family, especially the mother-daughter bond, as a purely loving and understanding entity. Anzaldúa thus appears as a pioneer of recent studies which argue that maternity is a complex, multifaceted phenomenon (see for example O'Reilly and Caporale-Bizzini [2009]).

Although lacking a circular pattern, "Serpent Woman" is another manuscript poem that was excluded from the *Borderlands* book, and which deals with family relations. In "Serpent," the lyric voice seems that of the very Coatlicue "whose eyes are mouths" (repeated twice). In the midst of a frenzied ecstasy, she says: "I dance on the corpse of my dead father." According to my reading, this "father" is a metaphor for any person with authority—a family member, a teacher—who subscribes to patriarchal tradition. Therefore, the speaker's dance seems a way of rejoicing the end of patriarchy, heterosexism, and family control. In fact, the last verse of the poem reads, "I am my own hearth." Using the term "hearth" multiplies the affective and caring connotations of "home." Finally, a speaker who affirms she is her own hearth is again criticizing established assumptions about family units.

All these poems must be read alongside the prose of the *Borderlands* book. In it, Anzaldúa praises one of her students for coming up with the idea that homophobia stems from a "fear of going home" (Anzaldúa 1999, 42); that is, fear of being rejected by one's family due to one's homosexual preferences. Here and in other places in the prose section of *Borderlands*, Anzaldúa continued her task to deconstruct the "home sweet home" ideal. As I suggested above, I suspect that Anzaldúa chose not to put the aforementioned poems in the *Borderlands* book to keep her family secrets; besides, she could have been trying to avoid talking about her lesbianism in a contentious manner. A less controversial reason, which I already pointed out, is shyness. It has always shocked me that Anzaldúa's most sensual poem, the lesboerotic "*Compañera, cuando amábamos*" (1999, 168-169), is written exclusively in Spanish. Was the author too shy to provide a translation? Was Spanish closer to her heart than English, so therefore, she chose to express herself only in that language? Hopefully, by writing these poems, Anzaldúa was able to exorcize some of the terrifying aspects of the domestic. Still, she kept answering the call of Tejas.

In "Tejas, why do you call me? Una cancion," Tejas is portrayed as a mean lover who demands everything and gives very little in return. The poem's refrain is rewritten in different ways. These changes evoke Anzaldúa's paradoxical feelings for a personification of her home state, whose behavior with her was also paradoxical. Hence the oxymoron between being given "mouth and feet"—with which to speak a bilingual tongue, kiss other women, tread on home ground, and walk freely—and being metaphorically "gagged and caged"—or silenced and forbidden to embody her Chicana academic lesbian identity. The poem portrays Anzaldúa's passionate feelings for Texas: her exile from it was as painful as leaving a "lover," which made her cry bitterly as she drove on the "highway."

Writing the poem in the song genre ("Una cancion") has folklore connotations, which remind us of the *corrido*. Therein, not only Anzaldúa's "Tejas," but also her other *canciones* corroborate the argument of José Limón, that Mexican *corridos* have influenced and continue to survive in Chicana/o literature (see Limón 1992). In this poem, Anzaldúa rewrites the *corrido* genre in her own Chicana feminist lesbian terms. For example, Anzaldúa uses the Spanish term *norias* (waterwheels) as a metaphor for her eyes, and the also Spanish *camposantos* (cemeteries) as a metaphor for her cheeks. These metaphors take us to a few exciting ideas, some of which have already been discussed. First, the use of Spanish words shows that Anzaldúa felt a strong emotional link to that language; second, what she elsewhere called her "Wild Tongue" (Anzaldúa 1999, 75) might also point at her lesbianism; third, her eyes can be read as the multiple eyes that populate her self—a self that, like a *noria*, often moved in circles; fourth, the *camposantos* of her cheeks can be read as the absence of affection (understood as no kisses on the cheek) which she received from her fellow Texans. As an example, Anzaldúa was not allowed to pursue a Ph.D. in Chicana Studies in her native state; consequently, she moved to California to carry out her research project.

Despite everything, and like the circling refrain of the Tejas "Cancion," Anzaldúa felt a passionate connection to her native valley in South Texas, to which she kept returning. To achieve this understanding, it is vital to read Anzaldúa's genealogy in "events outside of any monotonous finality ... in sentiments, love, conscience, instincts" (Foucault 76). As I noted earlier, the circular pattern suits both Anzaldúa's life and work well. Not surprisingly, the last poetry section of the *Borderlands* book is titled "*El Retorno*." Anzaldúa's working method was also circular, in the sense that she rewrote her texts over and over again. Several poems of the manuscript underwent this process too, as I show in the next section.

ADDICTIVE, RECURRING, GODDESS-LIKE POEMS

There are three poems, which appear both in the first manuscript and the poetry section of the later *Borderlands*, which Anzaldúa rewrote for several years: "*Antigua, mi diosa*," "Poets have strange eating habits," and "*Canción de la diosa de la noche*." As I previously stated, both the manuscript and the poetry part of the book start with poems that pay homage to Anzaldúa's *campesina* origins. Sadly, "A Sea of Cabbages," its translation, "Un Mar de Repollos," and "White-wing Season," describe doves that are caught either in a "net" or by white "hunters" (Anzaldúa 1999, 154 and 125). In contrast, "*Antigua*," "Poets," and "*Canción*" cherish the transformations Anzaldúa experienced as a mature person. As we will see in these three poems, Anzaldúa develops transformative *nagual* abilities thanks to the help of poetry. Thus, she goes from being a caged dove to feeling free.

"Poets have strange eating habits" was transformed in the passage from manuscript to book. The two verses added at the beginning reveal Anzaldúa's admiration for Lorca's nocturnal imagery: when facing the writing task, the poet finds "[d]ark windowless   no moon glides / across the nightsky" (Anzaldúa 1999, 162 space break in original).[8] At the end of the manuscript version, the poet is devoured by the abyss—"it swallows me whole." On the contrary, the book version reads "*me la tragó* [sic] *todita*" translated as "I swallow it   whole" (163, space break in orginal). This change empowers the poet as well as accounts for her strange eating habits.[9] In fact, "Poets" describes the writing of poetry as both an inner and outer task in which the poet must "plunge / off the high cliff" and "burrow deep into" herself (162-163).

Faithful to my intention of connecting poetry and prose, I must add another comment. Anzaldúa's poetry and prose often dig not only into the pains of creative writing (see chapter 6 of *Borderlands*), but also into the pains of a much tormented self. For instance, in the prose section, it says: "*Por que la vida me arremolina pa' ca y pa' ya, como hoja seca, me araña y me golpea, me deshuesa—mi culpa por que me desdeño*" (66); in the poem "Creature of Darkness," we read: "No, we like it here in the dark / we like sitting here with our grief / and our longing" (208). Being often expressionist, and at times very lyrical, these fragments are above all extremely honest. Reading such reflections from poet-philosopher Anzaldúa can enlighten us on how to manage moments of personal crisis.

A verse of "Poets" that is kept intact both in the manuscript and the book is: "feathers growing out of my skin" (Anzaldúa 1999, 162). The poet is a *nagual* who, as the Plumed Serpent, can work as a mediator to restore harmony between different worlds. As Anzaldúa explains in the prose of *Borderlands*: "the ancient Aztecs...believed that...by means of poetry and truth, communication with the Divine could be attained, and...[the] above...could be bridged with...[the] below" (91). Anzaldúa's well-known efforts to facilitate communication among worlds are celebrated by all her readers. There are poems which deal explicitly with Anzaldúa's attempts to communicate with the goddesses, and even to become a goddess herself.

In "*Antigua, mi diosa*" the lyrical voice sings her "*aflicción*" as she goes errant, hurting "*las plantas de [sus] pies*," looking for Antigua (Anzaldúa 1999, 210). The goddess of this poem, who dares to have very close relationships with humans ("*Me entraste por todas las rendijas / con tu luz llenaste el hueco de mi cuerpo*"), whose voice is "*un millón de alas*," and whose "*dedos canta[n]*" could be the very personification of poetry. In the prose part of *Borderlands*, Anzaldúa defines *Antigua* as "a greater power than the conscious I ... [her] inner self... the divine within" (72). The description of *Antigua* as the divine, the unconscious, and the inner self is coherent with my interpretation of it as personifying poetry or even the act of writing poetry. As we can learn from Anzaldúa's perspective in "Poets," poetry writing is a task which requires deep introspection; furthermore, poetry has the power to join the above and the below. In the poem "*Antigua*," one of the speaker's afflictions comes from the loss of inspiration to write poems. In the manuscript of this poem, the "*[d]eseos insepultos*" of the poet "*velan la noche eterna*." In the book, the night is no longer eternal but simply "*la noche*" (211), which gives hope to Anzaldúa so that she can finally write poetry by blooming again in *Antigua*'s darkest skin—i.e., "*brotar otra vez / en tu negrísima piel*" (211). Anzaldúa's desire becomes true in "*Canción de la diosa de la noche*."

A deliciously symbolic poem, "*Canción*" requires an article of its own. For my purposes here, I can say that the poem confirms as well as enacts the idea of poets as mediators. Anzaldúa wrote several versions of this poem; however, the version in the manuscript I am commenting upon here is almost identical to the one in the book.[10] Both versions present us with a mighty dialogical poet who can communicate both with "Isis," the above, and "Satan," the below (Anzaldúa 1999, 218-219). To achieve this multifold dialog, some transformations are necessary: first she blooms in the shape of "a vine / creeping down the moon" (218); then she "pass[es] / through the gate, / come[s] to the path on the left" and, finally, becomes "the gate." After inspiriting the readers with her metamorphosis, she tells us "You are the gate" (220), by which she ultimately encourages all poetry readers to participate in transformative ethical dialogs.[11]

The last verses are especially suggestive: "The moon eclipses the sun. / *La diosa* lifts us. / We don the feathered mantle / and charge our fate" (221). First, the patriarchal order (sun) is replaced by the matrilineal one (moon) thanks to the power of *la diosa*, who might again stand for poetry itself. Second, the "feathered mantle" joins the Christian tradition (*la Virgen de Guadalupe's* starry mantle) to the Aztec one (Coatlicue and the Plumed Serpent), putting forward an alternative Trinity from which to derive future rebellious gynealogies. As it is well known, fostering such a renewed *mestizo* encounter among cultures is one of the projects of *Borderlands*. Third, the verse "charge our fate" is especially intriguing given the unexpected use of the verb "charge" instead of "change," which invites readers to celebrate the transformative and empowering energies of poetry. Neither with simply a positive nor simply a negative "charge" but with both, the poetry reader is finally able to acquire the *mestiza's* "tolerance for ambiguity" which mediates between opposites (Anzaldúa 1999, 101).

Dedicated to Randy Conner in the *Borderlands* book, "*Canción*" is the poem that closes the manuscript, something that endows it with a special status. *Borderlands,* on the other hand, closes with the previously cited "Don't Give In, *Chicanita,*" a poem "*para* Missy Anzaldúa," the author's niece. Altruistically, Anzaldúa wrote none of these poems for herself and decided to finish the book version, once more drawing a circle back to her genealogical family.

CODA: POETRY AS TRANSFORMATIVE GYNEALOGY

As this article demonstrates, tracing the genealogy of *Borderlands* may lead us not only to poetry but also to Aztec culture. The epigraph of Anzaldúa's all-poetry manuscript says: "Xochicueponi in nocuic. / Brota, se desata como flor, mi canto. / My song puts forth shoots, breaks loose like a flower." This epigraph honors the Aztecs' floral games, known as *flor y canto*, which celebrated poetry's ability to facilitate the dialog between earth and heaven, body and soul, flower and song. According to Marta Sánchez, "forms of oral and popular culture" have had a great influence on Chicanos/as and Mexicans (12). Thus, both communities perceive poetry as a "vehicle not only for the rapid communication of a message but also for a quick audience response to social and personal concerns" (14). Putting Aztec wisdom and Sánchez's insightful comments together can help us to explain the reasons for Anzaldúa's initial decision to write an all-poetry book: first, to honor the festivals of her ancestors; second, to criticize the present situation of Chicanos/as while demanding social change; and, third, to communicate in a genre that can work as a bridge between people, and between people and the rest of the universe.

I will also argue that the genealogy of *Borderlands,* on the one hand, leads us to Anzaldúa's family tree; gynealogies, on the other, honor our female ancestors' contributions, combining them in *mestiza* ways, to achieve powerful transformations. Curiously enough, Anzaldúa's Basque last name somehow entails the harmonizing power of poetry; as she points out with pride, "Anzaldúa" means the union between the upper and lower worlds (see box 33, folder 2). In spite of its all-poetry origins, Anzaldúa transformed her manuscript into a multigenre text, *Borderlands*, which both accounts for the *mestizo* origins of Chicanos/as and promotes a *mestizo* future. In the next few paragraphs, I approach this future while circling back to the Spanish peninsula. I then offer another Trinity to be added to the one cited above (Guadalupe, Coatlicue, and the Plumed Serpent), and from which more gynealogies should arise.

It is pertinent, I believe, to explain why I link Anzaldúa to two authors from the Spanish peninsula: Rosalía de Castro and Itxaro Borda. Far from wishing to impose an imperialistic Eurocentric point of view, the purpose of this link is threefold: to not forget that, as Anzaldúa herself claims, part of her genealogy is in Spain; to share my perspective and genealogy as a scholar coming from that country; and to open a global dialog with other scholars. Regarding my last purpose, I wish to cherish Aztec wisdom by practicing a reading of poetry that breaks boundaries and forges connections not only among people, but also between people and the rest of the universe. Finally, in keeping with Anzaldúa's theory and practice of intersectionalities and connections, I believe that comparative readings of poetry can promote solidarity among all of us. Furthermore, doing comparative work is a way to continue Anzaldúan theories and practices, as I show below.

Second, Aztlán, Galicia, and the Basque Country share some similarities regarding their geographies, languages, histories, and cultural imaginaries. The three can be considered borderland regions located in larger territories: the U.S.A. in the first case, and Spain in the second and third. The three are also bilingual: Aztlán in English and Spanish, Galicia in Spanish and Galician, and the Basque Country in Spanish and Basque. The cultural movements of Galician *Rexurdimento* and Basque *Resurgimiento* arose in the nineteenth century, thanks to the promotion of Romantic ideas such as individual freedom. These movements, whose names might be translated as "Renaissance," tried to revitalize and dignify Galician and Basque cultures respectively—a situation which shares key parallelisms with El Movimiento Chicano. During the dictatorship of General Francisco Franco (1939-1975), Galician and Basque languages were forbidden and

Spanish was considered the official language in Spain. In the case of Chicanos/as, Anzaldúa reminds us that when she was caught speaking Spanish at school recess, she was given "three licks on the knuckles with a sharp ruler" (1999, 75).

Considering these issues, it is not surprising that the poets I compare each claim linguistic rights in their writings: Anzaldúa, by using either English or Spanish and mixing them up; de Castro, by writing either in Spanish or Galician; and Borda, by writing mainly in Basque and producing bilingual editions. Many writers of Aztlán, Galicia, and the Basque Country both write within their own cultural imaginations and rewrite the imaginations that were imposed by other cultures, be they Anglo or Spanish. Anzaldúa, de Castro, and Borda go even further by writing critically against the patriarchal imagination, which invades their cultures. Hence, de Castro has recently been claimed as a feminist (see García Negro 2010), and Borda is often praised for talking about her lesbianism in an open manner (see Ziga 2011). And in weaving they unweave, like Penelope herself.

Third, my proposal of alternative Trinities (Guadalupe, Coatlicue, and the Plumed Serpent on the one hand; Anzaldúa, de Castro, and Borda on the other) stems from the belief that Trinities must always proliferate for various reasons: to escape from the yoke of binaries, which ultimately lead to hierarchies; to avoid the creation of empires while the different Trinities take turns at performing leadership; and so forth. I close with a gynealogical reading of this Trinity of women poets with the hope that it will be continued by other readers.

Anzaldúa's poem "My Black *Angelos*," which is both in the manuscript and the *Borderlands* book, depicts the Mexican legend of La Llorona. Anzaldúa interprets La Llorona's crying as: "She is crying for the dead child / the lover gone, the lover not yet come" (Anzaldúa 1999, 206). In the nineteenth century, Galician poet Rosalía de Castro gave artistic form to the Galician concept of *saudade*—see *Cantares Gallegos*, first published in 1863. Nonexistent in both English and Spanish, de Castro's use of Galician *saudade* comprehends human beings' fears, dreams, frustrations, and aspirations about the present, the past, and the future. Very often de Castro's *saudade* is related to emigration, which is also a motif in Chicano/a writing. Thanks to de Castro, I read Anzaldúa's Llorona as suffering from *saudade*: crying for the present, the past, and the future—that is, for a happier future which may not come or which is not there yet.

Like Anzaldúa and de Castro, twenty-first century Basque poet Itxaro Borda often writes about human solitude. In "La porta oberta en el cel, I Aixo," she calls her own solitude "Una infinita no woman's land" (60). Moreover, in part six of this poem, Borda ponders over the term "frontera" in ways that are akin to Anzaldúa's concepts both of the borderland and the above-discussed "Otro Lado." Borda refers to the Basque people as "este pueblo" (58); her border is a way—"camino" (61)—which leads to both the future and the past, or the memory of a stolen kiss—"el recuerdo del beso que te hurté." Finally, Borda's "frontera" is the border between the Basque Country and the Spanish peninsula, the border inherent to a hybrid identity, either culturally or sexually defined, and the border between present realities and future possibilities.

If I were to put Anzaldúa, de Castro, and Borda in dialog with each other, it would be to transmit Anzaldúa's optimistic view of the future to the other two poets. Anzaldúa's optimism is shown in *Borderlands*, where the last prose sentence reads "*renacimientos de la tierra madre*" (1999, 113); and the last poem closes with "*la Raza* will rise up, tongue intact / carrying the best of all the cultures" (225). Ending with such positive notes gives readers the necessary hope to survive and strive for a better life. Furthermore, such endings promise a future in which several cultures—Chicano/a, Galician, Basque, feminist, lesbian, Anglo, and Spanish, among others—will be reborn and live together in dialog.

As I have emphasized, I agree with Foucault that the "search for descent ... disturbs what was previously considered immobile ... [and] shows the heterogeneity of what was imagined consistent with itself" (82). Hence my proposal of a further alternative gynealogical Trinity—Gloria Anzaldúa, Rosalía de Castro, and Itxaro Borda—from which to start a new poetic (dis)order. Based upon a proliferation of *mestiza* Trinities, such a (dis)order would rely on poetry as an Anzaldúan guide that can bridge feelings and ideas from different times and places. A poetic sensitivity is certainly needed to transform the political sphere through new dialogic attitudes that both respect and take care of difference. As her archived writings about *El Mundo Zurdo* reveal, Anzaldúa argued for the need to join "el cuerpo público con el privado" so as to start a "tribal communication" between "artists, writers, [and] political healers" among others early on (box 32, folder 2). I too hope we can achieve a new tribalism of this kind.

In conclusion, my comparative paper demonstrates the connections which exist beyond textual, human, temporal, and geographical borders. Comparing the poems in the G.E.A. papers with the ones published in *Borderlands* offers a more comprehensive reading of Anzaldúa's oeuvre. With this comparison, we learn, among other things, that Anzaldúa's respect for her family kept her from discussing their problems in public. This was probably one of the reasons Anzaldúa changed or softened some of her poems (e.g., the lesboerotic features) and left others unpublished. Fortunately, neither the conflicts with her family nor the ones with her native state discouraged Anzaldúa from using, defending, and loving the Spanish language. Moreover, my comparative reading between the unpublished and published poems delves into an analysis of Anzaldúa as a human being. In so doing, I have proved that the circle is a vital element not only in Anzaldúa's style of writing but also in her life. *Borderlands* starts and ends with poetry. A few pages after the opening poem, Anzaldúa writes in prose about the farmworker life of her family; finally, the book closes and circles back with a poem dedicated to Anzaldúa's niece.

Searching the genealogy of *Borderlands* led me to search the author's genealogy, part of which is in the Basque Country. To expand upon the comparative scope of the paper, I coined the term gynealogy and put Anzaldúa in dialog with two other poets, Galician Rosalía de Castro and Basque Itxaro Borda, while showing the similarities between them. My concept of a gynealogical Trinity is very close to Anzaldúa's *El Mundo Zurdo* from which she derived her *new tribalism*. That is, these three women write poetry from an-other sphere: that of goddesses who can remake the world. As has been argued by philosophy (see Foucault 1972), language creates identities, which implies it also creates worlds. The three poetry-goddesses thus recreate the world by creating poetic identities for themselves and the people living in their communities. Among other things, a poetic identity is subversive, creative, changeable, plural, comprehensive, contingent, and open to enter in dialog with other poetic identities—or *identities-alterities* (see endnote 1). To pay tribute to Anzaldúa's lessons in solidarity, it is about time to acknowledge similarity within difference to, hopefully, achieve dialog and cooperation among people on a global level. Let our dialogs treasure the intimacy, openness, and heterogeneity needed to achieve a poetic *mestiza* gynealogy.

ENDNOTES

1 Elsewhere I theorized on a similar concept, which I called identity-alterity. I coined this compound in 2003 to, among other reasons, address the dialogic interdependence between the other (e.g., another person, the body) and the self. In 2006, I wrote: "I suggest the term identity-alterity as an alternative to the concept of 'identity' as essential, unchangeable, etc. I write this term in italics to try to destabilize 'identity,' making it (look) more dynamic, as it moves into other time-spaces. An identity contains identities—age, physical appearance, nationality, profession, hobbies, 'sentimental status,' and others—that are susceptible to being altered. The hybridity of the compound enhances the relational possibilities of the self, as well as its openness to change into/being altered by another self, a self-other. This idea seeks to free the 'self' from the chain of unalterable 'identities,' the fixed hierarchies defined by patriarchy. Hopefully, identity-alterities, self-others are able to practice truly ethical relations of difference that confront all dualisms—man/woman, conscious/unconscious, reason/body, and so forth" (55).

2 The Benson library also has a copy of the late prose-and-poetry manuscript of the mentioned book, which I will not be discussing in this article.

3 A totalizing classificatory system would not please either Foucault or myself. Therefore, I wish that my classification of the poems to be open to criticism and improvement by other scholars.

4 Very few studies have been published on Anzaldúa's poetic identity/identity-alterity, among them by Freedman (1992), Garber (2005), and Saldívar-Hull (1999; 2000).

5 For more information on this genre alchemy, see Freedman 1992.

6 The Benson library holds two identical copies of the first all-poetry manuscript of *Borderlands*, which are archived in box 32, folder 9, and box 32, folder 10, respectively. Please bear in mind this endnote for my future references.

7 Some of the poems were published in other places. For example, "Del Otro Lado" appears in the anthology *Compañeras: Latina Lesbians* (1987) in revised form; "Del Otro Lado" has recently been reprinted in the *Gloria Anzaldúa Reader* (2009). Thanks to the editorial hand of AnaLouise Keating, the *Reader* includes other poems of the very first manuscript such as "Tihueque"—which, as Keating records, appeared also in the journal *Tejidos* in 1976 (see 2009, 19)—, "Enemy of the State," and "Encountering the Medusa."

8 Anzaldúa's love for Federico García Lorca is evident in her poem "La vulva es una herida abierta/The vulva is an open wound" (2009, 198-202). Hence "La vulva" starts with an epigraph taken from Lorca's poem "Llanto:" "¡Qué [sic.] no quiero verla! / Dile a la luna que venga, / que no quiero ver la sangre."

9 There must be a typo since, in order to keep the translation, it should say "*trago*" (1st person singular, present simple) instead of "*tragó*" (3rd person singular, past simple). As I found reading her papers, Anzaldúa re-accented her Spanish words over and over, which explains the typo.

10 In previous versions, the poem is titled "Cancion de Andres" and "Cancion de Andrea" (box 33, folder 15), which seem to be code names Anzaldúa liked for herself.

11 Being a dialogical feminist, I think ethical dialogs require that the self is open to be transformed or "altered" by the other—an "other" whose etymological root is the Latin word *alter*. See also endnote 1.

WORKS CITED

Alarcón, Norma. "Anzaldúa's *Frontera*: Inscribing Gynetics." *Displacement, Diaspora, and Geographies of Identity*. Smadar Lavie and Ted Swedenburgh, eds. Durham: Duke UP. 1996. 42-53. Print.

Anzaldúa, Gloria E. *Borderlands/La Frontera. The New Mestiza*. 2nd ed. San Francisco: Aunt Lute, 1999. Print.

---. Gloria Evangelina Anzaldúa Papers, Benson Latin American Collection, University of Texas Libraries, University of Texas at Austin.

---. "La Prieta." *This Bridge Called My Back: Writings by Radical Women of Color*. Cherríe Moraga and Gloria E. Anzaldúa, eds. Watertown: Persephone, 1983. 198-209. Print.

---. "(Un)Natural bridges, (Un)safe spaces." *The Gloria Anzaldúa Reader*. AnaLouise Keating, ed. Durham: Duke UP, 2009. 243-248. Print.

Borda, Itxaro. *Antología de poemas de Itxaro Borda*. Manu Lopez Gesani, trans. *Senez*, 40 (2010): 45-62. Print.

De Castro, Rosalía. *Cantares gallegos*. Vigo: Galaxia, 2008. Print.

Foucault, Michel. "The Discourse on Language." *The Archæology of Knowledge*. A. M. Sheridan Smith, trans. New York: Pantheon, 1972. 215-237. Print.

---. "Nietzsche, Genealogy, History." *Language, Counter-Memory, Practice: Selected Essays and Interviews*. Donald F. Bouchard, trans. and ed. Ithaca: Cornell UP, 1977. 139-164. Print.

Freedman, Diane P. *An Alchemy of Genres: Cross-Genre Writing by American Feminist Poet-Critics*. Charlottesville: University of Virginia Press, 1992. Print.

Garber, Linda. "Spirit, Culture, Sex: Elements of the Creative Process in Anzaldúa's Poetry." *Entremundos/Among Worlds: New Perspectives on Gloria E. Anzaldúa*. AnaLouise Keating, ed. New York: Palgrave, 2005. 213-226. Print.

García Negro, Pilar. *O clamor da rebeldía. Rosalía de Castro: ensaio e feminismo*. Santiago de Compostela: Sotelo Blanco, 2010. Print.

Keating, AnaLouise, ed. *The Gloria Anzaldúa Reader*. Durham: Duke UP, 2009. Print.

Limón, José. *Mexican Ballads, Chicano Poems: History and Influence in Mexican-American Social Poetry*. Berkeley: University of California Press, 1992. Print.

Núñez-Puente, Carolina. "Anzaldúa's Third Step: *Borderlands* beyond Deconstruction."*Fifty Years of English Studies in Spain (1952-2002): A Commemorative Volume*. Ignacio Palacios Martínez, ed. Santiago de Compostela: Universidade de Santiago de Compostela, 2003. 217-223. Print.

---. *Feminism and Dialogics: Charlotte Perkins Gilman, Meridel Le Sueur, Mikhail M. Bakhtin.* Valencia: PUV, 2006. Print.

O'Reilly, Andrea and Silvia Caporale-Bizzini, eds. *From the Personal to the Political: Towards a New Reading of Maternal Autobiographies.* Susquehanna: Susquehanna UP, 2009. Print.

Saldívar-Hull, Sonia. *Feminism on the Border: Chicana Gender Politics and Literature*. Berkeley: University of California Press, 2000.

---. "Introduction to the Second Edition." *Borderlands/La Frontera. The New Mestiza.* San Francisco: Aunt Lute, 1999. 1-15. Print.

Sánchez, Marta E. *Contemporary Chicana Poetry: A Critical Approach to an Emerging Literature.* Berkeley: University of California Press, 1986. Print.

Ziga, Itziar. *Sexual Herria*. Tafalla: Txalaparta, 2011. Print.

COMPULSORY HETEROSEXUALITY IN GLORIA ANZALDÚA'S "EL PAISANO IS A BIRD OF GOOD OMEN"

BETSY DAHMS

> I am concerned here with two other matters as well: first, how and why women's choice of women as passionate comrades, life partners, co-workers, lovers, tribe, has been crushed, invalidated, forced into hiding and disguise; and second, the virtual or total neglect of lesbian existence in a wide range of writings, including feminist scholarship. (Rich 632)

Adrienne Rich's essay "Compulsory Heterosexuality and Lesbian Existence" (1980) cited above, bemoans the lack of lesbian representation in literature as it exposes and critiques the institution of compulsory heterosexuality as a political and ideological phenomenon.[1] The following year witnessed the publication of *This Bridge Called My Back: Writings by Radical Women of Color* (1981) co-edited by Cherríe Moraga and Gloria Anzaldúa, whose many contributors expanded the universal view of "woman" to include women of color and non-heterosexual women. I would like to focus on the writings of Gloria Anzaldúa and her explorations of compulsory heterosexuality as Anzaldúa consistently employs lesbian and queer protagonists throughout her writing. To show that Anzaldúa was both conversant with contemporary theorizing and ahead of her time, I would like to read her understudied, yet recently republished short story "El Paisano is a bird of good omen" (1982)[2] alongside Rich's article to show how Anzaldúa fictionalizes the ramifications of and resistance to obligatory heterosexuality.

Archival correspondence shows a working relationship between Rich and Anzaldúa in 1981 when Rich was an editor at Sinister Wisdom and was publishing two of Anzaldúa's poems. Later correspondence in 1983 shows a turn from a working relationship to a more supportive friendship as the two share accounts of hospitalizations and funding opportunities for women writers. In one letter Anzaldúa tells Rich that she quoted Rich in the call for papers for *This Bridge Called My Back* (and got flack from African-American women for quoting a white woman), and, in another, Anzaldúa shares with Rich the fact that she had taped a picture of Rich, clipped from a newspaper, onto the bookshelf of her Texas bedroom. The intimacy evidenced in this correspondence (Box 19, Folder 7) would suggest that Anzaldúa was familiar with Rich's published work and probably read Rich's 1980 article mentioned above. According to Keating, however, "El Paisano" was first conceptualized by Anzaldúa in September of 1972, underwent many revisions, and was intended to be part of a novel that Anzaldúa referred to as "Andrea" (51). While Rich's influence of theorizing compulsory heterosexuality is apparent in Anzaldúa's short story, it should also be noted that Anzaldúa expands upon Rich's lesbian continuum to include effeminate males in her protagonist's affinity group and explores sexual relationships between women.

Published just two years after Rich's groundbreaking article, Anzaldúa addresses Rich's observed lack of lesbian representation and call for a critique of compulsory heterosexuality in her short story "El Paisano." Similar to other Anzaldúan protagonists, Andrea in "El Paisano" does not conform to her society's view of gender expression and condoned sexual desire. Yet the story revolves around the upcoming marriage of Andrea to her effeminate male friend Zenobio. Andrea and Zenobio are surrounded by other characters who exhibit same-sex desire: Don Efraín, Andrea's married uncle who flirts with Zenobio, Andrea's cousin, José Manuel, and Zenobio's ex-lover, Belinda López, who shows same-sex attraction by dancing with Andrea at her wedding reception. Ironically it is the compulsory heterosexuality of the time (set in 1940s-1950s Texas) that showcases the rural articulations of same-sex desire in the marriage of two non-heterosexual protagonists. This short story queers traditional marriage and disrupts societal norms both in content and form.

From the title of the story, the reader notes Anzaldúa's signature use of code switching between Spanish and English. The subject of the title, "El Paisano," is here a roadrunner but also a countryman, for Andrea is connected to the land and the animals that inhabit it. In keeping with Anzaldúa's larger project of disrupting and questioning assumptions, she does not italicize and rarely translates the Spanish in the short story.[3] Unlike in some of her other stories, Anzaldúa also does not provide a glossary for monolingual English speakers. The employment of Spanish in this text occurs mostly in dialogue, adding to the verisimilitude of the story: "Sí 'Amá, ¿qué quieres?," "No seas tonta, hijita...," and "Go and change, greñuda, muchacha chiflada... Tell them to bring out more tortillas de masa y la carne" ("El Paisano" 154, 155). She also uses Spanish to refer to the things Andrea is deeply connected to such as—"la tierra," The Papalote, and her body, ("Anda en la garra—on the rag") (153-4). Spanish thus serves as an intimate and daily language of the characters.

This first evidence of linguistic disruption in the story's title is followed by a formal disruption of non-traditional line breaks and spacing which on first notice complicate the reading process. Read more carefully, these non-traditional line breaks and spacing add a poetic dimension to the text and ironically serve to show the connection of the protagonist to the land and the omnipresent spirit with which she communes: the breaks connect and expand meaning rather than fragmenting it. In the following passage, for example, the nontraditional spacing allows the author to connect the protagonist to her surroundings by showing concentric circles of connectivity:

> Under her, the hard roundness of the mesquite post seems an appendage of herself, a fifth limb, one that's also part of the corral, the corral that's part
>
> of the land. The corral is a series... (153).

Still in other passages, the spacing emphasizes the second half of the space, enriching the experience of reading:

> Both connected...somehow. The trunk—a black wrung-out piece of cloth whose whorls and twists point toward some
>
> revelation (156).

This is a sampling of a literary technique found throughout the autohistoria that point to the author's willingness to take risks, both formally and in content.[4] My reading of the nontraditional line spacing, serving to connect rather than disconnect, is in line with Annamarie Jagose's interpretation of the use of the slash in *Borderlands/La Frontera: The New Mestiza* as both a technique of separation and a suturing of the words preceding and following the slash. This technique queers traditional line spacing and foreshadows the protagonist's queering of marriage and her resistance to social conformity.

In addition to the non-traditional line spacing that formally breaks up the text, Anzaldúa also inserts italicized dialogue of a wedding ceremony and social commentary on the ceremony to further disrupt linear conceptions of time and identity. These passages serve to show the many possibilities among which the protagonist has to choose. Passages in Latin, for example "*Ego jungo ves in matrimonium*" (156, italics in original), reminding the reader of the church sanctioning of the matrimony between one man and one woman, are interspersed with social commentary, "*You will go through this ceremony cabezona*" and "*You have to go through with it. You don't want to end up a solterona like your aunt Ramona*?" (159, italics in original). These parenthetical insertions remind the reader that time is not linear, but complex and layered. The italicization of these passages serves to highlight "the otherness" that they produce in Andrea. While Anzaldúa does not italicize Spanish words in the text, as the mixing of Spanish and English is natural for a Tejana character like Andrea, the language of the Church and of societal norms are indeed foreign to her. This literary technique of non-traditional spacing and non-traditional italicization challenges the rules of phallogocentrism.

Before the reader learns that Andrea prefers to wear men's pants (154), has hairy armpits, does "men's work," and notices the López girl for her "nice tits" (161), her connection to the land is made clear: atop a mesquite post of the corral, the post "seems an appendage of herself, a fifth limb, one that's also part of the corral, the corral that's part / of the land" (153).

Once the connection between Andrea and the corral/land is made, Anzaldúa includes the seemingly innocuous simile of relating the posts to people and the corral to society: "if the tops of the posts are not flush with the average height their heads are either lopped off to make a tidy corral or they are cast out as deficient, unsuitable" (153-4), thus foreshadowing the central conflict of the story—Andrea's resistance to compulsory heterosexuality. Andrea, for many reasons, is one of the "posts" that is not flush; she is defiant to her mother, she is mysterious and feared by her neighbors, and she is reluctantly marrying Zenobio, an effeminate male character, so that they "won't have to go through a 'real' marriage" (170). Anzaldúa further subverts the image of the fence post as a societal norm of compulsory heterosexuality by having Andrea reach orgasm atop one of the posts. Here, she challenges compulsory heterosexuality and men's power over women's body by defying strictures that prohibit female sexuality and masturbation. The imagery of the fence post serves as a visual articulation of socially sanctioned compulsory heterosexuality and drawings of this image accompany archival drafts, bringing attention to the centrality of the image to the short story. As noted in *Borderlands/La Frontera: The New Mestiza*, visual imagery is key to Anzaldúa's conceptualization of her stories:

> When I create stories in my head, that is, allow the voices and scenes to be projected in the inner screen of my mind, I 'trance.' I used to think I

was going crazy or that I was having hallucinations. But now I realize it is my job, my calling, to traffic in images. (69-70)

Anzaldúa's call to visual imagery is evidenced in her use of drawings in her lectures and her initial desire to be a visual artist. In an interview with Hector Torres, one of the few published pieces where Anzaldúa speaks about "El Paisano," she discusses the possibility of turning "El Paisano" into a screenplay for film (141).[5] And accompanying the archival draft below, Anzaldúa expresses her excitement that the drawing will be printed along with the text, adding that illustrating her stories is something that Anzaldúa would like to pursue. Anzaldúa's insistence on this image solidifies my reading of compulsory heterosexuality in "El Paisano."

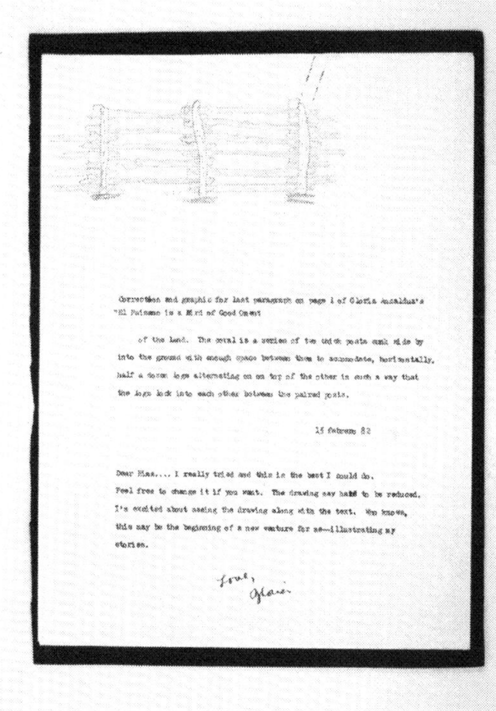
Correction and graphic for last paragraph on page 1 of Gloria Anzaldua's "El Paisano is a Bird of Good Omen"

of the land. The corral is a series of two thick posts sunk side by into the ground with enough space between them to accommodate, horizontally, half a dozen logs alternating on on top of the other in such a way that the logs lock into each other between the paired posts.

15 febrero 82

Dear Miss.... I really tried and this is the best I could do. Feel free to change it if you want. The drawing may have to be reduced. I'm excited about seeing the drawing along with the text. Who knows, this may be the beginning of a new venture for me—illustrating my stories.

Love,
Gloria

Gloria Anzaldúa Collection, Nettie Lee Benson Latin American Collection, U of Texas at Austin (Box 73, folder 19, image 3714)

The setting of the story, the dinner at the bride's house the night before a wedding in Texas, is created by compulsory heterosexuality imposed by society.

Marriage is one way to conform so that neither Andrea nor Zenobio is "lopped off" to fit in with the society or "cast out as deficient" (153-4). Rich explains how heteronormative and homophobic societies leave little option for non-conformists, and how those reared under these circumstances are guided from an early age to follow the path of heterosexuality and marriage regardless of personal sexual inclinations and desires. Both Andrea and Zenobio are engaging in a performance of compulsory heterosexuality, but this is a queer performance because both of them know that the ritual will only provide them with some social safety of superficially masking their same-sex desires that the family/town has already noticed. With the abundance of homosexual desire at the reception (Zenobio's sexual encounters with José Manuel, Don Efrain's tendency to stand too close to Zenobio and talk in whispers, Andrea dancing with Belinda López), Sedgwick's idea of a glass closet may support Rich's claims of the omnipresence of compulsory heterosexuality: while society will not allow the characters to live openly as sexual nonconformists, their difference is an open secret. The idea of a glass closet functions to mask difference while simultaneously denying the liberatory option of "coming out." The glass closet doesn't allow for a space to come out to, just as compulsory heterosexuality vilifies homosexuality and attempts to erase its history. Everyone in the town knows that Andrea and Zenobio are not heterosexual, so why go through with the wedding? For Andrea, this marriage will secure her future in terms of maintaining her land. As a female she is unable to inherit property and according to Rich's account of compulsory heterosexuality, is economically dependent on males. Her union with Zenobio will allow him to inherit her land for her and allow her to maintain her spiritual connection to it. For Zenobio, this marriage will compensate for his perceived "failed" gender expression and grant him full status as a Chicano male.

The author links this forced marriage to the makeshift construction of the portal, noting that both are temporary shelters from the dominating sun; here Anzaldúa puns the alternative spelling s-o-n, noting marriage's service to male control with s-u-n as the sun in Texas can be just as oppressive as patriarchy. Much like the portal, "erected with corrugated aluminum of different lengths and cedar branches that still distill their piney fragrance, looks unnatural," the marriage between Andrea and Zenobio is likewise constructed ("El Paisano" 156). And it is evident in archival manuscripts that Anzaldúa wanted to emphasize the portal. In her draft dated 1976, the word portal is consistently underlined.

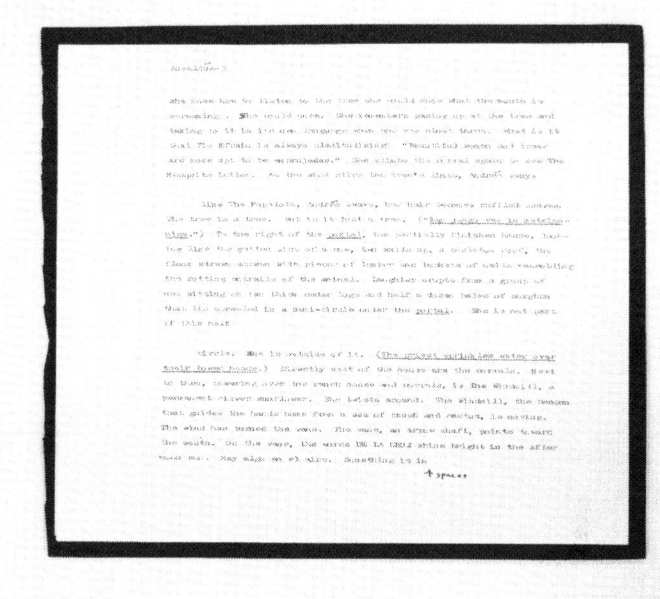

Gloria Anzaldúa Collection, Nettie Lee Benson Latin American Collection, U of Texas at Austin (Box 73, Folder 19, Image 3720)

COMPULSORY HETEROSEXUALITY HIGHLIGHTS DIFFERENCE

Ironically, it is within this site of compulsory heterosexuality where the non-heterosexual qualities of the society are most on display. In fact, Zenobio's former lover and Andrea's cousin, José Manuel, causes some of the main drama at the reception. Anzaldúa complicates the faux marriage between two homosexual characters by introducing a triangle of desire between José Manuel, Zenobio, and Andrea. This triangle of desire is a queered version of the triangle-of-desire motif Sedgwick discusses in *Between Men* (1985), where two men, who appear to be fighting over a woman, are really more concerned with each other than with the woman. Here, all three are characters with same-sex desires in a homophobic society, and the woman, rather than playing the role of an inconsequential actor, represents the biggest threat to the two men. Andrea has the power to expose José Manuel as a man who has sex with men, and she could also break off the marriage to Zenobio and force him to marry someone less understanding of his non-conforming gender expression and sexual desire. In Andrea's inner monologue, the reader learns that she questions Zenobio's choice of lover in José Manuel. She wonders, "What had ever possessed Zenobio. It's not like José

Manuel is the only one around. There's Pete and Mando" ("El Paisano" 167). Anzaldúa makes the reading of these characters as non-heterosexual explicit in a manuscript draft dated 6-6-1992.

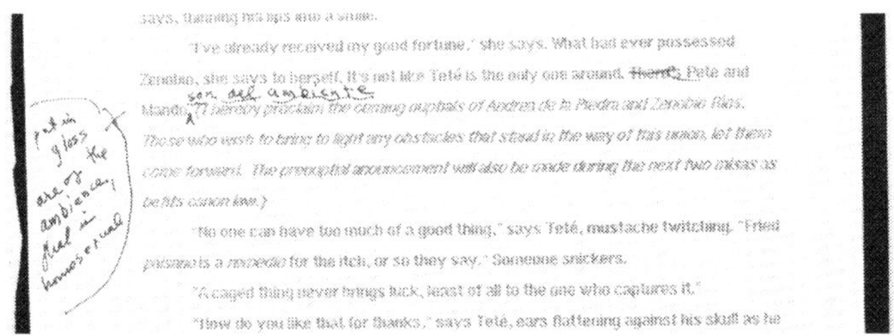
says, turning his lips into a smile.

"I've already received my good fortune," she says. What had ever possessed Zenobio, she says to herself. It's not like Teté is the only one around. ~~There's~~ Pete and Mando son del ambiente. *(I hereby proclaim the coming nuptials of Andrea de la Piedra and Zenobio Ríos. Those who wish to bring to light any obstacles that stand in the way of this union, let them come forward. The prenuptial announcement will also be made during the next two misas as befits canon law.)*

"No one can have too much of a good thing," says Teté, mustache twitching. "Fried *paisano* is a *remedio* for the itch, or so they say." Someone snickers.

"A caged thing never brings luck, least of all to the one who captures it."

"How do you like that for thanks," says Teté, ears flattening against his skull as he

Gloria Anzaldúa Collection, Nettie Lee Benson Latin American Collection, U of Texas at Austin (Box 73, folder 21, image 3789)

In this later version, after the 1982 publication in *Conditions* and the 1983 reprint in *Stories By Latinas*, Anzaldúa makes the character's non-heterosexuality explicit by adding "son del ambiente" with a note to add in the glossary the translated rendering of this colloquial phrase to the word "homosexual."

Andrea encounters José Manuel as he arrives to the dinner with a caged roadrunner as a wedding gift. When the verbal argument between Andrea and José Manuel escalates into a physical fight, Don Efraín, Andrea's gay but married uncle, intervenes, quietly imploring Andrea to "consider Zenobio" ("El Paisano" 168) as he whisks her from the site of conflict. As Andrea releases the captured bird, it is the boy in the purple shirt, who earlier in the story had released a horned toad from the cruelty of other children, who now asks Andrea to teach him how to commune with nature and animals. The color of his shirt is a thinly veiled reference to homosexuality and the "lavender menace"[6] that popularized the color purple as a homosexual signpost.

In a society where "people do not tolerate what's different" ("El Paisano" 169), the myth of heteronormativity is exposed by the presence of so many characters with homosexual desires and/or gender nonconformity. Andrea's masculine performance and Zenobio's feminine gender performance destabilize the notion that masculine is necessarily linked to male, or feminine to female. These "exceptions" to the gender rule are predated by elder homosexual role models like Don Efraín, who show how a Chicano male can perform life-long heterosexuality while simultaneously indulging in same-sex desire. Furthermore, Andrea and Zenobio serve as role models for younger gender/sex non-conformists such as the boy in the purple shirt.

Through two characters in particular, Andrea and the boy in the purple shirt, Anzaldúa links homosexual desire with a connection to nature. As a "masculine" female with same-sex desires, Andrea poses a threat to the heteronormative status quo, but her connection to nature is perhaps more threatening. It is this connection of spirituality and homosexuality that sets Andrea apart from the others and calls into question the possibilities of "coming out" as a lesbian, or "coming out" as spiritual, as feasible alternatives for the brown female protagonist. This connection to nature is perceived as threatening to others, especially the men, and among them, especially José Manuel, who through his macho gender performance and homosexual relationship with Zenobio has more to gain by cosmetically conforming to society's ideals of what a man should be. In fact, José Manuel brings up the right of inheritance in his confrontation with Andrea when she tells him that she will evict him from her land. He responds "Your land? You're a woman—or are you? Women don't inherit" (166-7). To hide his own social infractions, he attacks Andrea for her gender transgressions. Curiously, Andrea does not inflict harm; instead, José Manuel harms himself on her knife: "As he tries to push her a third time she takes a knife out of her jeans and his hand/runs into it" (168). José Manuel is pulled to the side by a friend and leaves Andrea staring at him. Her stare is accompanied by her inner monologue: "in the future I will not need a knife" (168), hinting at the potential development of her spiritual/supernatural powers.

José Manuel's performance of Chicano masculinities—by having (an) effeminate male lover(s), by confronting Andrea's perceived usurpation of masculine authority—inversely mirrors Zenobio's "failed" performance as a Chicano man. This failure to conform to the masculine code is evidenced by his mother's isolation at the party. Introduced alongside Andrea's mother who "made it a point to dress better than the other woman" (154), Zenobio's mother, Doña Inés, is first mentioned in her distinction from the other party guests. While Andrea's mother is dressed "in a pinstriped two-piece suit, white blouse, black hat veiled at the back, white open-toed pumps" (154), Doña Inés appears more austere: "under a crownless parachute hat her face is emaciated and passive. Her beige jacket hangs loose from her thin shoulders, her black wide hemmed skirt drags on the dirt" (155). Clearly the repercussions for raising a son who does not live up to society's standards have taken their toll on Zenobio's mother. Zenobio, however, never seems flustered or self-conscious, "he always looks beautiful" (169). He has found a sanctuary of sorts with Andrea since both can "hide" under the marriage they are about to enact; according to Andrea's mother, Zenobio "keeps himself hidden all afternoon in the house with [Andrea's] sisters draping themselves around him like an harem" (154-5). Just as the townspeople are unable or unwilling to acknowledge sexual and gender dissidents as homosexual, Andrea's mother is unable to see that Zenobio and Andrea's sisters inhabit more of a henhouse than a harem.

Andrea's mother is unnamed and serves as the transmitter of social and cultural norms: in Rich's terms, she is the "token torturer" because it is her duty to bind her daughter's mind to fit her into the institution of marriage (639). Because she is constantly challenged by Andrea and, to a certain point, acquiesces, her relationship with Andrea is complex. When Andrea's mother comments on Doña Inés—"All she talks about is how well her 'baby' can cook. I suppose if he wanted to she would let him take up sewing" ("El Paisano" 155)—Andrea speaks up for Zenobio, arguing with her mother that Zenobio should be allowed to do what he wants; she defies her mother's orders to make herself more presentable as a bride and to perform the role of a female by serving the wedding guests food (155). Andrea recognizes and blames her mother for perpetuating and reifying cultural gender norms.

Andrea's constant struggles with societal norms are alleviated by her connection to the land. Here same-sex desire and spirituality become linked for Andrea. It is Andrea's grandmother who immediately links Andrea's "poder" to commune with nature to her "querer" of women, the connection of spirituality and homosexuality that sets her apart from the others. Andrea and her grandmother share a rich emotional bond and both are thought to be brujas by the townspeople—a relationship that surely fits within Rich's lesbian continuum. Andrea's grandmother cautions her, "because you are wholly yourself. *That* terrifies people who are prisoners of others' upbringing, who are molded by others" (173, italics in original). Here her grandmother simultaneously observes Andrea's principal tension, between compulsory heterosexuality that "molds" society into a way of thinking and Andrea's dissident identity. Whereas Andrea's relationship with her grandmother fits within Rich's lesbian continuum as the two share experiences of being females with supernatural connection with the land, Andrea's sexualized relationship with Belinda López questions Rich's de-sexualized/non-physical conception of female bonds. After performing the perfunctory first dance with her groom-to-be, Andrea approaches Belinda López, who has been "turning down man after man, all bunched up around her like cattle around a salt lick, tongues falling out", to dance with her (171). Dancing with Belinda, Andrea becomes connected to the music and unaware that everyone else has left the dance floor, her "pelvis mak[ing] circles around Belinda's navel" (171). When Belinda urges her to stop, Andrea tells her "I'm tired of all the millions of things we're not supposed to do" highlighting her frustration with the status quo and foreshadowing her imminent departure (171). Ultimately, Andrea's respite in the bosom of the natural world proves too constricting for the masculine character with same-sex desires, who decides that she must leave the land to find a community that understands her many manifestations of otherness.

Heteronormativity becomes the cage that constrains dissident sexual desire and gender expression.[7] There is no discussion of the option to "come out"[8] as a homosexual or as a spiritual person or bruja. Andrea doesn't really have a choice but to marry because, as Efraín states, "it's all been decided for you" ("El Paisano" 160).[9] It is also Efraín who carves cattle bones found in the desert to show Andrea how to adapt and survive in an inhospitable climate like the homophobic one in which they both live. Andrea's linkage to the land and animals is what compels her to set the caged paisano wedding gift free, and this connection also complicates Andrea's decision at the end of the story to leave the land. Andrea foresees this departure in a dream where a third paisano, a roadrunner, is caught in the river and when thrown back, makes its way to the opposite bank in the form of Andrea's pet rattlesnake, Víbora. This rattlesnake,[10] Andrea's animal counterpart, symbolizes the forbidden knowledge that supplies Andrea her supernatural powers. This dream also foresees Andrea's victory over social conformity as José Manuel's wedding gift of a caged roadrunner, a "killer of rattlers" (168), is ultimately set free and her pet snake, Víbora, survives.

Andrea's inner struggle of whether or not to marry Zenobio and stay on her ranch changes Andrea's perception of her community. This change in perception makes Andrea more aware that she will be unable to live as herself, fully Andrea, as a married woman on the ranch. This perceptual shift necessitates social action. By seeing the inability of other homosexuals to enact social change in her environment (Don Efraín continues to be married to a woman while he flirts with Zenobio and counsels Andrea to do the same, José Manuel presumably will continue to engage in sex with men while publicly performing heterosexuality), Andrea decides that she must leave. The inner work of self-inspection has propelled her to make the public action of leaving her beloved land in an attempt to find a more hospitable climate.

As Andrea sets the wild paisano free from its cage, Andrea realizes she too must escape the narrow confines of her society. Where she will go is uncertain; she just knows that she needs to go "away from here" ("El Paisano" 175). She and Zenobio talk about the possibility of finding acceptance for their gender and sexual non-conformity in the "gavacho" (173) world, but given the racial climate of the 1940s-50s, it is unlikely that they will find peace in the "white" world. And given Andrea's spiritual connection to nature and supernatural powers with animals, it is unlikely that she will find a place where all of her is accepted and encouraged. Ultimately, Anzaldúa might posit "El Mundo Zurdo"[11] as her destination point. El Mundo Zurdo is, perhaps, the refuge for outsiders of all kinds to come together to construct a new world where differences are celebrated rather than erased or hidden under social constructions of compulsory heterosexuality and glass closets.

While Rich attempts to denaturalize heterosexuality as a preference in an effort to analyze its far-reaching effects, Anzaldúa's naturalization of same-sex desire is, perhaps, a reaction to the lack of lesbian representation in literature of the time. Anzaldúa's representation of same-sex desire does not fit common perceptions of lesbians in the early 1980s, but perhaps errs on making the representation of same-sex desire as natural as Andrea's connection to the land. The 1980s trend toward essentialism might account for this theoretic move. Yet, Anzaldúa's characters are not necessarily limited to Rich's lesbian continuum, as Andrea is able to conceive of a place, El Mundo Zurdo, which would not be limited to females. In this short story, Andrea is looking for a community of outsiders that would neither exclude Zenobio nor discredit her connection to the land. Here, Anzaldúa's utopic El Mundo Zurdo is inclusive of all forms of otherness, a vision perhaps unimaginable in the 1980s as lesbians were struggling for representation and validation. Nonetheless, Anzaldúa's theoretical contributions to identity negotiation in "El Paisano" offer a fictionalized account of the limitations of compulsory heterosexuality and her discussion of closeted desire merits recognition and further scrutiny.

ENDNOTES

1 I would like to thank Allison Santos-Martín for her help in unpacking the nuances of Rich's article for the present analysis.

2 "El Paisano is a bird of good omen" (1982) published in Conditions 8: 28-47, reprinted in Cuentos: Stories by Latinas. Eds. Alma Gómez, Cherríe Moraga and Mariana Romo-Carmona (1983) by Kitchen Table Women of Color Press. The version that Keating includes in the Gloria Anzaldúa Reader includes some translation of the Chicano Spanish and some alternative line spacing compared to the 1983 version published in Cuentos. All citations referenced will follow the 1983 version. I should also note that the subtitle to "El Paisano" in the 1983 version indicates that this is part of a larger work "Andrea: a novel in progress" that was never published.

3 In keeping with Anzaldúa's practice of not italicizing or otherwise othering non-English words, I do not italicize the Spanish words from the text. I join co-editors AnaLouise Keating and Gloria González-López when they state, "...the non-italicized format is our political and theoretical attempt to avoid the 'othering' of non-English language. And second, we follow Anzaldúa's own beliefs and practice. In her later works, she strongly preferred not to italicize Spanish or other non-English words" (Bridging 16).

4 The form of non-traditional line breaks is not a new invention on Anzaldúa's behalf; indeed this is a common feature of Avant Garde literature. However, I argue that the thematic intention of this form is new. Likewise, the effect on the reader is also a new contribution. It could also be argued that this non-traditional line spacing, the caligramatic writing, is meant to symbolize the spacing of fence posts and that it then becomes a sexual metaphor of openness to alternative sexualities, as evidenced by Andrea bringing herself to orgasm on a fence post.

5 My thanks to AnaLouise Keating for guiding me to this interview.

6 See Karla Jay's *Tales of the Lavender Menace: A Memoir of Liberation* (1999) for more discussion on the lavender menace. Randy Conner also mentions purple as a queer color: "Color symbolic of royalty, magic and spiritual enlightenment, frequently associated with androgyny and same-sex passion, its various hues including lavender, lilac, magenta, mauve and violet... In the early twentieth century, purple, especially violet, served in the West as a signifier of lesbian desire. As lavender, the color was claimed by the contemporary gay liberation movement..." (272).

7 Anzaldúa discusses cages as boundaries in her interview with Anne E. Reuman when discussing identity labels: "So I feel very close to the white dykes, and I have a love of them and their community and their art and their writing and their theories, but it began to be very constrictive in that I thought I was in a cage and they were defining the bars; and I needed to break out of that cage, just like I needed to break out of the cage of my family and the nationalistic cage of just being a Chicana and nothing more" (36).

8 For queers of color, there is rarely the option to "come out" and live as a homosexual in their communities. As McRuer notes, "coming out here becomes a suspiciously white and middle-class move toward 'self-respect,' not revolutionary social change, and many contemporary coming-out narratives might be seen as products of this shift toward individualism and essentialism" (McRuer 36).

9 For more on homophobia in Latina/o and Chicana/o culture, see Barbosa, Torres, Silva, and Khan's "Agapé Christian Reconciliation Conversations: Exploring the Intersections of Culture, Religiousness, and Homosexual Identity in Latino and European Americans" (2010), José Quiroga and Melanie López Frank's "Cultural Production of Knowledge on Latina/o Sexualities" and Lionel Cantú Jr.'s *The Sexuality of Migration: Border Crossings and Mexican Immigrant Men* (2009).

10 Anzaldúa's tono, her animal counterpart, is also a serpent, discussed in *Borderlands* (26); the snake is a recurrent image found throughout her corpus. See Zita's and Lioi's articles for a further discussion of the metaphorical use of serpents in *Borderlands*. Especially interesting is Lioi's claim that "the function of the snake in ancient Gnostic texts [was] as a female mediator of cosmic wisdom" (Lioi 81).

11 El Mundo Zurdo, as defined by AnaLouise Keating, "indicates communities based on commonalities, visionary locations where people from diverse backgrounds with diverse needs and concerns coexist and work together to bring about revolutionary change" (*The Gloria Anzaldúa Reader* 322). "El Mundo Surdo" is also the title given to reading series and writing workshops Anzaldúa initiated in the 1970s. The Chicano "S" was replaced to a "Z" in the printing of *This Bridge Called My Back* without the consent of the author.

WORKS CITED

Anzaldúa, Gloria, *Borderlands/La Frontera: The New Mestiza* 2nd ed. San Francisco: Spinsters/ Aunt Lute, 1999. Print.

---. Gloria Evangelina Anzaldúa Papers, Benson Latin American Collection, U of Texas Libraries, the U of Texas at Austin. Print.

---. "El Paisano is a Bird of Good Omen." *Conditions* 8 (1982): 28-47, reprinted in *Cuentos: Stories by Latinas.* Eds. Alma Gómez, Cherríe Moraga and Mariana Romo-Carmona New York: Kitchen Table Women of Color Press, 1983. Print.

Barbosa, Peter, Hector Torres, Marc Anthony Silva and Noshaba Khan. "Agapé Christian Reconciliation Conversations: Exploring the Intersections of Culture, Religiousness, and Homosexual Identity in Latino and European Americans." *Journal of Homosexuality* 57 (2010): 98-116.

Cantú Jr., Lionel. *The Sexuality of Migration: Border Crossings and Mexican Immigrant Men.* New York: New York UP, 2009.

Jagose, Annamarie. "Slash and Suture: The Border's Figuration of Colonialism, Phallocentrism, and Homophobia in *Borderlands/La Frontera.*" *Lesbian Utopics.* New York: Routledge, 1994. 137-58. Print.

Jay, Karla. *Tales of the Lavender Menace: A Memoir of Liberation.* New York: Basic Books, 1999. Print.

Keating, AnaLouise. Ed. *The Gloria Anzaldúa Reader.* Durham: Duke UP, 2009. Print.

Keating, AnaLouise, and Gloria González-López. Eds. *Bridging: How Gloria Anzaldúa's Life and Work Transformed Our Own.* Austin: U of Texas P, 2011. Print.

Lioi, Anthony. "The Best-Loved Bones: Spirit and History in Anzaldúa's 'Entering Into The Serpent.'" *Feminist Studies* 34:1-2 (2008): 73-98. Print.

McRuer, Robert. *Queer Renaissance: Contemporary American Literature and the Reinvention of Lesbian and Gay Identities.* New York: New York UP, 1997. Print.

Moraga, Cherríe, and Gloria Anzaldúa. *This Bridge Called My Back: Writings by Radical Women of Color*. Watertown, Mass.: Persephone Press, 1981. Print.

Quiroga, José and Melanie López Frank. "Cultural Production of Knowledge on Latina/o Sexualities." *Latina/o Sexualities: Probing Powers, Passions, Practices and Policies*. Ed. Marysol Asencio. New Jersey: Rutgers UP, 2010. 137-49. Print.

Reuman, Ann E. and Gloria E. Anzaldúa. "Coming into Play: An Interview with Gloria Anzaldúa." *MELUS* 25.2 (2000): 2-45. Print.

Rich, Adrienne. "Compulsory Heterosexuality and the Lesbian Existence." *Signs* 5.4 (1980): 631-60. Print.

Sedgwick, Eve Kosofksy. *Between Men: English Literature and Male Homosocial Desire*. New York: Columbia UP, 1985. Print.

---. *Epistemology of the Closet*. Berkeley: U of California P, 1990. Print.

Torres, Hector. "Gloria Anzaldúa: The Author Never Existed." *Conversations with Contemporary Chicana and Chicano Writers*. Albuquerque: U of New Mexico P, 2007. 115-145. Print.

Zita, Jacquelyn N. "The Anzaldúan Body." *Body Talk: Philosophical Reflections on Sex and Gender*. New York: Columbia UP, 1998: 165-83. Print.

ETHNICITY, NATIONALITY, AND RACE: TWO STORIES OF/ON BORDERS

TEREZA JIROUTOVÁ KYNČLOVÁ

A representative characteristic of Gloria Anzaldúa's masterpiece *Borderlands/ La Frontera: The New Mestiza* is the simultaneous coding of the author's personal life narrative with the historical and social context of her community at the geographical and cultural location on the U.S.-Mexico border in South Texas. The emphasis that the writer puts on the co-mingling and co-constituting of individual and communal stories and histories accentuates the significance of the geographical, social, and cultural networks within which one becomes a subject that may both consciously build her/his identity and, at the same time, contribute to positive and equality-oriented social and cultural changes on the communal level. As Anzaldúa tells us, "[n]othing happens in the...real world unless it happens in the images in our heads."[1] She learned from her experience and the history of her home and, as a result, vastly contributed to the transformation of Chicano/a studies and literature on the global level. On an individual level, Anzaldúa's work has provided me, as a teacher, with analytical tools for research in literary theory and gender studies.

In addition, there is another woman's individual, and no less intense, story that, in the same degree as Anzaldúa's writing, spurred my own coming to consciousness about the effect of borders. The woman's story, which I describe below, pertains to the history of the Czech borderlands, i.e., a location with cartography different from Anzaldúa's. Yet, what the Czech woman's narrative and Anzaldúa's theorizing bear most in common is the notion of intersecting individual experience and communal legacy. In other words, both Anzaldúa and the Czech woman narrator as individuals left a significant imprint in the histories of their communities and the borderlands that continuously shaped their lives.

It was the summer after I had graduated from high school and was about to commence my university studies when I met my intriguing narrator. I immediately was to learn she had influenced the demarcation lines of my homeland's borders. Her story is deeply Anzaldúan in the sense that it portrays a woman's unique resistance to oppressive historical powers and speaks eloquently about one's personal courage. In my constantly developing interpretation, the narrative also underscores an individual's significance on both the local and global levels—and most importantly it (literally) redraws the arbitrary givens of social and cultural boundaries and geographical borders.

A BORDER STORY

Even after the two decades since I listened to the narrator's voice, I still find it mesmerizing that the story embodies an ever-changing piece of life-as-art and art-as-life which metamorphosizes with the various paradigmatic and interpretative optics within which I can conceptualize it as I acquire knowledge of new epistemologies and theories while I navigate the maze of academia and thus my own mind. When the narrator finished her story, she once again recalled the onerous, yet transforming experience; I responded with utter awe and appreciation of the bravery she demonstrated. Later, I felt the story presented an image of sheer despair—what else could she have done to save her home? Then I conceived of the narration as defiant or even strategic, a reflected exploration and perusal of the (allegedly) female uncanny—that was my training in literary theory speaking. Nevertheless, it is undoubtedly a great story and as such it ought to be remembered as deliberate appropriation of history that anchors us in the places and bodies we call home, as Anzaldúa tells us in her writing as well as by the form of her writing. To my deep regret, I do not know the narrator's name.

Only about four years after I heard the story was I introduced to Anzaldúa's work. It was in a class on Contemporary American Women Writers at Charles University. Subsequently, during my study sojourn at University of New Orleans (right after 9/11), I was exposed to *Borderlands/La Frontera: The New Mestiza* and began to "read" the narrator's story as a *border story*. Obviously, my recognition of the border as a category of critical analysis which is "one of the most productive concepts of Western thought" and which is concurrently invested with a lot of emotional energy[2] was conditioned and prompted by my own crossing of the U.S. borders as a student of English and American Studies. Moreover, my acquaintance with Chicana/o evaluation, metaphorization, and investigation of the U.S-Mexico border and the radical theoretization of the present power relations has sensitized me to grasping the history of my own homeland's borders, which have shifted numerous times. Coming from the heart of Europe, I viewed this historical fact as a given, rather than as a potential focus of profound examination of one's cultural identity and position.

Thus, Anzaldúa's book did not teach me about my epistemic privilege as the concept is traditionally deemed within feminist standpoint theory;[3] instead, it taught me about my epistemic ignorance and unreflected blindness. Further, her work introduced me to *teorías* which may be employable not only in the context of U.S.-Mexican borderlands, but—if used reflexively and with respect to local situations and cartographies—elsewhere as well. Sometimes, as the hackneyed phrase goes, one just has to travel far from home to gain a deeper and a more-dimensional perspective on it. The story follows:

During my years in high school and the early years at the university, a group of my life-long friends and I would often go hiking in the mountainous region along the Czech-Polish border in the north of the Czech Republic, making our friend's parents' wooden cabin our base. There is a vast untended pasture with thick grasses in front of the cabin and a dense coniferous forest at its back that ascends for about a quarter of a mile and then drops sharply into a damp green valley. A well behind the only stone wall of the cabin is a generous supply of fresh water that seeps into a small pond next to it, especially in early spring after the snows melt. The pond always dries out completely during the hot summer months. Not being a biologist, I would wonder at the end of every summer what becomes of the newts that are abundant in the reeds-overgrown pool. The nearest settlement is almost three miles from the cabin, a good one-hour walk. To get to the cabin, we would never drive but take the train to the town of Teplice and Metují and then walk about four miles up, carrying food and blankets with us.

Once, it was late in August, a group of seven people came up the hill to the small cabin, asking whether they could just sit down for a while, enjoy the views and walk around the site. The group was a family accompanying their great grandmother, aged about ninety-two, who had wanted to come see the place for a long time, we were told. We struck up a conversation and asked the elderly lady why she had so much interest in seeing the place where the cabin was now located. She said, curiously enough, that she needed to see a sandstone post. We did not understand why, but immediately knew what pillar she meant and pointed it out to her. The sandstone post was buried deep in the ground and only about a half foot of it was peeking out of the lawn. The post was situated right behind the cabin, a mere two feet from its only stone-built wall. We were aware that such posts, usually two- to three-feet in length, had been used in the past for delineating land property areas or for marking the borders of countries. We had no idea what this particular post meant—whether it marked the farthest reach of the pasture and forest, or once represented a boundary of tended land, or even separated former Czechoslovakia from its historical and geographical neighbors. These posts are not infrequent in the region and for us it was just another mark in the surrounding landscape. For the lady, however, this very stone post signified a real milestone in all senses of the word.

Her story went back to 1938 when the Munich Agreement allowed for annexation of Czechoslovakian borderlands by Nazi Germany. Following this political settlement—which to this day represents one of the most traumatic events in Czech and Slovak history[4]—the Nazis declared that all areas (most of which were located along the then borders with Germany and Poland and had a high percentage of German-speaking population) be declared part of Nazi Germany and all Czech-speaking inhabitants gradually removed.[5] The area concerned, called Sudetenland, comprised almost a third of the country and in certain regions went as deep inland as 200 miles. The population of German-speaking citizens amounted to well over 3 million out of approximately 14 million inhabitants, which was the total population of Czechoslovakia at that time.[6] It also needs to be noted that a German-speaking population had been indigenous to the region for more than ten centuries and many of those people identified as citizens of Czechoslovakia and not necessarily as Germans by nationality, even though their linguistic identity did not correspond with the official language of the Czechoslovak Republic. In other words, the Munich Dictate disregarded nationality and self-identification in terms of geographical and cultural belonging.

The woman who came to see the site in the mountains had lived on that very place in 1939 when the consequences of the Munich Agreement were multiplied by the declaration of the Protectorate of Bohemia and Moravia—an institutionalized state that made Nazi occupation of Czechoslovakia official—and borders were being drawn once again. At that time, a large farmhouse stood where the cabin now was. Only the stone-built wall reminds us of what is now left of the farmhouse after it was burned to ashes at end of World War II. By that time, the woman no longer lived there, as she, her husband, and their three children had been evicted from their home by the Nazis in the early 1940s. This is not, however, why the woman and her beloved family came to the cabin.

She arrived to reminisce about one particular moment in which the sandstone post occupied a central position. It was early spring of 1939, the narrator recalled, when two young Nazi soldiers came by car to the farmhouse and called out for the husband, the owner of the property, to come out and present his identification documents. As it turned out, it was an immensely lucky coincidence that the lady's husband had gone to the village to run his errands and she was left in the farmhouse alone with their three little children. As a matter of fact, those two daughters and the son and their partners escorted their frail senior mother to the cabin and were thus present at her story-telling.

The woman recalled that she walked out of the farmhouse, walked up to the soldiers, and showed them her identification documents. While inspecting her papers, they said she need not worry; they were here just to mark the new Protectorate border. Having consulted a large unfolded map, they struggled and pulled a stone post from the car. Together they carried it closer to the farmhouse and positioned it about a yard in front of the entrance door. They walked back to the car and returned, carrying a spade and pickax.

Instantly, the woman understood this meant that the farmhouse had just been placed into Germany and removed from the map of Czechoslovakia, and that the family would be ordered to leave the farm immediately and settle in a town deeper inland, thereby losing their home, property, and the product of their work to the Nazi regime. The woman, being slightly older than the young soldiers, was outraged and protested. She recalled that she had grabbed the two-foot post and used all her physical strength and mental stamina to drag it just about a foot behind the back wall of the farmhouse, leaving a seven-yard-long groove in the soft and damp spring soil. She managed this successfully and dropped the post right at the back of the farmhouse, leaving it there as a way of symbolically redrawing the map back to what it had looked like before the soldiers' arrival. Her family's home thus remained in their homeland.

The soldiers, being young and therefore most likely inexperienced, had been sent to a remote, less populated region to perform their duties, and as the narrator implied, did not know what to do. They stared at her toiling with the stone and were speechless. Unquestionably, the orders must have been to kill anyone opposing the exertion of Nazi power. My view is that it was presumably because of their youth, lack of army experience, and/or possibly the fact she was a woman and a mother, that they did not follow their strict orders. The soldiers did not move the post from where she had dropped it and eventually left. Upon their departure, however, they said that had this been done by her husband or had the husband been present, they would have killed him and the family. Nevertheless, the farmhouse remained in Czechoslovakia and almost sixty years later, the woman who carried the post to Sudetenland came to see whether the stone was still there. It was. And still is. Although now it is just one milestone in the middle of the European Union where geographical state borders are expected not to matter, especially for citizens of E.U. member states, and especially for those who are white.

IN/VISIBLE RACE AND ETHNICITY: WHITE HAS MANY SHADES OF COLOR

The visitor's story is profoundly symbolic as it not only draws attention to the arbitrariness and constructedness of borders of states as historical entities that we are socialized to view as natural, given, and unchangeable, but also thoroughly demonstrates the instability and volatility of all boundaries and lines of normativity that Western thought draws to catalog the reality in clearly arranged binaries that are to help us navigate the world. Although the piece of the border in the narrative was not shifted in 1939 because of the narrator's immeasurable will, or despair that assisted her in taking the life-threatening risks, borders have, nevertheless, moved elsewhere and are not always marked by milestones or passports. Rather, they are marked by hierarchizations, power relations, and cultural prejudices inherent to our society.

One such border is the relationship of the Czech population towards the former German-speaking inhabitants of former Czechoslovakia and their descendants, who nowadays mostly live in Germany. Czechs tend to stereotype their former co-citizens as traitors who collaborated with Nazi Germany, and they do not wish to acknowledge the violence to which German-speaking Czechs living inland were exposed and became victims of after the Nazis surrendered in Europe. Further, the Czech views of the Holocaust frequently fail to recognize the fact that aside from Czech Jews, there were also Czech Roma who were sent to concentration camps in Poland and detention camps that were located *within* Czechoslovakia, which were at least partially operated by Czech-speaking staff who chose to side with the Nazis. Thus, the ethnic, racial, and linguistic issues pertaining to Czech Germans and Czech Roma have a long history that is based on discrimination and othering, derived from internal and mental borders deeply engrained in the minds of Czechs.

I deal with a border of this kind, a mental or epistemic barrier, in the university classroom where my courses that employ intersectionality are taught. I believe that in my teaching I have been successful in sensitizing my graduate students to gender and class issues. The students are able to deconstruct and use gender and/or class as categories of critical analysis—often within complex contexts—with a greater ease than they can actually *see* and *notice* race and/or ethnicity in the Czech society rather than in the Czech Roma minority only. Moreover, race and ethnicity—if discussed explicitly at all—are always talked about in reference to this group, but the general self-understanding of the Czech society tends to correspond with white myopia or, alternatively, color blindness.

The Czech Republic, not having been involved in colonial expansion unlike other West European countries, and only now being a target country of immigration, is predominantly a white society and by no means does it resemble the multiracial and multiethnic makeup of, for example, U.S., Belgian, Dutch or British societies. Thus, whiteness is what the students have been throughout their young lives socialized to *see* as a norm. In other words, due to the social context, racial or ethnic identities have been rendered *as if* nonexistent. Yet, these categories have not been deleted, they may only be seen as dormant and are waiting to be discovered, excavated, and recognized. Similarly, as one may gradually come to the awareness of inequalities pertaining to gender by being initiated into cultural norms and thereby socialized into a subject, rather than by being born a man or a woman (limited as these categories may be), the *seeing* and *noticing* and comprehending of racial and ethnic presence is a capability a person—a student, teacher, educator—consciously masters and learns.

In the Czech Republic, people of color are usually understood to be people from abroad, being foreigners and thus not Czechs. Consequently, many people and (some of) my students traditionally do not associate color with Czechness. If this is fact,[7] Czech Roma fall beyond the scope of critical thinking about race and ethnicity. At the same time, many people of color pass for white even though they identify as brown, African-American, or Asian. In other words, in the Czech Republic, white may have many shades "of color."

When teaching courses on postcolonial studies and literary theory from a gender studies perspective, I use relevant critical texts, for instance, bell hooks' work *Where We Stand: Class Matters*[8] which integrates a discussion of class and race in such a way that is approachable to my students and is comprehensible to readers who have had an experience with a communist regime that used class inequality as justification for honing social and global polarity between the "imperialist West" and the "socialist Soviet Bloc" during the Cold War. For the Chicana/o context, however, I employ short stories by Chicana writers, such as Anzaldúa, Cisneros, Valdés, and Viramontes to demonstrate how literature can be a means of liberation from rigid, hierarchical and discriminatory strictures derived from the racial and social organization of the society.

As much as students can identify with the "colored" nature of Chicana and/or African-American writing, they frequently seem unable to make the connection to Czech literature, as it is and historically has been, again, a white domain. There have been only a few books published by Czech Roma authors that were written in Czech or translated from the Roma language into Czech and thus could address and appeal to the dominant readership. While reading Roma women's stories in the class, students' reactions have been increasingly positive in terms of decoding the notions of class and gender conveyed by the texts. The racial and/or ethnic aspect is, however, viewed as one that is an exception to the character of the writing and therefore often falls by the wayside. In other words, it becomes difficult to maintain ethnicity and race as analytical categories for examining the multilayered identities portrayed in the works by Czech Roma writers.[9]

I have therefore also taken to relating the issues of race, ethnicity, class, and gender in literature to my students with the example of nineteenth century Czech National Revival. This movement, which set Czechs apart from the German-speaking "Significant Other" within the Austrian-Hungarian Empire, was a project that employed literature as a tool in its struggle for cultural and ethnolinguistic equality within the Empire.[10] In other words, literature was both the vehicle for Czech national self-identification and, at the same time, the very effect of this self-identification becoming gradually real; literature was both the means of identity production as well as the product of such identity manifesting itself as existent.

As opposed to the Chicana/o movement, which has used literature in a very similar, political way,[11] Czech National Revival was vastly represented by elite, upper-class, university-educated writers and politicians with power and direct political influence on the institutions of the society. Further, Revival representatives made the conscious choice of claiming Czech as their first language, thus thinking of their identity primary as Czech and not German-speaking Czech.[12] As Anzaldúa tells us, linguistic identity is what makes us whole—we are the language we speak.[13]

El Movimiento of the 1960s was faced with racial discrimination and linguistic terrorism, and was deeply gendered.[14] The Czech National Revival, on the other hand, encouraged women to become writers and to speak publicly and supported their political engagement in the making of the Czech nation and especially what we today understand as Czech literature. Nevertheless, it is impossible to speak of true gender equality on both the material as well as the symbolic level in this respect, as the presence and involvement of women writers was purely instrumental. In other words, women's roles and the ways in which femininity was constructed by patriotic discourse was, as Jitka Malečková has observed, "adapted to the needs of the national movement"[15] and not the goal of, for example, reaching equal standing between the sexes. Women served as a canvas that reflected images of national unity, patriotic ambition and the Czech society's cultured background, yet they were not free participants in this process of representation, as it was subject to the dominant nationalist discourse established on hierarchical views of national belonging, linguistic identity, and the presumed superiority of masculinity. The civilized character of the nation—which was to legitimize and justify its existence, integrity, and cultural independence—was evidenced by such pronouncements as "*even* women can write excellent Czech literature" which were aimed at the German-speaking majority.[16] The re-presentation of the progressiveness of Czech nationhood was to be supplied by female authors' writings, and the targets that were expected to *see* and *notice* were Germans and German-speaking Czechs.

Within the Czech writers' community, women were partners, but they were by no means equal partners. Also, Czech literature came out to be seen as white despite the fact that the Roma had already been settled in Europe for centuries. As nomadic subjects[17] the Roma were not thought of as members of society in general, for their home was on the road, in constant motion, in constant migration, and thereby disregarding the borders of evolving European nation states. It was only in the mid-1950s, when the laws of Czechoslovakia and other European countries made migration illegal and drove the Roma into housing projects and city margins, that the Roma became present in the minds of the majority population as a group suddenly contained and visible, for the Western eye finally *saw* and *noticed* the stable minority within the borders of their homelands and had to mentally incorporate them into the national "we." The Roma then belonged to a place that was understandable to the dominant culture; for as long as the Roma migrated, the notion of their belonging to the road was not perceived as existence rooted in one single place that could be located on a map and preserved by borders.

The Czech Roma Revival began in the 1970s as the Roma gradually moved from oral tradition and took to paper, thus challenging the idea of Czech literature as a white project relevant to the heart of Europe. Most significantly, Roma literature made it explicit that the Czechs and the Roma serve mutually as the Other for either of the communities.[18] This is also true of the Chicanas/os by white Americans, as the Mexican or the brown-bodied person for them is the utter Other for WASPS.[19] Further, the Roma are only now developing a myth that would serve as a foundation on which they could claim solidarity and common ties that would help the Roma community emancipate itself from the racialized conditions they face in the Czech Republic and Czech literature. In other words, the Roma are looking for their Aztlán.

Another parallel between Chicana/o literature and Roma literature is the wide division according to gender identity. Although Roma women writers, unlike Chicanas, have not been called Malinchistas for betraying the ideas of the emancipatory movement by portraying the gendered realities of family lives and voicing women's oppression by hyper-masculinity, the Roma family that extends to clans is both the means and the obstacle of Roma women's emancipation. Since the idea of family is one of the foundations of the Roma mutuality myth, it relegates women to the strictly defined confines of the private sphere and patriarchal rule. Consequently, it can be claimed there are two Roma literatures: women's and men's. This literary tradition is marked by gender division rather than the racial and ethnic lines which run between Czechs and the Roma. To add more complexity to the picture, many Roma, as implied above, actually pass for white and claim that they are not Roma or Gypsy, but identify as Czech *citizens*.

Gloria Anzaldúa's writing on Mestiza consciousness and postcolonial concepts of hybridity have helped me grasp the complexity of processual identity creation—one's self-reflective, conscious and utterly honest approach to one's introspection that acknowledges and—most importantly—embraces the contradictory aspects of one's identity, which is concurrently always perceived not only on an individualistic level, but as a part of a greater community, collective or even a global society. Moreover, Mestiza consciousness and *Borderlands/La Frontera: The New Mestiza* have also assisted me in understanding my home and my roots with a greater insight and opened new dimensions of perceiving and studying borders in my own geographical location, as well as my social and cultural environment. Reading Chicana literature has taught me a lesson about my own background and the historical influences that contributed to the shaping of the world into which I have been socialized. Chicanas' theoretical analyses of positionality have directed me to my own coordinates and are helping me be a resourceful teacher for my students. Further, Gloria Anzaldúa's and other Chicana authors' works elaborating on the U.S.-Mexico borderlands have inspired me to use the concept of borders as a tool for analyzing difference as a philosophical and social construction that in Western thought implies hierarchical oppositions and power relations, the character of which may be usefully accentuated by focusing on the act of drawing arbitrary dividing lines. This approach to the concept of the border overcomes the dualistic, either/or thinking and expands our notions of understanding and knowing, for it may employ the border *simultaneously* as a geographical location *and* epistemological position which are, at least from a feminist perspective, inseparable and always relevant to any given context. Such views help me and my students view our lives and our surroundings more critically and in more colorful and complex ways. Borders suddenly become ubiquitous—yet they no longer signify separation, but speak of a potential for analysis and invite us to uncover hidden histories and stories. Like the one told in the beginning of this text.

ENDNOTES

1 Gloria Anzaldúa, *Borderlands/La Frontera: The New Mestiza*, (San Francisco: Aunt Lute Books, 1987), 109.

2 Martin Procházka and Aleida Assmann, "Boundaries and Contact Zones." *Litteraria Pragensia* 13, no. 26(2003):1-7.

3 For discussion of feminist standpoint theory and epistemic privilege please consult: Sandra Harding, *Whose science? Whose knowledge?* Ithaca, N.Y.: Cornell University Press, 1991, or

Sandra Harding "Rethinking Standpoint Epistemology: 'What is Strong Objectivity?'" in *Feminist Epistemologies*, ed. Linda Alcoff, and Elizabeth Potter (New York: Routledge, 1993), 49-82 as well as Bat-Ami Bar On "Marginality and Epistemic Privilege" in *Feminist Epistemologies*, ed. Linda Alcoff, and Elizabeth Potter (New York: Routledge, 1993), 83-100.

4 Jan Tesař, *Mnichovský komplex: jeho příčiny a důsledky.* Prague: Prostor, 2000.

5 Jan Němeček, et al. *Mnichovská dohoda: cesta k destrukci demokracie v Evropě = Munich agreement : the way to destruction of democracy in Europe.* Prague: Karolinum, 2004.

Karel Zelený, *Vyhnání Čechů z pohraničí.* Prague: Ústav mezinárodních vztahů, 1996.

6 František Čapka, Dějiny zemí koruny české v datech, (Prague: Libri, 1999), 683.

7 As of now, there has not been any empirical research conducted that would support the argument which I present here. Drawing on discussions in my classes, I take the liberty of claiming that such an argument can provide an explanation for why race remains difficult to be taught, recognized and analyzed as a concept that *actually does* pertain to Czech society in the same degree as it concerns, for example, American society, which is commonly known for being racially and ethnically heterogeneous.

8 bell hooks, Where We Stand: Class Matters. New York, London: Routledge, 2000.

9 Alena Scheinostová, *Romipen: Literaturou k moderní identitě.* Prague: Athinganoi, 2006.

10 Marcin Filipowicz, "V jazyce naše… maskulinita: Případ obrozeneckého diskurzu." *Česká literatura* 60, no. 5(2012):665.

11 As much as I argue that literature was instrumental in the Chicano Movement, I also argue that literature authored by men was employed in a manner differing from that authored by women. Most importantly, Chicana writing that expressed gender-sensitive and feminist standpoints was viewed as one that betrayed the values of the Chicano nationalistic struggle.

12 Marcin Filipowicz, "V jazyce naše… maskulinita: Případ obrozeneckého diskurzu." *Česká literatura* 60, no. 5(2012):671.

13 Gloria Anzaldúa, *Borderlands/La Frontera: The New Mestiza*, (San Francisco: Aunt Lute Books, 1987), 80-81.

14 Anna NietoGomez, "Sexism in the Movimiento," In *Chicana Feminist Thought: The Basic Historical Writings*, edited by Alma García (New York and London: Routledge, 1997), 97-100.

15 Jitka Malečková, "Nationalizing Women and Engendering the Nation: The Czech National Movement," In *Gendered Nations: Nationalisms and Gender Order in the Long Nineteenth Century*, edited by Ida Blom, Karen Hageman, Catherine Hall (Oxford and New York: Berg, 2000), 293-310.

16 Jitka Malečková, "Nationalizing Women and Engendering the Nation: The Czech National Movement," In Gendered Nations: Nationalisms and Gender Order in the Long Nineteenth Century, edited by Ida Blom, Karen Hageman, Catherine Hall (Oxford and New York: Berg, 2000), 302.

17 Rosi Braidotti, *Nomadic Subjects: Embodiment and Sexual Difference in Contemporary Feminist Theory.* New York: Columbia UP, 2011.

18 Alena Scheinostová, *Romipen: Literaturou k moderní identitě,* (Prague: Athinganoi, 2006), 30.

19 Octavio Paz. *The Labyrinth of Solitude.* New York: Grove Press, 1985.

WORKS CITED

Anzaldúa, Gloria. *Borderlands/La Frontera: The New Mestiza.* San Francisco: Aunt Lute Books, 1987. Print.

Bar On, Bat-Ami. "Marginality and Epistemic Privilege." *Feminist Epistemologies. Ed.* Alcoff Linda and Elizabeth Potter. New York: Routledge, 1993. 83-100. Print.

Braidotti, Rosi. *Nomadic Subjects: Embodiment and Sexual Difference in Contemporary Feminist Theory.* New York: Columbia UP, 2011. Print.

Čapka, František. *Dějiny zemí koruny české v datech.* Prague: Libri, 1999. Print.

Filipowicz, Marcin. "V jazyce naše... maskulinita: Případ obrozeneckého diskurzu." *Česká literatura* 60, no. 5(2012):663-693.

Harding, Sandra. *Whose science? Whose knowledge?* Ithaca, N.Y.: Cornell UP, 1991. Print.

----. "Rethinking Standpoint Epistemology: 'What is Strong Objectivity?'" *Feminist Epistemologies. Ed.* Alcoff Linda and Elizabeth Potter. New York: Routledge, 1993. 49-82. Print.

hooks, bell. *Where We Stand: Class Matters.* New York, London: Routledge, 2000. Print.

Malečková, Jitka. "Nationalizing Women and Engendering the Nation: The Czech National Movement." In *Gendered Nations: Nationalisms and Gender Order in the Long Nineteenth Century*, edited by Ida Blom, Karen Hageman, Catherine Hall, 293-310. Oxford and New York: Berg, 2000. Print.

Němeček, Jan, et al. *Mnichovská dohoda : cesta k destrukci demokracie v Evropě = Munich agreement : the way to destruction of democracy in Europe.* Prague: Karolinum, 2004. Print.

Nieto Gomez, Anna. "Sexism in the Movimiento." In *Chicana Feminist Thought: The Basic Historical Writings*, edited by Alma García, 97-100. New York and London: Routledge, 1997. Print.

Paz, Octavio. *The Labyrinth of Solitude.* New York: Grove Press, 1985. Print.

Procházka, Martin and Aleida Assmann. "Boudaries and Contact Zones." *Litteraria Pragensia* 13, no. 26(2003):1-7. Print.

Scheinostová, Alena. *Romipen: Literaturou k moderní identitě.* Prague: Athinganoi, 2006. Print.

Tesař, Jan. *Mnichovský komplex : jeho příčiny a důsledky.* Praha: Prostor, 2000. Print.

Zelený, Karel. *Vyhnání Čechů z pohraničí,* Prague: Ústav mezinárodních vztahů, 1996. Print.

ACTIVIST POLITICS OF ART, PERFORMANCE, AND PEDAGOGY

FEELING THE RHYTHMS OF MY ROOTS: TOWARD PERSONAL TRANSFORMATION

RUSTY BARCELÓ

When I was asked to be a panelist on the subject of Chicanas, Music, and Consciousness, I was pretty apprehensive. I say this for three reasons: First, my talks are generally about multiculturalism and institutional transformation from an educational administrative perspective. That is where my expertise lies. Second, my songs are very personal, maybe even bordering on self-centeredness; they don't focus on "big themes." Third, I knew I would be sharing a panel with three accomplished musicians, one of whom is an ethnomusicologist! I cannot even read music, and I rely on a tuner to tune my guitar!

Nevertheless, I decided to take on the challenge because music has been such an important part of my life and, in particular, my Chicana transformation. Composing songs has helped me reconcile and embrace all of the identities that are so much a part of me today. In some ways, the simple tunes and words I pull together serve to deconstruct the contradictions and complexities of my life as it engages with the many borders I encounter. As a result, I better understand my own journey through this world and how I have changed, and must continue to change, to meet whatever challenges and opportunities cross my path. I have a deeper, and more deeply felt, understanding of what Gloria meant when she described *nepantla* as a site of transformation.

In many ways I consider myself more of a storyteller than a musician/songwriter. I do not think anyone would challenge the notion that songs are about stories. For me, stories are the weavings of my life. Putting stories to song helps me focus and see my own history in new ways. The creative process of interlacing words and music sharpens my vision, makes difficult subjects more manageable, and helps me resolve some of the contradictions that keep me stuck in the middle space—so I am able to move more freely within and beyond the boundaries that have defined me at any given moment of my life. And preparing for this talk helped me to see my songs in a new light.

As I prepared, I thought about my songs very differently, through a new lens, from a perspective that was both historical and quasi-scholarly. Studying them as a critic, I recognized for the first time that with each song I composed, I was not just telling a story or linking words to notes on a scale but also *processing* some "happening" in my life—like a war, racism, loves gained or lost, family issues, sexuality, identity, allies, and more. This processing, if you will, provided a "space" for those stories to come together in very deep and personal ways that would create a larger narrative that was both personal and cultural/historical.

In reviewing my songs, I was surprised to learn how closely they were connected to each other, and also how much they provided me with a platform to move in new directions. In a sense, they developed in me a new consciousness and the courage to "come out" on many fronts—as a Chicana, lesbian, activist, educator, daughter, and more. They even, I believe, helped me in my institutional leadership roles.

I have discovered that my music has gradually brought all of my identities together, in ways that are still evolving. Years ago, before I read and re-read *Borderlands*, I bought into the notion that I was not Chicana enough. Of course, no one ever told me precisely what that meant, beyond speaking Spanish and looking the part. I could do neither at the time, and being at Iowa in those days certainly didn't help. I did not think I was taken seriously as a Chicana.

At Iowa I was just someone named Rusty, a geographic and cultural outsider hovering on the borderlands and often feeling marginalized because I had no legitimate identity. I did not feel authentic. I knew how I was raised culturally, and to paraphrase Gloria, I was a turtle, carrying my family and all of my ancestors on my back. And yet, in my new space my heritage set me apart and made me all but invisible. And the stories that created me remained mostly unspoken. I didn't really have anyone to talk to about who I was, or about the racism that I had seen and experienced growing up in a Mexican-American family. I was stuck between worlds. Like others having or living in more than one culture, we get multiple, often opposing messages. The coming together of two self-consistent but habitually incomparable frames of reference causes "*un choque,* a cultural collision"(*Borderlands* 100).

Even as a child, I had often turned to song as a source of comfort and community, and I did so again during this trying time of my life. Music became a refuge, a safe space. It also became a space for identity formation. I began to learn how, through my music, all of my multiple identities could come together in a holistic way. (If you listen carefully to my lyrics, you will often find all my identities intermingled in a single song.)

I have often been asked which I identity I prefer: Chicana, lesbian, woman, person with disabilities. I tell those who ask that I must respond as a whole person. I cannot separate my identities to meet other people's needs or stereotypes. I do sometimes focus on one or the other in the context of a given conversation, but *always* from the sum of my identities. I am able to pick and choose on demand, in a way, *without losing myself.* My songs have enabled me to do this. They have been a powerful catalyst for understanding that my many different identities constitute a fully integrated self.

I have never considered myself a writer, but as I reflected on my history as a writer of songs, I realized that composing music is all about writing. And I was reminded of what Gloria wrote in her article "Speaking in Tongues": "Writing is dangerous because we are afraid of what the writing reveals: the fears, the angers, the strengths of woman under a triple or quadruple oppression. Yet in that very act lies our survival because a woman who writes has power. And a woman with power is feared" ("Speaking in Tongues" 33).

And I would add, *Women who sing have power!* I know that from my own experience. Singing and songwriting have empowered me. They are not just a creative outlet. They have given me strength and confidence, and helped give me agency in the world, ever since my earliest childhood.

Ever since I can remember, I have been singing. My family loved to dance, but I never could. I had polio when I was six, and I could never again dance without falling. So I would sit and watch, and dance in my head to the rhythms. And I would sing to myself. Sometimes I would pretend to be reading a book when everyone was dancing, but I was watching, and singing, and wanting to be part of it all.

Polio taught me to turn inward, to a place that felt both safe and generative. Even if I couldn't dance, song was still there, inside of me. And songwriting became my means of expression, my very own kind of dance, a means of finding my own rhythms in my family and community. In a way, it made me "part of it all."

It has only been within the last five years or so that I have actually been public about my music. For years, I was a closeted performer, sharing my music only with family and friends. In the 1970s and 1980s, I performed at protest rallies and take-back-the-night rallies, but mostly well-known protest songs. I just didn't think my songs were good enough to meet the standards of protest music of the day; and I *certainly* didn't think they were "real Chicana music." I composed and sang in English, and my songs were more in a traditional Western folk country tradition, seldom laced with the Spanish and Latin rhythms that are part of our lived experiences.

I was raised on rancheras, cumbias, corridos, mambos, jazz, and blues. This was the music of my childhood, my heritage, and my community. It was the music my parents played daily. But I also heard country and folk music, because my father was in the military, and our family lived in many different places around the world. In some ways, I felt a certain kind of privilege as the globetrotting child of a military father, but I also experienced the searing contradictions that I would later come to understand as bias, ethnic hatred, discrimination, and exclusion. All of these experiences are part of who I am today. They are the roots of my own transformation, and the source of the rhythms and words of my songs.

Those songs, while they often came out of struggle and pain, are also songs of affirmation and transformation. They are songs of myself, and also songs of my people. They are deeply personal, but also very political. They ask the world to take notice.

My friends Eden Torres and Norma Cantú were among the first to tell me that my music needed to be shared. They said the messages would resonate far beyond my inner circle. They said that by sharing my songs, I would empower others to take agency in their own lives. To paraphrase Eden's words, my songs tell the world I will no longer apologize for being the Chicana I am today. *I am Chicana, hear me sing!*

I heeded their advice, and I have never been sorry, even though I am still often a reluctant performer. Nothing has been more surprising and rewarding than to have my music valued by Chicanas. When Chicanas praise my music, I feel honored and blessed. After all these years, their appreciation still brings me out in new and exciting ways. And this circle of support helps me continue my transformation even today at sixty-five, pulled by the rhythms of my roots, writing and performing music as a bridge to somewhere new, to an even higher plane of *nepantla*.

Two songs [which I performed at the El Mundo Zurdo conference] bracket a long and important period of transformation in my life—nearly fifty years, in fact—and in my relationship with my mother, who moved on to the spirit world in 2003. I wrote the first song when I was eighteen years old as a first-year college student at Chico State in California. It had no title—like all my songs—and was written with only one chord, which I had learned earlier in the day on the guitar my brother gave me when I left for college. The song was to my mother, but I never sang it to her, for reasons revealed in the song written in 1966:

I sat my mother down
I looked at her and I said
Your daughter is a rambler
You might think of me dead

No grandchildren will I give you
Little love will you get from me
I'm just a plain old rambler
And I'll ramble where I please

Oh, please don't cry my mother
Oh, please don't cry no more
I'm grateful for what you have done
But I must follow the sun

Someday I might settle down
Till then I'll just roam around
Few letters will I write
I'm drifting out of sight

And now the time has come
I really must be gone
I see you at my judgment day
When God is melting my clay

More recently, I have been writing a follow-up song to my mother that was probably inspired by all the ads for Mother's Day. It has been ten years now since she left, and I can only hope that her troubled spirit has now found the peace she never enjoyed in this world.

Mama, Mama I am so sorry
I didn't mean to be

Your living, living memory
So sorry, I'm sorry

Mama, Mama I know you tried to tell me
But you would cry
And I would too
I only wanted the truth from you
So sorry, I'm sorry

Mama, mama you told me just enough to know
You said no
It was not your sin give it all back to him
So sorry, I'm sorry

Mama, Mama each day I grow stronger
I leave your pain far behind
Only because it is time
So sorry, I'm sorry

Mama, Mama I'm glad that you decided
To give me life,
To give me name
To give me love
To give me hope
To let me dream
So I might be one day me
Oh, mama

Mama, Mama I take your strength and courage
Your legacy
You left for me
Is now my living, living memory

So why do I write songs? Why does anyone write songs? Because writing is a performative, liberatory, clarifying, and integrative act. It bridges divides, bears witness, and moves us toward wholeness and authenticity—and transformation. As Gloria said, "Nothing happens in the 'real' world unless it first happens in the images in our heads" (*Borderlands* 109). And so the song I write is, to borrow again from Gloria, "the dialogue between my Self and *el espíritu del mundo.* I change myself, I change the world" (*Borderlands* 92).

I will end with the long answer from Gloria, who always said it better:

> Why am I compelled to write?... Because the world I create in the writing compensates for what the real world does not give me. By writing I put order in the world, give it a handle so I can grasp it. I write because life does not appease my appetites and anger... To become more intimate with myself and you. To discover myself, to preserve myself, to make myself, to achieve self-autonomy. To dispel the myths that I am a mad prophet or a poor suffering soul. To convince myself that I am worthy... Finally I write because I'm scared of writing, but I'm more scared of not writing. ("Speaking in Tongues" 30)

WORKS CITED

Anzaldúa, Gloria. *Borderlands/La Frontera: The New Mestiza.* 1987. San Francisco, CA: Aunt Lute Books, 1999. Print.

---. "Speaking in Tongues." *This Bridge Called My Back: Writings by Radical Women of Color.* Ed. Gloria Anzaldúa and Cherríe Moraga. New York: Kitchen Table: Women of Color Press, 1983. 165-74. Print.

MUSIC AND MY CHICANA IDENTITY

BRENDA M. ROMERO

Music has been an integral part of my Chicana identity. First there was my mother's singing; from her I learned my first song, the hymn "Bendito sea Dios" when I was two years old. I grew up listening to Gregorian chants at our little village church in New Mexico. This changed in the 1960s, with Pope John Paul's Vatican II decrees, and vernacular music began to be the basis of Catholic worship and folk songs became more commonly used in the Mass. In the 1960s I learned to sing protest folk songs, modeled on Joan Baez. Later I studied classical music and became a composer, then decided to become an ethnomusicologist.

I first learned to read music when I babysat for Mr. García, the band teacher at my elementary school; I was only eleven years old. After the Garcías' daughter went to sleep I sat at their piano and figured out how to play a short melody from her piano method book, using the right fingers and rhythms. At age thirteen, I bought a ukulele and learned to play it from a girl who lived across the street. At fifteen, a friend who traveled to Spain took my fifty dollars and brought me my own guitar from Salamanca. I taught myself to play mostly by imitating Joan Baez recordings and using her songbooks, as I learned to sing her songs. I also began to read notation and taught myself some easy classical pieces. I sang in the chorus starting in sixth grade and continued through high school. I did not study music formally until I was a freshman in college, however, but even then I thought I could not be a music major because I had not taken formal music lessons since I was a child. After one year at the University of New Mexico, I left school to explore the world...

Years passed. I was in Paris and was caught in the last student and working class demonstration on July 14 during the turbulent summer of 1968. That summer, living on a shoestring, hitchhiking in France and Spain, I read *Saint Francis* by Nikos Kazantzakis. I lived in a commune in Berkeley, California, and worked for the University of California as a typist. In 1973, I moved to Australia with my first husband and baby daughter and worked as a typist for the University of Queensland's Children's Hospital, a research center. During my lunch hour, I would regularly serenade those children who were there for months on end. In 1974, I was accepted to study voice at the then-called Brisbane Conservatory, with an Irish Australian woman, Margaret Dickson, with whom I shared an immigrant status in that country. I also studied composition privately with her adult son. Her husband was the director of the music program at the University of Queensland in Brisbane, which they referred to as "the Uni." Not long before I left Australia, this woman encouraged me to apply to the university's music program. All my life I had waited for the right person to encourage me to study music formally, and I owe Margaret Dickson the credit for giving me the conviction that I could in fact "make it" in a music program. Although this attitude about studying music is not limited to Chicanas by any means, it resonates all the more so with the internalized oppression that comes from the experience of being treated like an invisible entity because of the color of one's skin, and its associations with a lower socio-economic status.

> Deep in our hearts we believe that being Mexican has nothing to do with which country one lives in. Being Mexican is a state of soul—not one of mind, not one of citizenship. Neither eagle nor serpent, but both. And like the ocean, neither animal respects borders. (Anzaldúa 84)

An Irishwoman in Australia understood something about this and her encouragement eventually led me to my true calling. This was postponed for another two years because by the time we came back to the US my marriage was ending. Even as I worried about how this would affect my two daughters, I wrote a song, "A Time for Reflection," that began:

> A time for reflection, a time of new direction,
> I no longer feel that this is how our lives were meant to be,
> and when I look into your eyes, it's only you that I can see,
> not me, nor you and me.

I sang this song for a public audience for the first time at the SSGA conference in 2012.

I had managed to maintain my Spanish, and now I went back to school, along with my two daughters (ages five and fourteen months), in Quito, Ecuador, for a semester of Latin American Studies at the former Centro Andino of the University of New Mexico and Northwestern University. It wasn't until my marriage officially ended the next year that I decided music was something that no one would ever be able to take away from me. By then I was a student at the University of New Mexico; I transferred from Latin American Studies to Music. Even then, I declared the least demanding option, guitar pedagogy, as my major. As I gathered more confidence through my coursework, however, I switched to composition, where few Chicanos or Chicanas ever ventured. It is not often considered that indigenous and black people were not permitted to study composition during the colonial period, an unspoken legacy that lives on in "official" or academic music programs.

I completed my bachelor's degree in music theory and composition and took the Masters Preliminary Exams the day before we learned that one of my sisters had an inoperable brain tumor, a death sentence at age thirty-seven. I recalled the DDT that was introduced to our apple orchards in the 1950s, and how my sister loved green apples. It was the end of the thousands of fireflies we easily collected as children, and the end of giant bullfrogs in the *acacias*. The crawfish are only now starting to come back in 2013. My sister's condition resonated with countless stories of Mexican migrants condemned to an early death by pesticides.

> The U.S.–Mexican border *es una herida abierta* where the Third World grates against the first and bleeds. . . Tension grips the inhabitants of the borderlands like a virus. Ambivalence and unrest reside there and death is no stranger. (Anzaldúa 25-26)

Disappointment with music programs came in many ways over time, each requiring me to search deeper into myself. First of all, when I came back to New Mexico after a decade of being gone, which included three years in Australia, I wanted to learn about my own New Mexican *'Manito*[1] music culture and those of Pueblo, Navajo, and Apache people of the state—the people I'd gone to school with but never understood growing up. There weren't any classes offered on New Mexican music of any kind; instead all vernacular music was housed in the John Donald Robb Archive of Southwestern Music. Undaunted, as a Masters student in music theory and composition, I applied for a Graduate School Challenge Award, a grant that allowed me to help catalog the Robb Collection (much of it still in boxes) and listen to the hundreds of recordings of New Mexican folk music he and his wife collected from the 1930s on—a project he had converted into a hefty book, complete with musical transcriptions and translations into English, by 1980. I also taught a class on the subject through Chicano Studies during the year I finished the degree.

The most exciting of those songs were the ones called *inditas*. They provided a glimpse into a history that was never told in any of my classes. Following the 1998 meeting of NACCS in Mexico City, Norma E. Cantú and Olga Nájera-Ramírez asked to include an early presentation on *inditas* in their forthcoming *Chicana Traditions, Continuity and Change* (2002). This gave me the opportunity to further analyze this unique genre of New Mexican *inditas* as a means of understanding how the indigenous female body has been represented in New Mexico, via the emotional and spiritual elements that music provide. At the borderlands of New Mexico, the *indita* represents Our Lady of Guadalupe as much as she embodies vulnerability and a landscape that was rapidly disappearing from local control. The indigenous concept of the sacred earth is personified into the *indita* ballad tradition, some *inditas* appear to have been composed by indigenous people speaking and singing in Spanish (much as my earlier songs were written and sung in English). Here is a verse from the "Indita de Manuelito" (Robb 1980):

Yo soy el indio Manuel,	I am the Indian Manuel,
hermanito del Mariano,	little brother of Mariano,
que con mi flecha en la mano	who with my arrow in my hand
empalmo de dos a tres.	pierce two or three at a time.

In the New Mexican Danza de los Matachines, the Malinche character is not the traitoress she became in Mexico, via Octavio Paz and other male Mexican intellectuals of the past century. Here she is the first Christian convert, but nonetheless a symbol of submission to a dominant male order. Some of the most poignant *inditas* hold something of the pain and sorrow that native women have suffered. "La cautiva Marcelina" still speaks to the same pain and sorrow that many feel today as a result of war and internal conflicts over land and resources:

La cautiva Marcelina	Marcelina, the captive
cuando llegó al aguapá,	when she arrived at the cattail marsh,
volteó la cara llorando,	she turned her head, crying
—Matarón a mi papá,	—They've killed my father,
matarón a mi papá.	they've killed my father.

Coro:	Chorus:
Por eso ya no quiero	Because of this I no longer wish
en el mundo más amar	to love in this world,
de mi querida patria	from my beloved homeland
me van a retirar.	they are taking me away.

Gloria Anzaldúa wrote:

> My Chicana identity is grounded in the Indian woman's history of resistance. The Aztec female rites of mourning were rites of defiance protesting the cultural changes which disrupted the equality and balance between female and male, and protesting their demotion to a lesser status, their denigration. Like *la Llorona*, the Indian woman's only means of protest was wailing. (43)

Instead I have tried to transform my wailing into music. I have used music to encourage societal transformation by researching and singing *inditas.* I love the sound of the old archival recordings. I have tried to imitate those singers, because their songs and the way they sang them speak to my deepest sense of who I am. I hope that my performances of New Mexican *inditas* will bring a greater awareness of the complicated roles that indigenous people have played in local histories.

Music schools, like other Eurocentric establishments, are places where technical virtuosity is highly valued, and so is complicated "intellectual" music. By the time I was in the masters program in music theory and composition, as my sister's condition deteriorated, I was inspired to write a string trio for her; a piece that was performed and recorded and my final gift to her. Being Chicana I opted for a piece that recalled the Baroque idea called the Doctrine of Affections, which basically meant that they chose one mood and used only the tones that evoked that mood. The Doctrine of Affections probably recalls a time when the West was absorbing Arabic musical ideas from Spain. By focusing on only six tones, I sought to create a piece that would allow me to express most fully the growing sense of loss as I saw my sister slip away. But, as Dr. Aida Hurtado submits, a Chicana in the colonial gaze is useful for her brown, laboring body, but not as an intellectual person.[2] When I entered this piece, intellectually conceived, yet so full of heart and which my sister so loved, into the annual composition competition, only the youngest of three composers found the piece to have merit, exactly because it used only six notes. I realize in retrospect that if I had included notes talking about the Doctrine of Affections, the piece might have been more seriously considered. The composer who liked the piece commented on the passion the work communicated. Why didn't the others hear that, I still wonder?

Perhaps I just wasn't objective, but this convinced me that composition at the PhD level would only be more of the dry, competitive, unfeeling intellectual technical mastery that obliterates the connection to one's heart. As such, it is a fine emblem of colonial domination. Instead, I chose to study ethnomusicology at UCLA, which, for me, opened the door widely to learning about music through the heart versus the mind. This has proven to be true for me, but ethnomusicology is still the black sheep in the College of Music where I am enrolled, and where whiteness is the norm. As a dean once told me when I attempted to create an exchange program with music professors at UNAM, "There is status in going to Vienna; there is no status in going to Mexico City."

I am an ethnomusicologist and teach at a largely white institution, where being both an ethnomusicologist *and* Chicana often implies a struggle with Eurocentric patriarchal and institutional authority. Nowhere is this more difficult than in the traditional music department, my home unit, where, in the twenty four years I have been working toward more inclusive curriculum and participation, I am still the only Mexican-American woman who has been on the music faculty in the history of the institution, in spite of the 30 percent Hispano presence in the state of Colorado. Only two Chicanos have ever been enrolled, both specialists in Western art music.

Among my favorite of my compositions, is the woodwind quintet I composed for the Wheelwright Museum of the American Indian in Santa Fe for their 50th anniversary in 1987, because the flute player thought I was indigenous. I explained the situation, but they wanted the piece anyway. I based the work, titled *Native Winds,* on some songs documenting the nineteenth century Ghost Dance that I had taught at the Navajo Pine Hill School during my last semester at UNM for an end-of-year school play. Lakotas who came to the concert wept when they heard the old melodies that evoked their grandparents and the suffering that Wounded Knee brought to them in particular. When a group of Lakotas asked for help towards their annual Sundance a few months later, the Wheelwright donated all of the proceeds of that event to them.

Music has allowed me to express my indigenous ancestry, which is undocumented as it is for all but a few mestizos. When I was a graduate student in ethnomusicology at UCLA, one of my mentors Dr. Charlotte Heth (Cherokee), taught me that if I was to work with indigenous people I must give something back. In 1989, I began to play the violin for the "Matachina" (Danza de los Matachines) at the Pueblo of Jemez in New Mexico after their Hispano fiddler, Adelaido Martinez, who had played for their *danza* for thirty years, died of cancer. He came to me in a dream and told me that I would have to play violin for ten minutes a day. It took more time than that to learn the repertoire, but I made a promise to Our Lady of Guadalupe, since the Matachina is danced on her feast day of December 12. This helped me to calm the sense of the Spanish white guilt that is part of my identity, just as my indigenous self was able to find expression and satisfaction. As Saldívar-Hull notes in the Introduction to the second edition of *Borderlands,* "Part of the work of that *mestiza* consciousness is to break down dualities that serve to imprison women" (5). Even though Gloria was referring to being "both male and female," this also strengthens the Chicana's "internal critique of Chicano cultural practices that deny the indigenous part of the *mestizaje*" (5). Elsewhere I have written more about my ongoing work in Jemez, where I played the violin for nine years, until I had taught Adelaido's grandson to play the repertoire on his grandfather's old violin. Adelaido's grandson took my place in 1998, and I took off to do research on Matachines at the borderlands, later in Mexico, and most recently in Colombia. My challenge now is to finish the book on that subject.

Music programs are still a frontier for Chicanas and for Latinos in general. One thing I have learned from ethnomusicology is that music brings people together, but can also be used to form barriers to keep others out. The tight community of classical performers and composers in music institutions demonstrates this, as only those who participate are welcome—even musicians of color. But few people from disenfranchised populations get into music programs. Ethnomusicology, which calls attention to music in the rest of the world, is also undervalued and undermined. Given the benefits of playing and enjoying music for individual well-being, I find this unconscionable. The good news is that music continues to thrive among Chicanos and Chicanas in the US, as in Latin America. Eventually, a real presence will form in music departments.

ENDNOTES

1 See "New Mexico and '*Manitos* at the Borderlands of Popular Music in Greater Mexico," for *Transnational Encounters. Music and Performance at the U.S.-Mexico Border,* edited by Alejandro Madrid. New York: Oxford University Press, 2011:287-311.

2 Aida Hurtado. Public talk. May 16, 2012. University of Texas, Pan American campus, Edinburgh, Texas.

WORKS CITED

Anzaldúa, Gloria. *Borderlands/La frontera: the New Mestiza.* 3rd ed. San Francisco: Aunt Lute Books, 2007.

Robb, John Donald. *Hispanic Folk Music of New Mexico and the Southwest, A Self-Portrait of a People.* Norman: University of Oklahoma Press, 1980.

Romero, Brenda M. "*La Indita* of New Mexico: Gender and Cultural Identification," in *Chicana Traditions, Continuity and Change*, edited by Olga Najera-Ramirez and Norma E. Cantú. Chicago: University of Illinois Press, 2002.

---. "New Mexico and 'Manitos at the Borderlands of Popular Music in Greater Mexico," for *Transnational Encounters. Music and Performance at the U.S.-Mexico Border*, edited by Alejandro Madrid. New York: Oxford University Press, 2011.

CHICAN@ ARTIVISTAS AT THE INTERSECTION OF HOPE AND IMAGINATION

MARTHA GONZALEZ

This essay is informed by embodied knowledge and auto-ethnographic experience as a musician in a Chican@ rock group Quetzal and as an artivista (artist/activist) in East Los Angeles, CA. In keeping with the memory and teachings of Gloria Anzaldúa, I honor her by stating "I cannot separate my writing from any part of my life. It is all one."

"Invoked art is communal and speaks of everyday life" (Anzaldúa 67).

Like many, I have also experienced profound transformation through Gloria Anzaldúa's words. Anzaldúa's ability to imagine and construct images gave us tools of the mind but most of all of the spirit. Como dice ella misma, "The word, the image and the feeling have a palatable energy" (71). Much of her life's work was in articulating her creative process to us and in doing so, we were inspired and felt encouraged to find ways of expressing our multiple perceptions, visions, and realities. Anzaldúa stated, "Sometimes I put the imagination to a more rare use. I choose words, images, and body sensations and animate them to impress them on my consciousness, thereby making changes in my belief systems and reprogramming my consciousness" (70). I believe that words, images, and body sensations are best reached through creative expression. Imagination is at the forefront of this venture. It is no wonder then, how poetry, music, art, dance, and teatro are all intimate tools of this process.

This essay is a brief auto-ethnographic account of the catalysts that inspired a praxis and philosophy by which many East Los Angeles *artivistas* (artist/activists) continue to live. Chican@ *artivistas*[1] in Eastside Los Angeles neighborhoods utilize art and creative expression to deconstruct power, challenge multiple patriarchal systems, and build community. From renewed hope imaginaries erupt as *artivistas* channel the power and practice of music, art, and theatre, as tools of *convivencia* (deliberate convening). In dialogue with translocal Mexican communities, Chican@ *artivistas* have developed social techniques to harness artistic and creative power in order to transform and rebuild various sectors of their communities such as: food sovereignty, money recycling, self-sustained community services, and artistic networks. I suggest that by creating physical, spiritual, and ideological spaces through art and creative expression, *artivistas* operate at the intersection of hope and imagination. A discussion on the impact of Zapatista philosophy in Chican@ *artivista* praxis, and in particular, the organizing process and implementation of the 1997 *Encuentro Chican@ Indigen@ Para La Humanidad y Contra el Neoliberalismo*, will assist me in demonstrating the delicate balance and hermeneutics of Chican@ *artivistas* creative, professional, and community work; and how this process adheres to the kind of border consciousness Gloria Anzaldúa articulated in her work.

ZAPATISTA + ARTISTAS = ZAPARTISTA

On January 1, 1994, the day the North American Free Trade Agreement (NAFTA) was to go into effect, indigenous Mayan communities in Chiapas, Mexico took over four municipalities in the state including the city of San Cristobal de Las Casas. The *Ejercito Zapatista de Liberacion National* (E.Z.L.N), commonly known as the Zapatistas, was the first post-modern revolution that was *not* in search of governmental power. The Mayan communities claimed grievances with the Mexican government and the neo-colonial forces of globalization. Their uprising was an attempt to bring focus and attention to their struggle. Their tactics also significantly relied on building alliances with other communities in struggle around the globe.

Most unusual was the way in which they consistently appeared masked. Concealed by *pasa montañas, pañuelos or paliacates,* at no time did they allow their full faces to show in public.[2] Through their masks, the Zapatistas expressed to the world their struggles. However, the language in which they choose to communicate was not conventional political language. They often made their claims through poetic *dichos,* or sayings like, *"No tenemos que pedir permiso para ser libres!"*[3] *and "De tras de nosotros estamos ustedes!"*[4] In addition, they boldly and repeatedly declared their *mal govierno* corrupt.[5] In this sense, they avoided the traditional "discourse of power" and spoke to the heart, and from the heart (Muñoz 19). Among the constituency of male and female indigenous *comandantes* was a gentleman the Zapatistas called *Sub-comandante* Marcos. The media frenzy over these masked indigenous people soon turned their attention to this charismatic spokesperson. *Everyone* wondered, "Who is Marcos?" The Zapatistas responded:

> Marcos is gay in San Francisco, black in South Africa, an Asian in Europe, a Chicano in San Ysidro, an anarchist in Spain, a Palestinian in Israel, a Mayan Indian in the streets of San Cristobal, a gang member in Neza[6], a rocker in the National University, a Jew in Germany, an ombudsman in the Defense Ministry, a communist in the post-Cold War era, an artist without gallery or portfolio.... A pacifist in Bosnia, a housewife alone on Saturday night in any neighborhood in any city in Mexico, a striker in the CTM, a reporter writing filler stories for the back pages, a single woman on the subway at 10 pm, a peasant without land, an unemployed worker... an unhappy student, a dissident amid free market economics, a writer without books or readers, and, of course, a Zapatista in the mountains of southeast Mexico. So Marcos is a human being, any human being, in this world. Marcos is all the exploited, marginalized and oppressed minorities, resisting and saying, "Enough"! (Big Noise, "Zapatista")

The poetic, yet politically charged statement jolted the public's imagination. Understanding the way they might be read by the media and in attempts to engage the world to imagine beyond the masked indigenous subject, the Zapatistas released the above statement. Behind the *pasamontañas,* Marcos was and could be "any human being in the world" (*Green Left Online,* "Marcos is Gay"). By articulating multiple moments or varying global subjects in the midst of oppression—the "Palestinian in Israel," the "gay in San Francisco," a "black in South Africa"—they connected the common struggle amongst them all: neoliberalism. Furthermore, the act of describing common oppressions through the everyday experience and poetic-like prose further invoked their collective humanity. The Zapatistas not only made their point, but also refused to let the media mistakably seek "the one" person responsible for their uprising. They concluded their statement with; *"Todos somos Marcos!"*[7]

The world would come to realize that poetic prose would become a tactic for the Zapatistas. They unapologetically took and continued to engage in an exploration of subjectivities and discussions on economic and social oppression through multiple dialogues, poetry, *encuentros,* and other social technologies.[8] Furthermore, emphasizing a cosmic view of relationality, Zapatistas sought engagement/dialogue with their immediate and other struggling communities around the globe. They called for people and sites of resistance to come to the table to dialogue without false government language and discourse. Zapatistas believed then, like now, that *encuentros* can be important self-reflexive exercises that engender community building and critical consciousness.

Creative expression was and continues to be an effective way for the Zapatistas to articulate real and cosmic realities that include hope for local and global communities. I learned about the Zapatistas at the (now extinct) Popular Resource Center (PRC) in Highland Park, C.A. among the artists and activists that practiced out of this space in the late 90s. What was initially striking to me was precisely how the Zapatistas repeatedly used poetry-like expression to communicate their ideas. I remember thinking how poetry *was* the perfect tool. Subjectivity is an embodied reality. Both conscious and subconscious are often times articulated through creative expression. The creative process often draws out what Bakare-Yusuf articulates as "counter memory," which emerges through tangible modes of expression (182). Poetry and writing from Anzaldúa's perspective for example, was an "image-making practice" that can shape and transform what we imagine, what we are able to perceive, and what we are able to give material embodiment to (qtd. in Perez 317). Of course, art and culture production was an important force in *Movimiento* times.[9] However, art or cultural work was not centralized or taken as seriously as "political work." Meaning that art and music were often seen as ornamental rather than instrumental in a dialectic process that engaged community as more than an audience and spectators.[10] In this regard, Zapatista uprising was an inspiring moment in the Chican@ East L.A art scene in the mid-90s for reasons concerning both Zapatista methods as well as their tactics. The Zapatistas were unconventional, filled with compelling questions, and open to possibilities. Imagining creative expression—art, music, and culture—as a way to dialogue with other struggling communities could be more than a reality. Music did not have to be the "soundtrack" to the movement, or some entertainment you inserted between "important" speakers, but rather the music could be the movement itself—a dialectic tool. In this way, you could include others in the process, not just those who kept up with the latest political or theoretical material.

The Zapatista approach (*encuentros* etc.) to social movement also centered community assets and embodied knowledge, which intrinsically changed our self-judgment. Rather than conceive of our communities deprived and lacking resources, we acknowledged our experiences and valued the relationships and ways of organizing that were already underway in East L.A. In short, the Zapatista anti-imperialist message, as well their use of poetry-like approach to communicate their demands to the world, invigorated the Chican@ East L.A artistic scene in the late 90s. This inspiration was so profound that in 1997, 120 East *Los Artivistas* and the Zapatista Mayan community of *Oventic* organized *"El Primer Encuentro Cultural Chican@ Indigena por La Humanidad y Contra el Neoliberalismo."*

THE BIG FRENTE ZAPATISTA (BFZ)

> Chicana Art. . . has responded in greater or lesser measures, to the rise of particular social, economic and political forces. Some of the most salient of these have been the rise of post-industrialist, digital-based, production and distribution systems enabling accelerated, transnational flows of information; the restructuring of business labor; the dis-empowerment of workers and the growing relocation of unskilled manual labor jobs in manufacturing industries from the United States to the third world and elsewhere, including the Mexican side of the border. . . (Perez 11)

The Big Frente Zapatista (BFZ) became the organizing body for the proposed *encuentro.* The title of the organizing collective "The Big Frente" was playful, based on the Mexican organization called *La Frente Zapatista de Liberacion Nacional* (FZLN). *La Frente* was a civil society organization in support of the E.Z.L.N. As a collective we had experienced through our own communities how music and art were effective organizing tools. The conflation of two words, *artista* (artist) and *activista* (activist), the term *artivista* underlines Laura E. Perez's statement on Chicana artists as: "intellectuals whose work embody theories of resistance and visionary ideals of social change."[11] With *artivista* eyes on the Zapatista uprising, a call was disseminated to whomever was interested in planning an *encuentro* between Chican@s and Indigen@s. The call was circulated by word of mouth, email, and fax. It read:

> *El Big Frente Zapatista* invites you to participate in the First Cultural Gathering for Humanity and Against *Neoliberlaismo.* This *Encuentro* will take place in Chiapas, Mexico, between August 5-10... The Big Frente is a collective of artists, students, youth, workers, and cultural promoters from various communities and organizations. We work with all those who have been excluded and marginalized by neoliberalism and who have been inspired by the Zapatista movement. We are members of civil society, uniting in the efforts of Zapatismo, not only to support the EZLN in Mexico, but also to actively participate in our own transformation *"desde nuestra propia trinchera."*[12] The BFZ is dedicated to promote the work of the EZLN, FZLN, and any other organization working towards the creation of just societies for all humanity. In order to engage in this process we have organized the following Cultural *Encuentro* for Humanity and Against Neoliberalism. (Palomares personal collection)

The call also included a tentative schedule of activities for the *Encuentro*. Most of the participants that answered were college students between the ages of 18- 25 years of age.

The planning meetings were scheduled every Sunday for about a year. Meetings were mostly held at *Centro Regeneracion* in Highland Park. There were countless meetings and fundraising events that in retrospect strengthened the alliances between the participants. The informal network consisted of artists working in various mediums—visual and graffiti art, spoken word artists, bands, artisans, poets, and filmmakers. The BFZ also consisted of community organizers that may not have practiced artistic expression but rather appreciated creative/ artistic work and recognized the inherent power in the practice. Among the talented body of community organizers were Laura Palomares, Suyapa Portillo, and Miguel Rodriguez.

THE PROCESS

We utilized various social techniques to build trust among the *artivistas* and organizers. Although most artists were not "formally" trained, we each had the responsibility of facilitating creative ways of engaging group dialogue. We agreed to bring to the collective "ice-breakers," or trust exercises from our respective disciplines. The *teatro* group Chusma, for example, brought in various theatre exercises. We also studied and collectively discussed Zapatista philosophy and communiqués.

After a couple of weeks of meeting regularly, our discussions became more intimate. Sometimes the conversations brought up childhood memories of violence and sexual abuse. Some of the men also spoke up about spousal battery. The instilled trust initiated a kind of sharing that could have been incriminating or shameful for some of the participants. There was instead forgiveness and a kind of know-how amongst us that allowed these moments to come up without fear or shame.

Through this process, the BFZ came to realize that creating art that required constituent efforts to produce was more than a useful tool to get to know each other.

Stuart Hall states that, "without language meaning could not be exchanged in the world" ("Representation and the Media"). He goes on to stress that "without language there is no meaning." The BFZ extended the concept of "language" to apply to constituent efforts in collective culture production. Artistic mediums, after all, such as visual art, music and *teatro* are effective tools that can draw out important "sites of memory" in the body, where often times abstract theories speak to non-linear sensibilities capable of shifting consciousness and thus invoking critical change (Feldman 13).

Besides the weekly meetings, we also produced multi-media concerts to generate funds for the trip. We wanted all who wished to attend the *Encuentro* to be able to do so. The fundraising was constant. We held concerts, and even a "Zapatista run" where community and family sponsored participant runners. Some artists designed and sold merchandise. Local visual artists, Omar and Jose Ramirez for example, designed t-shirts that displayed the Zapatista Revolutionary Laws for Women or the "*Hymno Zapatista Nacional.*" Having raised enough funds, community organizers Laura Palomares and Suyapa Gris Portillo left two months earlier than the rest of *Encuentro* participants to make sure we were all settled and that we had personal contact with Zapatista organizers on the Mexican side of the border.

The rest of BFZ members stayed behind, but continued to fundraise. It was also important for us be able to pay for the cost of food for *Encuentro* participants as well as provide food and lodging for Palomares and Portillo. Furthermore, funds had to be distributed to the Zapatistas ahead of time so that they could purchase food supplies from their own community networks. The localized trust and cohesion built through this difficult yet powerful process allowed us to move on to a successful translocal dialogue with the Zapatistas. On August 2, 1997, one-hundred and twenty-seven Chican@ *artivistas* mostly from the Los Angeles area set out for Chiapas, Mexico to partake in the *Encuentro Cultural Chicano/Indigena Por La Humanidad y Contra El Neoliberalismo.*[13]

CHIAPAS, AGUASCALIENTES II: ENCUENTRO PROCESS

We decided to model the *Encuentro* after the dialogues and group work we had done amongst ourselves at the PRC. Once we arrived in Chiapas and the community of Oventic, Aguascalientes II,[14] we engaged in a similar format. The mornings consisted of *mesas de dialogo,* or dialogue tables concerning various topics. After the morning dialogues, we set to engage in communal creative expression. That is to say, we worked in different creative mediums based on the morning's discussions. The goal was to produce collective creative work that could be shared with others at the end of the day. *Encuentro* participants could choose workshops in *teatro,* poetry, music, graffiti/mural painting, and dance. The *artivistas* chose which workshops they would conduct. Janelle Gonzales and myself were in charge of the dance workshops. I was also able to participate in the music workshops. Chusma members such as Alberto Ibarra, Marisol Torres, Danny Torres, and Richard Montoya of *Culture Clash* ran the *teatro* workshops. The poetry workshops were conducted by Felicia Montes, Liza Hita, and Cristina Gorosica. Nuke, Omar Ramirez, Arnoldo "Zeta," and Rachael Velez Thorson were in charge of the mural painting workshops. And finally, Rosa Marta Zarate, Jose Q. Flores, Gabriel Tenorio, and Claudia Gonzalez conducted the music workshops.

There were additional members of the BFZ that also floated around to different workshops depending on where they were needed the most. Yaolt, Joe

"Peps" Galarza and D.J. Bean, from Aztlan Underground were multi-talented musicians and artists that were able to partake in more than one medium. Laura Palomares and Suyapa Portillo floated around making sure we stayed on schedule.

SONGWRITING WORKSHOP

Rosa Marta Zarate was a former nun who was invited by the Zapatista women to participate in the *encuentro.* Zarate had established her own relationship with the communities by supporting the cooperatives of artisans. Zarate, a talented singer and guitar player, facilitated the songwriting workshops, along with Jose Q. Flores and Gabriel Tenorio. Zarate was an effective leader as she encouraged and moderated the various silences and outbursts of ideas in the midst of creative energy. The workshop was filled with masked indigenous people and Chican@s that focused their attention towards a poster board mounted on the wall of the *cabaña.* Flores, Tenorio, and Enomoto worked along with the community and Zarate in the composition of music and melodies.

The process of writing song lyrics is a tedious task. We had previously discussed ideas in the dialogue sessions or *mesas* and now we were going to create music based on the discussions. *Nos Encontramos* was the topic of the day and we had spent an hour composing lyrical ideas. The cabaña was filled with chatter as the participants were attempting to come up with the next line to the composition. It was chaotic as the plethora of languages filled the room—Chican@s speaking English and broken Spanish, Zapatistas speaking Castellano, Tzotzil, Tzetzal and Tojolabal, and of course the Mexican observers speaking Spanish and broken English. Rosa Marta had a comedic way of diffusing opposing ideas on wording and phrasing. Every time we came to a consensus by a showing of hands, she would affirm our collective visions by writing the final lyric on the poster board. Soon we had completed our song and titled it *"El Grito de Alegria."*

Various Zapatista men and women voiced the style or genre of music they wanted the composition to be in. Some suggested a *corrido.*[15] The *corrido* was an informative and useful way of documenting this moment, but other Zapatistas felt our song should be more festive and danceable. Even though Chicanos wanted a little hip-hop feel, in the end, the group decided to make the first day's song a *Cumbia.* A portion of the lyrics read:

El pueblo con paso lento va ganando la lucha. La tristeza que hoy llevamos será un grito de alegría.

With a steady pace our pueblo wins this battle. The sadness we once held shall turn into cries of happiness!

El gobierno manipula, encarcela y asesina. Nosotros los Zapatistas romperemos las cadenas!	The government manipulates, encarcerates, and assassinates! We the Zapatistas shall break these chains!
Zapatistas somos todos y luchamos por la tierra. Dignidad, paz y justicia, libertad son nuestras metas.	We are all Zapatistas and we struggle for the land. Dignity, peace, justice and liberty are our goals.
Si nos robaron la tierra si nos quitaron el pan. El pueblo que marcha unido, lograra la libertad. El pueblo que marcha unido vencerá!	If they have taken our lands, if they have taken our bread, the pueblo who marches together shall win their liberty. The pueblo who marches together shall overcome!

The contents of the song reflect the day's discussion, which included our histories and all that our ancestors and people had been through. Colonization, war, disease, enslavement, and the loss of ancestral lands, were all common struggles among us. The song, however, takes a hopeful stance. Most importantly *"El Grito de Alegria"* is a re-articulation of the common phrase, "the cry of war." Amid the economic and political struggle for autonomy, *"El Grito de Alegria"* literally means "the cry of happiness"—a title celebrating the present, the process, the hope that we felt in each other's presence. Hope is after all an "ontological need" (Frieri 8). As Chican@s we were in Chiapas in solidarity with the Zapatistas, to dialogue, and thus fortify our own communities. Together we created a song for each day of the *Encuentro*, to commemorate the moment. But this song was also a way of producing community knowledge. My music group, Quetzal, recorded *"El Grito de Alegria"* on our debut album, which was released a year later. *"El Grito de Alegria*" has since been played in venues all over the U.S, Mexico, Japan, and Canada. We have also been informed that Mayan Encuentro participants have also continued to play it.

INDIGENOUS PEDAGOGY, HOPE AND IMAGINATION IN CHICAN@ ARTIVISTA PRAXIS

> "We could not be without being in relationship with everything that surrounds us and is within us. Our reality, our ontology is the relationships" (Wilson 76).

> "The land is paramount for all indigenous societies. Their relationship to that land, their experience on that land shapes everything that is around

> them. . . land is another word for place, environment, your reality, the space you're in" (Wilson 88).

The *Encuentro* demonstrated to us: (1) how music and or art could serve as tools of dialogue between communities and (2) how the process of collective communal engagement drew out multiple subjectivities between Chican@ and Mayan participants. Ultimately experiencing *convivencia* or the praxis of conviviality through music, art, poetry, and *teatro* in this *encuentro* initiated a critical consciousness. Furthermore, the convivial moments were in essence excavating ways that ceased to be relevant in a neo-liberal world. Beginning with colonization and well into the promises of modernity, human life has been slowly stripped of creative communal interactions or those indigena practices. There are very few communal efforts free of ties to state agendas. Most often-autonomous community efforts are unimaginable. Upon witnessing creative expression as a convivial tool, one is inevitably led to question capital markets' arrangement of one's own creative expression and in relation to one's community. The *Encuentro* experience generated a deep reflection on the status of creative expression in our lives. We found, as Anzaldúa had stated years earlier, "colonization could not eliminate the evolution of an indigenous psyche" (qtd. in Perez 2).

The 1997 *Encuentro* experience inspired us to ask: How do we engage more people in collective creative expression—especially in our own trenches? In this way, we opened up to an arena of hope. To express having hope in Spanish is to "abrigar esperanzas" (106). "Abrigar" is to shelter, to protect, to keep warm: Chican@ *artivistas* continuously nourish and protect these hopes. This is not a wide-eyed hope, but a hope that comes with a clear genesis and praxis. Importantly, love was a motivating factor in *artivista* processes.

Chela Sandoval discusses the hermeneutics of love as a "set of practices and procedures that can transit all subjects" (140). That is to say that love is something that can break through "whatever controls" to find an "understanding and community" (140). Much like love, creative expression when exercised as community is something that can "puncture" through narratives that "tie us to social time and space, to the descriptions, recital and plots that dull and order our senses insofar as such social narratives are tied to the law" (Sandoval 140). In this historic *Encuentro* between Chican@s and Zapatistas, art and creative expression transcended the laws of narratives. Combined with "risk and courage" we found that love, hope, and creative expression could generate the feeling and imagination that could "make anything possible" (Sandoval 140). Like Anzaldúa's work of looking back to "excavate hope for our future," Chican@ artivistas do the same in seeking dialogue with other communities in struggle (Perez 4).

Indeed anything seemed possible after having participated in this *Encuentro*. At present, embodied practices and art or creative expression as *the* critical tools of dialogue are centered in *artivista* praxis. Through a consciousness whose ultimate goal is to be accountable to one's community or to build community, music and art become more than my individual expression but rather a differential tool by which to engage social movement and liberatory consciousness.

I suggest that Chican@ *artivistas* engage in art practices in accordance with the cosmic view of relationality. Wilson states in the above passage "our ontology is the relationships," the *encuentro* clearly demonstrated to us how relationship building through artistic expression could be central in the ways in which Wilson describes (Wilson 76). Anzaldúa has also stated, "The religious, social and aesthetic purposes of art were all intertwined." *Artivistas* return to this practice in all its formations (66). As part and parcel to a *border consciousness,* creative expression is key in the tool of negotiating these worlds.

BORDER CONSCIOUSNESS: THE BODY AS KNOWLEDGE, IDEOLOGICAL, AND PHYSICAL SITE

Chicana modes of theorizing, epistemologies, praxis, and styles of resistance bare a historical trajectory (i.e., colonization, sexism, racism) that have given birth to ways of being and thinking needed to not only survive, but thrive amid a Eurocentric hegemony. Utilizing a differential strategy, Chicana *artivistas* center the body in academia and community art discourse. An understanding of the brown body and the regulations of its movements is "fundamental in the reclamation of narrative and the development of radical projects of transformation and liberation" (Cruz, 657). Art allows the body to articulate "that which is linked to whatever is not expressible through words" (Sandoval 139).

In this way Chicana *artivistas* claim an ideological, physical, and spiritual space from which to engage community with an understanding that a differential consciousness is accessed through "poetic modes of expression: gestures, music, images, sounds, words that plummet or rise through signification to find some void—some no place—to claim their due" (139).

THE BODY AND SPACE

Anzaldúa's articulation of *border consciousness* in her seminal work *Borderlands/ La Frontera: The New Mestiza* (1987) articulated *border consciousness.* Anzaldúa's work was groundbreaking as she utilized poetry to communicate, imagine, and thus claim spiritual, physical, and ideological space. *Border consciousness* was an innovative concept that articulated the psychosocial effects of what it means to live, struggle, and thrive as Chican@s amid a Eurocentric hegemony. Anzaldúa created a social theory that was metaphorically tied to a geopolitical site (the U.S./ Mexican border). Her poetic inscriptions and correlation of a *mestiza* consciousness to the physical U.S./Mexican border as "una herida abierta" or "the liminal space" was an important intervention in academia (Anzaldúa 10).

In this way, the brown body as a source of knowledge was the impetus surrounding a term that catapulted a Chicana feminist discourse worldwide. The discourse and body of work that *border consciousness* has since inspired is a prime example of the ways in which Chicana embodied knowledge, through the medium of poetry, can generate a theoretical space from which to counter Eurocentric paradigms of mind/body split. *Border consciousness* then became the differential strategy that unarmed Euro-racist academic paradigms (positivist, objectivity) while simultaneously creating a space from which to articulate the Chicana body's complex theories. Furthermore, Anzaldúa's epistemology also defied academic notions of style and instead introduced poetry to support her arguments. "For only through the body, through the pulling of flesh, can the human soul be transformed. And for images, words, stories to have this transformative power, they must arise from the human body—flesh and bone—and from the Earth's body—stone, sky, liquid, soil" (Anzaldúa 75).

CHICAN@ ARTIVISTA ES COMO EL TRAGAFUEGO

Individually and collectively we have continued to share the collective songwriting process, the *fandango* (participatory music and dance practice from Veracruz) as community building tools. As Anzaldúa stated, "I change myself. I change the world" (70). In this way as I travel and tour with Quetzal, I have also facilitated collective songwriting workshops in schools, prisons, correctional facilities, boys' homes, and church parishes in whatever city or country we find ourselves in.

When I write/compose my own creative work, I reflect on these experiences and the moments I have lived (as a sister, mother, wife, community member and scholar) and the great lessons I have learned in dialogue with communities. Such is the case with, *"El Tragafuego"* (Quetzal, "Imaginaries" 2009). This song was written after witnessing a firebreather in the streets of Veracruz. Witnessing the firebreather was a powerful testament to the kind of Hope that thrives amid economic hardship in the streets of Mexico. His presence was a strong reminder that imagination and hope take courage. It is the doing when there seems nothing left to be done. "*El Tragafuego*" is precisely about this kind of hope. Tied to this state of mind and emotion there is a dignity. I suggest that in communities, hope along with powerful social tools and techniques emanates a kind of wealth that dwarfs economic capital. The lyrics to *"El Tragafuego"* read

Lanza al aire el tragafuegos sus sueños por la noche! Mar de sueños que ilumina este oficio entre los coches.	The firebreather hurls dream-flames into the sky! A sea of dreams that illuminate this work among the vehicles!

Fuego! Fuego! La lumbre y su dueño!	Fire! Fire! The flames owner!
En cada pecho arde lagrimas risas y un sueño.	In every chest there thrives tears, laughter and a dream.[16]

Chican@ *artivistas* in East Los Angeles *son precisamente come el tragafuego.* The firebreathers who work in the streets for little to no pay, dodging cars at high speeds, while hurling fire out of their mouths, casting shadows, and truth-images into the darkness for all to see.

CONCLUSION

Chican@ *artivistas* attempt to strike a balance between commoditizing their art and engaging communities through it. Although they must survive, they are also consistently looking for ways to democratize the practice and engagement of art, music, and creative expression negating the capitalist impulse to sell everything we do. When we come to understand that "love is a powerful force that challenges and resists domination," hope is that which leads us to internalize this through our very actions (hooks 29). Hope must be acknowledged, valued, and freed from colonialist thought (cynicism, indifference) in order for imagination to be exercised. I suggest that Chican@ *artivista* praxis of community building through music and creative expression is precisely an exercise in hope. Existing in the liminal space, standing firmly in ambiguity, Chican@ *artivistas* enact a *border consciousness* via creative expression, and art practice methodologies. For we cannot imagine and dream without hope, and hope is contingent on believing that change is a possibility. For as Anzaldúa's epitaph clearly states, "the world becomes as we dream it."

ENDNOTES

1 I specifically refer to the Chicano artists that began to identify themselves with the term *artivista* beginning 1995 and into the present. I acknowledge that there were Chicano artists before this time in East L.A life. Indeed Chicanas and Chicanos have a long trajectory and history of arts in community. However the Chican@ art community that I am referring to is distinct by the ways in which they utilize their art and creative output.

2 Ski masks, handkerchiefs.

3 "We don't have to ask permission to be free!"

4 "Behind us, we are all."

5 "Bad government."

6 A Mexican barrio famous for its poverty and crime a few miles outside of Mexico City.

7 "We are all Marcos!"

8 The Zapatistas held local as well, "intergalactic" meetings or *encuentros* (encounters) to encourage dialogue for the purpose of building community.

9 The Chicano Movement of the 1960s is often referred to as "El Movimiento" or "The Movement."

10 There is a vast body of work that articulates how Chican@ art is reflective and an important part of instilling political consciousness in *Movimiento* times. Indeed we can think of public art such as murals, musicians, and the quintessential example of "El Teatro Campesino" as an important citation of this kind of work. However, there was still a sense of performer/audience divide. The participatory music and dance techniques that I highlight in this article as well as in my dissertation, introduces a new way of thinking about music as a dialectic tool in and of itself which disrupts the audience/performer divide, and a communities understanding of creative expression as a venture towards commodification.

11 Perez, *Chicana Art: The Politics of Spiritual and Aesthetic Alterities*, 11.

12 "From our own trenches."

13 Having answered the call the *Encuentro* also consisted of Chican@ participants from San Diego, Texas, and Long Beach, CA.

14 The Zapatista community we visited has since been renamed into Caracoles.

15 One of the many Mexican song-forms that have served as a historical document by way of sung oral tradition.

16 Quetzal. "Imaginaries." Smithsonian Folkways Recordings 2012.

WORKS CITED

Anzaldúa, Gloria. *Borderlands/La Frontera: The New Mestiza.* 1st ed. San Francisco: Aunt Lute Books, 1987. Print.

Esteva, Gustavo, and Madhu Suri Prakash. *Grassroots Post-Modernism: Remaking the Soil of Cultures.* London; New York: Zed Books; Distributed in the USA exclusively by St. Martin's Press, 1998. Print.

Feldman, Heidi. *Black Rhythms of Peru: Reviving African Musical Heritage in the Black Pacific.* Middletown, CT: Wesleyan UP, 2006. Print.

Freire, Paulo. *Pedagogy of the Oppressed.* New York: Continuum, 2000. Print.

Hall, Stuart, Sut Jhally, and Media Education Foundation. *Representation & The Media.* Northampton, MA: Media Education Foundation, 1997. Film.

Hooks, Bell. *Ain't I a Woman: Black Women and Feminism.* Boston MA: South End Press. 1981. Print.

"Marcos is Gay." *Green Left Online.* http://www.greenleft.org.au/1997/296/15601 (accessed April 28, 2009).

Perez, Emma. "Gloria Anzaldúa: La Gran Nueva Mestiza Theorist, Writer, Activist-Scholar." *National Women Studies Association (NWSA) Journal,* Vol. 17 No. 2 (Summer).

Pérez, Laura. *Chicana Art: The Politics of Spiritual and Aesthetic Altarities.* Durham: Duke University Press, 2007. Print.

Quetzal. "Imaginaries." Smithsonian Folkways Recordings 2012. Audio CD.

Sandoval, Chela. *Methodology of the Oppressed.* Minneapolis and London: U of Minnesota Press, 2000.

Wilson, Shawn. *Research is Ceremony: Indigenous Research Methods.* Black Point NS: Fernwood Pub. 2008. Print.

"Zapatista." *Big Noise.* http://www.youtube.com/watch?v=jlh5nY7QJD4 (accessed June 7, 2009).

GLORIA ANZALDÚA, NUESTRA GLORIA, NUESTRA HEROÍNA FRONTERIZA / OUR GLORY(A), OUR BORDERLANDS HEROINE: AN ART EXHIBIT AT ANZALDÚA'S ALMA MATER, THE UNIVERSITY OF TEXAS–PAN AMERICAN

STEPHANIE ALVAREZ, STEPHANIE BROCK, JANIE COVARRUBIAS, LAUREN ESPINOZA, AND ORQUIDEA MORALES

The *Gloria Anzaldúa: Nuestra Gloria, Nuestra Heroína Fronteriza / Our Glory(a), Our Borderlands Heroine* exhibit began as a single author course on Gloria Anzaldúa, taught by Dr. Stephanie Alvarez in Spring 2011. This class was the result of a petition process initiated by several Chicana graduate students who saw the need for an in-depth study of Anzaldúa's work at the University of Texas-Pan American (UTPA). Initially, Alvarez was hesitant because she was not scheduled to teach that semester because of a teaching overload the previous semester. She also hesitated because she felt that she was not the most qualified person on campus to teach what would be a very daunting class. After all, Emmy Pérez had done much more work and research on Anzaldúa. However, Alvarez agreed to teach the course because the students insisted and part of their argument was that many were to graduate the same semester. However, Alvarez understood her students' desires. She recalled her own transformative encounter with Anzaldúa's text, back in 1998, when she had taken a course with Denise Chávez at the University of Oklahoma. The profesora recognized that Anzaldúa meant even more to these Chicanas from the Valley and said yes with the blessing of Emmy Pérez. Furthermore, it was important to center Anzaldúa as a major academic and literary figure at the same university that she critiqued for its marginalization of her and other Chican@s. In *Borderlands*, Anzaldúa recalls that at "Pan American University, I, and all Chicano students were required to take two speech classes. Their purpose: to get rid of our accents" (76). The final project took the centering of Anzaldúa to an even greater level.

The initial leaders of the movement acquired the ten students necessary to make the class. On the first day of class, Dr. Alvarez informed the students that they would decide what the class would produce as a final project; the students chose to create an art exhibit. The idea behind adopting an art exhibit as the medium was to create and demonstrate a critical intervention and counter-space not only at the University of Texas-Pan American, but also in the Rio Grande Valley as a whole. After all, Anzaldúa observed, "conocimiento urges us to respond not just with the traditional practice of spirituality...or with the technologies of political activism...Conocimiento pushes us into engaging the spirit in confronting our social sickness with new tools and practices whose goal is to effect a shift" (*Reader* 311). The new tools and practice for us was the creation of the exhibit in the hopes to create a shift in us and the public.

Anzaldúa Pan American College yearbook pictures: 1966, 1967, 1968

Setting this art exhibit to the backdrop of the physical lands of the Rio Grande Valley was important and noteworthy as Anzaldúa herself was from the borderlands, Hargill, Texas; yet she is not celebrated enough nor known well in her homeland. The art exhibit became a visual way for community members to encounter and contemplate a text such as Borderlands/La Frontera: The New Mestiza. The fact that Anzaldúa is not widely known in the community also carries through to her alma mater—Pan American College (now UTPA). Unsurprisingly, there is no monument, plaque, or room on the UTPA campus named after Anzaldúa to commemorate her as a distinguished alumna. Because the community and UTPA both share a cultural history of exclusion and racialization, it was the hope that through the exhibit, we could move away from the physical intimacy of the page and create a more communal and public viewing of Anzaldúa's work, and the borders between "academia" and community be subverted and re-worked to introduce Anzaldúa's mestiza consciousness to a public that has not had access to it.

CONTEXTUALIZING THE EXHIBIT: MEXICAN AMERICAN STUDIES AND THE DREAM ACT

In order to understand the significance of this intervention, we would like to contextualize it within campus climate at the time. While students today at UTPA do not have to take the required speech class to erase their accents, rarely are their language, culture, or history honored as the center of study. One clear example of this is the state of Mexican American Studies around the time of the exhibit. In 2008, the Mexican American Heritage program at UTPA was revived by a faculty committee made up of all junior faculty Latinas. In 2009, the program was completely revised, and in 2010, it was officially approved and changed its name to Mexican American Studies (MAS). The MAS committee members restructured the curriculum of the program to better reflect the trans-disciplinarity of the major and minor as well as to cater to the needs of the students. In addition to these changes, a Mexican American Studies Graduate Certificate was created for graduate students.

One of the objectives of the MAS program is to study the experiences of Mexican American communities in the U.S. MAS students take a wide range of courses in many disciplines to study the political, cultural, social, economic, and artistic conditions and contributions of Mexican Americans, within a historical and contemporary context. Since UTPA is a Hispanic Serving Institution on the Texas-Mexico border that enrolls nearly 19,000 students, 89% of whom are classified as Mexican American and/or Latino, MAS can provide students with a culturally affirming education that allows them to critically assess Mexican American experiences through a transnational perspective. In the span of three years the program has grown exponentially, from zero to over thirty majors. In its previous thirty years, the program had graduated three majors. However, in the semester of the exhibit, the MAS major had been targeted by the Texas Higher Education Coordinating Board as a low producing major that should be cut. At the time of the exhibit, MAS had never received more than $2,000 in funding, had no full or joint faculty lines, and drew all of its classes from those offered in other programs. The lack of institutional support, faculty, and funding had marginalized MAS, making it very difficult to recruit and advise students. To help the program, students created the Mexican American Studies Club (MASC) in 2009. MASC was created specifically to bring awareness to the student body about the MAS program, in addition to past and present issues pertaining to Mexican American communities.

Unfortunately, the flyers posted around campus for the first meeting were vandalized on campus with the ethnic slur "MOJADOS!!" in late 2009. In 2010, two non-MASC flyers were also defaced with the words "NO MORE KITTIES NO MORE MOJADOS" and "YES TO THE BORDER WALL." The first flyer had images of cats that were available for adoption. The second flyer was a smaller one that was advertising a D.J. The final act of vandalism occurred in late 2010, in the women's bathroom of the College of Arts and Humanities building at the University of Texas-Pan American. The sink area was marred with the words "NO NO NO NO MORE MOJADOS." Later in Fall 2011, an undergraduate course dedicated to the study of Anzaldúa's work taught by Dr. Marci McMahon also held an art exhibit. Several English professors posted flyers advertising the exhibit. All of these were taken down from their doors by an unknown person, without permission.

A police report was filed for each individual event and the MASC officers also met with the Dean of Students and the Dean of the College of Arts and Humanities as well as the Interim Vice Provost to discuss a course of action. The students argued that this was hate speech and should not be tolerated. However, no action was ever taken by the administration. Additionally, in 2011, the Mexican American Studies Club organized a walk-out/teach-in on March 31st, César Chávez Day, to show student support for Mexican American Studies because they refused to sit by as the major was cut. The event featured a teach-in to educate the student body and community as a whole about the importance of a Mexican American Studies program at UTPA. Just moments before the event, one of the student organizers witnessed a key administrator remove one of the flyers and throw it in the trash.

The evolution of MAS and the actions taken against internal and external attacks has strengthened the program and its members, and it has also created a new consciousness for students who might not have been aware of their right to a fair and culturally affirming education. As many people assume that MAS is not a necessary program at the University of Texas-Pan American, the reception of the program and the club have been mixed with high running tensions. The mixed reaction is tied to a larger national rhetoric of fear and exclusion that marks those living along the borderlands as "alien."

Earlier the same year that the Mexican American Studies Club began to organize and suffered its first act of vandalism, its first and only Chicana President to date, Blandina Cárdenas, announced her resignation. Cárdenas[1] had been accused by some anonymous faculty members of plagiarizing in her dissertation just months earlier. While President Cárdenas did not directly address

1 Cárdenas co-authored with José A. Cárdenas the important report "The Theory of Incompatabilities: An Educational Framework for Responding to the Needs of Mexican American Children." Intercultural Development Research Association, Texas: 1977.

the allegations in her resignation letter, she referred to her recent heart surgery and stated, "I need to take greater care of this somewhat battered, mended heart."[2] Many Latinas on campus felt this was another case of a woman of color being presumed incompetent. While many people knew she was disliked, many further questioned what would motivate someone or people to undertake the specific task of reviewing a dissertation written some thirty-five years ago with the obvious intent of looking for acts of plagiarism. The assumption from the start must have been that she was not intellectually competent. This confirmed for many that there was a pervasive sense that Latinas were not intellectually competent and were underrepresented in the faculty. After all, 51% of all undergraduate and 48% of all graduate students at UTPA are Chicana or Latina. However, only 11.7% of the non-contingent faculty in the College of Arts and Humanities, the college in which MAS is housed, are Chicana or Latina. Just one month after President Cárdenas' resignation, a jury determined that UTPA willfully violated the Equal Pay Act in a suit filed by former Dean Hilda Medrano.

The campus spotlight shined on MAS once again in the Fall of 2010, just months before the exhibit, when a march in support of the DREAM Act and subsequent hunger strike took place at UTPA under the leadership of Alex Garrindo and the Coalition for Educational Opportunity Dream Act Project. Marches or protests at UTPA are not part of the present-day campus culture. A local article published online about this event was met with negative responses. The Development, Relief and Education for Alien Minors (DREAM) Act, a legislative proposal, offers undocumented students of good moral character who have lived in the United States for at least five years, immigrated before the age of sixteen, and have obtained a high school degree or its equivalent a path towards legal citizenship through attending college or completing two years of military service. The proposal was first introduced in August 2001; ten years later, there was still no legislation. Incensed by stagnant political bureaucracy, students of UTPA and members of surrounding communities organized rallies in October 2010 to support this act, raise awareness about the issue, and encourage people to vote. The UTPA President, Robert S. Nelsen, openly supported the legislation that would provide a path to citizenship for an estimated 602 UTPA students. However, the DREAM Act faces heavy opposition, even locally. This is evidenced in the following comment made on the website of the local newspaper, *The Monitor*:

> I guess the University of Texas Pan American has gone back to it's [sic] old name TACO TECH, thanks to all those ILLEGAL ALIENS [...]

2 Statement in her announcement of resignation on January 20, 2009. Her official statement can be read here: http://www.utpa.edu/documents/letter.htm

> VERONICA GONZALEZ, the CHIEF Border whatever she claims to be, has done a horrible job, look at all these illegals at a TACO TECH. Can you imagine how many are within the public schools? We are paying for their education and they are not even contributing to this country. WHAT A SHAME

Responses like this to the DREAM Act show how histories of colonization and institutionalized racism have shaped the conceptualization of race and citizenship in the Rio Grande Valley. Here we see the way students at UTPA and the University itself become marked as "others" outside of the realm of legality and therefore a threat to national security and economic stability. Through the MAS program and the exhibit, we try to address these issues and open up a dialogue between the community and academia. Gloria Anzaldúa's *Borderlands/La Frontera: The New Mestiza* was a logical choice to help us begin to develop this new consciousness that moved beyond binaries and (mis)understandings of nationality and citizenship and to make her work more accessible to a larger public.

FROM THE PAGE TO THE WALL: A (RE)FRAMING OF *BORDERLANDS/LA FRONTERA*

On any other day, walking into the Borderlands Room in the Education Complex at UTPA would not be something to write home about. The multipurpose space is commonly used for meetings and presentations. It is filled with comfortable seating and sometimes tables and chairs, depending on the occasion. The *Gloria Anzaldúa: Nuestra gloria/nuestra heroína Fronteriza/Our Glory(a), Our Borderlands Heroine* exhibit shifted the room's use to facilitate an art exhibit. The chairs and desks were cleared out; selected quotes paired with Anzaldúa's "pictograms / glifos" and poems from *Borderlands/La Frontera,* along with Anzaldúa's yearbook pictures and photographs of her grave site, were designed, printed, mounted, and ultimately hung on the walls. Because there was no budget for the exhibit, these images were printed using each student's one free print of one large poster in the media lab. After Dr. Alvarez purchased foam board and spray glue, she and the students occupied the hallways of the COAS building's third floor one Saturday afternoon carefully attaching the prints to the foam board with only a few casualties and wrinkles. Gloria Anzaldúa's published books were placed within glass cases (including all the editions of *Borderlands/La Frontera*), a computer was brought in to play the students' selections of music videos created to coincide with the exhibit, both a guest book and a look book were placed at the entrance of the room, a crossroads was taped along the floor and a stop sign was constructed and brought in.

Anzaldúa noted that the ideas of *Borderlands/La Frontera* "can't be melted down. The components are distinct; they're there to dialogue with one another" (*Reader* 211).

Therefore, all of these elements combined to bring critical ideas and concepts out from the pages of *Borderlands/La Frontera* so as to be embodied in a physical manifestation of Anzaldúa's ideology.

ON WHY YOU CAN'T PUT A WHOLE BOOK ON A WALL

Upon moving forward with the idea of translating the themes of *Borderlands/ La Frontera* into an art exhibit, many decisions had to be made; but of particular importance—the glue with which the exhibit would be held together—are the quotes chosen to be displayed. Ultimately, the nearly impossible goal of selecting quotes was to choose those that best exemplified, in their totality, the message Anzaldúa intended to communicate to the reader while also being true to the Rio Grande Valley community, the intended audience, who would be encountering the quotes outside of the book's framework. The quotes should disrupt, disturb or unsettle, while at the same time honor, affirm, and validate the lived experiences of the community.

The process for selecting the quotes was challenging. Not only because of the enormity of the task, but also the constant negotiating undertaken by the students with each other. The professor did not interfere with the decision-making process done without her presence; the students were to make the textual choices. Difficult conversations ensued and the quotes that were ultimately selected for the exhibit contributed to an effort to maintain a chapter's main message; at the same time, taken together, they attempted to convey the overall theory of praxis contained in Anzaldúa's book. The words selected (included below) for the exhibit are gateways into a book that creates, from the first chapter, an urge to delve into the history of borders: not only physical borders, but also social, economic, class, gender, ethnic, and racial borders. Anzaldúa invites the reader to become active, to redefine the notion of borders and to both fight against and embrace these *fronteras*: "Borders are set up to define the places that are safe and unsafe, to distinguish *us* from *them* [...] A borderland is a vague and undetermined place created by the emotional residue of an unnatural boundary. It is in a constant state of transition. The prohibited...are its inhabitants" (*Borderlands* 25). We hoped to convey the important message of the borderlands as a hybrid third space of strife and empowerment, where the experiences of its transcultural citizens are critiqued and valued as assets that allow one to develop la facultad.

Unrest, vulnerability and compassion flows throughout the book, particularly in chapter two, where the tyrannies and the stereotypes that need to be confronted and destroyed are brought to the forefront; which, for the exhibit, literally manifest as the walls of the room. Anzaldúa encourages the reader to redefine pre-existing conceptualizations. She aspires to find that rebellious courage to fight the established roles, to be conscious of the world we live in, to take risks:

> There is a rebel in me—the Shadow-Beast. It is a part of me that refuses to take orders from outside authorities. It refuses to take orders from my conscious will, it threatens the sovereignty of my rulership. It is that part of me that hates constraints of any kind, even those self-imposed. (38)

Thus, in chapter two we begin a move from the turbulent history of the colonization of the border to a reclamation of feminine figures in Chican@, Mexican and Aztec cultures that have been used to subjugate women. Here, Anzaldúa begins to break down the binaries that "[i]n trying to become 'objective,' Western culture made 'objects' of things and people when it distanced itself from them, thereby losing 'touch' with them. This dichotomy is the root of all violence" (59). These stopping points within the text are of particular importance to the community living in the Rio Grande Valley and other locales similar to it, which have been and currently are violent centers in need of continual push back against their oppressors.

Furthermore, Anzaldúa proposes that this rebellion manifests itself, in part, through language. She takes the reader through her own experiences with what she terms linguistic terrorism—a few of the experiences she describes even having their echoes in the halls of UTPA. For this reason (among others), one of her most recognizable quotes is included in the exhibit: "So, if you want to really hurt me, talk badly about my language. Ethnic identity is twin skin to linguistic identity—I am my language" (81). Her tongue is outlawed, cast as other, illegitimate, and her rebellion lies in her attempts to legitimize her language, thereby moving forward towards a new mestiza consciousness.

Gloria invites her readers to become conscious of themselves, to acknowledge obstacles and to cross over them, embrace their hybridity as a site of knowledge, compassion and empowerment. Anzaldúa reminds us that we all have the ability to *atravesarnos*, of showing those who hesitate, that not only do we possess the skills but the attitude to go beyond borders. In this way, putting the quotes in the context of an art exhibit allows for those experiencing the works to cross artistic borders into a theoretical landscape.

Including Anzaldúa's poetry in the exhibit was an extension of the idea of crossing artistic/theoretical borders. Taking specific poems out of their usual home between the pages of the book, emphasized the poems' existence as a literary extension of her theoretical framework, as they often recount and reconstruct the historical memory and trauma endured by Chican@s. In order to best convey this idea, the following poems were chosen to be displayed in the art exhibit in between the quotes. The following poems were displayed in the same order in between the above quotes which also appear in order of display; "To live in the Borderlands means you" (216), "The Cannibal's *Canción*" (165), "*mujer cacto*" (202), "We Call Them Greasers" (156), "*No se raje, chicanita*" (222), and "*Nopalitos*" (134). These poems were selected as representative of Anzaldúa's voice throughout *Borderlands/La Frontera*, and putting them right next to the quotes took away the dividing line between the theory and the text. Now both works are in a more sustained aesthetic conversation with one another.

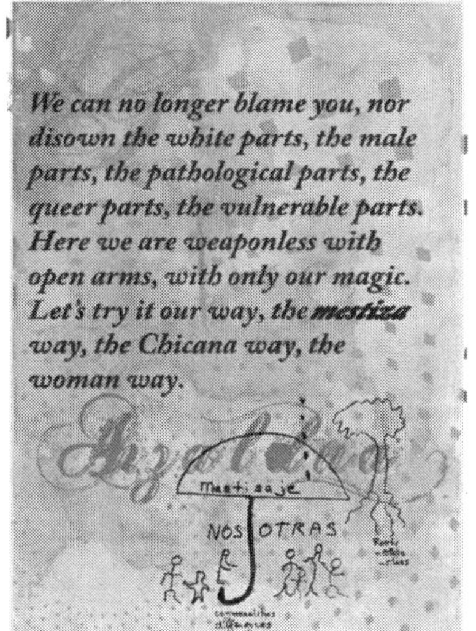

In "We Call Them Greasers" and "The Cannibal's *Canción*," the poetic voice finds the courage to expose injustices by refusing to ignore them. This speaker is re-embodied in "To live in the Borderlands means you" by continuing to challenge the present social norms through glimpses of Anzaldúa's own border theory. This carries through to "*mujer cacto*" and "*No se raje, chicanita*," where a hopeful future is identified and efforts are made to move past the nepantla state and toward a new mestiza consciousness. In combination, these poems paint a picture of past/present/future, and this is particularly important for the people who would be coming to view the exhibit, as they are still in the physical borderlands. Therefore, to see a historical trajectory (visually and textually) represented was an attempt to give current community members the tools to construct a future mestiza consciousness. In order to do that, though, a move had to be made to include the public viewing the work in what was being presented.

The location of all this text on the wall is not a traditional experience or practice of an art exhibit. In order to facilitate the viewers in creating a relationship between what is presented on the wall and their lived experiences, a way to bridge the gap between the text and viewer had to be included. One way this was done was through the graphic design created by Jessica Salinas behind each of the quotes or poems. The background design for both was continuous, but the display colors differed—the quotes were yellow while the poems were orange, giving a visual signifier to help the audience identify which was which, yet the graphic design pattern kept the continuity that they were one. As Anzaldúa notes, "[t]he components are distinct; they're there to dialogue with one another" (*Reader* 211). Another way that the border between text and "consumers" was crossed was through another element of Gloria's own creation: her doodles/glifos/pictograms. AnaLouise Keating tells us that Anzaldúa

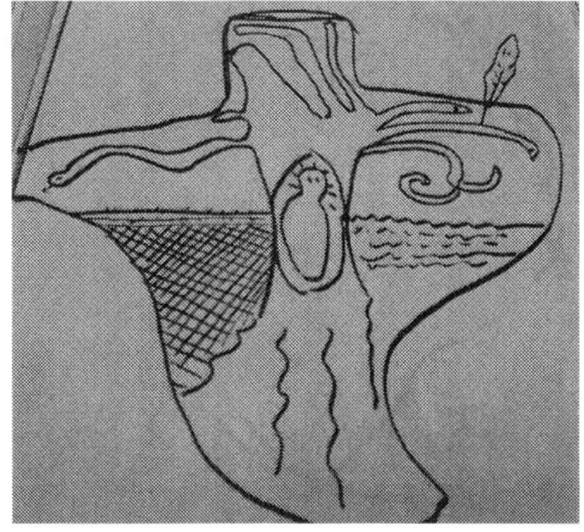

> seriously considered focusing her energies on painting or sculpting, rather than writing...she did not abandon the visual arts: she included many of her elaborate sketches and informal doodles in her journals; created flyers...added little drawings with her signature when autographing books or signing letters...and used what she called "pictograms" or "glifos" to illustrate her talks. (217)

Therefore, Lauren Espinoza visited the Bensen Library at the University of Texas at Austin to review Anzaldúa's papers in order to identify glifos that would be paired with the quotes.

Providing the visual images not only invites the viewer to step into the exhibit through the use of a familiar medium for an art exhibit, but also serves as an intellectual road map—an invitation for more people to follow Anzaldúa as she "enters the serpent." Particularly of note is that these images are line drawings—not (seeming) overly complex, but not so devastatingly simple as to be disengaging. After so much text, they are the vehicles used to invite the viewers to become more involved, and they provide a visual respite from the many words on the walls.

Taking the prose and poems of *Borderlands/La Frontera* in their 2D element leaves the reader to imagine theory for themselves, but when the words are taken out of that context and placed on walls, a visual space for meditation and reflection is added. Adding in a graphic design element and the pictograms are other ways to create a pause for the audience, and follows right in with Anzaldúa's lived theory because for "Anzaldúa, images and ideas are intimately interrelated" (*Reader* 217).

INTERTEXTUALITY AND TRAVESÍAS: MUSIC AND FOUND OBJECTS IN THE EXHIBIT

At the back center of the exhibit, facing the main door, stands a large stop sign at the physical crossroads created by yellow duct tape on the floor, in between the two walls that house her quotes and just behind all her displayed books. This is the object people first notice as they enter the exhibit space, both because of its size and because it is an everyday object that has been recontextualized. On the stop sign we included this quote from Anzaldúa: "Every increment of consciousness, every step forward is a *travesía*, a crossing" (70). The stop sign is a way to make the uncomfortable recognizable. By this we mean not only academia but also Anxaldúa's work, with which most of our audience was unfamiliar. The stop sign made people literally stop at a physical crossroads and face Anxaldúas words while at the same time guiding them through the space. The stop sign asks people to stop and think about their travesía, invites them into the state of nepantla in order to move into a new consciousness, but it does this through a recontextualization of an everyday object. Thus, our need to make this space accessible to a larger audience propelled us to include this found object constructed by Juan Cárdenas.

Similarly, to help transition between the public space outside of academia into an academic public space we incorporated music into the exhibit. This adds familiarity and a sense of home since many of the songs we chose were familiar to the intended audience. Through the music and the stop sign we created a safe space for people who don't have a relationship to academia. The music featured in the exhibit consisted of a collection of songs chosen by each of the students and the professor. Dr. Alvarez, was inspired by Calle 13's 2011 music video for the song "Vamo' a portarnos mal." As she viewed the video, she noted several correlations between the song, its visual representation and the themes we were discussing in class. She showed the class the video and suggested including a musical selection to complement the quotes, images, and poems that were being selected for the exhibit. Each student was charged with the task of finding a song and/or music video that equally embodied, from their point of view, Anzaldúa's ideology and works. As this was an individual undertaking, there are not only multiple perspectives but also various types of songs. For instance, the songs range in genre, gender of artists, language, and cultural meaning within the context of the border experience. A computer was set up to play the songs and videos, with a sheet indicating each song and the name of the person who chose it. Visitors were, therefore, able to play any song at any time.

Gloria Anzaldúa Playlist

1. "Vamo' a portarnos mal" - Calle 13
2. "One Love" - Playing for Change
3. "Somos más americanos" - Los Tigres del Norte
4. "Paso del norte" - Alejandro Fernández
5. "La Llorona" - Chavela Vargas
6. "I'm Just a Girl" - No Doubt
7. "Raindrops" - Rainbow Jaxx
8. "La niña" - Lila Downs
9. "Mojado" - Ricardo Arjona
10. "El rey" - Vicente Fernández
11. "Pastures of Plenty / This Land is my Land" - Lila Downs

The songs and videos used in the exhibit are just one example of the distinctive qualities that made "*Nuestra gloria, nuestra heroína fronteriza/Our glory(a), our borderlands heroine*" a unique cultural experience to not only honor Anzaldúa as a revolutionary scholar but also to promote awareness of the scholar-poet amongst the University of Texas Pan-American (UTPA) students, faculty, staff, and the community as a whole. Overall, the inclusion of the songs and, in most cases, their videos in our exhibit was of great benefit to its artistic development and a way for each student to further connect to Anzaldúa and her ideas on a personal level. In her essay "On the Process of Writing," Anzaldúa comments on the innovative developments that led to the formation of *Borderlands/La Frontera: The New Mestiza* and states, "Not only do I code-switch in language, but I jerk the reader around by also code-switching in genre: mixing genres, crossing genres from poetry to essay to narrative to a little bit of analysis and theory. The reader has to put it all together at the end" (*Reader* 190). This statement reflects the purpose of the playlist—to create a visual, auditory, and tactile experience for the audience as they reflect on Anzaldúa's work. This objective is a sign of the growing mestiza consciousness that each participant experienced and continues to experience as a result of this exhibit. After all, Anzaldúa herself incorporates music and text at various points in her most famous book:

> El otro México que acá hemos construido
> el espacio es lo que ha sido
> territorio nacional.
> Este es el esfuerzo de todos nuestros hermanos
> y latinoamericanos que han sabido
> progresar."
> —*Los Tigres del Norte* (Anzaldúa 23)

The excerpt comes from the song "El otro México" by the norteño band Los Tigres del Norte and are the lines with which Anzaldúa begins *Borderlands/La Frontera: The New Mestiza*. This intertextuality marks the song not only as a popular culture product but also signals Chican@ and Mexican@ music as a repository of knowledge(s) and the performers as producers of not just culture, but knowledge and (re)constructors of historical memory. The inclusion of the playlist in this exhibit is to include these different voices and experiences, thereby providing another layer from which the audience may pull. Accordingly, this entices the observers to connect what they see and hear at the exhibit to songs that have personal meaning to them, an idea that imitates Anzaldúa's point of view about her relationship with the reader, "In this way the reader brings into the text [exhibit] her own experience" (Keating 190). Overall, the inclusion of the playlist in the exhibit was of great benefit to its artistic development and an avenue not only for each participant to further connect Anzaldúa's thoughts to a larger transcultural framework but to promote awareness of the late Chicana poet.

POST EXHIBIT: RECEPTION, RE:SPONSE AND (RE)INSCRIPTION

Since the larger purpose of the exhibit was to help bridge the divide between community and academia, between Gloria Anzaldúa's work and her home, then it was necessary for us to collect the responses to the exhibit. Would the attendees connect to the exhibit? Was the exhibit successful in opening up a path of communication between these spaces? Thus, to facilitate our documentation of the responses, we provided attendees with two composition books or "libretas de comentarios" in which they were free to write their thoughts, comments, and concerns. Many of the guests did not know of Anzaldúa and her work prior to the exhibit and many did. Various professors brought their students. The plan was to obtain emotional, personal, critical, and social perspectives on the exhibit. Next to the libreta de comentarios we had two pens, one black and one red. These two colors were chosen because of their presence in *Borderlands*, specifically Chapter 6 "Tlilli, Tlapalli: The Path of the Red and Black Ink":

> For the ancient Aztecs, *tlilli, tlapalli, la tinta negra y roja de sus códices* (the black and red ink painted on codices) were the colors symbolizing *escritura y sabiduría* (writing and wisdom). They believed that through metaphor and symbol, by means of poetry and truth, communication with the Divine could be attained, and *topan* (that which is above—the gods and spirit world) could be bridged with mictlán (that which is below—the underworld and the region of the dead. (91)

It is important to note that during the five days of the exhibit and the event fifty-five people signed and/or left comments. A particularly interesting comment by Delia Pérez states:

> Great exhibition!
>
> My daughter dragged us parents here today for the MAS walkout—it was great. I wish more parents had attended with their kids. This is very important studies for our own kids to learn about—I tell her many past experiences from my life and through her class I have learned other important experiences of our people. What a shame to hear others—like my son or maybe my grandson will not have the opportunity—please join these people and talk to parents, friends and neighbors help out.
>
> PS I too was hit on my hands with a ruler in school for speaking Spanish—imagine that now…
>
> Thanks
>
> Delia
>
> a Chicana

Delia's statement that she is "a Chicana" should not be taken lightly. In the Rio Grande Valley it is not common for people to use this identifier. Others connected Anzaldúa's work with their own invisibility and voicelessness. Bianca writes:

> I didn't know when I picked up Gloria Anzaldúa's book 'Borderland' that she would widen my perspective of the World. It is so refreshing to see the female-latina-feminist. This exhibit + the MAS really are what make me believe I am getting somewhere in my education.

Abner relfects "It is good to see someone write for us when many of us can't." No comments were negative. "Viva la Gloria" —Teresa.

Furthermore, in order to share the exhibit with a larger audience, we created a look book. This format is a recontextualizing of the exhibit by using its original form, a book, to make it accessible to a larger audience outside of the Valley or those that were unable to attend the exhibit and would want to make similar critical interventions at their university. The purpose of the look book was to complement the *Gloria Anzaldúa: Nuestra Gloria Nuestra heorína fronteriza / Our glory(a), Our borderlands heroine* exhibit. Furthermore, the look book catalogs the images and text that were part of the exhibit and it includes the purpose of the exhibit, biographical information of the participants and the participants' personal explanation of the Gloria Anzaldúa playlist song choices. The intent is to make this look book available in an online format to reach a wider audience. As we worked on this part of the exhibit, we struggled in trying to label it. It is not a traditional art exhibit catalog that includes descriptions and scholarly essays about the exhibit but rather captures the exhibit and allows the viewer to interpret it on their own. The look book was part of the exhibit, our attempt to further document our project. We called it a look book instead of an exhibit catalog for various reasons. An exhibition catalogue is usually a book size format with color photographs, sometimes including other relevant work with short descriptions about the piece as well as interpretive text. The look book does not provide a critique of the text but is more of an homage to Anzaldúa's work. It keeps the exhibit alive once it no longer occupies the space on the walls of the ivory tower.

The look book, produced by Orquidea Morales, is a contribution to the mestiza nation for two important reasons: One, it is an extension of an exhibit that intervenes and creates new consciousness in a space that pushes out difference and secondly, the look book shifts the gaze, it changes the way people look at and understand Gloria Anzaldúa. Why was the look book necessary for a small exhibit at UTPA? The look book continues the legitimization of Anzaldúa's work that the exhibit began since it not only documents the exhibit and its purpose, but it also makes this information available to a wider audience, both inside and outside the university. In her essay "Border Arte," Gloria Anzaldúa writes that "Nepantla is the Nahuatl word for an in-between state, that uncertain terrain one crosses when moving from one place to another, when changing from one class, race, or sexual position to another, when traveling from the present identity into a new identity" (180). Through the look book, we are creating a space where awareness can occur, even for those who did not physically see the exhibit. It is through this awareness that we can enter into a nepantla state that encourages movement from one place to another. The look book creates a nepantla state at UTPA.

The look book is another interpretation of Anzaldúa's work both removed from the original texts but also part of it. The text has been moved from the book and placed in a museum setting. Later, the same text is then used to create the look book thus generating two shifts from the book to exhibit and exhibit to look book. One can argue that this constant sifting/shifting can distort Anzaldúa's original message. In her book *Borderlands/La Frontera,* Anzaldúa herself explores the fears of commodification and how museums distance the audience both from the physical object and its historical and cultural reality by placing it on display. In creating a look book to publicize the exhibit and even the exhibit itself are we selling Anzaldúa? Or are we institutionalizing Anzaldúa? Are we doing the same with the exhibit? These were questions we constantly addressed. In "Border Arte," Anzaldúa noted overhearing "the culturally ignorant words of the whites who...gape in vicarious wonder and voraciously consume the exoticized images" (108). She observed, "Though I, too, am a gaping consumer, I feel that these artworks are part of my legacy" (108). With those thoughts we felt comfortable moving forward with the look book and exhibit.

The look book does not distort the message but rather strengthens it since as nepantler@s we, through her concepts and theory, are now sharing our findings with others. Since we are from the frontera and at UTPA we can re-contextualize her work and use it as a way to fight against the institutions and set norms that she was writing against. Through the look book, we also center the gaze differently since it changes the way Anzaldúa's work is seen. By putting it in this "western" setting we are re-inscribing it, which is in itself a subversive act.

CONCLUSION

The libreta de comentarios has been a helpful tool for us as we rework the exhibit and think about how to further the project. Our goals are to eventually create a travelling exhibit. This essay we see as a reflection and also a possible guide for those interested in doing similar work. The exhibit is a critical intervention in how we talk about Anzaldúa in Chican@ Studies and how we think, or rather don't think, about the presence of Latin@s in museum studies. The Valley, 90% Mexican American and/or Latin@, is often romanticized today as a haven, but outsiders/insiders still do not understand that "whiteness" is very present in the infrastructure and mentality of the "brown" community. Centering Anzaldúa at UTPA through the exhibit requires all of us to question our positionality—physically, emotionally, and intellectually, in our communities, our university, and within Anzaldúa thought and art. As of today, spring 2012, the posters created for the exhibit continue to occupy the walls of the Borderlands room in the Education Building. ¡Qué viva nuestra Gloria!

WORKS CITED

Anzaldúa, Gloria. "Border arte : Nepantla, el lugar de la frontera." In La Frontera = The border: art about the Mexico/United States border experience. San Diego, CA : Centro Cultural de la Raza : The Museum of Contemporary Art, San Diego, 1993. 107-113. Web.

---. *Borderlands/La Frontera: The New Mestiza.* 2nd ed. San Francisco: Aunt Lute, 1999. Print.

---. *The Gloria Anzaldúa Reader.* Ed. AnaLouise Keating. Durham: Duke UP, 2009. Print.

Cárdenas, José and Blandina Cárdenas. *The Theory of Incompatibilities: An Educational Framework for Responding to the Needs of Mexican American Children.* Intercultural Development Research Association, Texas, 1977. Web.

"Gloria Evangelina Anzaldúa Papers." Benson Latin American Collection, University of Texas Libraries, the University of Texas at Austin. (Special Thanks to Christian Kelleher, Archivist).

"Welcome to Mexican American Studies." *Mexican American Studies.* University of Texas Pan American, 2011. Web. http://www.utpa.edu/documents/letter.htm

"NO TOPIC IS TOO TRIVIAL": FUSING ANZALDÚAN COMMITMENTS TO SOCIAL, POLITICAL, AND SPIRITUAL TRANSFORMATIONS IN ACADEMIA AS A CHICANA FACULTY MEMBER

KANDACE CREEL FALCÓN

My first reading of Gloria Anzaldúa's "Speaking in Tongues: A Letter to Third World Women Writers" validated my own experiences as a queer femme Chicana aspiring writer. I devoured her letter as if she were directly writing to me. By writing about the need to understand queer Chicana experiences in the context of white women spaces, white queer spaces, and heteronormative Chicana/o spaces, she validated the need for us to tell our stories. To claim our truths. And to do this through whatever means possible. She poses the question, "Who gave us permission to perform the act of writing?" (27). And in writing this letter she empowered me to do just that—write and explore how this approach to writing can be a pedagogical exercise for my Chicana/Latina and white students.

Gloria Anzaldúa's theories and methodologies like la conciencia de la mestiza, autoteoría, and nepantla emerge from a rooted critical connection to one's own observations about the world around us. This way of knowing, however, is often devalued and delegitimized within the space of the dominant, white, increasingly corporate academy. However, Chicanas and other women of color have been instrumental in interrupting these narratives through their inclusion of testimonio as both a methodological approach and an important space for knowledge production. Recent collectives of Chicana/Latina scholars have used testimonio in both of these ways: to highlight the process of sharing and writing one's own truth, and to theorize how powerful using testimonio as a pedagogical tool can be in the college classroom (The Latina Feminist Group, 2001 and Delgado Bernal, Elenes, Godinez & Villenas, 2006). Anzaldúa's work is deeply concerned with recognizing the value in exploring the personal, gaining meaning from everyday experiences, and reflecting on how these values can aid in our individual and collective social, political, and spiritual transformations. Thus, Anzaldúa's body of work becomes the entry point through which we can transform the politics of knowledge production within the space of the academy for theory and teaching.

I have always brought my experience as a femme Chicana feminist into the classroom with me. In my classrooms, I have utilized a feminist self-reflexive pedagogy. This means I reflect on my role and position as professor through my subjectivity as a queer Chicana while simultaneously asking my students to reflect on their own experiences and situated identities in relation to the subjects we cover. Oftentimes this has meant including vignettes about my life and experiences, while simultaneously remaining open and somewhat vulnerable to the consumption of those experiences by my largely white students. While I have found this to be a particularly valuable exercise for my white students, I do pause to think about the processes I undertake in my classroom as they operate through my experiences and body as one that can be dangerous for women of color. This modeling of using the self for experiential knowledge production also influences my pedagogical activities that rely on asking the same of my students.

Whereas many Chicana/Latina scholars have approached the tools of testimonio or autohístoria as an important part of integrating transformative and self-reflexive pedagogies in their classrooms with Latina/o students (see Delgado Bernal et. al., 2006), my classroom in Moorhead, Minnesota is one in which there are few students of color and fewer Chicana/o-Latina/o students. Thus, an investigation into how we integrate this kind of pedagogical approach with students, as women of color in predominately white classrooms, is necessary to explore. Norma E. Cantú suggests to us that "researchers who have studied diversity in classrooms may want to focus on the position of faculty of color at predominately white institutions versus those with a majority of students of color" (237-8). I am taking up this call as a Chicana in Moorhead, Minnesota.

More specifically, I discuss reflections guided by experiences I have had as a Chicana feminist faculty member in a predominately white university, both as scholar and teacher. I ground my discussion by exploring Anzaldúa's writings that focus on coalition building and the processes of writing: specifically the "Bridge, Drawbridge, Sandbar, or Island" (1990) speech and the longer written version from *The Gloria Anzaldúa Reader* (2009), as well as reading and teaching

"Speaking in Tongues" (1981) and "To(o) Queer the Writer—Loca, escritora y chicana" (1991). I use the methodology of storytelling in order to ground this juxtaposing of Anzaldúa's analyses in "Bridge" and "Speaking" to encourage reflection on the need to account for the struggles that Chicana faculty members continue to face within the academy as we work to transform our universities through multiracial feminist approaches within historically white institutions. Most importantly, I use Anzaldua's work to frame the value in cultivating an inclusive feminist politic through coalition and alliance building inside and outside the space of the classroom.

1. THE STRUGGLE FOR EXISTENCE AT A SMALL TOWN MIDWESTERN WHITE INSTITUTION

I began teaching as an adjunct instructor at Minnesota State University Moorhead, a small Midwestern university, in fall 2010. My position was split between American Multicultural Studies (AMCS) and Women's and Gender Studies (WGS). In the spring 2011 semester my position increased to a full-time "fixed-term" joint appointment still evenly split between these two areas. This was my employment situation until I applied and was hired for a tenure-track position in WGS in the fall of 2012. In my brief time at the university it was clear that both AMCS and WGS lacked significant institutional support. Two specific examples demonstrate the ways that both of these areas were, and continue to be, marginalized within the institution. While certainly not unique experiences for WGS and Ethnic Studies within the academy, both of these local examples include a lack of follow-through or commitment to areas that are invested in "diversity" within the institution.

The American Multicultural Studies Department houses two full time faculty members: one African American woman and one Asian American woman. While the program offers an AMCS major and minor, the program also provides students the opportunity to minor in area studies for each of the historically underrepresented racial/ethnic groups in the form of specialized minors in African American Studies, Asian American Studies, Chicana/o-Latina/o Studies, and American Indian Studies. As one might suspect, each faculty member of the department is responsible for their part of the specialized area studies in the field of their expertise, which also corresponds to their own racial/ethnic identity. In 2012, a Chicana professor moved her line from AMCS to a different department on campus, though she still teaches the courses in the Chicana/o-Latina/o Studies rubric for the department. Additionally, the Department once housed an American Indian woman professor who offered the American Indian Studies program, but she retired due to illness a few years ago and no efforts have been made to replace her or to revive American Indian Studies on campus. This is particularly upsetting because the area of West Central Minnesota, where our campus is located, should be serving the historically present American Indian communities of the Anishinaabe (Chippewa, Ojibwe) and Dakota (Sioux) nations.

The Women's and Gender Studies Program was established in 1971 and is often touted as one of the first women's studies programs in Minnesota. However, the program did not hold any full-time, tenure track lines until 2012 despite its existence in the university for 41 years. Furthermore, at the institution departments hold power, and thus the faculty members associated with WGS are often asked to legitimize our need for resources. This non-departmental status has meant that faculty in the program and our allies must remain hyper-vigilant against "attacks" or marginalization. For instance, at a faculty senate meeting for discussing the makeup of faculty representation for an interim dean search committee, a faculty member from a "traditional" discipline suggested that WGS should not have anyone serve on the committee because "they were not a department." This small example is one of many ways that WGS is seen as "less than" other departments on campus due to the status as a "program."

While it is commendable that the first WGS full-time tenure track hire is a woman of color, as Gabriella Gutiérrez y Muhs, Yolanda Flores Niemann, Carmen G. González, and Angela P. Harris note in *Presumed Incompetent: The Intersections of Race and Class for Women in Academia*, academic institutions create an inhospitable climate for women of color. Accordingly, "women of color must perform their social identities carefully and selectively to avoid being criticized, marginalized, dismissed, or rejected by colleagues and students. This performance may be particularly treacherous for women teaching or writing in disciplines (such as ethnic studies and women's studies) that challenge dominant ideas about equal opportunity" (8). This sentiment resonates strongly with me as a Chicana navigating this institutional landscape.

While this public state university serves approximately 7,000 students annually, the population of domestic Latina/o students only numbers between 130-140 students annually, despite the fact that the area has been a long-lived Mexican and Mexican American migrant worker settlement zone since the early 1900s and the neighboring northwestern towns/cities of Minnesota have experienced considerable Latina/o growth in populations. According to the most recent U.S. Census data, Minnesota's Latina/o population has increased 74.5% over the last ten years. With 250,258 self-identified "Hispanic or Latino" peoples counted, Latina/os make up 4.7% of the Minnesota statewide population (2010 Census Brief). While this proportion is similar in the Fargo/Moorhead area, our university is still far below "representative" of the general population of the area. After moving from the diverse urban area of Minneapolis to Moorhead, a rural city in north central Minnesota, I constantly bemoan the lack of diversity of this smaller city (the Fargo-Moorhead metropolitan area is about 215,000 people). In contrast, I am frequently informed by members of my community that Moorhead is much more diverse than it used to be. This area, then, does serve as the site of diversity for many students who move here from small, rural North Dakota and Minnesota towns to attend this university.

2. NO TOPIC IS TOO TRIVIAL AND THE ROLE OF COALITIONAL POLITICS

Anzaldúa's writings help us to understand the need for our experiences as Chicanas to be reflected in writing and in spaces from which we have been traditionally excluded. I believe her writings are a call to action. While grounding her call to action with her own position as a Chicana lesbiana she asks us (Chicanas and others) to recognize the need for Chicana experiences as legitimate and valuable sites of knowledge production. In each of the three articles I highlight in this reflection and use as pedagogical tools, she articulates the need for this process to be recognized as the cornerstone of coalitional engagements.

The essays I explore here span a decade of Anzaldúa's writings from the early 1980s to the early 1990s. Investigating these works in 2012 speaks to both their relevance and the resonance of her coalitional imperatives then and now. In "Speaking in Tongues" she articulates, "no topic is too trivial" (31) as that call to action to write about our lives. I write about my life as a Chicana faculty member highlighting that these topics are not trivial, and that we need to constantly continue to unravel our experiences in effort to uphold the power in diverse feminist coalitional politics.

AnaLouise Keating reminds us, as scholars of Anzaldúa's work, that she did not believe that any one person had "an exclusive, superior, insider perspective into her theories and writings" and furthermore that "Anzaldúa's inclusionary vision, coupled with her ability to create expansive new categories and interconnections, makes her work vital to contemporary social actors, thinkers, and scholars" (12). This speaks to Anzaldúa's scholarship as a powerful teaching tool and entry point into imagining and enacting inclusive feminist coalitional politics. Thus, my investment in interweaving storytelling, reflection, and closely reading Anzaldúa's own words shapes my own investment in coalitional politics from my location in Moorhead, Minnesota.

3. BRIDGE/DRAWBRIDGE

One of my white, anti-racist colleagues ran into me in the hall shortly after teaching her section of WS100, an eighty person topical survey of the introductions to the field of women's and gender studies. I consider her a white feminist ally who takes anti-racist work seriously, not just in rhetoric but also in action. She looked slightly worried as she asked if she could speak to me. "Kandace, I think I really messed up." I was confused as to what she messed up, I racked my brain about requests I had out to her on projects we were working on and I couldn't really think about anything too serious. After inquiring, "What's going on?" she launched into a story about how she asked her students to read an excerpt from Anzaldúa's Borderlands *from the textbook she assigned for her course. After presenting a lecture on what it meant for Anzaldúa to theorize* Borderlands, *her students, the majority of them white, began to claim that they were in the borderlands in myriad ways. She apologized profusely to me saying, "I shouldn't have introduced it in the way that she did, now all these entitled white students are using this term without even connecting it to the reality of Gloria Anzaldúa or Chicana experience!"*

Anzaldúa writes of the drawbridge that it "means having the option to take two courses of action. The first is being "up," i.e., withdrawing, pulling back from physically connecting with white people...The other option is "down"—that is, being a bridge. Being "down" might mean a partial loss of self" (147-8). Her thoughts on being a bridge means,

> ...being mediator between yourself and your community and white people, lesbians, feminists, white men. You select, consciously or unconsciously which group to bridge with—or they choose you. Often the "you" that's the mediator gets lost in the dichotomies, dualities, or contradictions you're mediating. You have to be flexible yet maintain your ground, or the pull in different directions will dismember you. It's a tough job; not many people can keep the bridge up. (147)

In this moment I found myself in these contradictory worlds; on the one hand I am the "expert" on Anzaldúa as I am a Chicana feminist and I utilize her theory as far as any of my white colleagues know, and yet in being asked to be the expert I am somehow more privileged to understand Anzaldúa's theory than others. The process of bridging then becomes complex; do I draw up the bridge, or keep it down in an effort to build solidarity with key allies on campus?

Because coalition, alliance, and solidarity are important goals to Anzaldúan theory, one way to achieve these efforts could be to look (respectfully and responsibly) at the ways that her theories might also impact or apply to one's own life, regardless of one's proximity to Chicana lesbian identity. In this case, there must be ways of being the bridge that helps others understand that they can use Anzaldúa's work without co-opting Chicana experience or seeking to own or claim it. In fact, this type of engagement with Anzaldúa's work becomes a potential site of transformation because we have centered a Chicana lesbian experience as the point around which our students want to connect. What becomes the danger is when the centering of those experiences gets conveniently erased. As Anzaldúa also reminds us, the only way to "transform our histories" is through alliances (155). Shouldn't we seek to find ways to connect our personal experiences to theories even when they are not our own? Doesn't this challenge traditional ways of knowing and knowledge production, realms where our theories are so often not present?

4. SANDBAR/ISLAND

Another white woman colleague who teaches in a Women's and Gender Studies program corners me at the National Women's Studies Association (NWSA) conference after she listened to my paper that engaged Anzaldúa's borderlands in relation to my oral history research with Midwestern Chicanas. Hastily between sessions she asks me if I can explain Anzaldúa's concept of la conciencia de la mestiza because she disagrees with it. She tells me, shouldn't we challenge notions of epistemic privilege? Isn't that what Anzaldúa's doing when she describes la mestiza?

Her questions take me aback. My use of Anzaldúa is rarely challenged by white feminists at NWSA. Once again, I am called upon as the expert on Anzaldúa but this time I mind it less. These questions of Anzaldúa's work feel like my colleague wants to exclude the coalitional aspect of her writings. The irony of Anzaldúa delivering the speech "Bridge, Drawbridge, Sandbar, or Island" at NWSA in 1988 does not elude me. But underneath my colleague's inquiries I cannot shake the feeling that there is something dangerous about her question. She doesn't understand, and yet she wants to know it in a way that she will never be able to know. And so, I push back. I do not exist within the academy as her endless fountain of knowledge of all things Chicana, or as the legitimizer of Chicana feminist theory and actions. Her questions push me to retreat to my Island, the place where there are no "causeways, no bridges—maybe no ferries, either—between [me] and whites" (148). But the islands are not sustainable, at least for me anyway. And so I become the sandbar, "a submerged or partly exposed ridge of sand built by waves offshore from a beach," a place where I can retreat from interactions like this and get "a breather from being a perpetual bridge without having to withdraw completely" (148). To withdraw completely means to sever the ties that are holding us together. My colleague supports me in many other ways; an ally on campus, a confidant through painful institutional experiences.

Anzaldúa reminds us that at the core of these various stages of "bridging" for lesbian women of color and white women that this is about alliance making. She tells us, "We may choose different options for different stages of our process," (149) but more importantly, "choosing to be a bridge, a drawbridge, and a sandbar allows us to connect, heart to heart, con corazónes abiertos" (149). I wrestle with my role as educator in all spaces. When students bring up these concerns I have answers, their micro-aggressions are a result of my presence as a queer Chicana professor and a consequence of teaching Chicana feminist theory; from white colleagues it can feel like a crushing blow. But like Anzaldúa, "I have been a persistent bridge," sometimes I feel as she was, "forced to 'draw the bridge,'" and sometimes still "driven to be an island" (149). But these strategic choices give queer Chicanas power in the academy, and like Anzladúa, I have purposefully chosen to embrace the bridge. While it may come with some costs, I believe the benefits overwhelmingly outweigh them.

5. BRIDGE

In spring of 2012 I taught the Women's and Gender Studies senior seminar course, which was also combined with the American Multicultural Studies senior seminar. As senior seminar topics are left up to the discretion of the faculty member who teaches it, I organized the course around the ways that women and feminists have theorized the personal. My approach was to ground our inquiries within how epistemological frameworks stemming from the personal are historically contextualized in the fields of WGS and ethnic studies. I also asked students to consider how the "personal" serves a bigger role within the academy at large.

For our section on Anzaldúa, (one three-hour class period) I asked my students to read several Anzaldúan works at the point in the semester where they began to start drafting their large research paper that fulfilled their capstone writing experience for the course. Before the specific class session, the students read "Bridge, Drawbridge, Sandbar, or Island" (1990), "Speaking in Tongues: A Letter to Third World Women Writers" (1981), "To(o) Queer the Writer – Loca, Escritora y Chicana" (1990), and her poem "The Coming of El Mundo Zurdo" (1977). In discussion I posed two main questions and asked the students to do a free write exercise on notecards for their responses. The goal was to think about how we could live Anzaldúa's words in our writing and in connection to our recurring course theme—the personal as epistemological and political. I asked them to think specifically about this line from "Speaking in Tongues" where Anzaldúa writes,

> ...the danger in writing is not fusing our personal experience and world view with the social reality we live in, with our inner life, our history, our economics, and our vision. What validates us as human beings validates us as writers. What matters to us is the relationships that are important to us whether with our self or with others. We must use what is important to us to get to the writing. No topic is too trivial. (31)

To ground this quote, I asked them to free write their answers in response to this question: "Thinking about Anzaldua's writings, how does an exploration of 'the trivial' become important for social, political, or spiritual transformations?" In this exercise I exposed my students to the importance of Anzaldúa's coalitional politics, purposefully engaged with my role as the bridge and asked them to think about the possibilities of social transformations from this approach.

I share some of my students' responses to this writing exercise to demonstrate the power in Anzaldúa's bridge-making commitment. By working through these responses we also collaboratively created a poem based on this notion to guide our writing process. The group of people who participated in this exercise included me, a WGS alumnus Teaching Assistant, who is a Transnational Desi woman, one Native woman, and twelve white women students. In their responses, which we discussed and mapped out on the board following the time to write, many reflected themes linked to identity, the importance of perspective and diversity, and social justice/activism in ways of knowing as they approached their understandings of Anzaldúa's texts. I focus on the "trivial" claim that Anzaldúa puts forth as the underpinning of Anzaldúa's teachings that connected to my course goals and my situated location in the academy—that claim would be the use of the personal as a means for social transformation.

When discussing the writing prompt I provided my students the option to connect their thoughts to social, political, or spiritual transformation. I was pleased with one student's response that fused these three areas together through an intersectional analysis. She wrote, "Identity is a process and cannot be trivial but must be expanded into the complexities of social, political and spiritual. We must take into account all aspects of women i.e. race, class, sex, as a whole intersecting, not just in one piece." In this student's understanding of Anzaldúa's quotation, I see her framing an intersectional understanding of identity via Anzaldúa's positionality. The student evokes Anzaldúa's intersectional identity to articulate the need for women's and gender studies as a space to be reflective on how the category of woman is contested and should be explored in relation to other identity categories. Anzaldúa's role as the bridge enabled this student to see the power in a vision of transformation that stems from identity; more specifically one that calls attention to alliance building through open hearts. It is on this trajectory that I articulate identity and the use of Anzaldúa's concepts like mestiza consciousness as non-essentialized understandings of identity. Understanding identity in intersectional ways enables us to work toward Anzaldúa's understanding of social transformation.

This is further reflected through another student's response to the writing prompt. She writes:

> Anzaldúa explores the trivial in the area of social transformation. Because whether or not something is trivial or important is relative to the person judging it. Therefore everything should be explored no matter how unimportant it may appear to be. Through this exploration, aspects of one's identity can be developed. Once everyone can feel that their ideas are valued, people can move forward to dive into this topic further.

This student articulates that we must see that the trivial is necessary in relation to our understandings of our identity. Furthermore, she articulates exploring the trivial as a valuable aspect of social transformation because, as Anzaldúa notes, "no topic is too trivial," meaning what we choose to explore can be the entry point for further valuable conversations about social transformation. It is also the way that others can be informed and invited to participate in thinking through the relation to the personal as political. So often within the space of the academy, some ideas or experiences are valued over others. Women's lives have frequently been constructed as engaged with "trivial" matters. Anzaldúa's assertion that "no topic is too trivial" becomes the radical catalyst for all women (in the most diverse understanding of that term) to claim the ability to explore how our lived (sometimes seen as "trivial") experiences can inform our social, political, and spiritual transformations. In her eternal position as bridge, she contrasts the way that Virginia Woolf writes of the need for "a room of one's own" for women writers to succeed. Again, Anzaldúa's work serves as a call to action for all women, not just a privileged few. Her success in this call to action emerges from a site of bridge-making. Furthermore, the articulations from a white woman student reading Anzaldúa enable us to see how centering Chicana lesbiana experience also serves as a means to begin thinking about coalitional politics. Grounding our own positionalities as we engage in shared struggles from unique locations can become a truly intersectional feminist politic.

The need for linking bridges to writing and to exploring the trivial as it pertains to societal transformation is multifaceted. A different student's response demonstrates a "Flowchart of Transformation" where she outlines her interpretations of Anzaldúa's spiritual, social, and political transformations in this multifaceted manner. She writes,

> Flowchart of Transformation:
>
> a) Spiritual: need to find peace with yourself before you can help another
>
> b) Social: work as a team, build trust
>
> c) Political: work with team for change to occur

Again, reiterating the sentiment the previous student's response elicits "What seems trivial to one individual may not be trivial to another." And she further writes, "All of society's 'norms' can be viewed as trivial if one steps outside the box they are living in. The trivial becomes political." This last line, "the trivial becomes political," encouraged me especially when we look at the larger themes of Anzaldúa's article, "To(o) Queer the Writer." She specifically ends that article with a vision of a multicultural rainbow bridge. She notes that "A bridge excludes racial separatism" and that she envisions a "rainbow serpent bridge composed of new mestizas/os, bi-and multi-racial queer people who are mixed and politicized will rise up and become important voices in our gay, ethnic, and other communities" (174). The politicizing of identities is important, and the ways that we as queer women of color facilitate these politicized processes can be valuable within the space of the classroom.

These articulations of the trivial as a beginning point help me to understand the power of the bridge. The bridge begins in coalition; it begins by drawing on our experiences that may be different from those with dominant identities. The trivial begins the conversation that allows bridging to take place. A different student sums this process up in her response to the in-class writing exercise in this way:

> Social is drawn together by trivial. It's how we build relationships. It creates a universal feeling that brings us together. Solidarity: social and political change is best grounded in relationship where we are able to identity with each other. We are best able to understand each other when understanding the 'trivial' parts of our lives and building from there it lays the groundwork for larger transformation.

Furthermore this student articulates, "Spirituality is grounded and created in everyday life or 'trivial' matters. 'We must use what is important to us to get to the writing' [means] living your life in your words and activism. Each piece brings us together."

These interpretations of Anzaldúa's texts compelled all of us to ground our understandings of the relationships between writing, identity, personal experience, and transformation. The power in doing this presents a lens through which we can see that social transformation is not limited to women of color but is rather our *collective* struggle that we must constantly work to define. Without political and spiritual transformation there will not be social transformation. Triviality is neither a luxury for third world women nor our only reality.

It is the potential of placing Anzaldúa's collaborative bridge building work at the center that enables us to see how white feminists might be able to approach her work in solidarity. It is this kind of response from my students both in their written form and in their verbal discussion of how much they enjoyed the texts that enable me to continue to be the bridge for them. After all, as professors who teach about gender, race, class, and sexuality, we are the bridge in these contexts. As such, we must be down to be walked on and enable these conversations to occur, grow, blossom, and die (though not necessarily always in that order). If we retreat and only seek solace in our islands, our tenuous programs will be swept under the rug in a quiet moment of our respite.

Social, political, and spiritual transformations as Anzaldúa writes provide the reader with a vision of hope. It is through being able to heal and be drawn-up bridges when we need to, but also through continuing to be open bridges that work to enable these kinds of transformative visions Anzaldúa holds in her writings. It becomes a beacon for how women of color, and Chicanas especially, can function within the space of the academy. It is only through recognizing the way that bridges must have two entrances to connect, can we imagine implementing Anzaldúa's feminist coalitional politics within the field of Women's and Gender Studies and the academy at large. This bridging is not the responsibility of women faculty of color alone. We see this when Anzaldúa poses this question in 1991 at NWSA, "Mujeres-de-color, mujeres blancas, ask yourselves what are you now, and is this something that you want to be for the next year or five years or ten? Ask yourself if you want to do alliance-coalition work and if so what kind and with whom" (149). While it is easy to see how bridging has often relied on women of color's openness to coalition and alliance building, it is also easy to see that if white women are not engaging in those same bridge building processes this will be a bridge to nowhere. Women of color will continue to be bridges to be walked on, as opposed to bridges seeking to connect shared struggles. The work we do in the classroom with white students, then, enables us to draw attention to those complex struggles and processes for bridge building while also asserting it is all of our shared responsibilities to work in coalition with one another.

In the spirit of Anzaldúa's combination of coalition building and her beautiful blending of poetry, prose, and analysis in her writing, my students constructed a community poem from our responses to the question, "What one word could summarize what you take away from Anzaldúa's ideas of social, political, and spiritual transformations?" We linked these one word summaries with their favorite Anzaldúan quote from that day's readings to bridge our understanding of her writing and the power of writing as a means toward social transformation with Anzaldúa's own enunciations. I choose to end this reflection with that poem, both because poetry is important to Anzaldúa's theory-making process and because it provides hopeful nods to the value of bridge work. In my experience as a bridge-maker there have been times when I have wanted to retreat, but the space of the classroom makes retreat nearly impossible (for effective dialogue at least). In sustained conversations about Anzaldúa's vision for scholarship and activism that emerges through creative approaches of writing we may be able to limit the other ways that Chicanas bear the brunt of bridge duties. We may also encourage white feminists to take part in these shared practices of bridging. We share our trivial truths here.

Goddess

"I am becoming-being/ the questor the questing/ the quest"

Vulnerable

"We go naked here"

Equal Experience

"Together we will walk"

Determined

"We can walk among each other talking of our writings, reading to each other."

Individual

"We go naked here"

Sharing identity

"Being a bridge means being mediator between yourself and your community and white

people, lesbians, feminists, white men"

Center

"And more and more when I'm alone, though still in communion with each other, the writing possesses me and propels me to leap into a timeless, spaceless no-place where I forget myself and feel I am the universe. This is power."

Flowing

"Identity is a river – a process."

Sandbar

"We not only need to look at who they are, the spaces they occupy… but also we have to look at our own motivations."

Creative

"We must use what is important to us to get to the writing."

Bridge

Spirited

Storyteller

"…I am thinking they lied, there is no separation between life and writing."

As we read this poem aloud, twice, as all good poems should be, we felt a collective sense of hope. We recognized the struggles that may lay ahead, but above all else, we breathed in a feeling of gratitude for the opportunity to think about our own writing as a means for social transformation, and how we might seek out bridging possibilities as a valuable part of an inclusive feminist coalitional politic.

WORKS CITED

Anzaldúa, Gloria. "Bridge, Drawbridge, Sandbar, or Island." *The Gloria Anzaldúa Reader*. Ed. AnaLouise Keating. Durham: Duke University Press, 2009. 140-156. Print.

---. "Speaking in Tongues: A Letter to Third World Women Writers." *The Gloria Anzaldúa Reader*. Ed. AnaLouise Keating. Durham: Duke University Press, 2009. 26-35. Print.

---. "To(o) Queer the Writer—Loca, Escritora y Chicana." *The Gloria Anzaldúa Reader*. Ed. AnaLouise Keating. Durham: Duke University Press, 2009. 163-175. Print.

---. "The Coming of El Mundo Surdo." *The Gloria Anzaldúa Reader*. Ed. AnaLouise Keating. Durham: Duke University Press, 2009. 36-7. Print.

Bureau of the Census. "The Hispanic Population: 2010," by Sharon R. Ennis, Merarys Ríos-Vargas, and Nora G. Albert. *Census Brief*, C2010BR-04 (May 2011). http://www.census.gov/prod/cen2010/briefs/c2010br-04.pdf (accessed December 17, 2012).

Cantú, Norma. "Centering the Margins: A Chicana in the English Classroom." *Race in the College Classroom: Pedagogy and Politics*. Eds. Bonnie Tusmith and Maureen T. Reddy. New Brunswick: Rutgers University Press, 2002. 226-238. Print.

Delgado Bernal, Dolores, Elenes, C. Alejandra, Godinez, Francisca E., and Sofia Villenas, eds. *Chicana/Latina Education in Everyday Life: Feminista Perspectives on Pedagogy and Epistemology*. Albany: State University of New York Press, 2006. Print.

Harris, Angela P., and Carmen G. González. "Introduction." *Presumed Incompetent: The Intersections of Race and Class for Women in Academia*. Eds. Gabriella Gutiérrez y Muhs, Yolanda Flores Niemann, Carmen G. González, and Angela P. Harris. Boulder: University Press of Colorado, 2012. 1-14. Print.

Keating, AnnaLouise. "Introduction: Reading Gloria Anzaldúa, Reading Ourselves... Complex Intimacies, Intricate Connections." *The Gloria Anzaldúa Reader*. Ed. AnaLouise Keating. Durham: Duke University Press, 2009. 1-15. Print.

The Latina Feminist Group, eds. *Telling to Live: Latina Feminist Testimonios*. Durham: Duke University Press, 2001. Print.

CUERPOS EN ESPIRAL: BODIES CROSSING BORDERS AND TRANSFORMING

MARÍA DEL SOCORRO GUTIÉRREZ MAGALLANES

"May our eyes open, may our hearts open"—Ancient wisdom

"Sensory Images: Images speak to us. They have their own meaning, and you sort of get behind the symbology and see what they are saying. Sometimes these images are very important because they connect different experiences that we have had, and give meaning to them."—Gloria Anzaldúa

IMAGES: SPIRAL & CUICUILCO

(Spiral)

(Cuicuilco)

We have a spiral: a curve on a plane that winds around a fixed center point at a continuously increasing or decreasing distance from the point; a symbol for a process of dialectics. We have a spiral where we imagine a body (our bodies) suspended and in a free fall gravitational trajectory which experiments a link between the internal and the external, of the physical body and the social body, of the inside and the outside, the public and the private, the aesthetic and the political, the straight lines and the curves, the visual and the sonorous, the confinement and the escape, the image and the word, the silence and the speech, and in this case, the triad: experience, reflection and theorization.

In 2011, the Programa Universitario de Estudios de Género at Universidad Nacional Autónoma de México, via a seminar entitled *Feminism in a Spiral,* made an open invitation to create a space in movement and to occupy it through dialogic learning processes. It was in this seminar that PUEG's director, Dr. Marisa Belausteguigoitia, presented us with a series of aesthetic interventions, theoretical reflections and pedagogical proposals to create and organize feminist language-grammars and new knowledge in an interdisciplinary platform. The first invitation in this seminar was to come out of the *encierros,* or confinements, metaphorically and epistemologically speaking. She referred to confinements or constraints of the episteme with a tunnel vision and of the restrictive disciplines we are trained in, of the theoretical "certainties" we are made to form throughout our academic schooling. She proposed we take the path via the spiral of multiple feminisms and to turn or take a gyration and allow our bodies to learn through articulate and politicized emotions. She guided us to think through pedagogies that could be thought of in terms of affective openings and fissures of the world through the act of questioning and, borrowing from Sara Ahmed, the emotion of wonder in the learning process. Wonder not as a private action but rather as an aperture to the possibilities of collective learning and to learn from the emotions emerging at the edges of ours kin.

Belausteguigoitia's feminist pedagogical proposals included the following:

1. Reflexive: the opening to the creation of a new body which means that the heterogeneous and radical pedagogical experiences are crucial in the learning *subject in process.*

2. Theoretical: to use the figure of the spiral as a pedagogical mechanism. The spiral compels us to twist, to queer, to turn around, to look inwards, to look outwards, to come in touch with our own bodies, with the world that hosts them, and with other bodies. Practices.

3. Methodological: to locate our bodies in the edges, the crossroads, the fissures, the voids, and the cuts of the spiral as points of departures to create new and critical knowledge to articulate theoretical reflections of our own experiences.

> 4. Praxis: to carry out actions and radical interventions in our works, in our research projects, in our academic endeavors and intellectual practices, to articulating and inventing new feminist grammars. To create new knowledge from the apparently unintelligible or untranslatable: subjectivity, the body, the emotions, the "un-representational," the invisible, the un-audible; To decipher and integrate the spoken and written word, the image and the sound, making of the spiral a recourse against constraint and confinement to recover the body and its individual and collective memory. And as Anzaldúa proposes, to heal the physical, individual and social body.

Dr. Belausteguigoitia's proposals helped me comprehend and articulate our experiences as Chicana students in Mexico, UNAM and PUEG. They helped me visualize our bodily and cultural dislocations to the curves and turns of the spiral way of thinking; they guided me to envision our bodies in new positions, in new ways, in new forms.

Thus I feel that in our presence at PUEG, we took on the challenge of Belausteguigoitia's propositions. Consequently, this graphic and visual essay is my intervention in an effort to record our experience as a Mexican born Chicana doctoral graduate student in my case, as a Colombian doctoral student in Selen Arango's case, and as Xicana doctoral graduate visiting researchers, in Cristina Serna and Sonia Mariscal's case, at UNAM's PUEG.

So in light of this intervention, I propose here that if for border artists all creation begins with an image (Anzaldúa, 2009), then also for the border theorists, the border historians, the border pedagogues, and the border feminists, our initiation image is that of a spiral. And it is in this spiral that our movement in our walk through PUEG, UNAM, and Mexico is serpentine – *a la Cuicuilco*. Our reflection is two ways, from Mexico to the United States, from the US to Mexico, and inside and outside. Our way of seeing in the spiral is situated in Nepantla and "upside down" as is that of the *flesh and bone butterflies* or the bat deities. The construction of our knowledge is transformed – *a la Coatlicue State* or the pain of personal pain; our bodies were re-membered and re-collected so that we could configure ourselves like *Coyolxauhquis*, like *Nepantleras*, like *Danzantes*, and like Snails.

An offering

> *As you walk across Lighthouse Field,* (PUEG, UNAM, México, Cuicuilco) *a glistening black ribbon undulates in the grass, crossing your path from right to left. You swallow air; your primal senses flare open. From the middle of your forehead, a reptilian eye blinks, surveys the terrain. This visual intuitive sense like the intellect of heart and gut reveals a discourse of signs, images, feelings, words that, once decoded, carry the power*

to startle you out of tunnel vision and habitual patterns of thought... (Anzaldúa 540)

IMAGE 1. SERPENTS

(Body painting by Trina Merry, 2012)

And we transformed into serpents. We were like serpents that held on the surface of the spiral to move around, to dislocate, re-situate in the curves, twist and open our eyes and our hearts; to open up to other forms of knowledge, other forms of wisdom, and other ways to create. Our meeting point: *Cuicuilco*. We situated ourselves in the curve. We walked to the threshold of the remains of this sacred site. Called by the crossroads of our lives, and helped by the bridges we created, we found our paths. Guided by Cristina Serna, we traversed the threshold and we walked the site in serpentine grace. We entered a sacred terrain, an ancient zone and a very important place for us and for Mexico: "Cuicuilco, a place of dance and chants" (Montemayor, 2008). The trajectory we took to get to the main edifice of the site was not a common path. Cristina Serna knew and led the way through another path. A serpentine and unknown path for us. The landscape continuously mesmerized us and challenged us. It alerted our senses. We observed flowers and cacti blossoming from the petrified lava. We saw big cacti in the shape of heart growing out of the volcanic rocks. We saw life and undulant movement making part of our walk. The introspection, the silence, and every now and then a word of amazement at the nature, accompanied us until we got to a small cave that hosted an *ofrenda*, an offering. There we dialogued about the energy of the ceremonial site and our sensations. We contributed to the *ofrenda* there; we offered our work, our thought and our writing to this sinuous path. Given this experience I consider that it was *Cuicuilco*, the place we traced our way of writing and of thinking about our experience, our time here and now in Mexico. Here we gathered strength to think and articulate with words, tones, and different intensities, our different and diverse ways to create as historians, theorists, pedagogues, sociologists and activists. *Cuicuilco* was for us a place where we transformed into serpents and shed our skin and tried to heal our wounds. Here we transformed our bodies on the surface of a spiral willing to twist, spin, and dislocate. Here we opened our eyes and hearts to be in touch with our feelings, and perceptions to integrate a full consciousness in communication with the external world. It was in the Cuicuilco-PUEG-UNAM-and-Mexico spiral that our bodies changed skin. Our bodies were transformed. Our sensations changed us. Our perception was transformed. Our vision changed. The way we view the world changed. And because of that, in and from diverse ways, we want to change how we live the world so that we can change the world.

IMAGE 2. *MARIPOSAS DE CARNE*

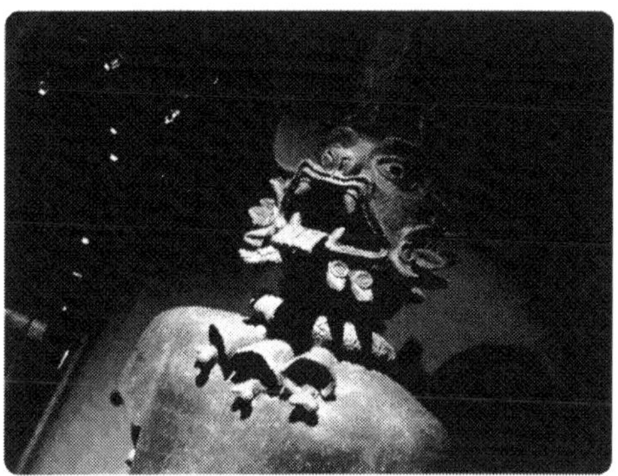

(Tzinacan in náhuatl; bigidiri beela, bigidri zinia and "mariposa de carne" in zapoteco)

We transformed into bat deities: *mariposas de carne*. In our path to *conocimiento*, crossing the threshold towards the spiral with our senses fully alert, we held on to the swirls of the different branches of knowledge. We began to experiment living in Nepantla, also in Mexico, and we transformed into *mariposas de carne*. We used our night vision to navigate the borderlands in multiple sites. The sites were not necessarily geographical, they were situational. Anzaldúa reminds us that to live in Nepantla means "to live *in-between*, in the border, in a locus of resistance, rupture, implosion and explosion, a state that allows us to shift perspectives to see through the past imposed on the present and helps us to recollect the fragments and create a new *assemblage*" (Anzaldúa 544). Nepantla is that terrain that we cross when we move from one place to another, when we shift from one situatedness to another, maybe from class, race, or sex, or when we shift from one present identity to a new one. In Nepantla the space between different perceptions and belief systems are juxtaposed. There is one that is conscious of the changing character of the categories of race, gender, sexuality and others that make conventional labeling obsolete.

For example, we the Chicanas and MeXicanas speak about when we were born in the US or crossed over, we self-identify as migrants, working class *women of color*, Latinas, Chicanas, Xicanas, or MeXicanas and the dominant culture denies our space in society. And when we "return to the homeland," to Mexico, although we self-identify in our difference as MeXicanas or Chicanas, we "pass" for Mexicanas. That is to say we go "unnoticed." But this usually changes when we open our mouths and speak; our tongue denounces us. Our tongue gives us away. Our tongue "betrays" us. So for the Chicano Spanish dialect we speak and the tones we use, we are called "*gringas*" or "*pochas*." The *criollo* dominant culture and the colonized mestiza culture in Mexico reject us, dis-recognize us. The people call us Chicanas only when our rebel tongue demands that specific recognition, or when someone knows the history of migrants, Mexicans in the Southwest of the US, or of people who have crossed the US-Mexico border. We move around and cross multiple borders. For us to move across these borders, be they physical, linguistic, cultural, disciplinary, or others, is to live in Nepantla. And it is in that border and the liminal spaces that we take on speech acts, we take on the spoken and the written word.

These speech acts transform us, as Anzaldúa states:

> Con la lengua hablamos, con la mano escribimos. Cuando la lengua y la mano trabajan juntas, unifican el arte y lo político y atacan la ideología dominante. Para muchas de nosotras los actos de escribir, pintar, hacer un performance, fotografíar y filmar son actos deliberados y determinaciones desesperadas de subvertir el *status quo*. Actos creativos son formas de activismo político que emplean estrategias estéticas definitivas para resistir normas culturales dominantes y no son meramente ejercicios estéticos. Creamos cultura en tanto que inscribimos estas formas variadas. (Milczarek-Desai 135)

Inspired by my experience of participating in a poetic anthology called *Las voces de las mariposas, 2011,* giving community recitals in various Mixtec pueblos in Oaxaca, and the excitement of the four of us becoming friends in Mexico, a Cuicuilco gathering was proposed to carry out a dialogue and poetry workshop. The four of us met and in the facilitation of the workshop, in part carried out by Selen Arango, several poems and drawings flourished. My poem was an epigram: an epigram in a curve.

> Epigrama en curva. Escribir sobre algo que se nos prohíbe. Escribimos en curva lo que deseamos: Infinitud. Imaginé que podría encontrarte en todas partes. Pensé: siempre, infinitamente. Descubrí que en la tierra no

> sería posible. Comprendí que sólo sería en el Universo... Te busco infinitamente... en el firmamento. Caían las palabras luminosas y yo las recogía.

It was in this creative writing meeting that the idea for this panel and intervention at the Mundo Zurdo Conference 2012 was proposed by Sonia Mariscal. It was through our dialogue and shared learning processes that we had already transformed ourselves into *mariposas de carne* that have the "night vision," the bat deities that have the quality to see the world "upside down." We spoke of our movements back and forth between Mexico and the US and Colombia and of how the people we had met in this movement and our culture shocks back and forth had transformed our way of seeing and ourselves. In some ways we imagined that through our speech acts we had also transformed those people we had contact with. It was then that we reminded ourselves of what Anzaldúa had said:

> *Tomar la palabra.* Despite language, class and identity differences and conflicts, there exists strong cultural links among Chicana, Mexicana, Latina, Native, Asian, Black, and other women. We can safeguard and strengthen these links through communications. People in possession of the vehicles of communications are, indeed, in partial possession of their lives. (Banerjee 122)

It is those back and forth movements that disorient us but at the same time they re-situate us in another place like the borders. These movements have pushed our transformation to *mariposas de carne,* bat deities. In this regard Anzaldúa refers to this bat deity or *mariposa de carne* as one associated "with nepantla stage of border artists—the dark cave of creativity where they hang upside down, turning the self upside down in order to see from another point of view, one thing that brings a new state of understanding... Perhaps the *murciélago goddess* questions the viewer's unconscious collective and personal identity and its ties to her/his ancestors" (184). As *diosas murciélago* we were able to see the world "upside down," with "night vision," with our ears wide open to listen, with our teeth sharpened to defend ourselves and with our tongue ready to speak: "*the soul speaks, the body acts.*"

IMAGE 3. COYOLXAUHQUI

(Coyolxauhqui in náhuatl: the goddess of the moon. The fragmented woman. Stone found in *Templo Mayor*, Mexico City, in 1978.)

Fragmented Woman, *Coyolxauhqui*, with the body, the head, arms and legs, separated around her upper body. The round shape of the stone, similar to the full moon indicates she is the moon goddess. Like the images of her mother Coatlicue, she has skulls tied to her waist. This is how we are in Mexico and the United States, like *Coyolxauhqui*. We are broken into pieces, broken by our tongues, by our class, by race, by gender, by sexuality and by "difference." When we opened ourselves to the spiral and we held upside down to have a different perspective, we opened our senses to *conocimiento* and we broke into body-mind-spirit-soul: we made ourselves vulnerable and we became fragmented. In the surface of the spiral path we transformed into *Coyolxauhqui*. In this state, it is our responsibility to recollect all the pieces of our bodies and to shift to new shapes. We must re-member and re-envision our bodies in this world. We must recover our pieces, and re-join and re-configure ourselves collectively. By the end of 2011, we gathered to celebrate our personal and collective transformations. On the day we celebrated there was a lunar eclipse and a strong earthquake. After the scare, we celebrated the closure of a painful yet transformative year of closing cycles in our lives. But above all we gathered to celebrate that we had met here in Mexico. During this year we collected ourselves into one piece and we gathered strength during our transformations to move on with our lives and projects.

IMAGE 4. *DANZANTES Y CARACOLES*

(Cristina Serna, Selen Arango, Sonia Marisca & María del Socorro (Coco) Gutiérrez Magallanes, Gathering for Dialogue and Poetry Workshop, Cuicuilco, Mexico, 2011. Drawing by Sonia Mariscal.)

In our recollection of our bodies, we danced to the rhythm of Nepantla and we transformed ourselves in *Danzantes and Caracoles*: dancers and snails. We danced and nepantleamos in search of new states of consciousness and new paths to *conocimientos*. In the surface of the spiral we became aware of the sonorous and visual realities that were imperceptible before. We became aware of the subjective experiences and of the external world. We let ourselves be guided to consciousness by the light of the moon, by the lunar eclipse, by Coyolxauhqui. We wanted to restore balance, equilibrium, the sense of belonging to a place in this universe, a sense of life on this earth. We entered and exited the spiral, like the head of the snail that goes in and out of its shell, its home. We listened to others and we want to be listened to. We learned from others by listening and we learn from our selves through our own speech acts. We learn to and from *tomar la palabra*. We resisted movement but also conceded to it. Like stones we threw ourselves to the spiral, we broke into pieces but we also reconstituted ourselves. We transformed ourselves. In 2011, at PUEG, at UNAM, and in Mexico, as Rusty Barceló's song says: "we danced to the joy of living, we danced to the joy of life, under the river moonlight."

We now have in our bodies the spiral shell like the snail, but we also maneuver strategies to go in and out when we decide to. We retract ourselves to ask the proper questions but we also extend ourselves to listen and learn from others. We move around, dislocate ourselves, dis-adjust and re-adjust, like the snails. In this journey, we have experimented transformations of the body-world-classroom-world-body nature.

We are artists, poets, feminists, theorists, historians, pedagogues and sociologists. We are as poet Roque Dalton says, "como los caracoles, que llevamos la casa móvil sobre las espaldas" (Dalton 196). We move and carry our homes in our backs: here, there, there, here, everywhere we go and everywhere we live.

We historically transform ourselves, as López Austin suggests:

> [L]a historia es un flujo de cuerpos de distinta resistencia al movimiento. Es como un torrente, como un torbellino, como una flama. Los hechos históricos – pesados, densos, y lentos unos, ágiles otros- se rayan las caras como las piedras de las morrenas. Cada hecho histórico es además de composición heterogénea. Sus partes se desplazan con ritmos diferentes en un continuo proceso de desajuste y reajuste. (209)

This is why we are *cuerpos en espiral*: bodies in spiral. We are *nepantleras, danzantes* and *caracoles* in a journey that proposes new metaphors to construct new knowledge. We are *cuerpos en espiral*, crossing borders and transforming, making history here and there and in-between, transforming ourselves and in doing so, transforming the world. May our upside-down vision help us navigate the *borderlands*, here, there, and in-between.

WORKS CITED

Ahmed, Sara. *The Cultural Politics of Emotion.* NY, Routledge, 2004. Print.

Anzaldúa, Gloria and AnaLouise Keating, ed. *The Anzaldúa Reader.* Duke University Press, 2009. Print.

Banerjee, Mita. "The Hipness of Mediation: A Hyphenated German Existence." *this bridge we call home: radical visions for transformation.* Eds. Gloria Anzaldúa and Analouise Keating. New York: Routledge, 2002. Print.

Barceló, Nancy Rusty. "Sing to the joy of living." Music recital: *Sex y Corazón Conference.* UCLA. 2009. Print.

Belausteguigoitia, Marisa and Lozano, Rian. *Pedagogías en Espiral. Experiencias y Prácticas.* México, Colección PUEG, UNAM, 2012. Print.

Dalton, Roque. *Pobrecito poeta que era yo.* El Salvador: UCA Editores, 2000. Print.

Las Voces de las Mariposas. Antología del XIX Encuentro Internacional: Mujeres poetas en el País de las Nubes. Secretaria de las Culturas y las Artes del Gobierno de Oaxaca. Centro de Estudios de la Cultura Mixteca, Colección Vidzu, 2011. Print.

Milczarek-Desai, Shefali. "Living Fearlessly With and Within Differences: My Search for Identity Beyond Categories and Contradictions." *this bridge we call home: radical visions for transformation.* Eds. Gloria Anzaldúa and Analouise Keating. New York: Routledge, 2002. Print.

Montemayor, Carlos. *Diccionario del nahuatl en el español en México.* Ciudad en Movimiento, Coordinación de Humanidades, UNAM, 2008. Print.

Muñoz Espinoza, Maria Teresa. "El culto al dios murciélago en Mesoamérica." Accessed: Web. 01, May, 2011. http://www.arqueomex.com/S2N3nMurcielago80.html.

Noguez, Javier and Austin, Alfredo López. Coords. *De hombres y dioses.* Zinancatepec, Estado de México, El Colegio Mexiquense; El Colegio de Michoacán, 1997.129. Print.

Villa R., Bernardo. *Los murciélagos de México.* Ciudad de México, UNAM, 1966. Print.

THE MAKING OF CULTURAL POETICS OF ENVIRONMENTAL JUSTICE: PEDAGOGIES AND PARADIGMS FOR ECOLOGICAL, CULTURAL & ECONOMIC TRANSFORMATIONS IN AN AGE OF GLOBAL WARMING

KAMALA PLATT

INTRODUCTION: GOING GLOBAL WITH GLORIA

> My job as an artist is to bear witness to what haunts us, to step back and attempt to see the pattern in these events (personal and societal), and how we can repair el daño (the damage) by using the imagination and its visions. I believe in the transformative power and medicine of art. As I see it, this country's real battle is with its shadow—its racism, propensity for violence, rapacity for consuming, neglect of its responsibility to global communities and the environment, and unjust treatment of dissenters and the disenfranchised, especially people of color. As an artist I feel compelled to expose this shadow side which the mainstream media and government denies. In order to understand our complicit and responsibility we must look at the shadow. (Anzaldúa, "Let us be the healing..." 93)

This essay begins with a crucial reality check—a glance at complicity with lados de sombras, shadow sides—born of five years teaching in the Rio Grande Valley (RGV/ El Valle): had Gloria Evangelina Anzaldúa not left El Valle, she would likely not hold the significance she holds, within and beyond this country, and we would not be artists, scholars, activists influenced by her tremendous work. *El Mundo Zurdo 3* would not exist, nor would the Society for the Study of Gloria Anzaldúa, nor the decades of conferences, speaker series, and volumes housed in disciplines across the social sciences, humanities, and beyond that have been dedicated to, or have drawn upon Gloria Anzaldúa's work. A haunting irony exists in the fact that in El Valle, today, we celebrate Gloria's name more than we try to change what made her leave, more than we acknowledge the horrendous realities from which some students in El Valle, living on ambos lados, cannot take leave. We know these realities of the shadow side exist, literally and figuratively: we know students who, by geography of birth, cannot go beyond the checkpoints, cannot be gainfully employed, and cannot continue their schooling outside the valle.[1] Many are Dreamers, caught in an immigration system-*beyond-reform* that needs dismantling. Others are from families caught in rounds of violence propelled by U.S.-sponsored Wars on Drugs and sustained by U.S.-attained guns and drug consumption. Still others experience the federal government's borderland militarization that walls off homelands and habitats and waives environmental, cultural, and religious rights. These are realities that we, as educators, have a role within, and we, as torch holders of Gloria Anzaldúa's legacies, strive to understand, to discern "our complicity and responsibility," and to discern when our work is compromised because we are trapped by the shadow side.

After five years of contingent teaching experience at University of Texas, Pan American (UTPA), an institution that can claim Gloria as an alumna, I am compelled to bear witness to the shadow realities: that her alma mater would likely not have hired Gloria Anzaldúa, and on the off chance it had hired her, it might have forced her out, as it has other forward-looking Chicanas.[2] It might have shunned the best of her work, as it has that of other women, ignored her stories as it has with the LGBT community, treated her as suspect in the covert culture of racism experienced by colleagues of deeper color,[3] or in the Intelligence Community culture installed with ICCAE.[4]

During the NACCS Tejas Foco 2013, a Librotraficante Underground Library named for Gloria Anzaldúa was launched. Tony Diaz, who initiated Librotraficante to smuggle banned books into Arizona during Spring Break 2012, notes that, saying Gloria Anzaldúa graduated from your school is "like saying that Emily Dickinson attended your school" and he continues "[t]hat's why I was stunned to find out that there was no monument to La Gloria at Pan Am, there was no building, there was no marker." Diaz is correct to note the formal lack of acknowledgment of Gloria Anzaldúa; however, there has been a continually growing celebration of her work by community, students, and faculty at UTPA and in the Rio Grande Valle, more broadly.[5]

In January 2012, when Librotraficante first responded to the banning of the Mexican American Studies (MAS) classes in Tucson, and the MAS/Raza Studies curriculum (which includes *Borderlands/La Frontera: The New Mestiza*), my classes viewed and discussed the on-line launch of the Librotraficante Movement; readings from banned books were on my syllabi and I introduced more that I became acquainted with through the list.[6] Although I tried for six years without success to get the Chican@ Database available in our library, and while a plethora of Intelligence Community Databases were introduced through our IGKNU program,[7] one email to our librarian ally, Virginia Gause, with the list of books banned in Tucson, brought her assurance that she would order the ones we did not have, so the beginnings of the Gloria Anzaldúa Under Ground Library should have been in place for Librotraficante's visit during NACCS. Working on the margins, we find support and respect for our dignity from those who have the most to offer, even if they are not writ large within the structures of power. Acknowledging their/our work is part of the repairing of el daño that Gloria advocates; it is also basic to the project of documenting cultural poetics of justice.

As I prepared this essay for publication, Texas higher education plans were unveiled: assuming Texas Legislature support, UTPA, at least in name, will soon no longer exist, subsumed alongside University of Texas, Brownsville (UTB), into a giant money-generating institution with a medical school attached; it was initially announced as "University of the Americas," chillingly reminiscent of another School of the Americas, with a name change to obscure its history.[8] Whether UTPA loses its history, and its connection to its alumni, along with its name, remains to be seen; perhaps the new beginnings can be transformative, reviving lost legacies, returning La Gloria to her beloved valley through the artworks she calls for.[9]

I wrote a grant proposal to help me begin the organization of my project. Because I did not receive funding and had to find time to work on this project while teaching five classes a semester, I submitted several conference abstracts that illuminated chapters I had planned. El Mundo Zurdo's abstract was the last of these in spring, 2012; I did not make a specific argument, but described the project as a work-in-progress that I would report upon. All my abstracts were accepted, but the email I got from *El Mundo Zurdo's* organizing committee said my acceptance was "conditional"—they wanted an argument, up front.

I felt discouraged and tired—I had done my own work, as a "Compustura," whom Anzaldúa describes as a seamstress who is "seaming together fragments to make a garment which you wear, which represents you, your identity and reality in the world" (qtd. in Lunsford 9), and it was seen as rags. Perhaps, miscommunication, or perhaps, the "weightiness" that Gloria describes when we, as family/

scholars, must negotiate for ourselves: "So there's a kind of weightiness on you *not* to write, not to do your art in as honest a way as possible." And I might add, not to teach, or speak as Compostura or as Nepantlera. Clearly, persistence got the better of my doubts—hence you are reading this article.

Recently, I browsed the used copies list of *Haciendo Caras* on Amazon—a very large number note that they contain highlighting and marginal notes—no surprise, I think—who would not, pen in hand, interact with this book? Books like *Haciendo Caras* make me wonder why anyone would choose to read an e-book.. I understand some e-books have writable margins, but Gloria brought together so many writers with much fuerza in that book, most of us need to scratch our passionate assent in our own hand, in the margins. When I first taught *Making Face, Making Soul/Haciendo Caras: Creative and Critical Perspectives by Feminists of Color*, it was for a Women and Gender Studies course at UTSA in 1999. Almost everyone in an auditorium classroom evaluated the book positively, even as I was terminated at the end of the semester from teaching women's studies (and anything but English, in the division) ostensibly for a few bad, early evaluations. Later, I am asked if I can make a connection between the termination and the teaching of *Hacienda Caras*. If I could have, it might have supported my eighteen page grievance that was not taken up by the administrative power structure of the university. *Hacienda Caras* operated as Anzaldúa's Trojan Horse that was able to infiltrate, letting ideas emerge into the belly of the university in the night as students encountered texts from people they were taught in the daylight not to trust. I was in front of the class teaching, so I was an easier target. To compare text and teacher in this instance is comparing apples and oranges. However, my shadowy termination experience adds grounding to my opening claim that Gloria's alma mater would not have invited or tolerated her teaching.[10]

Teaching as contingent labor, mostly in Texas higher education, the majority of my Women and Gender Studies Teaching has been covert; I am the Trojan *Burra*—in the last three years at UTPA, I was not sanctioned to teach Women's Studies (although I was when the previous director of our program who, ironically, knew me from UTSA, invited me) and because there is no funding for women's history month or other programming regarding women, no women's center/place to be, and little communication regarding women's issues. Not only was there little administrative/institutional support for women, there is little for LGBT solidarity, not to mention a studies program and until the recent renaissance of MAS which has struggled against state defunding and for any institutional support, less critical Ethnic Studies. Fortunately, at UTPA, the tentacles of control did not penetrate faculty determination of course curricula, even for contingent faculty. In my courses, we became involved in the poetics of environmental justice in the borderlands; my courses gained support from outside of the English Department when they became part of the Environmental Studies minor plan.

My first trip to UTPA was a campus visit for a professorship that included initiating a border studies program—based in the English Department—that never transpired; had it been initiated, it could have been a unique institute that would have done the borderlands work for which Gloria so clearly sees the need when she describes her love of and concern for El Valle—its peoples and environment—upon a return visit in "El Retorno."[11] I received the invitation for that campus visit partially because of my research of women promoting environmental justice in communities on the border, and beyond, work for which this article identifies a nexus with Anzaldúan cultural theory; yet, once I was there as a lecturer, I was up against a hierarchy I'd not experienced previously. I left UTPA as a lecturer whose composition and creative writing position was terminated for no identified reason. With ambivalence, but much gusto, I continue my real work, despite unemployment—and as time passes, UTPA's shadow lengthens.

Despite reluctance to ever teach another semester of five composition classes, I value the composition courses I have taught—a teacher can, as Anzaldúa advocates, invite a composition classroom to explore "postcolonial issues of identity" with students who might otherwise not be exposed to cultural studies theory, even as they are often *living* the issues we discuss, every day (Lunsford 9). In my classes, this takes a form that resembles the visions for the world that Gloria had—environment(al) matters—catchwords for change, templates for social and environmental justice that draw me back to her work, repeatedly; the transformations that are so slowly, but surely, in progress—like at UTPA. We *are building* in conjunction with those in the world who are artists, teachers, and scholars in the senses that Gloria describes.

Yet higher education in Texas, as elsewhere, seems bent on squelching out such gains, as K-12 pressure to teach to the tests makes headway in higher education, as budget cuts sear through innovative curricula, as Tejas legislation copycats Arizona's Raza Removal Act and does bidding of Right Wing PACs and pseudo-academic associations, such as the National Association of Scholars (NAS), to eradicate from history's accepted fold of CORE courses all Chican@, African American, Women's, LGTB, and other marginalized people's histories. Simultaneously, those faculty without the enfranchisement of tenure—those, like me, considered adjunct (to what?), contingent (on whose terms?), particularly those who teach subject matters that are also on the margins, are bled and then squeezed out. Arguably, the most widespread, interdisciplinary influence Anzaldúa's work has attained is in the very areas that today are under parallel, if not orchestrated attacks—in terms of subject matter, process, and ways of being.

I could not write this essay with its foundation in border-born conceptualizations of environmental justice and interwoven pedagogies and paradigms, without acknowledging these realities of higher education as they play out in the RGV, and without acknowledging that Gloria Anzaldúa belongs, not just in/to El Valle, not just in/to the fronteras—ambos lados—but also in/to the world. It is el mundo with all its heridas abiertas, and their subsequent scars, that Anzaldúa cares about most deeply in the epigraph above from one of the last publications of her (new) work, in an anthology whose title is taken from her words, collected and bound as *One Wound for Another, Una Herida Por Otra*; it offers Latin@ online responses to 9-11.

EL RETORNO

> Tierra natal. This is home, the small towns in the Valley, los pueblitos with chicken pens and goats picketed to mesquite shrubs... This land has survived possession and ill use by five countries..." ("El Retorno," 2007, 153-154).

As I look to the interstices of my interactions with Gloria Anzaldúa, her influence on the environmental justice cultural poetics unfolds through personal history as well as through coalescence of quotation and praxis. My involvement with women's creative work that addresses environmental issues impacting human communities, inequitably, is research I've involved myself with for nearly the time I've admired Gloria Anzaldúa's words. I first encountered her work in the form of *This Bridge Called My Back* as I was laying in the sand on Myrtle Beach, VA, over thirty years ago (Summer 1982). I had graduated from Bethel College in Kansas, moved to the Urban Life Center (ULC) in Chicago, and taken an impromptu trip to the east coast with new acquaintances. A fellow traveler was reading *Bridge* and shared the book.

Weeks before, I had celebrated graduation by joining the last week of the cross-continental Nuclear Freeze Walk (from Camden, NJ to NYC), had applied for a job with the Nuclear Freeze Campaign (and had the first of three decades of unfruitful job interviews), and was considering attending an anti-nuclear event near Chicago, when I was invited to the east coast. Upon return, my roommates said my mom had called: she'd seen me on national TV getting arrested at the anti-nuclear rally. Mom later told me she had been so sure that it was me because of how I smiled at the cop as he arrested me. Perhaps it was a fellow Nuclear Freeze Walk-er, who people swore was my twin sister, but could I doubt my mom's recognition of my smile? I have, since, settled on a compromise of interpretation: perhaps I had been transported to the protest, as I read *Bridge:* the palabras seemed that powerful! They formed a mezcla in my mind during years in Chicago, with other authors—Maxine Hong Kingston, Nikki Giovanni, Audre

Lorde, Gary Snyder, Malcolm X, Meridel Le Sueur come to mind—alongside murals, city politics, and tussles between magnetism of nature and of culture, of contemplation of my role as artist—the creation of the beautiful and condemnation of the unjust. And they would beckon me toward Chicana poetics, once I arrived at the University of Texas, Austin, a few years later.

Thirty years on, with more bumps than ever in our nation's, indeed our world's, nuclear paths, be they designed for threatening the "hostile," or heating the living room—or both, are best exemplified in depleted uranium, a waste product of energy recycled into weaponry that harms for generations to come, and *The Devil's Tango: How I Learned the Fukushima Step by Step*, Cecile Pineda's year-long manifesto recently published by Wings Press on the first anniversary of the Japanese nuclear plant catastrophe. The book is an act of vigilant art that "bear[s] witness to what haunts us...in order to understand our complicity and responsibility," a multi-genre offering toward Gloria's visionary melding of grassroots politics and culture, and a new work developing at the nexus of climate change and environmental justice, sometimes called climate justice. I read *The Devil's Tango* as I prepared an art installation about nuclear energy for *Glow: The Nuclear Show*, at Bihl Haus in San Antonio. "(Rock) Off Nuclear: Cradle to Burial Urn I" is the first in a land-based installation series that assembles items with figurative and literal powers of Satyagraha *against* nuclear energy and *toward* something aligned with mente y alma y cuerpo de la tierra.

Pineda's memoir of daily life observations in conjunction with nuclear realizations returns me to my past: meeting people thirty years ago who lived in what seemed an idyllic alternative/intentional community near Myrtle Beach, a place peopled with strangers, where I momentarily felt I'd like to belong. Juxtaposed in contrast is my not belonging: my traveling companion complains about nature and cicadas, and small towns, vowing unrequited love for the city, despite violence she'd encountered there; alienated by the binary stereotyping, I lacked vocabulary such as "urban nature." Later, environmental justice groups would analyze environmental racism's stereotyping when urban people of color and immigrants are seen as being against nature; they would provide a more extensive and inclusive definition of environment as neighborhoods, workplaces, playgrounds, places of worship, not just wilderness. The seventeen "Principles of Environmental Justice," would become the bedrock of my composition classes with umbrella topics of borderlands environmental justice, because the Rio Grande delta holds an all-encompassing landscape of environmental harm alongside its confluence of unique ecological communities. Anzaldúa affirms this broader spectrum of experience, inclusive of rural *and* urban communities when she writes: "Yes, the Chicano and Chicana have always taken care of growing things and the land" ("El Retorno," 2007, 155).

At the time however, I simply remember feeling the *connection* with the sense of nature and culture, men and women, and other perceived binaries as reciprocal, rather than always opposing forces, expressed by the writers in *Bridge*. I remember thinking I needed to keep my eye out for more of this writing by women of color theorists—somehow they went beyond the feminism I had been exposed to up to that time. They gave perspective to the small amount of Chicano writing I'd read, mostly in Indigenous publications such as *Akwesasne Notes.*[12] *This Bridge* and later *Hacienda Caras* helped me set expectations of writers who connect deeply theorized concerns of subject position in conjunction with their communities' desire for justice and rights, a healthy environment…a nexus of issues I would take up in my dissertation and share with my classes.

The connection was not only content-driven—I was also drawn to the genre. This Chicana mixed-genre work was part of a broader field of "experimental women's literature" I had studied while at Bowling Green State University (BGSU) for my MFA, but when as a doctoral student at UT, Austin, I proposed to teach such a course, I was told that "they could not afford the luxury" of teaching such women's work. Nonetheless, within the refuge of the "Ethnic and Third World" English classes at UT, we gained access to not only literary production that was marginalized elsewhere in academia, but to Cultural Studies theories that would connect literature and life/lived experience; our classes were where our professors honed the concepts that appeared in their internationally significant books, texts that stretched the academic envelope and, like Anzaldúa's, helped define the fields: *Resistance Literature, Chicano Narrative: The Dialectics of Difference*, and *Dancing With the Devil.*[13]

We benefitted not only from professors on-campus, but maestros en las calles, people like Chicanindio, Pinto Poet, and Raúl R. Salinas, at whose Resistencia Bookstore I spent volunteer time, and who later defended my dissertation[14], and organizations like PODER (People Organized in Defense of the Earth and her Resources) the group that sparked my interest in environmental justice with their fight against an oil tank farm in an East Austin neighborhood, and continues over two decades of "redefining environmental, economic and social justice issues" today.[15] My classmates from UT, Austin, now span the spectrum of academic success, our job titles range from adjuncts to administrators, but our scholarship, creative work, and teaching—rooted in the fertile ground of that particular time and space, encouraged by respectful engagement with, and mentoring from local elders, activists, and community organizations, as well as visiting scholars like Gloria Anzaldúa—has produced a groundswell of offerings. When, due to the often dire straits of contingent labor and unemployment cycles, I want to give up on my work, it is out of the respect I owe such mentors and the camaraderie of mi compas-y-colleagues, that I continue.

A classmate from that time would later describe the symbiotic relation of genre and content-driven concerns in work like Anzaldúa's when he noted:

> many Chicana writers…have contributed to an ongoing critique of Chicano historians and the Movement in their literature. In the process they have produced a body of work that defies traditional generic constraints. Moreover, in the popularization of multigeneric, multi-author anthologies advanced by women of color, they have also placed their writing at the service of a practical political agenda. (Mendoza 237)

The "cross-cultural cross-generic texts" and "autobiographical collections that assumed the same multigeneric form" he lists include those Gloria Anzaldúa wrote or had a hand in. Louis Mendoza's comments demonstrate the depth and breadth of the significance of bodies of work the English Department had dismissed as "luxurious," and in doing so, suggests that it may indeed be "unaffordable" for us *not* to study these texts that "bear witness," often in unconventional, perhaps eco gendered and cultured ways.

My first visual image of the earliest cover of *Borderlands* was as the book lay on the dashboard of a friend's borrowed car: the book, colorful on a gray day was making the rounds with the car: I am not sure whose copy it was, but conversation about the book ensued when we stopped to visit a friend from El Valle—was Gloria's book the stuff of the community or of academia? I listened, but was already dismissing such binaries as too often misleading us away from *La Puente*. We'd later read the book in class alongside *Loving in the War Years* and our professor would say as a postscript that Anzaldúa and Moraga were not representative Chicanas—was he concerned about our constructing a Chicana/o Literature syllabus without a straight Chicana?—I think about how we are always creating centers, and always some of us remain on the margins. I would encounter similar problems in a different way in my dissertation: yes, writing about the fiction writers and even the testimonio and spoken word artists, who dealt with environmental justice, could fit—albeit nontraditionally, for Comparative Literature, but despite all the cultural studies theory, there was discomfort: wasn't I pushing it looking at actos, demonstrations, murals, and T-shirts that exposed environmental racism?

Anzaldúa's writing bears the mark of the Trojan Horse she drew/drew upon by defying such categories. When she was rejected for such unconventionality, she looked to opportunity, creating it when it did not exist, and subsequently her trans-discipline work would speak to a broader spectrum of global, interdisciplinary gente. In this vein of cross genre and discipline, she, more than many contemporary Chicano/Tejano scholars may bear resemblance to, and the legacy of, the respected grandfather of Chicano/Tejano Literature, Américo Paredes.

Not long after I saw the cover of *Borderlands*, Gloria would come visit UT, Austin, and she would draw Trojan Horses on the black board, and talk of peaceable, creative interventions, so that I positioned her theory as part of the great Satyagraha artistry that is a primary legacy in the poetics of women in India as wall as the Chicanas promoting environmental justice; given my family legacy, I resonated with her words. As Gloria writes of the Trojan horse, years later, she states "The symbol is to see the university as this walled city, and somebody brings in the Trojan Horse, the Trojan *Burra*, into the city gates. At night the belly of the *burra* opens, and out comes the 'other' trying to make changes from inside. And I have a visual for that.... There's your Trojan *Burra*" (Lunsford, 13). She would talk about having been in the very UT graduate program I was in. Hearing her talk would foster my doubts about where I was studying, but it also gave precedence to work on the margins: the dissertation would focus on the literary examples of environmental justice writing, but I would make a case for receiving Chicana and South Asian environmental justice discourse and activism poetics as ecofeminism.

I share these personal memories to get at what lies within them, between the words: thirty years of an uneasy artistic kinship, of hearing palabras, insights, theory, voiced and re-voiced, of hearing others say what they believe Gloria meant, of transformations in who and where I am, who my communities are and what I am doing in them, of how I am trying to represent them honestly and usefully in words, of how I represent other women, am vigilant of repercussions, of how I represent myself as other, even to myself. In a way, this viajc is a trip back to that day on the beach with book & bridge in hand. It is my retorno, my seventh cycle. Having lived just over 52 years, I am on the cusp of a new cycle, as is the earth in its 2012 return. As when I had just graduated from college, I am jobless, but my time and mind and body are overbooked. I am multi-tasking ad infinitum, returning to *Bridge,* while unbeknownst to me, my smile at a cop who is arresting me is broadcast on national TV, or now, perhaps, tweeted, globally. Sometimes, as Gloria knew well, the "bridges" we build, lie between our multiple selves.

Y UN CHOQUE

> Like all people, we perceive the version of reality that our culture communicates. Like others having or living in more than one culture, we get multiple, often opposing messages. The coming together of two self-consistent but habitually incomparable frames of reference causes un choque, a cultural collision. (Gloria Anzaldúa, *Borderlands/ La Frontera: The New Mestiza*)

In 1992, as a Comparative Literature doctoral student wanting my dissertation to make both a scholarly contribution to social and environmental justice activism and community-informed contributions to the academic fields I inhabited, I began a study of cultural discourse promoting environmental justice from Chicanas and South Asian Women. After what I might—with generous optimism—call "un choque," my committee was reconstituted, my dissertation was refocused on literary work, and I produced *Women Write Environmental Justice: The Literary Tradition in India and Greater Mexico.* I was also still writing (and publishing) on the broader aspects of activism poetics. Subsequently, I expanded that study into *Environmental Justice Poetics: Cultural Representations of Environmental Racism from Chicanas and Women in India,* an interdisciplinary study of broader cultural poesis—novels to political tracts, poetry to wall art, blogs to brochures, philosophy to film—inspired and created by women and a few men who see the necessity of ***envisioning*** a future of global and local environmental wellbeing, and ***indicting*** harm that disenfranchises human communities with inequitable suffering born of environmental destruction, and of ***naming*** the detrimental effects of what Gloria Anzaldúa would later write of as the shadow side.

In a chapter that began as a *Frontiers* article on the Mothers of East Los Angeles I wrote:

> Gloria Anzaldúa's concept of being a bridge, which evokes connections initiated by members of a historically disempowered community with members of a dominant group as a means of dismantling domination, is activated in the interstices between community and corporation by the Mothers of East LA. ("Chicana Strategies for Success and Survival" 63)

I think of this now as I ruminate on how necessary climate justice transformations are ever going to make it through a society with corporate control written large on almost every bill legislators pass—should it serve them politically—or pass up or, should it benefit people and planet, but not short term, corporate profit maximization; surely such stymied ends are shadowed. Vandana Shiva, who contributes majorly to the South Asian component of my research, is one of the most prolific writers on environmental justice matters, particularly biopiracy and seed patenting, what she names "Columbus' second coming"; yet I've chosen a quote from her that speaks to activistas, in particular, but allows all of us to put things into perspective: "You are not Atlas carrying the world on your shoulder. It is good to remember that the planet is carrying you" (2009). We, as nepantleras—artists, academics, activistas, all of the above and more—bridge interstices that sometimes cover vast chasms of power differentials, and our work interconnects to promote local and planetary survival, if not well-being, and yet we work within a planetary system that magnifies the significance of our acts.

JUSTICIA AMBIENTAL Y POÉTICA

By moving from a militarized zone to a roundtable, nepantleras acknowledge an unmapped common ground: the humanity of the other. It works with las nepantleras, boundary-crossers, thresholders who initiate others in rites of passage, activistas who, from a listening, receptive, spiritual stance, rise to their own visions and shift into acting them out, hacienda mundo nuevo (introducing change) (*this bridge we call home* 570).

"Transformation," as Gloria Anzaldúa conceives it, must look both inward and outward, into the 99%, as well as the 1%... to use Occupy Movement terminology, into our selves and our communities, as well as outwardly, global. This holistic, interdisciplinary theoretical approach lends itself to elucidating ecological and social justice discourse: Anzaldúa's call, "now let us shift," offered in the final chapter of *this bridge we call home* is a template that could move us toward "healing the planet." Hence, Gloria Anzaldúa's "body of discourse" is the first bibliographic entry for my project proposal *"The Logic of Poetry, the Poetry of Ecology and the Ecology of Justice: Cultural Poetics of Environmental Justice and Paradigms for Ecological, Cultural & Economic Transformations in An Age of Global Warming"* a work-in-progress, incorporating the two decades of trans-disciplinary scholarship on women's cultural poetics of environmental justice described above, into a conversation on climate justice. In this work, women's texts provide a reading lens to examine a broad spectrum of current, environmental, and social "sustainability" discourse, to chart directions, to each move from where we stand.

Whether in writing or literature classes, we read and write about place and the subject positions of all stakeholders are examined through critical engagement in order to get a better sense of both the issue and the process that violates the communities' environmental well-being. Anzaldúa's theories contribute regional historicizing, and perception of subject position in conjunction with social and environmental matters such as environmental racism. Her stress on art as methodology by which to repair the world gives creative writing students further dimensions through which to engage their creative work.

In the introductory creative writing classes, we read books that are often not consciously nature writing—they may rub shoulders with nature, or it may aggravate their wounds, but our reading itself reinserts and examines the relationship between humans and the rest of the earth that sustains us. This critical work in environmental justice studies goes beyond most eco-criticism, uniting environmental justice with tenets of feminism and critical race theories; it goes beyond many creative writing courses in that it involves students in the creative and the critical, combined, examining writers' relationships with ecological justice and writing our own.

In Rhetoric and Composition, my writing students and I use the seventeen Principles of Environmental Justice adopted by the First National People of Color Environmental Leadership Summit in 1991, which have become mainstays in environmental justice organizing, in order to define environmental justice and even environmental issues;[16] these Principles are broad definitions that expand the physical definition of environmental beyond wilderness to where we work and play. They also expand the figurative definition of environmental. Students study, then identify and write about struggles for environmental justice including aspects of climate change in—or as they relate to—the borderlands where they live, using the Principles of Environmental Justice to define their issues as environmental justice concerns; they examine regional issues as environmental racism and injustice; these include the long-lasting, toxic shadows of a pesticide plant in Mission, TX, the negative environmental impacts of communities invaded by disruptive fossil fuel extraction,[17] of the effects of pesticide exposure, waste dumps, and other polluting entities on children's health and well-being, and the many detrimental implications of the border wall, and accompanying waivers.[18] We do get the sense, sometimes, that we are studying a peace-loving army of Atlases—women holding the world—both up and together—though our study of climate change alerted any who did not know, that the planet ultimately does hold us, and the fate of planet and humankind are intertwined. During my tenure at UTPA, the sense of the fuerza of activistas, who feel the responsibility of our mutual wellbeing with el mundo, was clear and articulate from Indigenous women on the border who make up the Lipan Apache Women Defense. In conjunction with the wall issues, the classes were presented with readings and web presence from Dr. Margo Tamez and her mother Dr. Eloisa Tamez, who protested through activism and the courts when their family land was seized for building the wall; they formed the Lipan Apache Women Defense and have built up the struggle against militarism and abuse of the well-being of Indigenous border communities to this day.[19] A hopeful emailed press release in March reported, "The U.N. Committee on the Elimination of Racial Discrimination (CERD), Early Warning and Urgent Action Procedures" has expressed "concern regarding the potentially discriminatory impact that the construction of a border wall might have on the Kikapoo, Ysleta del Sur Pueblo and Lipan Apache indigenous communities." However, this was followed by end of April, 2013 press release reporting

> While the U.S. forcibly took Indigenous and other vulnerable peoples' lands for the first round of border wall construction in 2009, it did not have the authority to dispossess Eloisa Garcia Tamez of her subsurface property rights, and the state aggression continues against an Indigenous property owner with deep ancestral ties to that land and what lies beneath.[20]

The introduction of this paper suggested that adulation must not overlook the necessity to address the issues that hold our community members down, from full expression of their identity, full rights and well-being, to environmental health and land rights, and that this applies vehemently in the RGV. Indigenous communities there, who retain their kinship and responsibilities toward the lands that their families have lived upon for centuries despite having their cultural identities and legacies removed by the state, deserve our vigilance, solidarity and respect. As Gloria wrote:

This land was Mexican once
was Indian always
and is.
And will be again.

(El Retorno 155)

CONCLUSIONS: FINAL THOUGHTS ABOUT GOING GLOBAL WITH GLORIA

This essay provides background to my larger project using environmental justice expression as a frame for ecologically, socially, and economically sustainable solutions that increase human rights, equity, and environmental well being on our small planet. It also points toward a nexus between cultural poetics promoting a wide range of environmental justice matters and Anzaldúan theory. Further, Anzaldúa's synthesis of non-violence, earth, and people justice joins those on the margins of dominant thought from both within and outside of intellectual traditions—those involved in nonviolent direct action (NVDA), what Bayard Rustin's pledge called "social peace," what Gandhi, evoking peace through social justice tradition, called Satyagraha. How do we sow influence back and forth across hemispheres? This trans-cultural/trans-hemispheric force has been present in political prisoner poetics and in Civil (Human) Rights and Independence Movements' discourse in the mid twentieth century, and in environmental justice movements throughout the world and it charts a path between historical resistance thought and the Arab (African) Spring (and beyond) and Los Indignados and Occupy/Decolonize/Wall Street-and-beyond Autumn movements begun in September, 2011. Anzaldúa's work has achieved a global status in some realms, but issues of planetary environmental/climate change require even further spread of discussion and action.

This trans-hemispheric work is particularly salient at Gloria's alma mater in the borderlands between worlds—as long as UTPA exists—and in El Valle communities far into nuestro futuro: similar to the solidarity work supporting those whose presence and education is under attack in Arizona, in El Valle, and in other parts of the world, those involved in cultural/artistic resistance to violence wrought on earth and all our relatives, both historically and currently, may provide perspective, unity, wisdom and educational resources to new struggles for climate justice, from ambos lados, no, from all sides, in the borderlands and beyond.

After 9-11, Gloria E. Anzaldúa predicted with typical acumen, "What we do now counts even more than the frightening event, close call, shock, violation, or loss that made cracks in our worlds.... May we do work that matters" (*One Wound* 27). She was prophetic in her sense that "what we do next" could be far more devastating than what had just happened, that the paralyzing shock and calm of most of the nation during the days when planes did not fly was only the eye of the storm. Only if we all attempt to be bridges across the shadow site chasms will we—as a myriad of communities—rise above the many forms of troubled waters of our time.

ENDNOTES

1 The number of unauthorized students was over 400 during my teaching stint at UTPA. The following paraphrases of student's comments suggest the fluidity of the border geography:

"My mother crossed the border to Mexico to give birth to me where she had reliable health care, hence I am a Dreamer."

"My cousins had come up and I was staying at my parents' home, but had a doctor's appointment, so we combined the trip with shopping after which I was tired and wanted to postpone the doctor's visit, but my mother convinced me we'd crossed already: when we got to the doctor's office, I was already dilated and the baby came within a couple hours! We'd have never gotten across the bridge...(from a student living in the U.S., with parents in México, who gave birth over Christmas break–she planned to give birth in the U.S. because it would be "so much easier for the child")

2 During time, most notably, President Bambina Cárdenas resigned following mean-spirited, truth-less attacks.

3 What was experienced was a culture of racism against people with darker skin color and African American cultural appearance. For a useful discussion of related issues and contemporary implications, see: Bim Adewenmi's article at http://www.guardian.co.uk/world/2011/oct/04/racism-skin-colour-shades-prejudice.

4 Intelligence Community Center for Academic Excellence, ICCAE program, is a federal grant program, which brought the CIA and other intelligence organizations into our classrooms. For my assessment of this program in 2008, see "Latino/a Students and Covert 'Securities': The Integration of Academic and Intelligence Communities" in VIVENCIAS: Reports from the field *Latino Studies* 6, (2008): 456-465.

5 While I could not name all of the UTPA community involved in educating about the famous alumna, two women from the broader community deserve recognition for their early and extensive work in promoting knowledge of Gloria's work, both on and off campus: in their celebration of her contributions from and to El Valle, Priscilla Celina Suarez and Noemi Martínez created just the kind of work Gloria advocates. I observed students gaze in awe at the altar they dedicated to her, hosted in a library showcase by Virginia Gause, at a time when only a handful of faculty were aware of her significance.

6 *Ocean Power: Poems from the Desert*, Ofelia Zepeda is a powerful example. Here is a little about the author: http://www.poetryfoundation.org/poem/239018.

7 IGKNU, UTPA's renaming of its Intelligence Community Center for Academic Excellence, ICCAE program.

8 A salient explanation of the School of the Americas comes from a work of fiction: Ana Castillo's character, Miguel, in *The Guardians*:

> It was a U.S. Army center located at Fort Benning in Columbus, Georgia, that trained more than sixty thousand soldiers and police, mostly from Latin America, in counterinsurgency and combat-related skills since 1946. Its graduates became experts in torture, murder, and political repression. Since the word got out on what the School of the Americas was really up to, in 2001 the school officially changed its name to the Western Hemisphere Institute for Security Cooperation. After 9/11 the government felt it could justifiably come out of its covert-training closet. (32)

9 I can see that Trojan *burra* already unloading in front of library now named after its foremost alumna, and now and I see the UTPA bronze bronco whinny a *bienvenidos*—yes, Gloria's influence shows up where we least expect.

10 When I was terminated, I was told it was for "student welfare"; I was not allowed to examine the offending evaluations, but could see them on the desk–the range spanned from 1 to 7—the entire spectrum of possible student response. I did not have to wonder which student's "welfare" were taken into consideration: The day the division's early evaluations had been conducted a student had come to my office hours, yelling so loudly that a colleague across the hall came to ask if he should call Security. Not wanting to escalate conflict, I declined his offer. The older white male student, retired from the military, wanted to see a military format in the classroom. I later learned that when I did not agree to comply with his demands in how my class was run, the student complained about me to the chair who, in terminating my classes for the following semester was only adding to a list of casualties that appears to continue to this day; I am in good company for highly accomplished teachers/scholars (many women of color) have had their work diminished or have been lost to this shadow side.

There were over 100 students in my auditorium classroom, but an ethnically-mixed group of mostly women consistently sat near the front, fully engaged, in range to make eye-contact with me and guest speakers. A few years later, I ran into one of these women who happily recognized me and asked if I was still teaching women's studies—she had referred friends to my classes, but they'd not found me listed. In that bittersweet moment—too short for me to speak a clear answer—all I could think was "what about her welfare?": I knew that like many of the women writing in *Hacienda Caras*, our welfare was in the shadows.

The termination continues to haunt me. With the rise of internet employment applications, the stock question has begun to arise: have you ever been terminated from a teaching position? Technically, I could probably get by with answering "no,"—I was not terminated from the course I was teaching, but, in effect, from further teaching in the social science portion of the division from that day forward—however, contingent labor cannot count on classes in subsequent semesters, anyhow. Yesterday, while filling out the form for a school where I have sought a position for years, I felt empowered by writing this article and left the question blank. My negation would protect me from the shadow side, but would do nothing to remove it. Were I questioned, I would speak my truth.

11 Originally a part of *Borderlands*, I used the reprint in *What Wilderness is this: Women Write about the Southwest in University Readers* (UR), I prepared for my classes. It was the single essay included in every UR I prepared while at UTPA; these included rhetoric and composition, literature, and creative writing courses.

12 See *Awkesasne Notes* (http://www.ratical.org/AkwesasneNs.html).

13 Texts by Barbara Harlow, Ramón Saldívar and José E. Limón, respectively; see details in Works Cited.

14 See http://av.vimeo.com/96375/880/26926857.mp4?token=1367941848_50d51d38e3c d4cbcd536b314738f43ddhttp://www.varelafilm.org/?page_id=84 among much web presence and many books.

15 See http://www.poder-texas.org/.

16 "The Principles..." from www.ejnet.org Delegates to the First National People of Color Environmental Leadership Summit held on October 24-27, 1991, in Washington DC, drafted and adopted 17 principles of Environmental Justice. Since then, The Principles have served as a defining document for the growing grassroots movement for environmental justice. This rendition of The Principles can be found at: www.ejnet.org. Five of the principles are listed below; other principles recognize "a special legal and natural relationship of Native Peoples;" oppose military occupation; call for education emphasizing "social and environmental issues;" and require that we consume and waste little, re-prioritizing "our lifestyles to ensure the health of the natural world for present and future generations."

1) affirms the sacredness of Mother Earth, ecological unity and the interdependence of all species, and the right to be free from ecological destruction.

3) mandates the right to ethical, balanced and responsible uses of land and renewable resources in the interest of a sustainable planet for humans and other living things.

6) demands the cessation of the production of all toxins, hazardous wastes, and radioactive materials, and that all past and current producers be held strictly accountable to the people for detoxification and the containment at the point of production.

8) affirms the right of all workers to a safe and healthy work environment without being forced to choose between an unsafe livelihood and unemployment. It also affirms the right of those who work at home to be free from environmental hazards.

10) considers governmental acts of environmental injustice a violation of international law, the Universal Declaration On Human Rights, and the United Nations Convention on Genocide.

17 One of the most significant of student studies, delivered to NACCS Foco in 2007, involved the community's response to the effects of what must have been "fracking" or hydraulic fracturing and/or horizontal drilling in the colonia where the student lived. This is early evidence of the injustice and ecological and infrastructural hazards of a globally significant environmental matter in South Texas: extraction of the Eagle Ford Shale oil fields; promoted as economical boom, it is having deleterious impacts on water, community/ human health and infrastructure, ecological habitats, and green house gas emissions and resulting climate change. Many of these effects were predictable from the small scale effects reported from my student's community.

18 The waiving of 36 Acts, particularly environmental (NEPA, Clean Water and Air, Native American religious freedom…) is one of the least known aspects of the border wall building. See http://dhswaivers.blogspot.com/for a blog that began to investigate the significance.

19 See the website that Margo created in conjunction with her work at Washington State University: https://mysite.wsu.edu/personal/mtamez/calaboz/default.aspx; her dissertation and several articles are on line as models of Indigenous resistance supported by academic work that stems from respect for the work of community elders. See also Lipan Apache Women Defense sites.

20 Even as this article's final draft is being polished, emails come in that Eloisa Tamez may have more land, and rights taken from her: "The U.S. Department of Justice and U.S. Department of Homeland Security will attempt to dispossess Tamez of her cultural, spiritual, economic, and social ownership of property in the subsurface–beneath the border wall" according to a Press Release, April 26, 2013. An April 30 Press Release explains further:

A statement issued by Daniel Romero, General Council Chairman for the Lipan Apache Band of Texas (Ndé) says, "We ask that the Obama Administration and Congress to incorporate [the United Nations] the CERD's demands for proper consultation and consideration of the Indigenous peoples and communities of the borderlands region. We request that the U.S. Government be inclusive of Ndés' ['Lipan Apache peoples'] request in current immigration reform and our proposal of the border lands policies that have negatively influenced the Ndé way of life."

WORKS CITED

Anzalúa, Gloria E. "Let us be the healing of the wound: The Coyolxauhqui Imperative" in *One Wound for Another/Una Herida Por Otra:Testimonios de Latin@s in the U.S. through Cyberspace (11 de septiembre de 2001-11 de marzo de 2002*, Claire Joysmith and Clara Lomas, eds., Mexico D.F.: Universidad Nacional Autónoma de México, 2005. 92-103. Print.

---. "El Retorno." *What Wilderness is this: Women Write about the Southwest.* Susan Wittig Albert and Susan Hanson, Austin: Univ. of Texas Press, 2007.153-155. Print.

---. Ed. *Making Face, Making Soul Hacienda Caras: Creative and Critical Perspectives by Women of Color.* San Francisco: Aunt Lute Books. 1990. Print.

---. *this bridge we call home: radical visions for transformation.* Gloria E. Anzaldúa and Analouise Keating, Eds. NY, NY: Routledge. 2002. Print.

---. *Borderlands/La Frontera: The New Mestiza.* San Francisco: Spinsters/ Aunt Lute. 1987.

Castillo, Ana. *The Guardians.* New York: Random House Publishing Group, 2007. Print.

Diaz, Tony. "The Gloria Anzaldúa Under Ground Library" *Huffington Post,* The Blog, 2-20-13.

Harlow, Barbara. *Resistance Literature.* New York: Metheum Press, 1987. Print.

Limón, José E. *Dancing With the Devil: Society and Cultural Poetics in Mexican-American South Texas* (New Directions in Anthropological Writings). Madison: University of Wisconsin Press, 1994. Print.

Lunsford, Andrea A. "Toward a Mestiza Rhetoric: Gloria Anzaldúa on Composition and Post-coloniality." *JAC* Vol. 18, No. 1, *Special Issue: Exploring Borderlands: Postcolonial and Composition Studies.* 1998: 1-27. Print.

Mendoza, Louis. *Historia: The Literary Making of Chicana & Chicano History.* College Station: Texas A &M University Press, 2001. Print.

Moraga, Cherríe & Gloria Anzaldúa. *This Bridge Called My Back: Writings by Radical Women of Color.* New York: Kitchen Table Press, 1981. Print.

Pineda, Cecile. *Devil's Tango: How I Learned the Fukushima Step by Step.* San Antonio: Wings Press, 2012. Print.

Platt, Kamala. "*The Logic of Poetry, the Poetry of Ecology and the Ecology of Justice: Cultural Poetics of Environmental Justice and Paradigms for Ecological, Cultural & Economic Transformations in An Age of Global Warming.*" Unpublished manuscript. 2010-12.

---. *(Rock) Off Nuclear: Cradle to Burial Urn I,* June 2012, installed at Bihl Haus for Glow: The Nuclear Show. David Zamora Caseras, curator, June 15, 2012. San Antonio, TX.

---. Environmental Health Grant (SALUD) Proposal, submitted to NIEHS, with The Esperanza Center, October 2003.

---. "Chicana Strategies for Success and Survival: Cultural Poetics of Environmental Justice from the Mothers of East Los Angeles." *Frontiers: A Journal of Women Studies*. Volume xviii, Number 2 1997. 48-72. Print.

Saldivar, Ramón. *Chicano Narrative: The Dialectics of Difference*. Madison: University of Wisconsin Press, 1990. Print.

Shiva, Vandana. The Green Interview, Thimpu, Bhutan, December, 2009. Web. http://www.thegreeninterview.com/t/aznobycthq/VandanaShivaTranscript.pdf

ANZALDÚAN THEORY AND PHILOSOPHY ACROSS TIME, SPACE, AND THE ACADEMY

ANZALDÚAN TEXTUALITIES: A HERMENEUTIC OF THE SELF AND THE COYOLXAUHQUI IMPERATIVE

NORMA ALARCÓN

If I had the words for all of the images in my head, life would be much easier.
—stated by a young girl in my critical literacy workshop for middle school girls

INTRODUCTION

The following critical essay is a preliminary and provisional attempt to bring into relief what I think are the structures and theory of praxis in the work of Gloria Anzaldúa as it is currently given to us in the corpus of her published work.[1] Ironically, Anzaldúa does not appear to have mentioned the concept-metaphor[2] of decolonization for her life-long project to heal the inner wounds and the sociopolitical and economic wounds of colonization. In fact, however, I think that her project's *telos* was a quest for personal and political decolonization, a project that begins with processes entailed in a self-reconstruction of a damaged self due to trauma suffered. Chela Sandoval writes, "We had each tasted the shards of 'difference' until they had carved up our insides; now we were asking ourselves what shapes our healing would take" (*Making Face, Making Soul*, Anzaldúa xxvii). With few exceptions, such as the concept-metaphors of psyche, spirit, being, self, other, and consciousness, Anzaldúa deeply distrusts and often rejects epistemologies offered by white hegemonic Western forms of Reason. These forms, in fact, cannot help the speaking subject[3] of color make sense of her experience. In the process, Anzaldúa develops her own concept-metaphors by (largely) drawing on her readings of Jung and Jungian-style notions of the psyche-spirit, symbols, and shadow; the pre-Colombian legacy of cosmological and mythographic figures and terms; and her personal experience that is often narrated in a testimonial and anecdotal style in her early work, from *Bridge* to *Borderlands*. In my view, these texts provide a narrative praxis entwined with theory of praxis that become the initial ground for the later development of her thought. Further, these texts, combined with interviews of that period, are, in my estimation, continuously and diversely rethought and reinscribed in later work as she relentlessly pursues meanings for experiences both personal and political. For Anzaldúa, one's experiences must not be let go without inquiry as to their meanings.

At a minimum through this conjunctive assemblage that structures praxis and theory of praxis, Anzaldúa tries to transform the chaos of experiences into order—an order which, in effect, is constantly in peril of becoming once again an agonistic chaos as she depicts, for example, in La Facultad and The Coatlicue State (*Borderlands*, 38-39 & 41-51, respectively). As attentive readers of Anzaldúa's work in print know, her writings are a cornucopia of possibilities for lines of inquiry, as such what I do in this essay represents what I believe to be one important "line." Thus, Anzaldúa's philosophical grounding in the inner and outer experiences of the self remains to be explored further. In brief, Anzaldúa draws from a variety of systems of knowledge to achieve her own "system," to achieve what she projected for herself in El Mundo Zurdo section of "La Prieta" (*Bridge*) and in *Borderlands*, where she states that she wants

> the freedom to carve and chisel my own face, to staunch the bleeding with ashes, to fashion my own gods out of my entrails. And if going home is denied me then I will have to stand and claim my own space, making a new culture—*una cultura mestiza*—with my own lumber, my own bricks and mortar and my own feminist architecture. (44)

Indeed, she did.

THEORY-IN-THE-FLESH

The invocation for "theory-in-the-flesh" put forth by Cherríe Moraga was one that referred to the contributors of the section "Entering the Lives of Others: Theory in the Flesh" in *This Bridge Called My Back* (21-23). It also prompted readers to explore their personal and political structures of experience. For many, it was an understanding that it was these very personal and political structures of experience, memory and history that conditioned an outsidedness rooted in the violence of slavery and colonization within the Anglo-American nation-state, though not limited to it. Hence, for example, Audre Lorde's title for her collection of essays, *Sister Outsider* (1984), has been virtually as foundational to a queer and feminist women-of-color consciousness as *Bridge* has been.

The interpellation to do "theory-in-the-flesh" was responded to by many who understood and knew that their work was being carried out on the outer margins of the socioeconomic, political, and academic weave. Laboring from the outer margins of a highly stratified society, these women-of-color understood that if their work was heard at all, it was in sound bytes that dehistoricized and dematerialized their work, thereby silencing it—with a few exceptions. However, many queer and feminist women-of-color in general heard what they had to say between and amongst each other, as Chela Sandoval analyzes in her work, *Methodology of the Oppressed,* and reiterates in her more recent essay, "AfterBridge: Technologies of Crossing," (21-26) in *This Bridge We Call Home* (2002), Anzaldúa's last edited book with AnaLouise Keating.

At the 2010 meeting of the Society for the Study of Gloria Anzaldúa, for example, Laura E. Pérez commented that *Borderlands* "was an invitation into the deeper recesses of the margins," which at the time she could not bear (*El Mundo Zurdo 2:* 13). However, a few years later she had embraced the book and was claiming that Anzaldúa "presents us with a new philosophical framework outside of Western binary thought" (*El Mundo Zurdo 2*:14). It is a claim that I think first returns us to that invitation to delve "into the deeper recesses of the margins" which in Anzaldúa's work are structured by a confrontation with her internalized otherness, the source of her trauma and wound.[4]

CONFRONTING INTERNALIZED OTHERNESS

For Anzaldúa, "theory-in-the-flesh" emerges from her confrontation with her trauma and wound that has also generated what she names a Shadow Beast, that is, the negativity within the self that threatens her quest for self-integration, healing and wholeness every step of the way. Eventually, as I will discuss, that quest is mediated by the concept-metaphors of Coatlicue, Nepantla, and Coyolxauhqui and the practice of making and unmaking and remaking as a lived necessity. In an early interview (1983) with Christine Weiland, Anzaldúa gives us a glimpse of a theoretical view of the praxis towards self-transformation and self-reintegration that she subsequently details in The Coatlicue State in *Borderlands*. It entails a confrontation with the negative and violent otherness of self in its interiority—"You make the inner changes first, and then you make the other changes...Sometimes you can do both at the same time: work to create outer change, through political movement, at the same time that you're trying to do meditation and developing yourself" (101). For Anzaldúa, confronting the internalized otherness opens the possibility of self-transformation, as it can become a transition from wallowing in a state of victimhood by diminishing the internalized self-contempt. However, that confrontation may have to be repeated as internalized otherness, is not easily swept away completely, if ever.

Western philosophy can be said to "begin" and end with the question of the Other[5]. Anzaldúa's psychic, spiritual, political and intellectual journey, however, starts with inquiries into her own otherness within that compels her to pierce the "mystery of the self" and to explore "the center of the self" (*Bridge* 169). In effect, there is a double alienation at work—the one that alienates her from a desired integral interiority of self and the alienation and exile from society and the world. In the healing work for the interiority of self, Anzaldúa recognizes her double alienation. She says:

> I feel a great isolation and separateness and *differentness* from everyone, even though I have many allies. Yet as soon as I have these thoughts—that I'm in this alone, that I have to stand on the ground of my own being, that I have to create my own separate space—the exact opposite thoughts come to me: that we are all in this together, juntas, that the ground of our being is a common ground, la Tierra. ("Bridge, Drawbridge, Sandbar, or Island"141)

To assuage that loneliness she has to both create and imagine a community for herself.

What are the sources of that doubled alienation and that sense of living in exile, which are the product of the traumatic wound? They are multiple—as a colonized-raced-daughter, as a colonized-raced-student, as a colonized-raced-woman, as queer and poor in short, as a social being in the world where her very interiority and exteriority of self is other. Also, she is the other of multiple communities and least the other in a "community of women of color writers" (*Bridge* 171). Though this may provide solace, it does not eradicate the otherness experienced within—inside herself. That internalized multiple sense of otherness is agonistic and a result of damage, injury, and woundedness arising from her own structures of experience, many of which are narrativized in her writings. However, she believes that through writing she will achieve the expulsion of that other within her (the Shadow Beast) by putting into praxis and theory of praxis the overarching Coyolxauhqui "method," which she subsequently transforms into "the Coyolxauhqui imperative"—the vision of reaching out, of being all in this together. Thus to Spivak's question "Can the Subaltern Speak?" Anzaldúa juxtaposes "Can the Subaltern Write?" She gives an affirmative answer to both questions, and urges women to speak and write in "Speaking in Tongues: A Letter to 3rd World Women Writers" (*Bridge* 165-173).

She wills herself to write, "Because the world I create in the writing compensates for what the real world doesn't give me" (*Bridge* 169). In fact, the real world produces in her the experience of inner-otherness-in-the-flesh which threatens to overwhelm and devour her, as depicted in The Coatlicue State. In brief, I think that her project is to decolonize herself and reach out to others to do the same through both speaking and writing—to exorcize otherness by transcoding it into language. She insists, "And as we internalized this exile we came to see the alien within us and too often as a result, we split away from ourselves and each other" (*Bridge*, 169). Speaking and writing are the tools for piercing that mystery...it is the quest for an integral self, for the center of the self, which we women-of-color have to think as 'other...' " (*Bridge*, 169). It is a process of self-disalienation. In order to get rid of that otherness, we must confront it and revolt. Her project for excavating and disclosing this otherness diverges quite a bit from that of Simone de Beauvoir in *The Second Sex* by focusing on the resultant inner structures of experience first, which are not those of a white bourgeois privileged woman. In fact, de Beauvoir's theorization of being Other is one of white women in relation to a European white heteropatriarchy.

Though Anzaldúa succeeds in writing and speaking "about life on the borders, life in the shadows" (*Borderlands* preface), she puts in question towards the end of her life her success in having dissolved the Western body/mind/spirit split, which was one of her goals, and states, "Though your body is still la otra and though pensamientos dualisticos still keep you from embracing and writing corporally con esa otra, you dream of the possibility of wholeness." ("now let us shift..." 563). The structured inner and outer experience of otherness must be confronted and dissolved through acts of decolonization over and over again through the positional locations she elaborates for this confrontational act—largely The Coatlicue State, Nepantla, and the Coyolxauhqui method and imperative. Nepantla is an "in-between" space through which a "third critical space" is seized and pivoted to encompass diverse situations and worlds. It is an interstitial space, a space in-between multiple social worlds. Caught between multiple sociopolitical and cultural worlds, the interfaces of lifeworlds are a consistent current and undercurrent in Anzaldúa's development and hermeneutic of the self. Though initially Nepantla is a "liminal state between worlds, between realities, between systems of knowledge, between symbology" ("Toward a Mestiza Rhetoric" 268), thus elaborating the praxis of self-healing by creating an "in-between" space that facilitates self-transformation (*Entrevistas* 5), the concept-metaphor of Nepantla is also reframed for her vision of public acts by Nepantleras, a correlative concept-metaphor coined by Anzaldúa.

BETWEEN CHAOS AND ORDER/BETWEEN IMAGINAL CONSCIOUSNESS AND REASONING CONSCIOUSNESS

It is not inaccurate to say that Anzaldúa waged a life-long battle to dissolve the Western Cartesian split of body-mind-spirit.[6] She did so by first focusing on her own embodied life formation and situation. Very distrustful of the western academy's alienating forms of reason, she says, "Something has to emerge out of the chaos and raw material of your life" ("Putting Coyoxauhqui Together" 259). This is a major reason for her call to "de-academize" theory and construct theories of our own, a decolonial project to say the least (*Making Face, Making Soul* xxvi).

Though she starts her devotion to writing the colonized body, calling it "autohistoria," it is also clear that she was evolving an "automythography," which, entwined in process, would eventually yield a visionary philosophy of the personal and the political. In *Borderlands*, she declares, "I write the myths in me, the myths I am, the myths I want to become" (93). Fifteen years later in "now let us shift...the path of conocimiento...inner work, public acts," she tells us, "As a modern-day Coyolxauhqui, you search for an account that encapsulates your life, and finding no ready-made story, you trust her light in the darkness to help you bring forth (from the remnants of the old personal/collective autohistoria), a new personal myth" (559-560). Through the 80s and 90s, Anzaldúa continued pivoting Coyolxauhqui's meanings for her and the centrality of this concept-metaphor in her work. From the position of an in-between Nepantla consciousness, Coyolxauhqui is a theory and praxis and theory of praxis encompassed by compostura and descompostura, which is subject to revision as an ultimate compostura proves elusive. That is, it may have to be performed over and over again (6).

Though many of her early writings tend to emphasize testimonio and autohistoria, by the time she publishes *Borderlands* the entwinement with an automythography begins in earnest. They are, in effect, assembled and interwoven currents that feed each other—autohistoria and automythography. One could also say that an automythography envisioned earlier by Anzaldúa reaches an elaborated vision that culminates in the three essays I will be discussing. However, a sample of an earlier vision is thematized in the section of "La Prieta" (*Bridge*) called "El Mundo Zurdo (The Left-Handed World)," where she states:

> I believe that by changing ourselves we change the world, that travelling El Mundo Zurdo path is the path of a two-way movement—a going deep into the self and an expanding out into the world, a simultaneous recreation of the self and a reconstruction of society. And yet I am confused as to how to accomplish this...I build my own universe, El Mundo Zurdo. (232-233)

By the time she publishes the last essay completed in her lifetime ("Let us be the healing of the wound: The Coyolxauqui imperative—la sombra y el sueno"), the confusion has been dispelled and she has built her own universe, which she continually offers to her listeners and readers. That universe entwines autohistoria and automythography, and she resolves the confusion for herself in a visionary political philosophy drawn from praxis and theory of praxis. One could also say it is drawn from experience and theory of experience, which she depicts and analyzes as a speaking subject in a process of reconstructing the self and its constructed heterogeneity.

In her essay, "Putting Coyolxauhqui Together: A Creative Process," Anzaldúa appears to have for the first time pulled the "bones" together which she articulates into a skeletal architecture, thereby providing an epistemologic/automythographic structure for her creative process which she had already rehearsed in "Tlilli, Tlapalli: The Path of the Red and Black Ink" (*Borderlands* 65-75). Through that structure she depicts and details her embodied internal struggle to pull the "bones" together. It is an agonizing effort to produce any piece of the embodied writing she desires in the finished product given the interruptive force of the chaotic emotions undergone in the process of weaving writing itself. In her eyes, these products of writing are always flawed in the face of the ideal perfection she seeks and which blocks her repeatedly in the effort to write. As readers we can empathize with the arduous processes undertaken and in fact come to understand why so much written material remained either in her computer or files, now relegated to the Anzaldúa Archives, which I am sure many will consult in years to come.

In this essay, she gathers the "bones" for structuring the skeletal articulation, which are represented by the concept-metaphors of La Llorona, la naguala, el cenote, nepantla, the shadow [elsewhere noted as Shadow Beast], and Coyolxauhqui, who has the healing powers of a shaman. These guide her in the fleshing out of the text as well as herself. Though she does not mention Coatlicue by name, she addresses brooding depressions for which Coatlicue is the salient figure and at times a metonym of La Llorona. With the exception of the Shadow Beast, all of these concept-metaphors, figures and symbols have been appropriated from the pre-Colombian indigenous mythographic narrative tradition and legacy. However, Anzaldúa recodifies these for herself with the exception of La Llorona, who retains her salient post-conquest meanings, especially grief. She is still a woman who wails for the loss of her children and is condemned to a perpetual grief in her search for them. Anzaldúa says, "My symbol for la herida de colonialism and the trauma of Conquest is La Llorona" (*EntreMundos* 55).

For Anzaldúa, the call to write comes from La Llorona, "the dark mother... the ghost woman who wails the loss of her children." She is closely linked to la naguala, the virtual twin "musa bruja...that incites [her] to write...[and] will carry [her] through from beginning to end" ("Putting Coyolxauhqui Together" 242). The response to the call is motivated by the need to make sense and give meaning to the chaos and raw materials of her life which have been constituted by the founding wound and trauma of her personal experience as initially narrated in "La Prieta" and scattered throughout subsequent interviews and writings. It is important to note that in the creative process depicted in this essay, Coyolxauhqui in pieces is closely linked to La Llorona and la naguala. It is the call to put Coyolxauhqui together again and restore her to wholeness from the dismemberment and fragmentation she underwent at the hands of her brother, the God of War. From this point of view, Coyolxauhqui's disarticulated body is put in tension with the desire to reassemble her own body in pieces into a wholeness which will be represented by the final written product, from descompostura to compostura, and back again as required by situation. Through this internal tension, Anzaldúa maps her strenuous inner struggle to write her "entrails." That mapping entails a diving into El Cenote, the concept-metaphor or symbol for the inner recesses of the self, including the unconscious when possible and in a fully conscious way. The praxis of confronting the violent inner recesses of the self as depicted in The Coatlicue State have evolved into a theory of praxis for embodied writing which is now represented by El Cenote as the cavern for the imaginal—El Cenote, which in other texts Anzaldúa also refers to as the dark cave, marks the site of "the cavernous theater of dreams" (245), a state of awake-dreaming. El Cenote yields "visual, aural, or olfactory memory of some trivial incident [that] triggers a stream of images. Subliminal events in your body or sensations provoked by its organs appear and vanish like fleeting fish, leaving behind a flash of el cuerpo's knowledge" (245).

To begin the work of deciphering and organizing the "bones" and to capture the awake-dreaming stream of inner focused Nepantla consciousness, she invokes la naguala, who enables talking "about the work of embodying consciousness" (249) and capturing that stream in her "net of words" ("Putting Coyolxauhqui Together" 247). That is, she attends "to the imaginal with the goal of translating it on paper" (244) and catches it in her "net of words." La naguala, musa bruja, is, however, also linked to Nepantla, which in a relay play together begin to decipher and organize the contents of El Cenote, "a mental network of subterranean rivers of information that converge and well up to the surface" (244). In naguala space, her perception is "hyperempathic" and she becomes "shifting and fluid, the boundaries of self-identity blur…" This state alternates between "hyperempathy and excessive detachment, a seamless change from one to the other" (250).

Nepantla is invoked to create "a wider space in [her] mind…" ("Putting Coyolxauhqui Together" 252). The Nepantla liminal position assists Anzaldúa in fielding the confusion and disorder, as "[i]t enables switching from one perception channel to another" (252). Nepantla's wider scope allows her "to make connections, allowing the various scenarios to merge and come into focus." Nepantla is shaman-like. Its work "is a mysterious dreaming or perception which registers the workings of all states of consciousness...moves from rational to visionary states, from logics to poetics, from focused to unfocused perception, from inner to outer world. Nepantla is the twilight landscape between self and the world, between imagery of the imagination and the harsh light of reality" (252). Nepantla in this creative process operates "in the liminal spaces" (252), navigating the interstice between an overly ordered side and "bacchanalian chaos, always attempting to join the two in a seamless web" (252). "Nepantla averigua el conflicto. It provides associations and connective tissue...and interweaves multiple, superimposed strands of thought... The imaginal consciousness, the dreaming naguala, seizes the booty that El Cenote renders up and turns into sentient worlds, while Nepantla interlaces those worlds into a coherent whole" (252-253).

However, the achievement of "a coherent whole," the one that will be the reassembling of Coyolxauhqui, is not without obstacles. The naguala can shape shift into a virulent musa bruja who has the capacity to "rise up from the depths" and drag her "into the deep waters of the cave" (255). In that cave she becomes possessed by the Shadow Beast which she "can't deny, can't hide from the shadow side of writing" (255). She is in effect thrown into chaos, which throws her into depression, or the Coatlicue state. She feels that she must confront the dark cave and the Shadow Beast and admit that it's part of her. She posits that it is her own "irrationality" that catapults her into the Coatlicue state and fears that she may not "emerge with the message from the source," suspecting that her "irrationality" arises from a desconocimiento (ignorance or denial) of herself, which she has to confront. In brief, she will have "to accept the imperfections" (259) in the work, "accept its partial incoherences...like a person's life all art is a work in progress" (259). Thus she hopes that "[t]his Coyolxauhqui will emerge from the cave's cauldron" (259); that is, from El Cenote, which is both the source for creativity and the source that may envelop her in a chaos that she must process.

Throughout this creative process, Anzaldúa's high intensity self-questioning continually begs the question of whether she has succeeded in putting Coyolxauhqui together again from the depths of El Cenote, the dark cave. The cave, the cauldron, is always at play. Has Coyolxauhqui been reassembled without succumbing to white western modes of rationality which would disembody the work? Resisting the epistemological methodologies of white Western rationality, she wants to give coherence and order to the chaos on her own terms, constructing her own universe, her own concept-metaphors (epistemologies). She wants to capture the language of the awake-dreaming of the inner imaginal world into a "net of words" that does not mimic white western rationality. In this fashion, she moves from a first semiological plane of disorder to a second semiological order that is all her own construction.[7]

CONOCIMIENTO

In "now let us shift...the path of conocimiento...inner work, public acts," Anzaldúa reiterates and restages some of the key concept-metaphors mapped out in the depiction of the creative process as well as in *Borderlands*. These are aligned with the "path of conocimiento.... Conocimiento questions conventional knowledge's current categories, ossifications, and contents" (541). "Conocimiento comes from opening all your senses, consciously inhabiting your body and decoding its symptoms" (542). For Anzaldúa, conocimiento is an "overarching theory of consciousness, of how the mind works" (*Interviews*, 177). It is a concept-metaphor that she recodifies from the Spanish language's customary usages. It reflects

> an awareness, the awareness of facultad [as depicted in La Facultad in *Borderlands*] that sees through all human acts whether of the individual mind and spirit or the collective, social body. The work of conocimiento—consciousness work—connects the inner life of the mind and the spirit to the outer worlds of action. In the struggle for social change I call this particular aspect of conocimiento spiritual activism.[8] (*Interviews* 178)

Traumatic events such as an earthquake or an encounter have the power to throw her into chaos, "shattering the mythology that grounds [her]" ("now let us shift," 544), which had already been depicted and rehearsed in "La Facultad" in *Borderlands*. That is, the contingent narrative of the self that grants a precarious sense of wholeness is always liable to interruption and disruption. In fact, though unmentioned, La Facultad's irruption is the first stage-space of conocimiento[9]. This type of chaotic disruption catapults her into Nepantla. The shattering emerges from the outer world and in Nepantla, the second stage-space of conocimiento, she is situated in the liminal space "where the outer boundaries of the mind's inner life meet the outer world of reality, in a zone of possibility" (544). In restaging the concept-metaphors used for mapping the creative process, here Coatlicue represents "depths of despair, self-loathing and helplessness" which is the third stage-space of conocimiento. Earlier I referred to this as self-contempt, which encompasses the emotions listed here (545). Through some form of action (the fourth stage-space of conocimiento), she can work herself out of depression, and her "desire for order" (fifth stage-space of conocimiento) leads to restructuring the pieces together "to create a new narrative articulating [her] personal reality" (545). If you will, this will be administered by the Nepantla state of consciousness. Each "arrebatamiento"—that is, shock, susto, and trauma—reopens the wound. It constitutes a "loss of the familiar," which motivates the effort to reintegrate herself or put Coyolxauhqui together, which in this instance is herself. It instantiates the sixth stage-space of conocimiento. However, the resulting reintegration and reinscription in the Coyolxauhqui stage-space may fail as it is tested out in the world and may not "live up to your ideals... Disappointed with self and others, angry and then terrified at the depth of your anger, you swallow your emotions, hold them in, blocked from your own power, you are unable to activate the inner resources that could mobilize you." (545) The Shadow Beast and the Coatlicue State recur, bringing forth an embattlement with the unwanted aspects of the self, which can be paralyzing. These unwanted aspects of the self have, in effect, been constituted by that internalized otherness that may require repeated confrontation.

The seventh stage-space, after failure, can bring forth a new development in her self-narrativization/automythography. It is a critical turning point of transformation:

> you shift realities, develop an ethical, compassionate strategy with which to negotiate conflict and difference within self and between others, and find common ground by forming holistic alliances. You include these practices in your daily life, act on your vision—enacting spiritual activism. ("now let us shift" 545)

In fact, in the previous passage Anzaldúa is more fully narrativizing the transformation that is possible after each "fall" into the Coatlicue State (545). Throughout, she struggles with the shadow/Shadow Beast, that is, "the unwanted aspects of the self" (545). Simultaneously throughout, she maintains the liminal space of Nepantla, which does the liminal work that pivots the inner-outer consciousness. Thus each arrebatamiento is a "chance to reconstruct yourself" (547). She is bound to rewrite and re-interpret "the story you imagined yourself living in..." (547).

In this essay, the concept-metaphor of Nepantla receives a broader and larger characterization and definition than ever before in the Anzaldúan corpus. It is home, and it represents both transition and "site of transformation" (548). If earlier in "Putting Coyolxauhqui Together..." she had stated "nepantla averigua el conflicto," within, now it is the liminal space "where different perspectives come into conflict...[it] is the zone between changes where you struggle to find equilibrium between the outer expression of change and your inner relationship to it" (548-49). She realizes, however, that though "your head and heart decry the mind/body dichotomy, the conflict in your mind makes your body a battlefield where beliefs fight each other" (549). I think that the different perspectives that come into conflict and make themselves evident to Nepantla consciousness are a restaging of Anzaldúa's theory of Mestiza Consciousness; however, the specific mestizaje of that theory in *Borderlands* is now hybridized beyond the specificity of Mexican history of mestizaje itself. That is, she is expanding the earlier theory to encompass other possibilities.

As she restages the Coatlicue State and the Shadow Beast (550-551), "being lost in chaos occurs when you are between 'stories' before you shift from one set of perceptions and beliefs to another, from one mood to another" (553), she insists, however, that "the body is the basis for the conscious sense of self, the representation of self in the mind" (555), though not without question, always tripping into self-doubt and negativity. Nevertheless, she goes forth continuously "re-interpreting [her] past…reshap[ing] her present" (556). "You are sure of one thing: the consciousness that's created our social ills (dualistic and misogynist) cannot solve them—we need a more expansive conocimiento, [that is, as stated earlier. a more expansive consciousness.] The new stories must partially come from outside the system of ruling powers" (562). She is quite clear that

> Coyolxauhqui personifies the wish to repair and heal as well as re-write the stories of loss and recovery, exile and homecoming…stories that lead out of passivity and into agency, out of devalued into valued lives. Coyolxauhqui represents the search for new [concept-] metaphors to tell you what you need to know, how to connect and use the information gained, and, with intelligence, imagination, and grace, solve your problems and create intercultural communities. (563)

The politico-spiritual activism of knowledge, outside of religious metaphysics, sharing and exchange that the concept-metaphor of Nepantla represents becomes the neologism of Nepantleras. They can function as mediators that "averiguan el conflicto," inner and outer, and call "on the connectionist faculty to show the deep common ground and interwoven affinities among all things and people" (567-568). Nepantla is the pivoting liminal space where Nepantleras can operate to effect that politico-spiritual activism. Are these politico-spiritual activists to be the leaders of a "new tribalism" that Anzaldúa invokes? The ones who "begin building spiritual/political communities" (576)? She says, "By compartiendo historias, ideas, las Nepantleras forge bonds across race, gender and other lines, thus creating a new tribalism" (574). I interpret the possibility of creating a "new tribalism" as the construction of an alternate spatio-temporality that remains to be elaborated further as Anzaldúa is no longer just speaking of a "cultura mestiza" that only refers to people of Mexican descent as in *Borderlands,* but is now a formulation that shows "the deep common ground and interwoven kinship among all things and people" as cited above. It would be a "new tribalism" of the excluded and the outcasts from the white hegemonic Anglo-European world and heteronormative patriarchy.

THE COYOLXAUHQUI IMPERATIVE

In "Let us be the healing of the wound: The Coyolxauhqui Imperative—la sombra y el sueño," Anzaldúa begins by saying, "the day the towers fell [reference to 9/11/01], me sentí como Coyolxauhqui, la luna. I fell in pieces into that pitch-black brooding place" (303). La Llorona howls with grief and loss and Anzaldúa feels the imperative to "speak" esta herida abierta. Most of the concept-metaphors and symbols discussed in "Putting Coyolxauhqui Together: Creative Process" are restaged and reiterated here as they also were in "now let us shift..." The key concept-metaphors elaborated upon to depict the creative process in the exploration of the structure of inner experience are again deployed here, to reiterate the path of transformation we must take not just in healing our personal inner wounds, but also our political wounds which are caused by the leaders of exploitation, injury and imperialism. That is, I think, that imperialism's inner Shadow Beast produces an exteriority of sheer destructiveness that affects us all—the outcasts, the excluded, the dispossessed, and the atravesados, all of which are addressed in *Bridge* and *Borderlands*, and reiterated throughout her work.

In depicting the shadow (alternately in other texts Shadow Beast), which is a negativistic and violent form of embodied consciousness, Anzaldúa states

> As I see it, this country's real battle is with its shadow—its racism, propensity for violence, rapacity for consuming, neglect of its responsibility to global communities and the environment, and unjust treatment of dissenters and the disenfranchised, especially people of color... In order to understand our complicity and responsibility we must look at the shadow. (304)

There's ambiguity in the latter statement as one is not quite clear if that "shadow" is our own that depicts our complicity, or the "shadow" of perpetrators of destruction. Both, I would say.

Throughout the piece, she interweaves a detailing of the predatory logic of Imperialism's actions both locally and globally with the concept-metaphors and symbolic figures she had elaborated for processes of creativity, healing and transformation. Now, however, as in "now let us shift..." she invokes these to help us "to put a psycho-spiritual-political frame on our lives' journeys" (314). Just as she had confronted her Shadow Beast at every turn (a self-wounding negative consciousness), which is closely linked to the wound of trauma, shock or susto, she calls upon us to now also perceive it as a "collective shadow—made up of the destructive aspects, psychic wounds, and splits in our own culture" (311).

Though we can perceive the destructive effects of Imperialism's shadow (Beast) upon all of us, what could possibly be the wound to be healed that spurs the emergence of the Shadow Beast within predatory imperialists? It is difficult to imagine healing the wound of the predator, even if we can speculate about it as we would that of a serial killer. Following Anzaldúa's thought, its very predatoriness is conditioned by the wound (trauma) that generates imperialism's Shadow (Beast). It's like calling upon us to discover and heal the wound of our rapists, whose act of rape is a product of their own Shadow, which is not analogous to that of his victims and in fact is producing it for his victims. Would there be a relationality that needs to be discerned so that we are not complicit due to ignorance or desconocimiento? But in fact, that is what Anzaldúa appears to be calling upon us to do through the path of conocimiento, as mediated by Nepantla and Coyolxauhqui positions and generating the Nepantleras who will carry out through conocimiento the assemblage of a psycho-spiritual-political frame. Though this interpretation may disturb some of us, it is possible. However, I think, it is possible as well to imagine a correlative interpretation based on alternate thinking posed in this essay as well. That is, we must avoid taking a vengeful position, which spells more destruction, for we must not exchange "one wound for another" (307).

Conocimiento, which emerges from our confrontation with our personal wounds and Shadow Beasts, will not necessarily be an option chosen by Imperialism and its supporters. As such it must be our conocimientos. Anzaldúa transfers the path of conocimiento, drawn from the structures of her inner experiences, into the public realm. We have allowed Bush to "kill off the dream (el sueño) of what our culture could be—a model of democracy" (307). Through desconocimiento (ignorance and/or denial) we have been complicitous, and it is now time to take responsibility as we continually work as well on the conocimientos that emerge for us in the public sphere.

To that end, Nepantla and Coyolxauhqui are involved with the transition from lethal crisis to transformation:

> The Coyolxauhqui imperative is to heal and achieve integration... Coyolxauhqui is my symbol for the necessary process of dismemberment and fragmentation, of seeing that self or the situations you're embroiled in differently. It is also my symbol for reconstruction and reframing, one that allows for putting the pieces together in a new way. The Coyolxauhqui imperative is an ongoing process of making and unmaking. (312)

Let us remember that the "unmaking" is a result of repeated traumatic assaults and of desconocimiento, an aspect of the Shadow (Beast) that has not been confronted. Without confrontation there's no conocimiento. Since it is doubtful that Imperialism will confront its Shadow (Beast) and miraculously reach conocimiento of the destructive force embedded in its logical forms of thought and doing, we must begin "to think not in terms of 'my' country, or 'your' nation but 'our planet'" (312). And with our conocimientos in hand of both inner and outer structures of experience, "let us be the healing of the wound" (314). Let us bring a different future into being. Just as we confront our personal wound/Shadow Beast to yield conocimiento for ourselves, transferring the "method" to the public realm demands that we become aware of Imperialism's path and logic of destruction and combine a psycho-spiritual-political activism that can lead us to confront our social sickness, much of it a result of predatory actions and forms of thinking. It is up to us to do it.

Through conocimientos—that is, the knowledge we produce—and psycho-spiritual-political activism (non-religious), we can confront the Shadow Beast, the negative and nihilistic consciousness of Imperialism's predators, which can be seen, I think, as serial killers and mutilators. Build a "new tribalism" dedicated to discovering our interconnectedness across race, gender, class, sexuality and ethnicities to bring forth the "new stories from outside ruling powers." Let us remember that Anzaldúa uses the terms story and stories in ways that also invoke non-fictional stories, and invoke the idea of putting information together, for which Nepantla and Coyolxauhqui go hand in hand. Thus, whether they be factual or fictive, the stories can disclose the logic and structures of predatoriness and the wound that motivates and defines it, as simultaneously we give structure to the "new tribalism" (politics) based on our human interconnectedness, which may assist in disclosing the logic of predatoriness—that is Empire's own criminal mind. Does this heal the predator's wound too? If it does not, we can at a minimum persuade many to confront their inner and outer desconocimientos in order to create a different future and an alternate world for ourselves, which may include the dream of a people's democracy that changes the current character of the Imperialist Corporate State. Can we do that Nepantler@s through the Nepantla and Coyolxauhqui imperative and method? Can we starve the destructive political spirit of the predator with our own political thought and action?

CONCLUSION

The Twenty-first Century appears to be inaugurated by a "decolonial turn." Taking the lead in the Americas, for example, there has been The Zapatista Movement (EZLN) launched in 1994. The anti-colonial movements of the Twentieth Century from India to Cuba and U.S. Civil Rights Movements, which include subsequent post-colonial critical thought, which in effect are still engaging forms of resistance to the Corporate State's local and global neo-colonialism but have not done enough to reach "l@s de abajo." The relentless machine of the Corporate State's neocolonialist operations continue to fiercely recolonize "l@s de abajo" as well as others who have not thought of themselves as colonized such as white people in the U.S. L@s de abajo, if you will, in recent decades have been pursuing another line of inquiry in an effort to free themselves from colonial structures of experience and knowledge. L@s de abajo have been formulating praxes and theory of praxes in order to generate alternative spaces for new forms of political thought and action and Gloria Anzaldúa is one of them.

There is work being done to this end, for example, in Bolivia and other parts of South America. In the United States, the effort in decolonizing knowledge has been spearheaded by Anzaldúa and Moraga's *This Bridge Called My Back* and scholars such as Emma Pérez, Chela Sandoval, Arturo Aldama, and Naomi Quiñones in their published work to name a few. The work of New Zealander Linda Tuhiwai Smith and other indigenous-based scholars have also been taking a lead in the decolonizing of praxis and knowledge. Recently Paola Bacchetta has transnationalized the decolonial thought of Anzaldúa in her essay "Transnational Borderlands: Gloria Anzaldúa's Epistemologies of Resistance and Lesbians 'of color' in Paris (*El Mundo Zurdo* 2010) and with her colleague Jules Falquet in Paris she has translated into French the decolonial work of Chicanas and Latinas in *Les Cahiers du CEDREF.*

In brief, I cannot do justice to the proliferating bibliography of the "decolonial turn" at this time. However, it could be that our earlier focus on anti-colonial movements and resistance has not been well understood as also including decolonizing forms of thought and action, and the implications in the context of the stratification of academically produced knowledge and of capitalist structures of power. I believe so.

ENDNOTES

1 I want to thank and acknowledge the work of AnaLouise Keating, who has been bringing to our attention through edited collections some of the scattered publications by Gloria Anzaldúa, and Norma Cantú's foundational work in the formation of the Society for the Study of Gloria Anzaldúa. I also want to thank and acknowledge Steve Martinot's published work on the formation and structures of White Identity in the U.S. Moreover, I could not have finished this piece without the assistance of Christina Gutierrez.

2 Scattered in her critical work Gayatri Spivak uses the hyphenated notion of "Concept-Metaphor." I have decided to deploy it in this essay because I think that Anzaldúa is constructing her own "concept-metaphor" epistemology which she appropriates from pre-Columbian mythography and terms. Through that appropriation she recodes them for her creative and philosophical vision. I interpret "concept-metaphor" through the hyphen as Spivak's effort to bring into relief the relationality and/or correlativity between terms that are customarily used separately in the Anglo-European critical corpus and production of knowledge. Both terms signal a substitution for differently situated "referents" that may be erased depending on the specified genre of the text from philosophy to science. Anzaldúa herself states, "I have to have a central metaphor like La Llorona or La Prieta. Within that central metaphor are these concepts, like working within the interface between different realities—nepantla space" (*Interviews* 176). Thus, in order to provide critical consistency to my structuration of this

particular line of thought in Anzaldúa's work, I will be adhering to this "concept-metaphor" theoretical perspective as much as is possible. I was able to find at least one reference to the idea of decolonization when Anzaldúa points to the ways "we attempt to decolonize ourselves" as we work through the violence internalized from the societies we live in,"Anzaldúa (*Making Face, Making Soul* xxvi).

3 For elaboration of the notion of the "speaking subject" see Julia Kristeva's "The System and the Speaking Subject," in *The Kristeva Reader*, ed. Toril Moi.

4 From the beginning of her published work Anzaldúa launches a testimonial and anecdotal inquiry of the Self in the flesh, for example in *Bridge* "La Prieta" where she first speaks of her vision of El Mundo Zurdo (208-209) for transcending her agonistic life formation, and "Speaking in Tongues: A Letter to 3rd World Women Writers." Also in *Borderlands*, the turmoil of the internalized unwanted otherness is given greater personal depth as torment of the self, for example, the chapter called "La Herencia de Coatlicue: The Coatlicue State" (41-51) as well as interviews of that period which depict, reinscribe and rescript her agony. A recent book by the noted neurobiologist Antonio Damasio, *Self Comes to Mind: Constructing the Conscious Brain* (2012), maps the ways in which indeed one can insist on the idea of "theory-in-the-flesh" from the bottom up of the organism's knowledges. Also the work of noted neurophysiologist Candace B. Pert lends itself to idea of "theory-in-the-flesh" in her book *Molecules of Emotion: Why You Feel the Way You Feel* (1997).

5 Though Western philosophy may "begin" and continue to our day with the question of the Other, its focus has been Anglo-European. In fact, though the concept and practice of othering has been deployed against the enslaved and colonized people of color, locally and globally, the effects of that theory and practice have not been reckoned with, unpacked, nor engaged by whites in general—men or women. A self-decolonizing praxis and theory of praxis is now being formulated by some people of color, especially queer feminists of color.

6 For a fascinating account of this process as "selfcraft" see Chapter 6 of Edwina Barvosa's *Wealth of Selves: Multiple Identities, Mestiza Consciousness and the Subject of Politics* (2008).

7 For further elaboration on this issue against the grain of Western "rationalist epistemology," see Amala Levine's "Champion of the Spirit: Anzaldúa's critique of Rationalist Empistemology," in *EntreMundos/Among Worlds*.

8 This is a restaged conceptualization inspired by Roland Barthes' euro-centered theorization in "Myth Today" collected in his book *Mythologies* as well as Jacques Derrida's theorization and critique of Levi-Strauss's theorization of myth in "Structure, Sign, and Play in the Discourse of the Human Sciences," collected in *Writing and Difference*. In brief, by reading Anzaldúa through her cultural location I transfer euro-centered critical theory to the U.S. That is, it crosses the Atlantic.

9 AnaLouise Keating has been expanding and critiquing in her work Anzaldúa's notion of "spiritual activism." I refer the reader especially to her edited collections of Anzaldúa's work. For additional reflections on conocimiento and Coyolxauhqui consciousness, see Irene Lara's "Daughter of Coatlicue: An Interview with Gloria Anzaldúa" in *EntreMundos*. Also many of the essays collected in *this bridge we call home* critically rethink aspects and influence of Anzaldúa's work and *Bridge*, as well as essays collected in *El Mundo Zurdo* and *El Mundo Zurdo 2*.

WORKS CITED

Anzaldúa, Gloria. *Borderlands/La Frontera: The New Mestiza.* San Francisco: Aunt Lute, 1987.

---. "Bridge, Drawbridge, Sandbar, or Island." *The Gloria Anzaldúa Reader.* Ed. AnaLouise Keating. Durham: Duke UP, 2009. 140-56. Print.

---. *Making Face, Making Soul: Haciendo Caras: Creative and Critical Perspectives by Women of Color.* San Francisco: Aunt Lute, 1990. Print.

---. Interview. "Daughter of Coatlicue: An Interview with Gloria Anzaldúa." By Irene Lara. *Entre Mundos/Among Worlds: New Perspectives on Gloria Anzaldúa.* Ed. AnaLouise Keating. New York: Palgrave Macmillan, 2008. 41-55. Print.

---. "now let us shift…the path of conocimiento…inner work, public acts." *This Bridge We Call Home: Radical Visions for Transformation.* Ed. Gloria Anzaldúa and AnaLouise Keating. New York: Routledge, 2002. 540-78. Print.

---. Interview. "Within the Crossroads: Lesbian/Feminist/Spiritual Development." By Christine Weiland. *Gloria Anzaldúa: Interviews/Entrevistas.* Ed. AnaLouise Keating. New York: Routledge, 2000. 72-127. Print.

---. Interview. "Quincentennial: From Victimhood to Active Resistance." By AnaLouise Keating. *Gloria Anzaldúa: Interviews/Entrevistas.* Ed. AnaLouise Keating. New York: Routledge, 2000. 177-78. Print.

---. Interview. "Toward a Mestiza Rhetoric: Gloria Anzaldúa on Composition, Postcoloniality, and the Spiritual." By Andrea Lunsford. *Gloria Anzaldúa: Interviews/Entrevistas.* Ed. AnaLouise Keating. New York: Routledge, 2000. 251-80. Print.

---. "Putting Coyolxauhqui Together: A Creative Process." *How We Work.* Ed. Marla Morris, Mary Aswell Doll, and William F. Pinar. New York: Peter Lang, 1999. 241-62. Print.

---. "Speaking in Tongues." *This Bridge Called My Back: Writings by Radical Women of Color.* Ed. Gloria Anzaldúa and Cherríe Moraga. New York: Kitchen Table: Women of Color Press, 1983. 165-74. Print.

---. "La Prieta." *This Bridge Called My Back: Writings by Radical Women of Color.* Ed. Gloria Anzaldúa and Cherríe Moraga. New York: Kitchen Table: Women of Color Press, 1983. 198-209. Print.

Anzaldúa, Gloria, and Cherríe Moraga, eds. *This Bridge Called My Back: Writings by Radical Women of Color.* New York: Kitchen Table: Women of Color Press, 1983. Print.

Keating, AnaLouise, ed. *The Gloria Anzaldúa Reader.* Durham, NC: Duke UP, 2009. Print.

---. "Risking the Personal: An Introduction." *Gloria Anzaldúa: Interviews/Entrevistas.* Ed. AnaLouise Keating. New York: Routledge, 2000. 1-15. Print.

Lorde, Audre. *Sister Outsider: Essays and Speeches.* Freedom, CA: The Crossing Press, 1984. Print.

Pérez, Laura E. "The Performance of Spirituality and Visionary Politics in the Work of Gloria Anzaldúa." *El Mundo Zurdo 2: Selected Works From the 2010 Meetings of the Society for the Study of Gloria Anzaldúa.* Ed. Sonia Saldívar-Hull, Norma Alarcón, and Rita Urquijo-Ruiz. San Francisco: Aunt Lute Books, 2012. 13-27. Print.

Saldívar-Hull, Sonia, Norma Alarcón, and Rita Urquijo-Ruiz, eds. *El Mundo Zurdo 2: Selected Works from the 2010 Meeting of the Society for the Study of Gloria Anzaldúa.* San Francisco: Aunt Lute Books, 2012. Print.

A CASE FOR THE SELF-IN-COALITION: EXPLORING ANZALDÚA'S LEGACY OF LA NAGUALA WITH LUGONES' COMPLEX COMMUNICATION

KELLI ZAYTOUN

"An inclusive movement cannot emerge from the search for a common good...but only from careful attention by each vulnerable social segment to the specific experience and vulnerabilities of the others."—Iris Young, "The Complexities of Coalition"

"For nepantleras to bridge is an act of will, an act of love, an attempt toward compassion and reconciliation, and a promise to be present with the pain of others without losing themselves to it."—Gloria Anzaldúa, "(Un)natural Bridges, (Un)safe Spaces"

Feminist positions on the role of identity politics in coalition work are varied.[1] In a 2010 Feminist Studies article, Elizabeth R. Cole and Zakiya T. Luna identified a split in the literature between those who emphasize the importance of naming and utilizing their identities in work across difference (i.e., Gloria Anzaldúa, Combahee River Collective, Diane Fowlkes) and those who warn that an emphasis on identity can normalize, privilege, or dismiss some identities at the expense of others (i.e., Floya Anthias, Judith Butler, Kimberlé Crenshaw, Andrea Smith) (75-77). According to the authors, "there is a tension between those who claim that an appreciation for the complexity of identity is a central tool for struggle and those who caution that as a political tool, any identity claim simultaneously engages otherness and exclusion and thus may be an obstacle to successful coalition" (76). Cole and Luna later confirmed that new social movement[2] literature and their own research exploring activist narratives revealed that "social change organizations actively construct, rather than reflect, a fixed or ascribed social identity" (77). More specifically, they claimed the work itself, particularly the work of not dismissing but dealing directly with differences in experience among group members, created opportunities for the development of new political identities that served as critical tools in coalitional strategies (96). Such findings suggest, therefore, that to dismiss or ignore the selfhoods[3] and identities of members of the coalition, even doing so in the search for commonalities, is contrary to the group's function. Furthermore, lack of consideration of the multiply, socially constructed identities within the group is a missed opportunity to deepen awareness of processes critical to the success of coalitional movements. In this paper I turn our attention to the complex experiences through which self and identity are created in coalition. I seek to continue Cole and Luna's important work by offering an expanded theoretical analysis, including practical examples, of how a lived sense of selfhood and identity are negotiated in solidarity with others, and how what I term the "self-in-coalition" contributes to the identity and effectiveness of the collective. My analysis builds on Gloria Anzaldúa's legacy of conocimiento, particularly the concept of "la naguala." In what became one of Anzaldúa's final published works, "now let us shift…the path of conocimiento… inner work, public acts," she explains la naguala in a way that appears for the first, and last, time.[4] She says la naguala, which in Náhuatl means shape-shifter, is "the function that arouses the awareness that beneath individual separateness lies a deeper interrelatedness" (569). Although her discussion of la naguala here is brief, its significance and potential are notable and, I argue, worth exploring and expanding in conversations on feminist coalitions. I then place Anzaldúa's work in conversation with Maria Lugones' theory of complex communication in coalitional limens to strengthen what I see as the essential communicative conditions for the functioning of la naguala. I argue that the self-in-coalition necessarily engages in both la naguala and complex communication. Together Anzaldúa and Lugones' theories strengthen my claim that in coalition the self is continuously changing but not dissolving; the self-in-coalition seeks a deep sense of relationality but not sameness with others, and functions best when difference, identity, and oppression are understood as situated yet shifting experiences of the self and the collective. Lastly, I will describe examples of narratives[5] that indicate the construction of the self-in-coalition; these offer evidence for Anzaldúa's vision of conocimiento at work.

In their review of the literature on feminist coalitions, Cole and Luna address Diane Fowlkes' claim that Anzaldúa employed "complex identity narration" in her work across difference (Cole75). Anzaldúa's mestiza consciousness is recalled in this context; however, I offer a look beyond Fowlkes' 1997 analysis to Anzaldúa's later thinking.

LA NAGUALA INVOKED

Gloria Anzaldúa's essay "now let us shift" showcases her work on "conocimiento," the journey one takes through the personal and the social dimensions of life by alternating one's concentration between "inner work" and "public acts" (540). To Anzaldúa, inner work refers to emotional, cognitive, bodily, imaginal, and spiritual efforts (542). Conocimiento, or "reflective consciousness," is gained from "opening all your senses" to the struggle to know a rich, situated, physical, and mindful sense of self as well as one's potential to act to make a positive difference in the social world (542). Although numbered, the stages are not linear; Anzaldúa explains that the stages, or "stations," or "spaces," can occur simultaneously, and that one may work through all seven stages in one day yet dwell in one for months, as the stages represent "a meditation on the rites of passage, the transitions of life from birth to death, and all the daily births and deaths in-between. Bits of your self die and are reborn in each step" (546). A process through which individual and collective knowing grow more inclusive, creative, and revolutionary than ever before, conocimiento ultimately creates a "shift in reality" that brings forth "an ethical, compassionate strategy with which to negotiate conflict and difference within self and between others" (545). Very briefly, I will describe the stages of conocimiento as they lead to stage seven, where the potential for la naguala and coalition work is reached.

In the first stage of conocimiento, *el arrebato*, an upheaval in one's view, in one's complacency, occurs. This experience moves one into second stage, *nepantla*, or transition, where one is aware that change is required, as Anzaldúa said, "yesterday's mode of consciousness pinches like an outgrown shoe" (549). In the third stage, *Coatlicue*, one slips into an incapacitating state spurred by the burden of change. Within stages four, five, and six are an emergence from despair and the engagement in the recreating of self in relationship to others. Stage seven of conocimiento, "shifting realities," is where conditions for coalition work are favorable. "Shifting realities" entails a transformation that Anzaldúa described as follows:

> When a change occurs your consciousness (awareness of your sense of self and your response to self, others, and surroundings) becomes cognizant that it has a point of view and the ability to act from choice. (568-569)[6]

So, the "knower" according to Anzaldúa that has been born out of the change in consciousness has several functions. More specifically, she said that this "knower" is always with you but has been "displaced by the ego," evidence that Anzaldúa saw some continuity of the self but she also saw it as an ever-shifting, unbound, unstable, phenomenon (569). The knower can see the self as a system of relational parts. In an interview with Inés Hernández-Ávila, Anzaldúa said the following:

> When you watch yourself and observe your mind at work you find that behind your acts and your temporary sense of self (identities) is a state of awareness that, if you allow it, keeps you from getting completely caught up in that particular identity or emotional state. (Keating 177)

What she described here is a very complex system—three dimensional if you will—the knower, self (identity/emotions), and others/world. I will return to the concept of "the knower" later, as I will argue that my idea of the self-in-coalition is closely aligned with Anzaldúa's knower. First, I want to bring attention to la naguala as a *function* critical to the knower's ability to act in coalition. La naguala, the shape-shifter, is indeed responsible for the change in consciousness that constitutes stage seven of conocimiento, shifting realities. Perhaps Anzaldúa's emphasis on the language of "shifting," exemplified in her choice of the essay's and stage seven's titles, were inspired by the idea of la naguala, yet little critical attention has been given to its significance and its influence on her work toward the end of her life. She described the shape-shifting function of la naguala in this way:

> This conocimiento gives you the flexibility to swing from your intense feelings to those of the other without being hijacked by either. When confronted with the other's fear, you note her emotional arousal, allow her feelings/words to enter your body,[7] then you shift to the neutral place of la naguala. You detach so those feelings won't inhabit your body for long. (569)

La naguala, therefore, generates the complicated awareness of separateness *and* deep interconnectivity simultaneously.

CONNECTING LA NAGUALA AND COMPLEX COMMUNICATION

I am interested in looking more carefully, and expanding using primarily Lugones' work, at how this "awareness" of interrelatedness brought about by la naguala occurs. Two reasons motivate this inquiry: First, Anzaldúa did not provide a deep description of the conditions under which the knower shifts its attention from having a point of view (ego) to a sense of deeper interrelatedness. Secondly, in considering the conditions for this shift, more attention must be paid to what Lugones calls "the logic of narrow identity" that historically and currently exists in the US today (75). Its dismantling is required to provide an opening for the function of la naguala and the complex communication, as described by Lugones, which must follow. According to Lugones, restrictive understanding of our own and others' identities and oppressive situations keep us from communicating and strategizing beyond oppression's reach.

Lugones argued that complex communication in liminal spaces is necessary and difficult in two ways: it requires "recognition of the intersectionality of oppressions as real and important for struggle and it requires a movement outward toward other affiliative groups recognized as resistant" (76). Simply changing our point of view and inhabiting liminal space are not enough (placing ourselves there by taking a stance against all oppressions); liminal spaces are *enacted* by reading the opacity of others, the peculiarities of their resistant strategies, and "developing forms of communication that signal disruption of the reduction attempted by the oppressor" (84). Transparency of others and our commonalities with them cannot be assumed because we cannot presuppose the meanings of each particular liminal encounter. According to Lugones, "the key that opens the door to the limen is not resistance to oppression per se, but rather resistance to particular forms of oppression at particular times in particular spaces" (77).

Drawing on the work of Alfred Arteaga, Lugones suggested that the "speech act" in a limen is a site of "formation for contestatory discourse" that has a three-fold form (82). First, it communicates disruption of the colonizer's monologue; secondly, it provides an opening to "life lived differently," and third, it is a coalitional form that communicates an invitation to other disruptors (of the colonizer's monologism)/other resisters to make the limen more inclusive (82). Lugones argues that in the limen "[w]e speak to power backed up, grounded, in each other's meaning" (82). Resistance, therefore, involves an act of "intercultural polyglossia" (83).

According to Lugones, complex communication involves a continual reconstruction of the self, a self not limited or eliminated by domination. Liminal spaces exist in particular spacialities and times; they are communicative achievements. So, like Anzaldúa, Lugones argued that a shift in "self" (to the "knower" in Anzaldúa's terms) is necessary in order to recognize deep interrelatedness; however, she added that this reconstruction can only truly occur in coalitional limens, in the process of discovering our own multiplicity and each others' opacity. Both shifts in consciousness and communication work together in the limens to inform and develop the other. I argue they occur cyclically, and sometimes even simultaneously, like the stages of conocimiento themselves. More specifically, I assert that it is in the limen that the function of la naguala, that which alerts knower to new forms of interrelatedness, takes place. La naguala, the shape shifter, is the creator of new forms of being, new forms of relational selves, new forms of resisting oppression. To use another Anzaldúan metaphor if I may, la naguala is a bridge to new forms of individual and collective consciousness, to the self-in-coalition.

In the next section I situate the concept of "shifting consciousness" in feminist accounts of subjectivity and selfhood. Anzaldúa's discussion of "consciousness" raises some questions of agency and responsibility that, by engaging them, give us an opportunity to enter what Mariana Ortega called "a space between the accounts of the traditional subject...and those accounts that move so far away from subjectivity that, in the end, they leave us with our hands tied as far as possibilities for political resistance go" (19). I will examine Anzaldúa's account of "knower" with other feminist accounts of relational selfhood, including my own account of self-in-coalition, to help create a more complex and specific connection between the transformation of consciousness and the development of the function of la naguala in liminal spaces.

RELATIONAL SELF-IN-COALITION

A comprehensive exploration of the immense terrain of contemporary self and subjectivity discourse is beyond the scope of this essay; however, some discussion of notions of self is critical to its arguments. As Katherine Adams pointed out, Anzaldúa used the juxtaposition of coalition work with mestiza subjectivity to demonstrate that "cross-difference alliances must predicate themselves upon an understanding of identity as always fractured by multiple, shifting, and contradictory identifications with and against surrounding material contexts and people" (3). Effective coalition deeply depends on the understanding that a sense of self is a changing, situated locality for consciousness. Adams refers to this concept as the "indeterminancy of 'selfhood'" (3). Indeed, many contemporary feminist approaches to self align with phenomenological accounts that describe subjects as intersubjective. To clarify, Adams claimed that such approaches depict the self as "fundamentally intersubjective in its identity—or constituted through rather than in advance to association with others—and constantly open to revision" (3; emphasis in orig.). Mariana Ortega argued for considerations of a multiplicitous self (which is distinct from the idea of "multiple selves") in light of a Heideggerian phenomenological account of self-in-the making and of Lugones' notion of "world"-traveling (3). She explored notions of self emerging from the work of Lugones and other Latina scholars, where the self is consistently negotiating uncertainties and inconsistencies, bringing forth what she called a "new consciousness," similar to ones described by Anzaldúa (mestiza consciousness) and Chela Sandoval (differential consciousness).[8]

In a more recent account of relational selfhood, Alexis Shotwell and Trevor Sangrey pointed out that although most feminist relational theories of self emphasize how self-statements are influenced by engagement with others, the reverse has not been explored; they contend "that it is equally important to attend to how one's self-expression, which is always social, changes other people's experience of themselves" (59). Identifying a problematic trend in contemporary theorizing in which trans and genderqueer people serve as objects through which gender is conceived, Shotwell and Sangrey explain the importance of recognizing that "trans existence" impacts the gender identity of non-trans people (57); they argue that "[trans and non trans] gender formation is mutually, and multiply informed" (60); it is ever-shifting within the context of interaction. According to the authors, "trans people's existence itself creates non-trans people as something new: as not transgender" (69). Exposing how gender normalization and objectification occurs in common narratives about trans people, such as those related to the concept of "gender transition" and the reduction of gender experience across race, culture, and other difference, Shotwell and Sangrey offer several examples of the relationality of what is regarded as "normal" and "deviant" gender identity and behavior (61). Gender is not simply communicated by an individual; it is supported, rejected, misunderstood, and more, by those around the individual, in ways that usually reinforce heterosexuality. And, importantly, the authors argue that a gendered consciousness or self is formed co-constitutively with others through lived experiences of the body in particular social conditions in particular moments in time.

Shotwell and Sangrey's "relational self" argument is important to the discussion on feminist coalitions and the self-in-coalition for at least two reasons. First, by demonstrating how "interactive gender [and gendering] actually is," we are reminded of the work yet to do in including not only trans persons in feminist coalitional work, but in imagining and acting on an understanding of gender (including our own) that is more fluid and complex than what has been constructed in the past in self-proclaimed feminist scholarship (72). This point might appear at this juncture to be a distraction from my paper's main argument; however, it is such a critical detail in the larger issue of feminist coalitions I mention it here. Secondly, Shotwell and Sangrey suggest that in a relational model of selfhood, individuals are "optic(s) by which to understand the world," and that "focusing on one person…is only really effective when individuals are understood as a way to see the intersecting worlds that make them up" (71). Understanding the self in this regard can help to move us as individuals into the "liminal, border-dwelling situation," called for by Lugones, where "the oppressed will understand each other even though their struggles against various forms of oppression have mostly led them to look inward, to their group of narrow resistant identity" (78).

What I label as a "self-in-coalition" looks outward, and sees the self and its identities as constructed with others, and sees oppression as constructed as well; importantly, looking outward requires a willingness to explore our own and each other's specific journeys and situations and the inextricable connections between them. This willingness is spurred by the function of la naguala, and the liminal situation described by Lugones is the space within which individual expressions of la naguala can become a collective of coalitional action. The self-in-coalition has the capacity to see itself as incomplete, its identities relational, multiple, and shifting. As I mentioned earlier, the self-in-coalition possesses the capacity inherent in Anzaldúa's "knower," or the ability to step away from its identities and emotional states and see them as temporary. This allows room for the awareness of deep interrelatedness that is invested in a "connectionist," not a defensive, individualist view ("now let us shift" 569). Lastly and critically, I argue that stories about the self in the relational processes described above are not distractions from our larger, collective causes, but instead provide a richness that informs our struggles and strategies.

Before discussing some concrete examples of self-in-coalition, I'd like to make the general comment that another major value of the notion of a multiplicitous, relational self is that it offers an alternative to what AnaLouise Keating refers to as the dangers of "self-enclosed individualism," or the view that "each individual has a unitary, unchanging core self that must be nurtured, protected, and in other ways honored at all cost" (26). With this view comes an attitude that "...if each individual is fully responsible for his or her own life, there is no need for collective action or systemic change" (27). This binary construction of self and society serves as an obstacle to imagining our interrelatedness; because it also reinforces normalized ideas of what individuals should be, the self/society binary also keeps us from seeing our identities in complex ways, as explained in more detail below.

Like Keating, Shotwell and Sangrey discuss and defend the dangers of individualism, or what they refer to as "inadequate liberal-individualist models of selfhood" in their critique of the US medical system and focus on individual rights (57-58). They argue, citing Sylvia Rivera's and Cressida Heyes's work, that the current medicalized model of trans people's lives, which focuses on and assumes that trans people desire sex reassignment surgery, for example, does not account for the complexity of gender formation in not only trans people's lives, but non-trans lives as well. By emphasizing access to individual medical care in our advocacy for trans existence, in a society that imagines gender as *either* male or female, we can unwittingly reinforce that binary, reinforce a trans person's assumed need to transition into a particular, normalized sex—the "opposite" of the sex into which they were born. Indeed, we become a participant in what Lugones has called "the oppressor's imaginative construction of us" (79). Shotwell and Sangrey in part offer a relational model of self in order to respond to the need for a more adequate and complex way of understanding gender formation, and gender normativity, than what the individualist model provides.

SHIFTING SELF-IN-COALITION ILLUSTRATED

According to Shotwell and Sangrey, "self-identification" is "a narrative that in its telling constitutes the self" (71). The stories that follow are intended to provide examples of selves-in-coalition in the making. I begin with a narrative by Judith Ezekiel, a scholar of women's and American studies at the University of Toulouse. In describing her struggle to understand her own and others' multiply constructed identities, she explained:

> I grew up white. Not just white. I grew up *neon* white. I grew up marshmallow-in-the-hot-chocolate white. And then I changed. I wasn't actually born neon white, just plain white. You know, that white that is not visible to, or problematized by whites, but is ever-so-visible to people of color, that default white of the "un-othered." (1)

Ezekiel, who refers to herself as an ethnic Jew, grew up in an African-American neighborhood in the Midwest US in the 1960s, in the height of Black Power. She sees race as a historical construction, and references French theoretician Collette Guillaumin, in commenting that, "race is not the basis for racism—*racism* and the appropriation of the bodies and labor of a class of people, *creates and defines 'race,'* and naturalizes it rather than the opposite... They (meaning race and other categories of identities) are biological myths constructed to reinforce sociological, material realities" (2; emphasis in orig.). She goes on to describe how, after moving to France thirty years ago, she was faced, given the historical and contemporary political climate in France, with anti-Semitism in more frequent and intense ways than she faced in the US, and had been in France constructed as Moroccan, Algerian, and Tunisian, or "not-white." Schooled in Black Power, she always thought it was important to claim that she was "white," to acknowledge the privileges (though they dwindled in France) that came with it, but, as Judith, whose scholarship and activism focuses on anti-racist social movements, participated in her research groups and anti-racist coalitions, her colleagues referred to her as non-white, and asked her why she was afraid of identifying as a person of color. She was left wondering if they were charging her with "betraying them and trying to 'pass'" (9). She closes her story by acknowledging that although she thinks she has had some agency in constructing her ethnicity, ultimately, she, explains, "it is in the gaze of others that I have been placed in positions that I do not control...My fluidity in race is not contradictory with rigid, material repercussions of a racist system; to the contrary, it is this fluidity that has exposed me...to racism first hand" (10). I tell this story as an example of how identities shift—personally and socially—

and the hard work required in this two-fold process of, in Anzaldúa's words, "inner work" and "public acts" and in Lugones' call for coalition that recognizes intersectionality of oppressions and makes a movement outward toward other resistant affiliative groups.

Ezekiel recognized that although her race and her identity were not concrete, the oppression that she faced was. She acknowledged that it was her not being perceived as white by others that had a far more profound effect on her than her being Jewish. Interacting with other affiliative groups (such as those inhabited by women of color) outside the Jewish community is what changed her sense of self. Interestingly, this "change" motivated her to tell her story and to continue her coalition work in more complex ways.

Adams mentions a self-statement similar to Ezekiel's in her remark that Anzaldúa is credited for "offering one of the earliest and most influential discussions" of the self-in-coalition when, at the 1988 meeting of the NWSA she opened by saying, "This morning I looked in the mirror to see who I was (I keep changing)" (qtd. in Adams 3). Anzaldúa's talk was about coalition politics, what she described as "the need to form alliances without subordinating differences" —or, in Anzaldúa's words, without forgetting "la mierda between us" (qtd. in Adams 3). Both ideas of multiplicity of self and opacity of others are mentioned here.

In an essay written with AnaLouise Keating in *This Bridge We Call Home: Radical Visions for Transformation*, Deborah Miranda recognized that within the fluidity of identity lies the possibility of connecting with and opening to others. She came to a new, broader understanding of "mestiza" as she attempted to see the similarities between US Indian and Chicana experience. In her realization she stated:

> I suddenly realize that it [*mestiza*] is much larger than simply blood or genetics: 'Mestiza' is even larger than gender, despite its gendered origins. Mestiza means that which does not obey or even see boundaries; that which blurs sharp distinctions in favor of what is best or most appropriate; that which thrives in ambiguity because ambiguity means survival, creation, movement. (206-207)

I note here that Miranda's understanding developed in conversation with Keating within which she seemed to shift her perspective from one focused on a particular identity to a more inclusive one. She continued, "After all this time! I am finally beginning to understand what Gloria meant by the term 'mestiza consciousness.' We are just beginning to form the Mestiza Nation that she saw twenty years ago" (207). Commenting earlier in her piece that to deny Indianness would be a heresy, she concluded by saying that denying mestiza consciousness "would be the ultimate in heresies" (207). Published in a dialogue format, the essay speaks to the importance the authors placed on the process of the formulation, or co-construction, of their ideas. I think it also serves as evidence for the mobilization of la naguala and the forms of complex communication outlined by Lugones.

Cole and Luna, who collected oral histories of scholar-activists in four countries, provided evidence for how new and inclusive identities were formed by those they interviewed. Activists described discovering a link between themselves and those who had a common experience of marginalization, but not necessarily a common identity. In fact, one activist, Cathy Cohen, reconstructed the meaning of the term "queer" to include "women who are resource-poor and have children" because they are "marginalized by their sexual decisions" (qtd. in Cole and Luna 80). Cohen, therefore, reconceived "queer" in a broader way that could potentially help to build a bigger, expansive movement among people with similar experiences and political goals. Cole and Luna discovered that activists built new identities through "reflection," "nurtured alliances," and "expansive imagination" (such as Cohen's reconstruction of the term "queer") (81). They also reported that working across difference was facilitated by childhood experiences in which one engaged across difference, and that all expressed a sense of responsibility for helping to end oppression imposed by the "First World," or a sense of global citizenry. Overall, Cole and Luna concluded that activists relied on their own histories and creativity, perhaps what Anzaldúa might say was their la naguala, to produce new identities, and that openly dealing with difference was critical for effective coalition work. Rich with insight and evidence from each of their twelve participants' interviews, Cole and Luna confirm that studying narratives proves to be a useful tool in understanding coalition work.

Telling more stories of shifting self-in-coalition journeys can help open the communicative spaces called for by Lugones. The accounts of self that I have mentioned here help lay a foundation for, and provide concrete examples of, how the creation, and re-creation, of consciousness interacts in relationship to others to mobilize la naguala and create liminal spaces.

CONCLUSION

Not surprisingly, working on this essay called on me to reflect on the complexities of my own identities. I recalled the first time I prepared a paper on the concept of self and coalition, which was for the Roundtable on Latina Feminism; I assumed I would be the only participant of Arab decent. I discovered after presenting my paper that another participant and friend, whom I knew only as Argentinean, was also Lebanese. I don't speak Spanish, although my Portuguese (gained years ago while living in Brazil with my coincidently Lebanese host family) helped me to understand many of the conversations going on around me that weekend. But I realized, with the concept of reading others' opacity on my mind, that even the identities that I shared with many of the roundtable scholars—woman, feminist, parent, academic, for example—were gained along very different paths, still somehow, we were connected to each other in profound ways. I realized that although we cannot claim a bond of common experiences, we can claim interrelated ones.

Feminist coalitions engage in the complicated mission of simultaneously working on, *and* moving beyond, the goals of our particular identity groups to form larger, more inclusive communities. Anzaldúa reflected on this point in her final comments in "now let us shift": "You wonder when others will, like nepantleras, hand themselves to a larger vision, a less-defended identity" (571). La naguala and complex communication will require much work and flexibility. Lugones says that it requires creativity. Similarly, Anzaldúa states the following, what might be read as her parting vision, in "now let us shift":

> Las nepantleras envision a time when the bridge will no longer be needed—we'll have shifted to a seamless nosotras. This move requires a different way of thinking and relating to others; it requires that we act on our interconnectivity, a mode of connecting similar to hypertexts' multiple links—it includes diverse others and does not depend on traditional categories or sameness. (570)

The self-in-coalition engages in the difficult but critical work of recognizing and paying careful attention to the differences in our stories of oppression, to the shifts in our multiply, simultaneously experienced identities, and, very critically, to creating new relational identities within the many moments of the journey towards resistance and, ultimately, justice and harmony. I close with the proposal that work across difference requires conditions that simultaneously nurture the self and the feminist coalitional projects in which we are invested. As M. Jacqui Alexander stated, "any alienation from self is alienation from the collectivity" (18). I contend that further work on feminist coalitions must defend yet complicate the role of self and complex identity politics in work across difference.

ENDNOTES

1 I refer to "coalition work" here as Cole and Luna defined it: "the process through which groups that define themselves as different work together politically, either long or short term, in the service of some mutually valued end" (71).

2 Cole and Luna describe the "new social movements" as "the non-class-based social movements that emerged beginning in the 1960s" (75).

3 I refer to "selfhood" or "self" broadly as, what Linda Martín Alcoff has called, "lived subjectivity" or "how we experience being ourselves" in specific places and times (93). My definition

is generally consistent with feminist phenomenological accounts of self. Self in this context is interchangeable with Erin Tarver's recent use of the term "subjectivity," which she describes as "the first-person, bodily/cognitive experiences of self that arise in and through particular relations of power, and that are differently privileged or oppressed by virtue of their particular situations with respect to those relations" (815). Tarver's work notably focuses on philosophical and political articulations of the relational self. In my work, I focus, as Anzaldúa did, on selfhood as an emotional, cognitive, physical, and spiritual experience, as a body in motion with all that surrounds it, seen and unseen, and certainly felt. I use the term "identities" in reference to parts of the self, what Tracy Robinson called "both visible and invisible domains of the self that influence self-construction" (85). Identities are created, not naturally acquired. They are personal and social, individually claimed by selves, and used socially to label groups in which individual members participate.

4 Prior to the essay "now let us shift," Anzaldúa makes reference to the concept of "la naguala" in several essays and interviews, most extensively so in the article "Putting Coyolxauhqui Together" (242, 249 – 250, 253, 254). She also mentions "la naguala" in the articles "Speaking Across the Divide" (293) and "The New Mestiza Nation" (211). Anzaldúa's use of la naguala is connected to the "nagual" or, according to nagualism, the shape shifter. Traditionally the nagual refers to a human who shifts to animal forms, or an animal that serves as a companion or spirit guide. Brinton reported that in the Náhuatl language, all words with the root "na" referenced "knowing" and/or knowledge (13). Anzaldúa makes use of all three of these definitions in her descriptions of la naguala prior to "now let us shift." In "Putting Coyolxauhqui Together," an essay about the writing process, she refers to la naguala as "animal in you and your animal-companion, yourself and other" (249) and "a hyperempathetic perception (that) fuses you with your surroundings" (250); however, in this essay she does not expand on la naguala's ability to connect humans with each other. The essay does describe in detail the process of "embodying consciousness," making mind, emotions, body, and writing, one (250). Only in "now let us shift" does Anzaldúa define the role of la naguala in the process of conocimiento and coalition, or la naguala as a specific function of the self, a type of shape shifting, yes, but what's shifting is the self's perception of its connectedness *to other beings* and the world. I believe that Anzaldúa was again honoring all three traditional definitions of nagual in "now let us shift": the nagual as shape shifter, the nagual as inextricable companion, and nagual as knower. But la naguala, in this essay, refers to a shifting consciousness, a consciousness, a knowledge-base that can *only be gained in relation to others.*

5 One way we come to know selfhood, our own and others', is through the written and oral narratives. I am interested in how self-narratives are used as means for not only making sense of experience, relationships, and identities, but for creating them. I will argue that narratives not only reveal but are a part of how one negotiates a lived sense of self *with* their solidarity with others and that this process is an important part of the journey of working with diverse

others to end multiple forms of oppression and privilege. Although narratives may be written in isolation, they are always constructed in conversation with the world around us; narratives are living tools through which selves in relationship are discovered and understood. Therefore, my considerations of selfhood are theoretical and narrative in nature.

6 I will go into more detail about Anzaldúa's notion of consciousness further into the paper because I realize this claim, particularly as it has been pulled out of its context, may seem to have some problematic or at least complicated elements, like its assumption of agency. But I argue later that this emphasis on consciousness is a component worthy of consideration in deepening discourse on coalition.

7 In the previous paragraph, Anzaldúa refers to this moment as a "merger" of la naguala and "the object observed" (569). Here one can see clearly the connection between this new usage of la naguala and its traditional Náhuatl meaning.

8 For a description of Anzaldúa's concept of mestiza consciousness see *Borderlands: La Frontera* and for Sandoval's differential consciousness see *Methodology of the Oppressed.* Both argue that a particular consciousness is created through the lived experience multiple oppressions.

WORKS CITED

Adams, Katherine. "At the Table with Arendt: Toward a Self-interested Practice of Coalition Discourse." *Hypatia* 17.1 (2001): 1-33. Print.

Alcoff, Linda Martín. *Visible Identities: Race, Gender, and the Self.* New York: Oxford University Press, 2006. Print.

Anzaldúa, Gloria E. *Borderlands: La Frontera.* San Francisco: Aunt Lute Books, 1987. Print.

---. "now let us shift...the path of conocimiento...inner work, public acts" *This Bridge We Call Home: Radical Visions for Transformation.* Eds. AnaLouise Keating and Gloria Anzaldúa. New York: Routledge, 2002. Print.

---. "Putting Coyolxauhqui Together: A Creative Process." *How We Work.* Eds. Marla Morris, Mary Aswell Doll, and William F. Pinar. New York: Peter Lang, 1999. Print.

---. "(Un)natural Bridges, (Un)safe Spaces." *The Gloria Anzaldúa Reader.* Ed. AnaLouise Keating. Durham: Duke University Press, 2009. Print.

Brinton, Daniel G. Nagualism. "A Study in Native American Folk-Lore and History." *Proceedings of the American Philosophical Society* 33.144 (1894): 11-73. Web. 14 Oct. 2012.

Cole, Elizabeth and Zakiya Luna. "Making Coalitions Work: Solidarity across Differenc within US Feminism." *Feminist Studies.* 36.10 (2010): 71-97. Print.

Ezekiel, Judith. "I Grew up White: Dayton Girl Crosses Borders, Changes Race." Women's Studies Lecture Series. Wright State University, Dayton, OH. 6 April 2007. Address.

Fowlkes, Diane. "Moving from Feminist Identity Politics to Coalition Politics through a Feminist Materialist Standpoint of Intersubjectivity in Gloria Anzaldúa's *Borderlands/La Frontera: The New Mestiza.*" *Hypatia.* 2:2 (1997): 105-124. Print.

Keating, AnaLouise, ed. *Gloria E. Anzaldúa: Interviews/Entrevistas.* New York: Routledge, 2000. Print.

---. *Teaching Transformation: Transcultural Classroom Dialogues.* NY: Palgrave MacMillan, 2007. Print.

Lugones, María. "On Complex Communication." *Hypatia.* 21.3 (2006): 75-85. Print.

Miranda, Deborah and AnaLouise Keating. "Footnoting Heresies: Email Dialogues." *This Bridge We Call Home Radical Visions for Transformation.* Eds. AnaLouise Keating and Gloria Anzaldúa. New York: Routledge, 2002. Print.

Ortega, Mariana. "'New Mestizas,' 'World-Travelers,' and 'Dasein': Phenomenology and the Multi-voiced, Multi-cultural Self." *Hypatia.* 16.3 (2001): 1-29. Print.

Sandoval, Chela. *Methodology of the Oppressed.* Minneapolis: University of Minnesota Press, 2000. Print.

Shotwell, Alexis and Trevor Sangrey. "Resisting Definition: Gendering through Interaction and Relational Selfhood." *Hypatia.* 24.3 (2009): 56-76. Print.

Tarver, Erin. "New Forms of Subjectivity: Theorizing the Relational Self with Foucault and Alcoff." *Hypatia.* 26.4 (2011): 804-825. Print.

Young, Iris. "The Complexities of Coalition." *Dissent: A Quarterly of Politics and Culture.* (1997). Web. 4 May 2012.

I want to thank Jen McWeeny and Amy Morgenstern for their invaluable comments on drafts of this paper.

HAUNTED BY VOICES: HISTORICAL IM/MATERIALISM AND GLORIA ANZALDÚA'S MESTIZA CONSCIOUSNESS

CATHRYN J. MERLA-WATSON

What is considered theory in the dominant academic community is not necessarily what counts as theory for women-of-color...Necesitamos teorías that will rewrite history using race, class, gender and ethnicity as categories of analysis, theories that cross borders, that blur boundaries—new kinds of theories with new theorizing methods. We need theories that will point out ways to maneuver between our particular experiences and the necessity of forming our own categories and theoretical models for the patterns we uncover.

— Gloria Anzaldúa *(Making Face, Making Soul)*

In the introduction to the watershed 1990 anthology *Making Face, Making Soul/Haciendo Caras: Creative and Critical Perspectives by Women of Color*, from which the above quotation is taken, Gloria Anzaldúa exhorts women of color to forge their own theories that refuse the imperative of western universalism. Instead, she encourages them to speak to and illuminate their own lived experiences, ways of understanding that give insight into our diverse histories, hopes, dreams, desires, even our espantos or ghosts—that which invisibly, yet palpably, structures our lifeworlds and construct particular horizons of possibility. The role of theory, which Anzaldúa conceives as a "mental viewing" or "formulation of apparent relationships," is to unravel the complex threads with which we compose various "masks" as an interface between the subject and various systems of power, as well as to begin to re-member identity, or what she terms "making faces" or "haciendo caras." This revisioning of theory, though, also implies that we must grapple with the slippery matter of the unapparent, the shadowy "membrane of the past superimposed on the present", without letting it consume or derail us (xxvii). Doing so requires that we learn to bridge, to learn to live and reckon with our ghosts and to traverse and connect multiple terrains of power by fashioning "theories that overlap many 'worlds'" (xxvi). The domain of theory, then, should be a collective enterprise of suturing multiple constituent elements of identity and lived experience, in addition to recomposing a radical "altarity," borrowing from Laura E. Pérez, that includes the seemingly dead, to re-engage new pasts and re-imagine and co-construct new presents and futures.[1] I argue here that Anzaldúa in her reconceiving of theory, and more specifically her articulation of mestiza consciousness and ontology, enunciates a more holistic alt*a*rnative interpretative practice for understanding Latina/o cultural production that brings into relief how materiality is animated by the seemingly immaterial or invisible armature that concretely gives shape and signification to social life. In this way, Anzaldúa radically re-energizes how we might understand and approach the complexities and entanglements of materiality, memory, and history in the way in which she underscores how the material is always already to some extent infused by that which resists easy legibility, including the psychological, spiritual, and the socially spectral more generally.

Anzaldúa's intuitive and holistic hermeneutic of new mestiza consciousness indexes not only this mutually informing relationship between the material and so-called immaterial or what I term an "historical im/materialism," but also concomitantly enacts an alternative to the Hegelian-Marxist dialectic,[2] which has occupied a central role in gleaning meaning from Latina/o cultural production since the 1970s.[3] Because of its reliance upon the visual and its binary parameters, the dialectic proves inadequate in the analysis of the unruly and multivalent forces of what sociologist Avery Gordon calls "ghostly matters," which, at least in part, composes the new mestiza and perhaps all post/modern subjectivity.[4] And while the dialectic has undoubtedly functioned as a preliminary useful tool for understanding the social or ideological (de)construction of aesthetics and canon and social transformation, it delimits in advance what composes meaning, or what can be gathered, albeit oppositionally, whether it be within the proper home of canon or in creating interpretive lenses for understanding power in our social worlds. In contradistinction to the dialectical approach, to reiterate, Anzaldúa's conceptualization of mestiza consciousness responds to and incorporates the spectral in understanding subjectivity by valorizing and making "count" what is not readily seen—though profoundly felt and sensed—and uncertain within the shadows, absences, and aporias of texts, broadly conceived, in service of formulating and enacting oppositional consciousness and social transformation. This historical im/materialism gestures toward and involves nontransparent forces and structures that guide thought, action, and desire—unruly, eccentric, indiscrete, and fluid spectral matter that cannot be routed by the bifurcated channels of the dialectic.

In the first section I sketch a brief definition of the dialectic, as well as provide a cursory overview of how this approach has informed and predominated the analysis of Latina/o texts, and how this approach precludes engagement with ghostly matters beyond "social death." I then segue to explore how Anzaldúa provides a radically more inclusive and holistic alt*a*rnative to the dialectic through her enunciation of mestiza consciousness and cognate theorizations. By way of closing, or rather carving out new vistas for apprehending subjectivity and lived experiences, I examine how we might apply Anzaldúa's theory of mestiza consciousness to understand the role of spectral matter to an excerpt from queer Chicana playwright Virginia Grise's recent play *blu,* as well as to recent Chicana literary production more broadly. In doing so, I further suggest that such a theoretical approach articulates concurrently new sites and interpretive mechanisms for recuperating queer Chican@[5] history.

LIMITS OF THE DIALECTIC

In the nineteenth century, Karl Marx retooled the dialectic of Hegel, who understood history as emerging from "Spirit" in his forging of a "materialist conception of history," which posited opposing forces of class struggle within particular contexts as a driving force or teleology of history. Its basic formula includes merging a thesis and antithesis into a synthesis through a process of negation, wherein one part or half of this dichotomy sublates the other, although some interpret this process of synthesis to mean that the two parts are held in tension within a coherent totality. Based in the Hegelian philosophy of internal relations, in which reality is understood to be comprised of various parts or elements, the dialectic necessarily involves a process of division and selection to identify the preconditions for capital and wage labor, and to construct tools for the dismantling and overthrow of this capitalist mode of production. As Marxian scholar Bertell Ollman elaborates, the dialectic "provides a perspective for viewing and evaluating" social phenomena through, in Marx's own words "observation and deduction" (118-19). However, many scholars ranging from postmodernist theory, affective studies, and post-humanist theory to neo-Marxist thought have critiqued the dialectic in three central ways that are relevant to how the dialectic has been taken up in Chicana/o-Latina/o literary and cultural studies. The dialectic not only creates a limited binary perspective of the world, or divides it into two parts, but also, and relatedly, understands those two parts as discrete and homogenous. In other words, the dialectic precludes *in advance* the proliferation and heterogeneity of social difference, and it does not account for the complexities and contingencies of our social worlds. Finally, the dialectic privileges the visual: it is an optic that assumes transparency and legibility and occludes other sensual or embodied ways of knowing and approaching the lived world.

By the late 1970s, Marxist criticism and the dialectical approach had already infused Chicano cultural criticism; however, in the early 1980s, Chicana feminism launched powerful critiques to Marxism, particularly in regard to the way in which it elided forms of difference. For example, Sonia Saldívar-Hull underlines how

> Chicana readings of *color blindness* instead of color consciousness in "politically correct" feminist essays indicate the extent to which the issue of race and ethnicity are ignored in feminist and Marxist theories. Theorists such as Rosaura Sánchez, Alma Gómez, Cherríe Moraga, Mariana Romo-Carmona, Gloria Anzaldúa, and Helena María Viramontes, working collectively as in *Cuentos* (Gómez, Moraga, and Romo-Carmona, 1983) and individually as in *Borderlands* (Anzaldúa 1987), insist on illuminating the complications and intersections of multiple systems of exploitation: capitalism, patriarchy, and white supremacy. (204)

Yet, despite such critiques of the ways in which Marxism and white feminism ignore how systems of power work through heterogeneous categories of difference, by the early 1990s, Marxism and its dialectical approach took firm hold within Chicana/o-Latina/o literary studies as a primary mode of inquiry for understanding the ways in which Chicana/o-Latina/o literature is embedded within and challenges particular socio-historical conditions of the Southwest and the Americas, as evidenced with the 1991 publication of the anthology *Criticism In The Borderlands: Studies in Chicano Literature, Culture, and Ideology.* Ramón Saldívar's chapter, for instance, promised a more inclusive pan-American literary canon through "critical dialectical awareness" ("Narrative" 11). While hegemonic narratives under the guise of the all mighty signifier present reality as a universal truth or dictate what appears natural, a dialectical approach exposes and contextualizes their ideological underpinnings in order to carve out space for other perspectives. Narrative, to restate, frames out direct insight into the "ideological formations that concrete situations have produced" ("Narrative" 16). And although he understands narratives as heterogeneous, the dialectical approach obscures this heterogeneity embedded in texts through its binary structure and dependency on the visual aspects of ideology.

Around the same time of the publication of this anthology, José David Saldívar and Ramón Saldívar published their own highly influential scholarly monographs, *The Dialectics of Our America: Genealogy, Cultural Critique and Literary History* and *Chicano Narrative: The Dialectics of Difference,* that espoused a dialectical approach to Chicana/o and Latina/o literature as well as literatures of the Americas more broadly. Inspired by 1980s New Historicism's emphasis on the way in which expressive acts, including texts, are embedded within a network of material practices, they argue in various manners that meaning should be gleaned from narrative through a dialectical relationship to particular socio-political and cultural histories. More specifically, they draw upon Fredric Jameson's *The Political Unconscious: Narrative as a Socially Symbolic Act,* published in 1981, in which he attempts to bridge literary theory and history through dialectical materialism, arguing that literary texts are "socially symbolic acts" that emerge from particular ideologies and contexts, informing Jameson's now eponymous imperative: "Always historicize!" (9). Literature, then, is not a passive text, but rather an active mechanism that mediates the Real, and must therefore be recognized as allegorical to reveal ideological contradictions and tensions within the real world. Calling upon psychoanalytic theory, Jameson proposes that identifying contradictions within the formal elements of text etches out a temporary window into an underlying political unconscious, "the unity of a single great collective story" (19). Jameson writes:

> Only Marxism can give us an adequate account of the essential *mystery* of the cultural past, which, like Tiresias drinking the blood, is momentarily returned to life and warmth and allowed once more to speak, and to deliver its long-forgotten message in surroundings utterly alien to it. This mystery can be reenacted only if the human adventure is one. (19)

However, not only does Jameson reduce and essentialize all history to that of a singular and homogenous class struggle or unity, but also, in doing so, assumes that once "long-dead issues" that return to and haunt the present, or the "intangible historicity of concepts and categories" (9), are always immediately legible and accessible through language or discourse. Through his reliance on legibility and ideology, Jameson thus dangerously reinscribes the very silences to which he seeks to give voice. Many of the tensions surrounding visibility, wholeness, and homogeneity that haunt and trouble Jameson's dialectical account of narrative also inhere in dialectical analyses of Chicana/o and Latina/o literature.

The dialectic, moreover, has largely shaped work on identity, history, and social consciousness in relation to urban space and place in Chicana/o-Latina/o literary and cultural studies. In *Barrio Logos: Space and Place in Urban Chicano Literature and Culture,* for example, Raúl Homero Villa analyzes Chicana/o cultural production in relationship to urban geographies through what he calls "barriology," a form of knowledge produced through the interplay or dialectic between "socially deforming (barrioizing) and culturally affirming (barriological) spatial practices" (8). This analytic, though, presumes that the ostensibly socially deforming and affirming are mutually exclusive of one another, and forecloses recognizing the ways in which each "side" is complexly or multiply composed. As Mary Pat Brady notes, places function through myriad and simultaneous interactions or "as nodes in articulated networks" (127). Consequently, Villa's dialectic consigns the ghostly to the realm of social death, erasure, or that which functions as a solely deconstructive force, as demonstrated in his reading of the ghostly in the literary work of Helena María Viramontes and Lorna Dee Cervantes. But as Avery Gordon reminds us, the ghost is also a social figure, an absent presence that also functions as a marker of hope and reconstruction through what she calls "transformative recognition" that is not necessarily circumscribed within the visual. The specterly also functions, particularly in the writing of women of color,[6] as an entanglement of loss and desire, past traumas and present yearnings, the embodied and disembodied, or, to restate, structures of lived experience that coalesce in sometimes unexpected and previously unthinkable ways that are not necessarily antithetical or mutually exclusive.

MEMBRANES OF THE PAST: HISTORICAL IM/MATERIALISM

In contradistinction to the historical or dialectical materialism that has dominated Chicana/o Studies for roughly the past two decades, the work of Anzaldúa, particularly her formulation of new mestiza consciousness and ontology, articulates a powerful and alternative methodology for reckoning with the spectral matters of Chicana/o cultural production. Further, it galvanizes a more holistic, intuitive, embodied theorization of subjectivity, textuality, and materiality in relationship to history and lived experience that does not depend on ready transparency, binary divisions, or unified wholes. Her work summons the specters of lived experience and the socially spectral more generally, or, that is, incorporates the unseen, yet felt, into knowledge production. As Jorge Capetillo-Ponce posits, Anzaldúa's theorization of the new mestiza only superficially resembles Marx's dialectic in that it coheres two seemingly disparate elements and produces a new third composition ("On Borderlands and Bridges"). However, in this synthesis, I would add, one element does not sublate the other, but rather the very terms of the seeming binary are deconstructed and undermined in order to understand mestiza subjectivity and ontology. This embodied and affective register of knowledge production refuses and confuses the binary logic of the dialectic, the thesis and antithesis, which in turn corroborate through antagonism and sublation to produce synthesis. The new mestiza functions as a dynamic and contingent assemblage who does not deny her constituent parts or "worlds," but rather actively works through and among them in a reconstructive project of healing and surviving through re-membering, whereby engendering a "metaphysics of interconnectivity" (Keating 13). As such, Capetillo-Ponce identifies a central tension of conceiving mestiza consciousness through the dialectic:

> What sets Anzaldúa apart from Marx, however, is her disinclination to draw any clear-cut distinction between the material world below and ideas hovering above. It is as if she is telling us that ideas and the material world are so intimately intertwined that it is impossible to pry the two apart. And here we encounter a problem, for in the absence of sustained efforts to divide the world into opposing categories by which the thinker can then see the march of events as slowly synthesizing, can a thinker's method truly be called "dialectical"? (169)

For many materialists, though, the very mention of spirituality or metaphysics is enough to conjure the hoary phantasm of Hegelian idealism and provoke thinly veiled disdain and automatic distrust, if not downright hostility. And while it is not my intention to define or wholly circumscribe Anzaldúa's spirituality or metaphysics, it is my aim to underline the ways in which Anzaldúa explores how the material is always already infused by the seemingly immaterial (as well as the inverse) and radical heterogeneity, and in doing so, disintegrating the binary division between them.

In resituating an Anzaldúan "mestiza metaphysics" in relation to dominant queer theory, Mikko Tuhkanen asserts that the new mestiza names a "metaphysics of not only interconnectedness, but of constitutive crossing" between worlds, and that "'bridging' of entities, their hybridization, enables an evolutionary deformation of current existence and a becoming-other of what is presently available" (270, 271). Anzaldúa does not signal an idealism detached from the here and now, but rather indexes a Borderlands ontology by mining lived experience for its "virtual past" to enunciate a "a future uncontained in the repertoire of present possibilities" (271). In a similar vein, in her monograph *Chicana Art*, Laura E. Pérez examines how several Chicana artists and writers, including Anzaldúa, from the 1970s to 2000 call upon the spiritual and non-western epistemologies to challenge Eurocentric and imperialist worldviews to tap into "a new resource of politics," and to imagine new grounds for politic practice or "spirit work" (3). Pérez reflects how within this diverse corpus she

> perceived a language of the ephemeral, the unseen, and the half-present that expressed the spiritual as a reference either to the divine or to that which is socially ghostly—certain bodies, desires, cultures, even locations. In this sense, the artwork itself was altar-like, a site where

> the disembodied—divine, emotional, or social—was acknowledged, invoked, mediated upon, and released as a shared offering. (5-6)

These artists thus intertwine the material and immaterial or the seemingly insignificant within Eurocentric registers of meaning-making in order to more fully re-assemble and communicate their own particular and collective lived experiences and political struggles.

In her articulation and re-assemblage of the new mestiza in *Borderlands/ La Frontera,* Anzaldúa grounds and connects her to the complex geography of Borderlands. She commences with a poetic description of the ways in which the new mestiza identity is embodied, fluid, and haunted by the "emotional residue of an unnatural boundary" between the U.S. and Mexico: "1,950 mile long open wound / dividing a *pueblo,* a culture, / running down the length of my body, / staking fence rods in my flesh / splits me splits me / *me raja me raja* / This is my home / this thin edge of / barbed wire" (24-25). Anzaldúa poetically renders here how the new mestiza social body is mutilated and dismembered by the violent legacies of colonialism, tangible forces that "split her": "The U.S.-Mexican border *es una herida abierta* where the Third World grates against the first and bleeds" (25). The land, figured as female and penetrable within imperialist discourses, is conceived as an "open wound" that is also intimately tethered to the new mestiza social body. This liminal space, moreover, is home to "los atravesados": "the squint-eyed, the perverse, the queer, the troublesome, the mulato, the half-breed, the half dead" (25). The Borderlands are indeed not only connected to and embodied within the new mestiza, but are also a geography inhabited and animated by the socially spectral, or in the words of French philosopher Jacques Rancière, "the part which has no part": what is present, perhaps even at the "center," but not visible or accounted for (or held accountable to) by those in power. They are shadowy half-present figures who have been historically allocated to the invisible or unintelligible within the hegemonic distribution of common sense.

Yet, the new mestiza does not solely index a "state of injury" or a reactive *being,* but also is simultaneously elaborated as productive *becoming,* a subjectivity whose matter and becoming extends beyond violently imposed borders, or what escapes binary mechanisms of divide and conquer. The poem continues: "But the skin of the earth is seamless. / The sea cannot be fenced, / *el mar* does not stop at the borders" (25). She is formed in the interstice in the "lifeblood" "in between," "a vague and undetermined place created by the emotional residue of an unnatural boundary. It is in a constant state of transition" (25). She is thus continually shifting and crossing, embodying a subjectivity-on-the-move, for she continually traverses and bridges various physical, spiritual, and psychological worlds and thresholds, never allowing herself to remain too comfortable or safe. In various works, Anzaldúa thus turns to the Mesoamerican goddesses Coatlicue and her daughter Coyolxauhqui as figures of consciousness and healing through re-membering the Chicana social body. While Coatlicue represents "a third perspective" or more than "a synthesis of duality" (68) as well as the potential or germinal that must be activated in order to reckon with the violences of conquest and bridge cognitive worlds and her constituent parts, including ghosts of the past, to reconstitute the self, Coyolxauhqui, who was dismembered by her brother Huitzilopochtli, is re-imagined as an empowered figure of perpetual recomposition and spiritual growth, a model for "temporarily restoring your balance and wounded psyche" ("now let us shift" 562). In a 1994 interview with Debra Blake and Carmen Abrego, Anzaldúa states:

> I think the reason this image [Coyolxauhqui] is so important to me is that when you take a person and divide her up, you disempower her. She's no longer a threat. My whole struggle in writing, in this anticolonial struggle, has been to put us back together again. To connect up the body with the soul and the mind with the spirit. That's why for me there's such a link between the text and the body, between textuality and sexuality, between the body and the spirit. (220)

This recuperation of female deities, and particularly Coyolxauhqui, works to resist Cartesian dualisms and bring into relief the way in which mestiza identity, and all subjectivity, is multiply constituted and evolving.

And yet, as queer of color studies scholar Rod Ferguson argues, no subjectivity is "innocent" or free from the ever-reaching grasp of capitalism because "capital is based on a logic of reproduction that fundamentally overrides and violates heteropatriarchy's logic," or, to restate, capital and the state rely on and hail "aberrations" for the continuation of capitalist modes of production (16). Many scholars have also inveighed against the overly celebratory discourses of hybridity and flexibility in postmodern theory, underscoring how these theories deracinate difference as well as unintentionally rehearse the co-optive logics of global capitalism that target contingent or "flexible" labor, as the ongoing femicides of maquila workers in Ciudad Juárez horrifically demonstrate. While I agree that no subject formation is ever fully immune to interpellation, I would argue, though, that Anzaldúa constructs a larger theory or metaphysics of knowledge production that emphasizes cognitive dexterity, spectral and embodied ways of knowing, and bridging that characterizes Chicana third space feminism more generally. In the introduction to the watershed anthology *Making Face, Making Soul,* Anzaldúa expounds upon this dynamic and shifting mode of knowledge production enacted by mestizas and radical women of color:

> Wherever we are, we make sure there are several entrances and exits, that our homes have alternative escape routes, and we don't let ourselves

> get painted into corners...Our strength lies in shifting perspectives, in our capacity to shift, in our 'seeing through' the membrane of the past superimposed on the present, in looking at our shadows and dealing with them...*Encrucijadas,* haunted by voices and images that violated us, bearing the pains of the past, we are slowly acquiring the tools to change the disabling images and memories, to replace them with self-affirming ones, to recreate our pasts and alter them—for the past can be as malleable as the present. (xxvi-xxvii)

When occupying cramped spaces the new mestiza and other marginalized social positions, according to Anzaldúa, possess (though "latent" in us all) an extrasensory faculty or "facultad": "the capacity to see in surface phenomena the meaning of deeper reality" (60). It enables the subject to pierce through taut surfaces, textual or otherwise, to recognize and engage with the various constituent components, including shadowy specters, that configure social positionality and lived experience, so as to excavate what moves us, what informs differential horizons of possibility. These ghosts may compose alternative knowledges in pursuit of bridging and social transformation.

In contradistinction to the dialectic, which engenders a static and discrete "synthesis," the ontology of the new mestiza is cognitively agile, for "rigidity means death," and decidedly haunted and porous (Anzaldúa, *Borderlands/La Frontera* 101). Rejecting Cartesian dualisms in addition to western deductive reasoning "that tends to use rationality to move toward a single goal" or synthesis, mestiza consciousness is animated by "divergent thinking, characterized by movement away from set patterns and goals and towards a more whole perspective, one that includes rather than excludes" (101). In this way, mestiza consciousness underlines how the production of meaning and knowledge is not always a transparent and straight-forward process, but rather an inductive and intuitive one, an "assembly" or assemblage of meaning, embodied and textual, that is galvanized by lived experience and genealogies of desire:

> This assembly is not one where severed or separate pieces merely come together. Nor is it a balancing act of opposing powers. In attempting to work out a synthesis, the self has a third element which is greater than the sum of its severed parts. That third element is a new consciousness—a *mestiza* consciousness—and through it is a source of intense pain, its energy comes from continual creative motions that keeps breaking down the unitary aspect of each new paradigm. (101-102)

Though Anzaldúa gestures toward the dialectical through the use of "synthesis," contends Marcial González, the new mestiza consciousness is not "truly dialectical" because, quoting Ramón Saldívar, "a true dialectic necessarily involves us in a negation. In a relationship between opposed terms, one annuls the other and lifts it up into a higher sphere of existence: development through opposition and conflict" (171). However, whereas González dismisses Anzaldúa's new mestiza consciousness as symptomatic of what he diagnoses as general postmodern condition of schizophrenia, postmodern geographer Edward Soja in *Thirdspace* employs Anzaldúa's theorizations of the Borderlands precisely because her work incorporates various voices, images, and other constituent parts of lived experience so as to formulate a "recombinatorial and radically open perspective of space," what he terms "thirding" or the "trialectics of spatiality" that accounts for various overlapping categories of social difference (5, 6-7).

Anzaldúa's new mestiza consciousness theorizes, in summary, a borderlands assemblage or subjectivity and mode of knowledge production that bridges and manifests through the interstices of thesis and antithesis, first and third world, self and other. It authorizes a more holistic and embodied perspective, including the socially spectral, that not only undermines binaries by connecting and refashioning them, but also calls into question the very power relations that carve out and maintain those binaries.

QUEER HISTORIAS AND NEW MESTIZA INSURGENCIES

In closing, I briefly demonstrate the transformative interpretive possibilities in employing mestiza consciousness as a theoretical lens—though it is by no means limited by the ocular—for understanding subjectivity, social life, and queer Chican@ history in the recent play *blu,* by Virginia Grise, which won the 2010 Yale Drama Award, and its implications for making sense of recent ghostly Chicana literature in relation to the recuperation of queer history more generally. Inspired by Grise's own lived experience as a queer Chicana, the play *blu* renders an intimate portrayal of how the nation-state and global capitalism cooperate to subsume and devalue particular lives along the mutually informing axes of race, class, gender, sexuality, and citizenship. The play evinces a pervasive claustrophobia as the prison and military industrial complexes, the demand for a global and flexible labor force, and repressive cultural nationalist imaginaries encroach upon and close in on each of the characters' lifeworlds. Focusing on two queer Chicana lovers and partners, Soledad and Hailstorm, and their children, (Soledad's biological children), Blu, Gemini, and Lunatico, and their father, Eme, *blu* unearths intertwined structures of affect and lived experience to reconstitute Chicana subjectivity. As the play's barrio setting virtually encroaches upon and suffocates the characters, ghosts, and the socially spectral are partially brought into relief, foregrounding the ways in which geography is experienced affectively and differentially, albeit in no automatically legible or intelligible manner.

The following passage occurs near the conclusion of the play and follows in tandem with traumatic flashbacks of the rape of Soledad's daughter and her son's death in Iraq. Soledad recounts to her partner Hailstorm:

> you know sometimes after work, after work, I drive, drive into the hills. turn off my headlights. stare at the lights. city lights from the hill's terrace. just think how big the world is you know. wonder how I got here. why here? this neighborhood, this street. sometimes I walk in the hills, underneath a full moon. can hear the wailing at night behind the mission walls still standing. see the white horses disappear between buildings. there's that spot where the tracks are at. a crossroads at the bottom of the hill. they call that spot ghost town. say that in ghost town, the children will push you over the railroad tracks. the handprints of children left in dust, the handprints of dead children, ghost children. i go up there. try to listen to the voices of the ancestors in the trains passing…i ain't ever been alone. not really. first baby at seventeen. moved from my father's house to my man's house. to a house with my children. to a house with my children and my lover. (54-55)

This site is haunted by an invisible net of history and embodied memory, specters of colonialism and misogynist transnational imaginaries—the (tri)strangulation of La Llorona, and by symbolic extension, Malinche and Cihuacoatl—the children of the Ghost Tracks out by the San Antonio missions, a Native American horse ghost of the Alamo. They give sense to both loss and desire, what we cannot always say or write, or even admit to ourselves, but what we know deep down in our huesos anyway, what we profoundly *feel*. They are revelatory of not just impending social death or necropolitics, but they additionally gesture toward an assemblage of im/material relationships that immobilize and move individuals and communities toward constituent horizons of possibility through a "continual creative motion" of simultaneous re- and deconstruction (Anzaldúa, *Borderlands/La Frontera* 80). In the final moments of the play, Soledad sits upon the roof, gazing toward the horizon, and tries to make sense of her tragedy by re-membering her kin, and, by metonymic association, a community besieged simultaneously by overlapping forces of neocolonialism, securitization and a so-called war on terror, and global postmodern capitalism that targets and leeches sexualized, gendered, and racialized labor from "los atravesdos." Here Soledad calls for "ocean waters" to "carry us home," simultaneously real and imagined matter that interconnects various bodies and lived experiences,[7] an im/material force that surges through and beyond the binaries of the dialectic, for "*el mar* does not stop at the borders" (Anzaldúa, *Borderlands/La Frontera* 25).

In her essay "Queering the Borderlands: The Challenges of Excavating the Invisible and Unheard," theorist and historian Emma Pérez reflects upon the various impasses of recovering queer Borderlands histories, such as a lack of "proper" archival documents or texts, which only reinforce the "colonial heteronormative gaze." She describes this "colonial imaginary" as a rigid optic that understands categories of difference and identity as well as national identity as singular, homogenous, and static. For this reason, she became "impatient" and contested the colonial imaginary by writing her novel *Forgetting the Alamo, Or Blood Memory*, which featured her own "*tejana* baby butch, named Micaela Campos, who must avenge her father's death at the Battle of San Jacinto, just a month after the fall of the Alamo" (122). Pérez continues: "And so, we will make her up or locate documents to uncover a history of sexuality on the borderlands that is hidden from the untrained *eye*" (124; emphasis mine). As literary and cultural studies scholar Louis Mendoza has noted, not only is the writing of history a literary endeavor, but also that literature, and particularly Chicana/o literature, necessarily functions as an alternative archive of "historical evidence" due to the ways in which systemic national and colonial violences have rendered the voices of this group silent and marginalized (19). However written texts, and especially recent Chicana/o literary expression, offer us more than just that or what we can *see*, but that which invisibly structures affect, something ghostly that grabs, arrests us, and ruptures our normative ways of seeing, feeling, and being. While Micaela is haunted by various interrelated misogynist colonial imaginaries, she herself becomes a ghostly narrator, whereby foregrounding the subjective nature of the telling of history. Turtle, a homeless and transgender character in Helena María Viramontes's novel *Their Dogs Came With Them*, remains socially spectral throughout the novel as she wanders the apocalyptic streets of East Los Angeles during the late 1960s and early 1970s, as this area is "quarantined" for ostensibly rabid dogs that are symbolic of the novel's dehumanized and dispossessed Chicana/o characters. This chorus of queer characters—Soledad, Micaela, and Turtle—thus together beg the questions: How do we respond to their complex predicaments and historias, their ghostly matter, or how is it that they differentially "feel brown," to borrow from José Esteban Muñoz ("Feeling Brown")? And more pointedly, how do we feel them, their absent presence, and become responsible to them and, in doing so, maybe ourselves? As I have suggested here, Anzaldúa's new mestiza consciousness helps us to holistically and intuitively make *sense* of them beyond the strangulation of the dialectic and social death, and enables us to become haunted by their voices so as to let them guide us toward a "minoritarian theory of affect" (Muñoz 71), as well as the concrete horizons of possibility they signal—though in no certain terms or terrains.

ENDNOTES

1 See *Chicana Art: The Politics of Spiritual and Aesthetic Altarities.*

2 In his most recent monograph *Trans-Americanity*, José David Saldívar notes, for example, in an interview with Mónica González García that through the title of *Dialectics of Our America* that he references "the study of Hegelian-Marxist dialectic (and immanent critique)" (184).

3 For the purposes of this essay, I focus mainly on how Marxism infuses the study of Chicana/o-Latina/o literature since the late 1990s, particularly through the lens of New Historicism. But as José David Saldívar argues in the first part of *The Dialectics of Our America*, writers such as José Martí, Roberto Fernández Retamar, Gabriel García Márquez, and Rolando Hinojosa constellate a larger oppositional American literary history as well as a transnational and transhistorical Marxist critique through their interrogation of dependency theory by dramatizing how surplus value is created in the periphery or border zones and then expropriated by the center. Building on the work of Jean Franco and Fernández Retamar, Saldívar contends that José Martí's "Nuestra América" wages a powerful critique of U.S. imperialism and Manifest Destiny, and opened up space for understanding Latin American literature as an amalgamation of Spanish and indigenous perspectives, thereby rewriting American literary history. In his examination of Retamar's critical corpus, such as his autobiographical pamphlet *Caliban*, his essay "Nuestra América y Occidente," and his *Casa de las Américas* essays, Saldívar also situates Retamar as an intellectual of the American hemisphere, and identifies him as advocate of critical cosmopolitanism and pan-American politics. Saldívar posits, too, that Retamar's leadership in the Casa de las Américas in Havana, which formally recognized Chicano letters as constitutive of this Latin American "new narrative," was central to resisting the hegemony of Eurocentric literary canon and forging an oppositional American literary history. The Casa, furthermore, enabled various cultural, political, and national crosspollinations that helped progress this pan-American "new narrative," which draws upon various and diverse pan-American literary styles, as evident in the fiction of Gabriel García Márquez and Rolando Hinojosa. In addition, just as García Márquez in his early novels concerning the mythical pueblo Macondo highlights the parasitical nature of the core in relationship to the periphery and critiques Western imperialism, Chicano writer Rolando Hinojosa, such as in the *Klail City Death Trap* series, illuminates the disintegration of Mexican ranch society and the emergence of new (Anglo) dominant social and economic order in the Borderlands. According to Saldívar, in summary, many of the writers associated with the Casa not only brought to light the multicultural, transnational, and dialogical nature of American literary history and canon, but also radically undermined U.S. imperialism and modernity as well as critiqued dependency theory.

4 See *Ghostly Matters: Haunting and the Sociological Imagination.*

5 I take a cue here from Sandra K. Soto in *Reading Chican@ Like a Queer: The De-Mastery of Desire* in which she uses "Chican@" to disrupt the gender normative signifiers "Chicana" and

"Chicano." This is particularly important to my analysis in the final section as I conceptualize the spectralization of the transgender character Turtle in the novel *Their Dogs Came With Them*, by Helena María Viramontes.

6 For an extended discussion of how writing by U.S. women and people of color use the spectral as a vehicle for addressing collective historical trauma, see, for example, Kathleen Brogan's *Cultural Haunting: Ghosts and Ethnicity in Recent American Literature* and Patricia Holland's *Raising the Dead: Readings of Death and (Black) Subjectivity*.

7 The play links the diasporic experiences of African Americans and Mexican Americans through metaphors of water, or what black queers studies scholar Omise'eke Natasha Tinsley calls the "materiality of water," in her reconceiving of a queer black Atlantic (212).

WORKS CITED

Anzaldúa, Gloria. *Borderlands/La Frontera: The New Mestiza.* 2nd ed. San Francisco: Aunt Lute Books, 1999. Print.

---. "Doing Gigs: Speaking, Writing, and Change, An Interview with Debbie Blake and Carmen Abrego (1994)." *Gloria E. Anzaldúa: Interviews/Entrevistas.* Ed. AnaLouise Keating. 211-33. Print.

---. "Haciendo caras, un entrada." *Making Face, Making Soul*/Haciendo Caras: *Creative and Critical Perspectives by Women of Color.* San Francisco: Aunt Lute Press, 1990. xv-xxviii. Print.

---. "now let us shift...the path of conocimiento...inner work, public acts." *this bridge we call home: radical visions for transformation.* Ed. Gloria E. Anzaldúa and AnaLouise Keating. New York: Routledge, 2002. 540-78. Print.

Brady, Mary Pat. *Extinct Lands, Temporal Geographies: Chicana Literature and the Urgency of Space.* Durham: Duke UP, 2002. Print.

Brogan, Kathleen. *Cultural Haunting: Ghosts and Ethnicity in Recent American Literature.* Charlottesville: UP of Virginia, 1998. Print.

Capetillo-Ponce, Jorge. "On Borderlands and Bridges: An Inquiry into Gloria Anzaldúa's Methodology." *Bridging: How Gloria Anzaldúa's Life and Work Transformed Our Own.* Ed. AnaLouise Keating and Gloria González-López. Austin: U of Texas P, 2011. 165-71. Print.

Ferguson, Roderick A. *Aberrations in Black: Toward a Queer of Color Critique.* Minneapolis: U of Minnesota P, 2004. Print.

González, Marcial. "Postmodernism, Historical Materialism and Chicana/o Cultural Studies." *Science & Society* 68.2 (2004): 161-86. Print.

Gordon, Avery. *Ghostly Matters: Haunting and the Sociological Imagination.* Minneapolis: U of Minnesota P, 1997. Print.

Grise, Virgina. *blu.* New Haven: Yale UP, 2011. Print.

Holland, Patricia. *Raising the Dead: Readings of Death and (Black) Subjectivity.* Durham: Duke UP, 2000. Print.

Jameson, Fredric. *The Political Unconscious: Narrative as a Socially Symbolic Act.* Ithaca: Cornell UP, 1982. Print.

Keating, AnaLouise. "From Borderlands and New Mestizas to Nepantlas and Nepantleras: Anzaldúan Theories for Social Change." *Human Architecture: Journal of the Sociology of Self-Knowledge* 4.3 (2006): 5-16. Print.

Mendoza, Louis Gerard. *Historia: The Literary Making of Chicana & Chicano History.* College Station: Texas A&M UP, 2001. Print.

Muñoz, José Esteban. "Feeling Brown: Ethnicity and Affect in Ricardo Bracho's *The Sweetest Hangover (and Other STDs).*" *Theater Journal* 52.1 (2000): 67-79. Print.

Ollman, Bertell. *Dance of the Dialectic: Steps in Marx's Method.* Champaign: U of Illinois P, 2003. Print.

Pérez, Emma. "Queering the Borderlands: The Challenges of Excavating the Invisible and Unheard." *Gender On the Borderlands: The* Frontiers *Reader.* Ed. Antonia Casteñeda et al. Lincoln: U of Nebraska P, 2007. 122-31. Print.

Pérez, Laura E. *Chicana Art: The Politics of Spiritual and Aesthetic Altarities.* Durham: Duke UP, 2007. Print.

Rancière, Jacques. *Aesthetics and Its Discontents.* Trans. Steven Corcoran. Cambridge: Polity Press, 2009. Print.

Saldívar, José David. *The Dialectics of Our America: Genealogy, Cultural Critique, and Literary History.* Durham: Duke UP, 1991. Print.

---. *Trans-Americanity: Subaltern Modernities, Global Coloniality, and the Cultures of Greater Mexico.* Durham: Duke UP, 2012. Print.

Saldívar, Ramón. *Chicano Narrative: The Dialectics of Difference.* Madison: U of Wisconsin Press, 1990. Print.

---. "Narrative, Ideology, and the Reconstruction of American Literary History." *Criticism in the Borderlands: Studies in Chicano Literature, Culture, and Ideology.* Ed. Héctor Calderón and José David Saldívar. Durham: Duke UP, 1991. 11-20. Print.

Saldívar-Hull, Sonia. "Feminism on the Border: From Gender Politics to Geopolitics." *Criticism in the Borderlands: Studies in Chicano Literature, Culture, and Ideology*. Ed. Héctor Calderón and José David Saldívar. Durham: Duke UP, 1991. 203-20. Print.

Soja, Edward W. *Thirdspace: Journeys to Los Angeles and Other Real-And-Imagined Places.* Malden, MA: Blackwell Publishing, 1996. Print.

Soto, Sandra K. *Reading Like a Queer: The De-Mastery of Desire.* Austin: U of Texas P, 2010. Print.

Tinsley, Omise'eke Natasha. "Black Atlantic, Queer Atlantic: Queer Imaginings of the Middle Passage." *GLQ: A Journal of Lesbian and Gay Studies* 14.2-3 (2008): 191-215. Print.

Tuhkanen, Mikko. "Mestiza Metaphysics." *Queer Times, Queer Becomings*. Ed. E.L. McCallum and Mikko Tuhkanen. State U of New York P, 2011. 259-94. Print.

Villa, Raúl Homero. *Barrio-Logos: Space and Place in Urban Chicano Literature and Culture.* Austin: U of Texas P, 2000. Print.

SHOCK AND COFFEE: ELABORATING THE SUBTLETIES OF ANZALDÚA'S THEORY OF "INTIMATE TERRORISM"

MEGAN SIBBETT

Through *Borderlands/La Frontera: The New Mestiza* and her other work, Anzaldúa creates a multitude of theoretical paradigms: *mestiza* consciousness, *facultad*, *conocimiento*, and so on. The more we look and understand, the more we realize the depth of Anzaldúan theory. While a theorization of terrorism may not be readily apparent in *Borderlands*, I argue that Anzaldúa creates a dynamic theorization of "intimate terrorism," a concept she situates in profound ways, drawing attention to terrorism within the mundane, historically and contemporarily. The intimacy and persistence of violence becomes evident through her autobiographical and historical (re)counting of the *mundane* aspects of "intimate terrorism," especially as they are entangled with cultural beliefs and historical narratives that cloak violence in protection, normalcy, and a visible invisibility.

While I argue that Anzaldúa's work complicates and critiques mainstream concepts of terrorism, I contend that this is not just an argument that intimate terror exists and should be included in defining terrorism. Rather, I propose, as the *recognition* of such violence develops into a *theorization* of "intimate terrorism" we gain a larger more complex understanding of "terrorism" and violence in U.S. imperializing patterns and projects externally and internally. This theorization and its praxis further enable us to see how the hegemonic, colonial concepts of "terrorism" are challenged and problematized. Through a close and dexterous reading of her work, her theorization of "intimate terrorism" thickens in profound ways. Through such a reading I focus an Anzaldúan concept of "intimate terrorism" that (1) relies on the recognition of intimate and mundane violence, (2) implicates both people (and groups of people) as well as complex systems, (3) identifies violence within perpetual, sustainable systems, and (4) resists victimology as she couches her analysis within a concrete theorization of feminist rebellion.

The phrase "intimate terrorism" occurs in the second chapter of *Borderlands*, a chapter housed under the title "Movimientos de rebeldía y las culturas que traicionan" (rebellious movements and traitorous cultures) (38). In the section titled "Intimate Terrorism: Life in the Borderlands," Anzaldúa has loaded each sentence with multiple layers of meaning. The careful crafting of this section significantly reveals how Anzaldúa conceptualizes "intimate terrorism." All four of the conceptual points mentioned above make up the cartography of this section, though her concept of "intimate terrorism" is not confined to this particular section alone, as she further fleshes out those four components in the larger context of *Borderlands* and in her other work as well.

MUNDANE, INTIMATE VIOLENCE AND TERRORISM

There is no doubt that Anzaldúa's account of life within the borderlands is rife with violence. Prior to her section on "intimate terrorism," her text begins with a historically situated chapter where she accounts for the tumultuous genealogy of the tejana/os who were violently displaced and continually brutalized in the acquisition of land and the creation of a border, "an unnatural boundary" (25). While violence is a constant, as Anzaldúa subtly demonstrates with a historical and contemporary recounting of life in the borderlands, the violence is also varied and applied to multiple groups and individuals. Yet what also accompanies these acts of violence is the incessant *threat of violence* and the accompanying terror. "Tension grips the inhabitants of the borderlands like a virus," Anzaldúa further explains, "Ambivalence and unrest reside there and death is no stranger" (26). As she describes her own lived experience, as well as those of her family and all others who dwell in the borderlands, she not only draws attention to the ongoing violence, she repeatedly underscores the terrorizing threat of constant, daily violence. The pattern she establishes in the first chapter is repeated throughout the text and signifies the presence of not just violence but an "intimate terrorism"—the residual fallout that contaminates the everyday.

Anzaldúa situates this anxiogenic violence in the first paragraph of the "Intimate Terrorism: Life in the Borderlands" section. She begins:

> The world is not a safe place to live in. We shiver in separate cells in enclosed cities, shoulders hunched, barely keeping the panic below the surface of the skin, daily drinking shock along with our morning coffee, fearing the torches being set to our buildings, the attacks in the streets. (42)

The violence described here is an intimate and mundane violence that resonates as a constant threat rather than a singular instance of violence. I contend that Anzaldúa's articulation of such violence, one that is demonstrated through brutal actions *as well as* the maintenance of a constant threatening environment, creates an important divergence among violence and terrorism, and answers why the section is titled "intimate terrorism" rather than "intimate violence." Without creating a false dichotomy of terrorism and violence, Anzaldúa relates the two while also establishing the perpetual terrorizing threat of violence that distinguishes terrorism from violence in specific ways.

Within *Borderlands*, Anzaldúa's poem "Cervicide" illustrates these layers of daily violence, terror, and brutality within a domestic space surrounded by the mundane. The poem's title, Anzaldúa explains, means "the killing of a deer" (127). In order to make sure the metaphorical meaning is not confused, she adds, "In archetypal symbology the Self appears as a deer for women" (127). Through the poem she recounts the killing of Venadita, the pet fawn, by Prieta, the young girl. Both Prieta and her pet fawn are described as dark (prieta), tawny, and spotted (venadita); they mirror each other's movements and emotions while emitting a haunting ordinariness that dramatizes the mundane tone of the poem.

Despite the seemingly methodical killing of Venadita, Anzaldúa situates the poem within a space of perpetual tension—"They had to kill their pet, the fawn. The game warden was on the way with his hounds" (126). With no given explanation, the game warden patrols and surveils Prieta's home—not for the first time either, because both Prieta and her mother are familiar with the sound of his truck. If they are caught with the fawn, Prieta's father will face a fine and go to jail. The absurdity of this law contrasts sharply with the reason why they are raising the fawn—a hunter had killed the fawn's mother and the children found Venadita hours after her birth. The law situates the nurturing of the fawn as a crime and not the brutal killing of her mother. Doomed from the moment of birth and in constant danger in the space in which she survives, Venadita reflects Anzaldúa's earlier description of border dwellers who are also perpetually targeted with exterminating violence. In contrast to Venadita and Prieta, the hunter, sanctioned or at least ignored by the state, and the game warden, the representative of the state, help perpetuate a system where survival is illegal for Venadita and Prieta.

Anzaldúa carefully, but quickly draws attention to Prieta's options for killing the fawn. She cannot turn her loose in the woods, knowing Venadita will come back after having been forced at birth into a system she depends upon for her survivability, which ironically also limits and endangers her. Prieta also cannot shoot Venadita because the warden will hear; demonstrating that the potential violence he can inflict on them is not reciprocal. Instead Prieta must club her fawn to death. Anzaldúa intermixes the brutality of this scene with the details of finding the hours-old fawn and the death of the fawn's mother, blending a scene of inescapable violence from birth to early death. The weight of the hammer folds Prieta's "body backwards" just as the infant fawn had stood, shaking on "her long thin legs [that] were on the edge of buckling" (126). With each blow of the hammer, Venadita and Prieta stare at each other's faces: "Though Venadita's long lashes quivered, her eyes never left Prieta's face. Another thud, another tremor. *La guadria* and his hounds were driving up the front yard. The *venadita* looked up at her, the hammer rose and fell. Neither made a sound" (126). Their silence and knowing looks are not reflective of their passivity or lack of rebellion; instead the silence, punctuated only with the blows of the hammer, indicates the invisible violence that pervades the borderlands, as Anzaldúa demonstrates throughout the entire text of *Borderlands*. This violence also happens in the shed, a familiar everyday space but one tucked away from the eyes of the public and unseen by the warden. Prieta digs a hole in the same shed and rolls Venadita into the hole, along with the empty bottle they used to feed her. This burial of the bottle and the deer symbolizes that nothing can sustain Venadita or Prieta in their world of constant threatening violence. When the warden enters the shed, his hounds claw at the dirt, but the warden jerks them away, no longer interested in patrolling the shed. He has accomplished his task as the violence he came to inflict has already taken place. He leaves to again come unannounced another day. The space, silence, and regular patrolling of the warden contribute to the mundane tone of the poem.

Perhaps sensing that skeptical readers would dismiss the connection between the warden and the killing of Venadita, Anzaldúa's footnote reminds readers of the additional layers of meaning for the poem as Venadita represents not only Prieta, but also the larger category of women. Anzaldúa makes it clear that while violence exists in the borderlands for all genders, women, as subjects further disenfranchised from the state, more often confront daily, perpetual violence that tries to control their reproductive bodies. The construction of the poem exemplifies the point Anzaldúa makes regarding "intimate terror" and violence. Prieta killing the deer is an act of violence, but it is one created and instigated by the larger, daily presence of an "intimate terror" through an oppressive system and its actor, the warden, maintaining a threatening, destructive, and powerful presence.

Like the poem, Anzaldúa's theorization in connection to themes of violence and terrorism in the larger body of her work function as a critique of mainstream recognitions of "terrorism" and "violence." In U.S. media, "acts of terrorism" are often described as the result of an inexplicable and undeserved hatred toward an exceptional nation. Generally the motivation for "terrorism" is either perceived as stemming from general anti-American beliefs or because the "terrorist" is understood to be a monstrous psychopath. "Terrorism" is rarely portrayed as an act of violence backed by a history of living in intimate terror. "Cervicide" illustrates this important but complex point: terrorism, rather than being an inexplicable occurrence, is backed by systems of "intimate terrorism." "Intimate terrorism" is a perpetual state of living with brutal acts of violence *as well as* the daily, haunting presence of violence within the mundane.

Accordingly, in addition to the distinction of terror, terrorism, and violence, Anzaldúa outlines the *daily* violence within the systems of "intimate terrorism." Her phrase "daily drinking shock along with our morning coffee" not only signifies a persistent violence, but also anchors it in a commodity, coffee, that is inscribed with exploitation, power, and imperialism. While this reference is undoubtedly subtle, it is important in understanding how Anzaldúa conceptualizes "intimate terrorism." The notion of mundane violence in no way suggests that such violence is "less" harmful or insignificant. Its quotidian presence often goes unrecognized even though it is as dramatic as Anzaldúa describes. In turning attention toward terrorism in such a way, she enables a scathing critique of the very systems (and people) that position terrorism in ways that hope to avoid implication.

IMPLICATING PEOPLE AND COMPLEX SYSTEMS

Anzaldúa's attention to local and global localities extends her critique of terrorism toward implicating instigators and perpetrators of violence. Because her methodology is situated in a simultaneous local/global analysis, she propels her theorization into locating and naming people, groups, and systems. One of the paragraphs in the "Intimate Terrorism" section begins with the phrase "Not me sold out my people but they me," which Anzaldúa repeats at the beginning of two other paragraphs in the final section of the chapter. Each of these three paragraphs focus on a reversal of betrayal where Anzaldúa, accused of betraying her own home, culture, and history in her feminist and queer rebellion, argues against the act of "glorify[ing] aspects of [her] culture" that harm her in the guise of protection (44). Far from glorification, she demonstrates how particular people and systems create and perpetuate "intimate terrorism." In each of the three paragraphs, her repeating phrase "Not me sold out my people but they me" references three different yet interrelated groups—her *mexicano* culture, Chicano nationalism, and colonizing white Anglo culture. The "my people" travels between these groups as different cultural aspects, namely the "crippling" of women by *mexicano*/border culture, the misogynist portrayal and historicization of *Malinali Tenepal* by Chicano nationalism,[1] and the 300 years of brutal colonization of women of color by Anglo culture (in collusion with Spaniard, Mexican, and Chicano culture, she adds). Such a strategy is invested in critiquing specific systems and groups of people in order to demonstrate more fully and profoundly the long presence of "intimate terrorism."

Anzaldúa's details of her particular phrasing "Not me...but...they" become an intricate and powerfully compact index of her theorization of "intimate terrorism." While at first it may appear that Anzaldúa creates her own "us and them" binary, she in fact confounds it with "my people," especially as those she is referring to as her "people" travel through at least three different groups of people. Moreover, in the use of "my people" she situates herself within them, not apart from them. The illusion of the binary becomes hazy as the phrase takes on multiple meanings and implicates multiple groups that Anzaldúa still claims with the combination of "my people" and "they me." Not only does she upset the false binary that the majority of U.S. "terrorism" tropes rely on, she also emphasizes a local self-scrutiny and a sense of responsibility. While the sense of responsibility factors into the fourth component of her theorization, the strategic rebellion that works against victimology, the self-scrutinizing aspect of involvement within oppressive systems represents the movement toward a localized analysis of various people's involvement in "intimate terrorism."

In her first reference of "Not me sold out my people but they me," Anzaldúa, after emphasizing how "'home' permeates every sinew and cartilage in [her] body," condemns the strategy of "protection" (43). As part of the theorization of "intimate terrorism," her attention to those cultural beliefs carried out in the name of protection reveals the subterfuge of the terrorism tropes situated in an easy binary of "us and them." Suddenly we see terrorism perpetuated within those spaces that were staked out as protective and "anti-terror." Through such theorization Anzaldúa demonstrates the need to turn attention onto the "protectors" in order to gain a greater understanding of terrorism. The significance of this strategy can be further represented in analyzing the definition of terrorism according to the U.S. Code, the official code of laws used by the U.S., the CIA, and the State Department ("Combating Terrorism" 12-13).

---

1 Of course the vilification of *Malinali Tenepal* is not exclusive to Chicano nationalist tropes. Anzaldúa also works against Octavio Paz's construction of "la Malinche" as "la Chingada," a passive, historical object in *The Labyrinth of Solitude*. Other Chicana feminist scholars take up these critiques as well. Norma Alarcón points out that Paz "has displaced the myth of Guadalupe, not with history, but with a neomyth," one that was adopted by Chicano nationals. ("Traddutora, Traditora" 65).

I argue that in the context of post 9/11 mainstream tropes of "terrorism," the significance of Anzaldúa's conceptualization of "intimate terrorism" offers a contrapuntal reading regarding the debates around the standard definitions of terrorism. According to the U.S. Code, "terrorism means premeditated, politically motivated violence perpetrated against noncombatant targets by subnational groups or clandestine agents" ("U.S. Code"). Within the last decade there has been enormous debate and production of scholarship over the definition of terrorism and what definition is appropriate for the U.S.[2] What makes an "official" definition so tricky for the U.S. is the need for a definition that not only ignores self-reflexivity but also eradicates the notion of it. An "official" definition requires a global application as well as a domestic application, but not a "local" application where groups and systems working under the name of "protection" are implicated, whether that protection is in the name of individuals (American citizens, Afghan women) or spaces, commodities, and ideas (the U.S./Mexico border, fossil fuels, "liberty"). Ultimately an "official" working definition cannot implicate particular agents and systems within the U.S. in the ways that Anzaldúa does through her analysis of protection. Neither can it call up a sense of responsibility, an understanding that Anzaldúa demands through her conceptualization of "intimate terrorism."

Anzaldúa's conceptualization of "intimate terror" calls for a breakdown of the "us and them" binary that looks at the intimate terror we carry out on others and ourselves. She turns a gaze not only onto the borderlands outside or in contention with the U.S. but also on the intimate borderlands—the psychological, the personal, the local and the domestic. As we have seen, Anzaldúa's "Intimate Terrorism: Life on the Borderlands" conceptualizes "intimate terrorism" in a way that emphasizes the benign nature and "protective" guise of power's beneficiaries while also refocusing attention on the people and systems that traffic in such terrorism.

Despite the brevity of this particular section, Anzaldúa's conceptualization is far from vague; furthermore, she insists on its application to her own culture. She is not interested in creating a theory that simply celebrates her roots or even

2 Much of this scholarship stems from the discipline of terrorism studies, which emerged after 9/11 as a stand alone academic and research field, a field that receives a great deal of funding (Shepherd; Jackson et. al.). The director of terrorism studies at the University of East London claims that "a new book on terrorism is published every six hours in the English Language" (Shepherd). In a critique of the field, queer theorists Jasbir Puar and Amit Rai argue that terrorism studies relies on a history that "ties the image of the modern terrorist to a much older figure, the racial and sexual monsters of the eighteenth and nineteenth centuries," and that such pathologizing reinforces "an aggressive heterosexual patriotism" (Puar and Rai 117).

her multiple cultures. By utilizing a more Anzaldúan definition of terrorism, we would better understand the complexity of terrorism as well as its intimate and mundane prevalence. We would also have a more keen understanding of the ethereal framing of the "War on Terror." Most importantly, we would better recognize terrorizing systems located in and through the U.S.

As mentioned above, Anzaldúa's framework of "intimate terrorism" implicates multiple groups of people, and it is applicable to multiple systems of oppression as well, systems that Anzaldúa indicts for the ways they manufacture "intimate terrorism." One of the first systems Anzaldúa explicates is dominant culture. "Culture forms our beliefs," Anzaldúa writes in the section on "Cultural Tyranny," a section that precedes the "Intimate Terrorism" analysis (38). She explains: "We perceive the version of reality that it communicates. Dominant paradigms, predefined concepts that exist as unquestionable, unchallengeable, are transmitted to us through culture" (38). Though many may not question or even notice the dominant tyrannical acts of culture, especially on a daily basis, Anzaldúa makes an obvious effort to situate her analysis of culture within spaces of violence.

However it should be noted that while she argues "Culture is made by those in power—men," she does not leave her analysis within a reductive binary where men are to blame and women are innocently and passively submissive, incapable of participating within or perpetuating violence within patriarchal culture. In putting emphasis on males she does not hesitate to call out the greatest benefactors of patriarchy, yet she also establishes patriarchy as a system that we participate in, regardless of our gender. In understanding patriarchy as a system, Anzaldúa creates a more accurate space in which to critique dominant culture and how cultural tyranny is maintained.

Anzaldúa's analysis thickens as her theorization of culture, violence, and power is applied not only on the individual level but also on the tribal/community, national, and global levels. One of the key aspects in the theorization of "intimate terrorism" is this telescoping of the local with the global. She explains that behaviors such as selfishness (or looking after the self) in women are condemned through culture, and she situates this condemnation in the priority of tribal warfare. She writes:

> Tribal rights over those of the individual insured the survival of the tribe and were necessary then, and, as in the case of all indigenous peoples in the world who are still fighting off intentional, premeditated murder (genocide), they are still necessary. (40)

A preliminary reading might criticize Anzaldúa as justifying the very system she critiques—showing why domestic tyranny ultimately is "necessary" (40). I argue, however, that this is not Anzaldúa's intention. Rather she shows how tyranny and colonial violence are maintained in mutually reinforcing oppressive systems. While some of the domestic tyrannical requirements may seem innocuous, particularly in the face of threatened colonial genocide, including the condemnation of female selfishness and ambition—"set[s] of rules so that social categories and hierarchies will be kept in order"—Anzaldúa highlights the inherent violence of casting female care of self as a deviant act. She writes, "Deviance is whatever is condemned by the community. Most societies try to get rid of their deviants," adding, "[m]ost cultures have [also] burned and beaten their homosexuals and others who deviate from the sexual common. (40) Tyranny, then, is maintained not through singular acts of brutality but through policing "deviant" bodies and behaviors that occur within the everyday.

The theorization of "intimate terrorism" thus involves the pairing of sometimes subtle, mundane violences with larger systems of more stark violences. Anzaldúa does not separate these multiple violences into separate systems or analyses. She goes to extra lengths in her writing to avoid creating a hierarchy of more terrible violences. By refusing to rank violences and levels of oppression, Anzaldúa creates a complex, interwoven analysis that refuses to situate violence and terrorism in the hands of a few perpetrators. Rather, she draws attention to multiplicities of oppressors and situates violence and terrorism within a system that is often under-theorized or over-simplified, even in feminist or post-colonial analyses.

PERPETUAL, SUSTAINABLE SYSTEMS

In conceptualizing "intimate terrorism" as perpetuated both by individuals and groups, Anzaldúa also recognizes how complex, competing and interwoven systems can sustain mundane violence. Her example of the survival of the group over the gendered individual demonstrates that such violences do not exist in isolation, but instead are perpetual parts of overlapping systems. Her inclusive critique of Anglo, Chicano, and *Mexicano* culture involves the theoretical application of conceiving "intimate terrorism" as perpetual. In order to meet such an overwhelming presence of violences, she creates a theoretical paradigm that maintains an equally sustainable applicability through its maneuverability amongst the local and global.

To this end Anzaldúa interweaves her critique of multiple cultures, creating a theoretical impetus that applies to multiple spaces within those cultures. For example, the patriarchal system of "protecting" women, Anzaldúa explains, is a system of men "protecting" women and girls from other men. She writes, "don't poach on my preserves, only I can touch my child's body," couching multiple violences that confine women to patriarchally endorsed spaces, roles, and behaviors while simultaneously situating them as constant potential victims of both others and those doing the "preserving." She consequently elaborates the understanding that the system is perpetual—reproducing patriarchal power and, of course, more violence. She overlays this critique of protection with another system of "protection" through religious ideology. While the two justifications for patriarchal protection and religious protection contradict each other, they also work in tandem within "intimate terrorism."

Oppressive power dynamics in patriarchal culture and religion, she argues, specifically rely on the rhetoric of protection. Because women are recognized in "Christianity and most other major religions" as "the stranger, the other" and "closer to the undivine" due to their abilities to create life and menstruate, religious logic situates them as needing protection paradoxically from themselves. She writes, "Humans fear the supernatural, both the undivine (the animal impulses such as sexuality, the unconscious, the unknown, the alien) and the divine (the superhuman, the god in us)" (39). Yet, at the same time, women are seen in need of protection by men from other men. Both patriarchal religions and men benefit from the "protection" scheme, even as the logic behind the two simultaneously portray women as all too powerful and as the male's weak counterpart. She ultimately shows that such systems stifle the ability to react and act, which for Anzaldúa demands active and focused rebellion. As she proclaims, "Our cultures take away our ability to act—shackle us in the name of protection" (42-43). While the two justifications for patriarchal protection and religious protection contradict each other, they also work in tandem within "intimate terrorism."

Through the placement of each section in the second chapter of *Borderlands*, Anzaldúa focuses an analysis on how intimate terrorism is manufactured. Such an understanding recognizes the production and sustainability of "intimate terrorism" in a structural, as well as an ideological, sense therefore enabling its theorization. Prior to the "intimate terrorism" section, she begins by fore-grounding her rebellion and then immediately focuses on "cultural tyranny." As I have argued, the broadly specific scope creates an attention on culture that carries over into "intimate terrorism." When she begins the section with the assertion, "The world is not a safe place to live in," she does not offer the sentence as an abstraction or hyperbole. By weaving specific critiques of multiple cultures, groups, and people with a conceptualization of terrorism and violence, Anzaldúa demonstrates what Cherríe Moraga calls for in avoiding the problem of dealing with oppression from a theoretical base. The most significant aspect of Anzaldúa's conceptualization of "intimate terrorism" is therefore the movement from recognition, to understanding, to rebellion. Her project here is not a simple explanation or portrayal of life in the Borderlands or life in the borderlands with "intimate terrorism"; she is developing a theoretical paradigm for rebellion against such terrorism. In order to understand her rebellion, we must also understand the sustainable nature of the systems that produce "intimate terrorism." Creating a working and adequate method of rebellion requires a non-linear, complex, and interwoven approach, as well as a recognition of the chain reactions between groups, systems, and the advantages those systems bring for those in power.

Through her specific examples, which of course are not an exhaustive listing of contributors to "intimate terrorism," but function as actual and theoretical examples, Anzaldúa accordingly situates terrorism away from a vague, indiscriminate point of origin. She shows how "intimate terrorism" functions within perpetual systems and is enacted by individuals, groups, and systems in order to solidify mechanisms of privilege. Most significantly she demonstrates that such terrorism is situated within our immediate realm, not as something "foreign" or far away.

ASPECTS OF ANZALDÚAN REBELLION AGAINST "INTIMATE TERROR"

Anzaldúa begins and ends her second chapter, "*Movimientos de rebeldía y las culturas que traicionan*," not only with the notion of rebellion, but with its theorization. Through the chapter's title, she places emphasis on framing rebellious movements within a slippery notion of traitorous cultures. The plurality of movements and cultures signifies what I earlier referred to as a sustainable critique of violence and terror. Her use of the phrase "*las culturas que traicionan*" resists the static arena of a binary because, as she demonstrates in this chapter, the cultures examined are multiple, as is the meaning of traitor (37). Therefore the phrase reflects an assembly of dominant, oppressive cultures, groups, and practices; yet, it also enables a feminist, decolonial method that seeks out female and queer icons of rebellion deemed traitorous by various dominant aspects of cultures. Anzaldúa draws out the "feminist architecture" of her rebellion theoretically in three central ways: first, by recognizing the necessary inclusion of the history of indigenous female resistance; second, by inserting a personal, queer, and intimately focused identity of rebellion; and third, by emphasizing a sense of responsibility that rejects victimology and defeatism even while avoiding the oversimplification of violence and resistance (44).

The first aspect of her theorization of rebellion against "intimate terrorism" involves her reclaiming and recovery of indigenous women's histories. As an example, in the final section of the second chapter, titled "The Wounding of the *india*-Mestiza," Anzaldúa explains that through the misogynist historicization of *Malinali Tenepal* within Chicano nationalist memory and naming, that "the worst kind of betrayal lies in making us believe that the Indian woman in us is the betrayer. We, *indias y mestizas*, police the Indian in us, brutalize and condemn her. Male culture has done a good job on us" (44). In her introduction to

Borderlands, Sonia Saldívar-Hull states, "[r]eclaiming and reinventing *Coatlicue*, Malintzín, and *la Llorona/Cihuacoatl* in New Mestiza narratives elaborates the constant shifting identity formations of Anzaldúa's Chicana/mestiza feminist" (7). These female persons and deities of rebellion are theoretically accompanied by other women and Anzaldúa herself. Of course, and obviously, Anzaldúa's project is not to portray herself as the new *Coyolxauhqui* in a self-celebratory text on her feminist accomplishments. Rather, she shows theoretically how indigenous women's rebellious movements are global and local, historical and contemporary, and as personal and intimate as they are abstract and ancient. With such an amalgam of rebels and traitors, she confounds the traitor/rebel binary through a New Mestiza consciousness.

This theme of historical rebellion is accompanied by Anzaldúa's own memory of her rebellion beginning with a snapshot of her six year old self. Yet the personal and intimate nature of her recounting of her own rebellious history goes even deeper. In the first section, "The Strength of My Rebellion," she situates her own intimately focused identity of rebellion. Throughout the chapter she highlights a rebellion that works against a profusion of tyrannies: culture, gender, sexuality, religion, and patriarchy. In a multiplicitous confrontation, Anzaldúa shapes her theory of rebellion through her concept of the "shadow beast" and by queering her rebellion. After describing her "stubborn will" in childhood, she writes: "There is a rebel in me—the Shadow-Beast. It is a part of me that refuses to take orders from outside authorities," but it also "refuses to take orders from my conscious will, it threatens the sovereignty of my rulership" (38). While the "shadow beast" should not be situated as the singular core of Anzaldúa's rebellion, it should be understood as a passionate and difficult part of a personal and collective rebellion.

After the section titled "Half and Half," where she rebels against the "despot duality" of gender, she introduces a queer rebellion that embraces the "shadow beast" in order to recover the "unacceptable parts" people push into the shadows in fear of rejection (38). Queerness is a key component of this aspect of her rebellion. After exploring the active "choice to be queer," she writes that queerness is "an interesting path, one that continually slips in and out of the white, the Catholic, the Mexican, the indigenous, the instincts...It is a path of knowledge—one of knowing (and learning) the history of oppression of our *raza*. It is a way of balancing, of mitigating duality" (41).

This queer political approach and the "shadow-beast" have everything to do with her theory of "intimate terrorism" and the rebellious ways we can situate, understand, and respond to cultures of terrorism.

The "shadow beast" as a component of Anzaldúa's theorization of rebellion is complex, and I only spend time here in drawing attention to its meaning within the specific context of understanding "intimate terrorism." Throughout her work the meaning of the "shadow beast" is illusive. It is a space, a shadow, where we push parts of ourselves, our cultures, histories, or ideas that obstruct the path to assimilation—heteronormativity, U.S. patriotism, and patriarchy. Yet the "shadow beast" is also a rebellious (sense of) being. Anzaldúa elaborates on the varied results or consequences of "[wakening] the Shadow-Beast inside us" (42). In the act of pushing contradictory, unruly parts of ourselves and our histories into the shadow or in ignoring our own shadows, the "shadow beast" personifies a dangerous consequence of willful amnesia.

In "Let Us Be the Healing of the Wound: The Coyolxauhqui Imperative—la sombra y el sueño," an essay she wrote following the attacks on the World Trade Center and the Pentagon on September 11, 2001, Anzaldúa elaborates on her own state of being and her attempts to move "into another state of mind" (304). She explains, "I'm still trying to escape my shadow beasts (desconocimientos): numbness, anger, and disillusionment" (304). In equating "shadow beasts" with *desconocimientos*, she links the "shadow beasts" with a majority of the national emotion and confusion following 9/11. She explains later that such violence and trauma "force us to confront our desconocimientos, our sombras—the unacceptable attributes and unconscious forces that a person must wrestle with to achieve integration" (309). Yet rather than staying within a state of mind dwelling on disillusionment, Anzaldúa follows through on her theory of rebellion and stares the "shadow beast," or in this case disillusionment and anger, in the face. In *Borderlands* she writes that some people, when they gaze upon the "shadow beast," see "not lust but tenderness; on its face we have uncovered the lie" (42). "The lie" in Anzaldúan theory is not meant to be a constant but something that is recognized, learned, or remembered in following a rebellious path that involves recognition.

In "Let Us Be," Anzaldúa is specific about what lies must be uncovered in order to grapple with understanding 9/11 and how "terrorism" was and is constructed at and after that event. She writes, "Bush and half of US Americans fell into fear and hate. The instinct toward violence has become so normalized in this country that many succumbed to reacting inhumanly instead of responding compassionately" (309). Her words directly connect with the notion of intimate terrorism and mundane violence, as epitomized and effaced in the daily cup of coffee, which is normalized in order to sustain more obvious forms of violence. She continues:

> It's unfortunate that we get our national identity and narrative from this majority who refuse to recognize that conflict is not resolved through war. They refuse el conocimiento (spiritual knowledge) that we're connected by invisible fibers to everyone on the planet and that each person's actions impact the rest of the world. (309)

Yet rather than leaving her explication on mundane violence here within what some might consider an abstract or sentimental, multicultural pep talk of "we are all one family and we should learn to love each other," she draws attention to some tangible specifics:

> Putting gas in our cars connects us to the Middle East. Take a shower squandering water and someone on the planet goes thirsty; waste food and someone starves to death. Though we comprise approximately 4.5% of the people on the planet we consume 82% of its resources. And fear, ignorance, greed, over-consumption of resources, and a voracious appetite for power is what this war is about…[W]estern neo-colonialism sucks the resources (life force) of third world countries. (309)

Within this excerpt Anzaldúa brings the theorization for "intimate terrorism" forward and confounds the Bush doctrine binary of "us and them," especially as she does not evade the responsibility for mundane violence that disseminates through U.S. consumerism and imperialism. Rather than succumb to *desconocimiento*, she looks beyond the national narrative of disillusionment and into a more complex understanding of reasons for the "War on Terror," thereby looking the "shadow beast" in the face. In the process of complicating terrorism and 9/11, she draws upon many other instances of perpetual violence through U.S. imperialism in order to better frame the 9/11 rhetoric and policies of the Bush Administration. She describes CIA and U.S.-backed regimes in the past that overthrew independent governments in Chile, El Salvador, Nicaragua, Iraq, Guatemala, Saudi Arabia, South Africa, Indonesia, and the Philippines (306).

Furthermore she confounds the binaries of us/them and traitor/patriot, especially as it is framed within US exceptionalism, by undermining the cowboy hero image of George W. Bush. Throughout the essay she repeatedly draws attention to the cowboy-Bush image, writing, "Bush comes riding in on his white horse, a gunslinger at high noon, bragging that he'll bring in Osama bin Laden 'dead or alive' and save the world for us" (307). However, in her critique she avoids characterizing Bush within just another good/evil binary. While acknowledging that probably "all of us harbor a Bush-type raptor within our psyches," she writes that she knows that he is neither "totally evil nor one-dimensional" (310). Yet by locating the cowboy-Bush image within the national rhetoric and response following 9/11 and the war in Afghanistan, she avoids the orientalist and nationalist binaries that fuel the *desconocimiento* relating to 9/11.

In one paragraph in particular she critiques the cowboy image in a few strategic ways. She begins by critiquing the bombing of Afghanistan and the pseudo-feminist rationale for the war in Afghanistan: "Bush assumes a feministic guise and intimates he'll emancipate the Afghan women from their backward and uncivilized third world culture" (307). She scoffs and ridicules the idea of

Bush's innocent and heroic interest in women's rights, adding "Oh yeah, sure he'll save those women behind veils whom *our* policy silenced, reduced to meeting in secret to learn and teach, diminished to begging in the streets" (307). Similar to the work of feminists critiquing the "War on Terror" and the Bush Doctrine, namely Lila Abu-Lughod, Nadje Al-Ali, and Nicola Pratt, she points toward an absent historical memory of US policy in Afghanistan and other countries. With the terms "backward" and "uncivilized third world culture," she uncomfortably but familiarly aligns the western emancipatory hero with orientalist discourses. With such wording, Anzaldúa reveals that the "feminism" of the Bush administration is not feminist at all but an objectifying, orientalist gaze on women.

In her following sentence in the same paragraph she turns her attention to local oppression within the US. She writes, "He ignores our own culture's attempt to silence and gag women and men of color" (307). Instead of ignoring the oppressive ploys of these same binaries here in the US, Anzaldúa creates a larger, more complex understanding of terrorism, violence, and histories of oppression. She puts pressure on the easy binaries of the terrorism tropes by including US oppression in Afghanistan and the US.

The final aspect of her rebellion is the importance of taking responsibility and rejecting victimology, or being unable to work against oppression. She approaches the subject of responsibility in a way that does not deny the realities of multiple violences. In the third paragraph in the "Intimate Terrorism" section of *Borderlands*, Anzaldúa writes, "The ability to respond is what is meant by responsibility, yet our cultures take away our ability to act" (42). Yet in creating her own "*cultura mestiza*," her self-made culture and space through her "own feminist architecture," she does not leave her indictment of "intimate terrorism" as a mere recognition, but an active plan against it (44). In the fourth paragraph she writes, "We do not engage fully. We do not make full use of our faculties. We abnegate" (43). While she refers to our individual abilities and faculties, she also alludes to the faculties within her body of work, which consist of several theoretical paradigms and ways of seeing and being.

She undertakes this responsible aspect of her theorization of violence and rebellion against it throughout the majority of her theoretical work. In *Borderlands* Anzaldúa gives us the starting point of many of these theories and ways of being and knowing. In the "Intimate Terrorism" section in *Borderlands*, she explains, "there in front of us is the crossroads and choice: to feel a victim where someone else is in control and therefore responsible and to blame...or to feel strong, and, for the most part, in control" (43). In engaging fully, she emphasizes the theoretical theme throughout her work of overcoming dualities while paying attention to multiplicities that are intimate, mundane, and local, as well as global.

CONCLUSION: THEORIZING "INTIMATE TERRORISM" BEFORE AND BEYOND 9/11

In the project of examining the concept of terrorism, it would be problematic to reify September 11, 2001 as *the* defining moment in situating and understanding terrorism. Following 9/11 and in the yearly tributes since, the media is filled with bold headlines that 9/11 changed the world or "changed everything" as Dick Cheney stated during *Meet the Press* in September of 2003 ("Transcript"). Blinded by U.S. exceptionalism, such an approach to terrorism fails to include the complexities that Anzaldúa addresses. While the post 9/11 world is brimming with many more images and examples of "terrorism," especially in U.S. popular culture, it is important to recognize a theorization of terrorism that occurs before 9/11/2001. Anzaldúa writing about "intimate terrorism" in the 1980s challenges the constraints of a post 9/11 theorization of terrorism, as she points toward traditions and patterns of terrorism that have long existed in the US. Her theorization enables a recognition of how mainstream tropes of terrorism post 9/11 become imbued with particular meanings and functionality in U.S., especially as they are tied traditions of racism, sexism, homophobia, classism, and patriotism.

Despite the concise crafting of the "Intimate Terrorism" section, Anzaldúa's theorization is far from vague even as it retains an elasticity that allows for its multiple applications. If the people that make up the U.S. population utilized a more Anzaldúan definition of terrorism, we could better confront the complexity of terrorism as well as its intimate and mundane prevalence. We would also have a more keen understanding of the nebulous framing of the "War on Terror" by acquainting ourselves with "intimate terrorism" in our own nation, families, and selves, along with the oppressive practices carried out in the name of U.S. exceptionalism.

WORKS CITED

Alarcón, Norma. "Traddutora, Traditora: A Paradigmatic Figure of Chicana Feminism." *Cultural Critique* 13 (1989): 57-87. Web. 2 Feb. 2008.

Anzaldúa, Gloria. *Borderlands/La Frontera: The New Mestiza.* 3rd ed. San Francisco: Aunt Lute, 2007. Print.

---. "Let us be the Healing of the Wound: The Coyolxauqui Imparative—la Sombra y el Sueño." *One Wound for Another/Una Herida Por Otra: Testimonios de Latin@s in the U.S. through Cyberspace (11 de septiembre de 2001-11 de marzo de 2002).* Eds. Claire Joysmith and Clara Lomas. México D.F.: Universidad Nacional Autónoma de México, 2005.

"Combating Terrorism: Interagency Framework and the Agency Programs to Address the Overseas Threat." United States General Accounting Office. May 2003. Web. 10 Sept. 2008.

Jackson, Richard, Breen Smyth Marie and Jeroen Gunning. *Critical Terrorism Studies: A New Research Agenda.* Hoboken: Routledge, 2009. Ebook Library. Web. 07 Sep. 2012.

Puar, Jasbir, and Amit Rai. "Monster, Terrorist, Fag: The War on Terrorism and the Production of Docile Patriots." *Social Text* 20.3 (2002): 117-148. Web. 10 Oct. 2010.

Shepherd, Jessica. "The Rise and Rise of Terrorism Studies." *The Guardian.* 2 July 2007. Web. 10 June 2012.

"Transcript for Sept. 14." *Meet the Press.* MSNBC. Web. 14 Sept. 2003. 31 May 2012.

"U.S. Code Collection: Title 22 Chapter 38. 2656f." Legal Information Institute. Cornell University Law School.Web. 1 Dec. 2008.

AN ECOLOGY OF HEALING: AN ANZALDÚAN READING OF MORALES'S *THE RAG DOLL PLAGUES*

CORDELIA E. BARRERA

INTRODUCTION

Alejandro Morales's highly symbolic novel *The Rag Doll Plagues* directs our understanding of the great potential in unearthing ecological concerns and themes of coming to consciousness along the US-Mexico borderlands. In her *Borderlands/La Frontera: The New Mestiza* subsection titled "El retorno," Anzaldúa charts an ecological awareness that juxtaposes the exploitation of the borderlands with the oppression of its native peoples. In this paper, I will delineate what I call an "ecology of return," an archetypal trajectory that develops ideas enmeshed in Anzaldúa's Coatlicue state to underscore the means by which Morales develops the idea of Nature, or the natural world, as our own instinctual nature.

The Rag Doll Plagues sustains a narrative structure that underscores a political ecology of dispossession; individual bodies, however, suffer a homologous alienation. The three plagues in the novel underscore a biopolitics steeped in the ill treatment of a Borderlands landscape by various and shifting political regimes. This historical exploitation of a Borderlands landscape parallels major elements of Gloria Anzaldúa's mestiza consciousness, as she describes it in the subsection of *Borderlands* titled "El retorno." When she visits the Rio Grande of her home terrain, she references the great river as a symbol of the natural environment.

Significant to the present study is Anzaldúa's depiction of the river as a serpent nailed to a fence. The river is her means to assert the interdependence, the reciprocity, between humans and nonhuman nature. In *The Rag Doll Plagues,* the ecological nightmares of human waste, filth, and mounting garbage directly correlate to diseased bodies; contaminated bodies are a signifier for ecological abuses that occur through time.

NEW MEETING GROUNDS: CHICANA/O ENVIRONMENTAL THOUGHT

Chicanas/os are a people with a long established land ethic rooted in communal expressions of identity. In groundbreaking works of Chicana/o fiction by authors as diverse as Arturo Islas, Helena Maria Viramontes, and Ana Castillo, renewal and rebirth are often central aspects of consciousness that connect us with our forgotten histories as well as forge sustainable paths for the future. The road, however, that brings Chicana/o and environmental studies together is not clearly paved. However, works by Devon G. Peña, Laura Pulido, and Arturo Longoria—to name a few—address issues of the natural environment as they relate to broader social and environmental justice priorities.

In an effort to expand the theoretical base of Anzaldúan studies into the realm of current ecocritical thinking, this essay explores the fluidity between conocimiento and nepantla, post-*Borderlands* epistemologies that I argue underpin Anzaldúa's environmental thinking. Drawing from the relational theories of conocimiento and neplanta is the catalyst that moves us beyond a Western logic of domination towards what might be called a "queering" of established binaries embedded in Western ideas of the nature/culture and body/spirit split—bisections that have reinforced a destructive pattern of human separation from nature. This essay engages the points at which these connectionist ways of knowing enter into an ecocritical dialogue to speculate on a fertile, future direction of Anzalduán studies. A position that embraces the sacred and mythic dimensions of living in the world effectively queers mainstream ecocritical thinking. To use Judith Butler's term, when we "trouble" or "queer" prevalent American ecocriticism, we begin to understand how we may re-gather and re-conceptualize our spirits and energies to awaken a localized, place-based consciousness that is radical, antiracist, and nonheterosexist, and, as such, well-positioned to destabilize hegemonic regimes and systems of knowledge via engaged methodologies of collective action in the name of egalitarian living and democracy.

Gloria Anzaldúa's environmentalism holds the promise of psychic integration seeded in an awareness of a mythic interconnectedness between people, nature, and all things. In "Let us be the healing of the wound: The Coyolxauhqui imperative," Anzaldúa discusses her desire to pass onto future generations the spiritual activism that she has inherited from her cultures. Spiritual mestizaje underscores the negotiations and connectionist modes of thinking found in her theories of conocimiento and nepantla. These post-*Borderlands* epistemologies entwine Anzaldúa's palimpsestic consciousness; they are like the unbounded spirals and waves we find scattered throughout her drawings and works of art, many of which remain unpublished. Significantly, Chicana/o literature is poised to show how "racism and the challenge of environmental sustainability have been intertwined for more than a century" (Ybarra, "Walden Pond in Aztlán" 18). Early examples can be found within the pages of the first Chicano anthology of literature, *El Espejo/The Mirror* (1969), in the works of José Montoya, for instance. José David Saldívar argues that Montoya's early poetry—such as "Pobre Viejo Walt Whitman"—successfully concretizes theories of social resistance alongside "epiphanic revelations about the self" to "establish and generate a socially disciplined paradigm" while working to decenter Euro-American literary traditions (11). Mainstream American environmentalism has, nonetheless, often isolated Chicana/o environmentalism and ecocritical precedents in its discourses. There are many reasons for this, not the least of which surrounds divergent ways of living in and knowing the world.

For instance, mainstream US environmentalism is often thought to be concerned with narrowly defined quality of life issues (Pulido 5) and the vision of individuals exercising freedom in their various interactions with nature (Ybarra, "Walden Pond in Aztlán" 19). A compelling pattern emerges when we compare mainstream US environmental writing—from early works by Henry David Thoreau and John Muir to later works by Edward Abbey—to Chicana/o works that engage an environmental perspective. US environmental writing often features the removal of an individual, whether this be the author him or herself, from an urban locale of everyday social contexts and concerns, to the realm of nature. In nature, one is isolated, or distanced, so to speak, from contemporary technologies and economic developments. In US environmental writing, the human spirit, once disassociated from an urbanized setting, becomes free to disengage from constructs of self-determinism borne of a spirit of Manifest Destiny that underscores progress and development in terms of land ownership and the civilizing transformation of so-called "empty" spaces. US environmentalism often strives to isolate nature from human impact. The wilderness ideal at the heart of the establishment of many of the United States' earliest National Parks helped root a national ideal and a national identity that reinforced a dualistic separation of humans from nature.

Conversely, "Chicana/o environmental writing exhibits a steady consciousness of colonization as well as a continuing awareness of an ever-evolving ethnic identity" (Ybarra, "Walden Pond in Aztlán" 5). Themes that emerge from such works often engage a social justice agenda, the legacy of the Mexican Revolution, and the political ecology of dispossession (Marcone and Ybarra 93). A clear example of Chicana environmental writing aligned with this trajectory is found in Cherríe Moraga's *The Last Generation* (1999), in which she writes:

> "As a Chicana lesbian, I know that the struggle I share with all Chicanos and Indigenous peoples is truly one of sovereignty, the sovereign right to wholly inhabit oneself (*cuerpo y alma*) and one's territory (*pan y tierra*)." (173-4)

For Moraga, territory—land—is not just a place on a map to be plotted, or a nation-state from which to extract life-giving resources; her expanded definition of land extends to one's right to wholly inhabit one's body as well as the natural world. Land and bodies are conflated to signify a common ground for radical action. Priscilla Solis Ybarra writes that, in her poetry, Moraga links oppressed bodies with the landscape in an effort to critique a "parallel exploitation" that "recuperates the sense of an alienated right by recognizing the connections it forges" (Ybarra, "Lo que quiero" 241-242). For Moraga, physical territory—including one's home and job—as well one's own body, not only signify that which an individual can become wrested or alienated from, but, more importantly, sites of reparation.

Chicanas/os and other people of color in the US, such as the many Indian nations that once roamed their native lands freely, have fostered and maintained relationships with the natural world. Devon G. Peña describes this "land ethic" as one in which the natural world, the landscape—*la tierra*—is a member of the community of life, and as such, worthy of respect and protection. Peña adds that Mexican Americans and Chicanas/os tend to "define nature as homeland, not natural resources or wilderness" (*Mexican Americans* xxxiii). In his discussions of the ecological politics entwined in identity, place, and community of hispano-mexicano settlers in Colorado's San Luis Valley, an original Spanish land grant settlement, Peña discusses the loss of historic cultural landscapes in terms of the recovery of a hispano-mexicano environmental ethics of place ("Endangered Landscapes" 64). A significant aspect of his research focuses on "cognitive maps"—mental pictures of home places encased in a "tapestry" of "resistance identity," wherein place-based knowledge of locality is combined with critical consciousness of the threats posed by the modernist projects of a globalized political economy ("Endangered Landscapes" 65). Although Peña's main focus is to discuss resistance identity in terms of local farming and acequia communities that are inextricably bound to farmers' livelihoods, he concludes that ultimately the land ethics of hispano farmers appear to revolve around "the critique of the global economy to the extent that it manifests as a threat to the well-being and integrity of the local community" ("Endangered Landscapes" 65). It is at the local, community level that Peña roots hispano-mexicano environmental ethics, which he writes are "governed by an intense and even militant attachment to place (and to staying in place) and therefore by an unwavering commitment to the principle of local autonomy" (65). An ethics of place, then, is derived from localized identities inextricably bound to a politics of landscape.

This paper is part of a larger project in which I hope to situate Gloria Anzaldúa's ecological and environmental writings in the broader context of 21st century social and environmental justice movements. This first task seems straightforward enough, as Anzaldúa's work contains the seeds of burgeoning environmental thoughts and speculations that encompass ecological concerns and themes of spirituality bound in her vision of an ancestral and egalitarian homeland on the US-Mexico borderlands. My second task, however, is more elusive, as I ultimately wish to broaden the playing field of Chicana/o environmental literary production to show how core trends and issues might inform a transnational, global ecology of healing based in 21st century ideologies of decolonization and coming to consciousness. In this regard, there appear to be a number of viable paths, as there are multiple environmentally based precedents concerning Chicanas/os and people of color that are both wide-ranging and far-reaching. These efforts include, among others, the nationally recognized environmental organization, "The Mothers of East LA", the Southwest Network for Environmental and Economic Justice (SNEEJ), a group of 60 grassroots indigenous and labor groups dedicated to environmental and economic justice in the American southwest and northern Mexico, and broader policy efforts of Chicanas like Theresa Cordova, who currently serves as the Director of the Resource Center for Raza Planning at The University of New Mexico, a center that enables students to engage in research and policy analysis on issues affecting traditional communities in New Mexico.

Additionally, when we consider the example of Teresa Leal, an early activist who struggled for farmworker rights alongside Cesar Chavez and other members of the United Farm Workers Union (UFWU) in the 1960s, we find a trajectory of activism that begins with what Leal has called quite simply, "survival. Back then," she continues, "we did not call it an environmental movement (referring to her early experience with the UFWU), we just called it survival" (Adamson 46). In the twenty-first century, Leal remains an outspoken voice for interconnected movements devoted to "human rights, labor rights, gender rights, and environmental rights" as well as SNEEJ (Adamson 47).

Chicana/o environmental activism is historically associated with environmental justice and social justice movements, and although such efforts are significant in that they are inextricably linked to colonizing agendas and practices, they are not necessarily bound by a spiritual, place-based ethics, which

I argue is necessary to what Anzaldúa has called "coming to consciousness." My ultimate goal is to develop a praxis—a methodology aligned with broader trends and imaginings espoused by feminists such as Chandra Talpade Mohanty, Chela Sandoval, and Emma Pérez. But there is much at stake here, and there are myriad trajectories and possibilities I have yet to explore. For instance, is it productive to engage Pérez's decolonial imaginary in working to re-inscribe practices of eco-criticism that naturally extend to Chicana/o texts? For Mohanty, decolonization, anticapitalist critique, and solidarity anchor an antiracist feminist framework, an inclusive feminism attentive to borders and the necessary transcendence of borders. How might we engage these ideas, which are all bound within a theory of social and economic justice, to frame a broader contextualization of ecosocial experience (Mohanty 107) where diversity and difference are central values? More importantly, where do these ideas and practices fit into nascent, but rapidly developing decolonizing movements of a global environmental ethics rooted in more equitable and sustainable alternatives to global capitalism?

A crucial aspect of this research pertains to Anzaldúa's privileging of the spiritual when writing about ideas of nationhood and the egalitarian coexistence of different peoples. I believe that a re-imagining of Anzaldúa's writings regarding the spiritual, the shamanistic, the fantastic, and the monstrous enable a trajectory of thinking aligned with what environmental historian Carolyn Merchant calls ecological revolutions: "Ecological revolutions are major transformations in human relations with nonhuman nature" that arise from "changes, tensions, and contradictions that develop between society's mode of production and its ecology," as well as between its modes of production and reproduction (3). These dynamics support the acceptance of new forms of consciousness, ideas, images, and worldviews. These forms of consciousness represent power structures. As such, when one worldview is challenged and replaced by another during a scientific or ecological revolution, power over society, nature, and space is at stake. With this in mind, when we prioritize Anzaldúa's ideas that suggest a conflation of physical bodies with the body of the earth, we begin to work towards situating her untethered environmentalism to material acts of recovery that may effectively de-colonize mainstream environmental thought in quite revolutionary ways.

A CHICANO ECOLOGICAL TRAJECTORY OF RETURN

Maria Herrera-Sobek argues that Alejandro Morales is the "first Chicano novelist to systematically sustain an ecological perspective throughout" (100). With this in mind, Morales's highly symbolic, dystopian novel, *The Rag Doll Plagues,* is a model place to begin identifying trends and key issues relevant to the practice of ecocriticism within Chicana/o literary productions. Because the novel engages broader ideas of decolonization rooted in the historical exploitation of indigenous bodies, and consequently, indigenous landscapes, the novel delineates what I call an "ecology of return," an archetypal trajectory that develops ideas enmeshed in Anzaldúa's Coatlicue State to underscore the means by which the author develops the idea of Nature, or the natural world, as our own instinctual nature.

The Rag Doll Plagues directs our understanding of the great potential in unearthing ecological concerns and themes of coming to consciousness along the US-Mexico borderlands. When we engage Anzaldúa's *Borderlands* susbsection titled "El retorno," we understand how she charts an ecological awareness that juxtaposes the exploitation of the borderlands with the oppression of its native peoples, a theme that exhibits a consciousness of colonization as well as an awareness of an ever-evolving ethnic identity.

Anzaldúa positions the US-Mexico border as a distinct bioregion in chapter three of *Borderlands,* entitled "Entering into the Serpent." Here, she likens the Earth, the South Texas landscape in particular, to a coiled serpent: "I know Earth is a coiled Serpent," she writes. "Forty years it's taken me to enter the Serpent, to acknowledge that I have a body, that I am a body and to assimilate the animal body, the animal soul" (48). Later, in "El retorno," she returns to the South Texas Valley after having left the region to pursue an education and career. She visits the great river, a symbol of the natural environment, to "watch the curling, twisting serpent, a serpent nailed to the fence where the mouth of the Rio Grande empties into the Gulf" (111). When Anzaldúa depicts the river as "a serpent nailed to the fence," the river is not merely a symbol of the natural environment unnaturally staked. It is rather Anzaldúa's means to assert the interdependence, the reciprocity, between humans and nonhuman nature. Her depiction leaves us with a vision of the region and its people nailed to the unnatural built environment of a border fence that cuts and separates rather than heals and unites. Because Anzaldúa locates her bodily materiality only when she enters "into the Serpent," this conflation of her physical body with the body of the earth enables us to understand the complex nature of her ecological and spatial awareness as well as how the land's exploitation has historically and directly related to injustices in the human community. For Anzaldúa, "[t]he snake is a symbol of awakening consciousness—the potential of knowing within, an awareness and intelligence not grasped by logical thought" ("now let us shift" 540).

When we combine these ideas with Anzaldúa's thoughts on conocimiento, a key component of her post-*Borderlands* epistemology, we prioritize a deepening of perception that underscores the imaginal, spiritual-activist and radically inclusionary possibilities implicit in her more-widely known theories of la facultad and a mestiza consciousness. Conocimiento represents a non-binary, connectionist mode of thinking, and entails a deepening of perception. It is a spiritual capacity bound by the knowledge "that we're connected by invisible fibers to everyone on the planet and that each person's actions impact the rest of the world" ("let us be the healing of the wound" 309).

Morales's novel emphasizes human relationships as bound within the ecosystems they inhabit. Throughout the novel, we wander alongside the protagonist—Dr. Gregorio Revueltas—through space and time to underscore how we create the past and not the future in the present (141-2). In Book 1, Gregorio transforms from a racist Peninsular to a more compassionate Mexican émigré; in Book 2, he harmoniously communes with both the female body and a historical consciousness seeded in traditional environmental knowledge; in Book 3, he is transfigured into all who have gone before him—he is all men (which I take to signify all men and women). His name in all 3 books—Gregorio Revueltas—signifies return, or more precisely, a turning over, or revolving. *The Rag Doll Plagues* is a New Historical novel that does not merely reproduce history, but transcends it, much in the same way the protagonist transcends his own history from one epoch to the next. More importantly, in the novel, the search for knowledge—signified at the simplest level as the search to find a cure for recurring plagues—is linked to environmental issues, as ecological nightmares of human waste, filth, and mounting garbage directly correlate to diseased bodies; contaminated bodies are a signifier for ecological abuses that occur through time.

Morales foregrounds the relationship between the environment and social improvements, but he makes clear that these are entwined in changing discourses of knowledge. In the novel, Morales reveals knowledge and knowing as a palimpsest. When it appears that Dr. Revueltas has reached the limits of Western rationalism, forms of traditional environmental knowledge and place-based knowledge grounded in a communal land ethic begin to shape the impetus that will in a sense, bring him full circle, towards a new consciousness. Dr. Revuletas participates in an "ecology of return," an archetypal trajectory that reinscribes environmental ideas enmeshed in Anzaldúa's theory of conocimiento. In this way, the author develops the idea of Nature, or the natural world, as a mirror of our own instinctual nature.

Pushing the field of ecocriticism even further, we see how Dr. Revueltas may be termed a neplantero, a term coined by Anzaldúa to describe a unique type of mediator who facilitates passages between worlds. Neplanteros are "agents of awakening…who think in terms of the planet, not just their own racial group" ("Speaking across" 293). A scientist and a *mestizo,* Dr. Revueltas's trajectory through time represents a non-binary connectionist mode of environmental thinking and knowing.

The science in *The Rag Doll Plagues* points to an alternative cultural project, one that indicates that there are limits to Western scientific knowledge. Because the subaltern occupy a position that is different from traditional environmentalists, they express new articulations of issues and problems. The path of conocimiento, then, reminds us of systems of knowledge that force us to become agile in more than one mode or approach of living in and knowing the world. Nepantla occurs during the many transitional phases of life, but it is the task of individuals—people—to invent holistic, relational theories and practices—tactics—that will transform the many worlds in which we dwell. Like Dr. Revueltas, when we entertain ideas that contradict the accumulated knowledge of the system from which we are enculturated, we become the translators and diplomats that occupy the space between seemingly contradictory systems of knowledge.

When we reverse the camera angle of mainstream environmental and ecocritical thinking, we risk being swallowed whole by the earth's mouth as Anzaldúa describes in "The Coatlicue State." When we break holes in the old boundaries we unrest "that which abides" (*Borderlands* 73) to become a thousand sleepless serpent eyes. We awaken. As we inscribe a place-based ethics and traditional forms of knowledge supported by a holistic indigenous ancestry, one rooted in communal expressions of identity, we ignite nothing less than the promise of psychic integration seeded in an awareness of "the interconnectedness of people and nature and all things" ("Speaking across" 282).

Anzaldúa acknowledges that it "is time for us to move beyond confining parameters of what qualifies as knowledge," beginning with a consideration of "the value of knowledge that is rooted in the body" ("Let us be the healing of the wound" 229). In *The Rag Doll Plagues*, Gregorio Revueltas "awakens" when he puts his "history through a sieve" (Anzaldúa, *Borderlands* 104) and re-learns to embrace his indigenous ties to the landscape. For Anzaldúa, when we put history through a sieve and reinterpret history through the use of new symbols and the shaping of new myths—as she says we must—we can trace the trajectory of those who aim to communicate such a rupture in the hope of deconstructing identities with the goal of re-constructing them so as to work to "transform the small 'I' into the total Self" (*Borderlands* 104-105). The total Self is achieved only as it is contained within a viable relationship to the terrain. Transformation, emergence and renewal occur—just as does consciousness—*within*; such changes, however, are reflected in, and reflective of, outer terrains. This trajectory is evident in *The Rag Doll Plagues*, as Dr. Revuelta's conscious rupture with an oppressive cultural tradition, signified by Western medicinal practices that encourage a mind/body split, is the catalyst that propels him to embrace a new way of thinking and living. This is evident in the final lines of the novel, when he states: "I am no longer me. I am transfigured into all those that have gone before me: my progenitors, my hopeful ever-surviving race" (200). For Anzaldúa, only when we come to grips with our desconocimientos, can we re-think the borders of our bodies, our identities, to engage strategic acts of reparation.

Chicana/o environmentalism has much to offer mainstream US environmentalism, not the least of which is how we may re-gather and re-conceptualize our spirits and our energies to awaken a planetary consciousness that is radical, antiracist, and nonheterosexist, and, as such, well-positioned to destabilize hegemonic regimes and systems of knowledge via engaged methodologies of collective action in the name of egalitarian living and democracy for all.

WORKS CITED

Adamson, Joni. "Throwing Stones at the Sun: An Interview with Teresa Leal." *The Environmental Justice Reader: Politics, Poetics & Pedagogy.* Eds. Joni Adamson, Mei Mei Evans, and Rachel Stein. Tucson: U Arizona Press, 2002. 44-57. Print.

Anzaldúa, Gloria. *Borderlands La Frontera: The New Mestiza,* 2nd ed. San Francisco: Aunt Lute Press, 1999. Print.

---. "now let us shift...the path of conocimiento...inner work, public acts." *This Bridge We Call Home: Radical Visions for Transformation.* Eds. Gloria E. Anzaldúa and AnaLouise Keating. New York: Routledge, 2002. 540-576. Print.

---."Let us be the healing of the wound: *The Coyolxauhqui imperative—la sombra y el sueño.*" *The Gloria Anzaldúa Reader.* Ed. AnaLouise Keating. Durham: Duke U Press, 2009. 303-317. Print.

---."Speaking across the Divide." *The Gloria Anzaldúa Reader.* Ed. AnaLouise Keating. Durham: Duke U Press, 2009. 282-294. Print.

---."(un)natural bridges, (Un)safe spaces." *The Gloria Anzaldúa Reader.* Ed. AnaLouise Keating. Durham: Duke U Press, 2009. 243-248. Print.

Butler, Judith, *Gender Trouble: Feminism and the Subversion of Identity.* New York: Routledge, 2006.

Castillo, Ana. *So Far From God: A Novel.* New York: Penguin, 1994.

Herrera-Sobek, Marie. "Epidemics, Epistemophilia, and Racism: Ecological Literary Criticism and *The Rag Doll Plagues.*" *Alejandro Morales and His Work.* Ed. José Antonio Gurpegui. Tempe: Bilingual Review Press, 1996. 99-108. Print.

Islas, Arturo. *The Rain God.* New York: Harper, 1991.

Longoria, Arturo. *Adios to the Brushlands.* College Station: Texas A & M Press, 1997.

Marcone, Jorge and Priscilla Solis Ybarra. "Mexican and Chicana/o Environmental Writing: Unearthing and Inhabiting." *Teaching North American Environmental Literature.* Eds. Laird Christensen, Mark C. Long, and Fred Waage. New York: MLA, 2008. 93-111. Print.

Merchant, Carolyn. *Ecological Revolutions: Nature, Gender, and Science in New England.* Chapel Hill: U of North Carolina Press, 1989. Print.

Mohanty, Chandra Talpade. *Feminism Without Borders: Decolonizing Theory, Practicing Solidarity.* Durham: Duke U Press, 2003. Print.

Moraga, Cherríe. *The Last Generation: Prose and Poetry.* Brooklyn: South End Press, 1999. Print.

Morales, Alejandro. *The Rag Doll Plagues.* Houston: Arte Público Press, 1991. Print

Peña, Devon G. "Endangered Landscapes and Disappearing Peoples? Identity, Place, and Community in Ecological Politics. *The Environmental Justice Reader.* Eds. Joni Adamson, Mei Mei Evans, and Rachel Stein. Tucson: U of Arizona Press, 2002. 58-81. Print.

---. *Mexican Americans and the Environment: Tierra y Vida.* Tucson: U of Arizona Press, 2005. Print.

Pulido, Laura. *Environmentalism and Economic Justice: Two Chicano Struggles in the Southwest.* Tucson, U of Arizona Press, 1996.

Saldívar, José David. "Towards a Chicano Poetics: The Making of a Chicano Subject, 1969-1982. *Confluencia.* 1.2 (Spring 1986): 10-17.

Solis Ybarra, Priscilla."Lo que quierro es tierra: Longing and Belonging in Cherríe Moraga's Ecological Vision." *New Perspectives on Environmental Justice.* Ed. Rachel Stein. New Brusnwick: Rutgers U Press, 2004. 240-248. Print.

---. *Walden Pond in Aztlan? A Literary History of Chicana/o Environmental Writing Since 1848.* Diss. Rice University, Houston, 2006.

Viramontes, Helena Maria. *Under the Feet of Jesus.* New York: Plume, 1996.

BREAKING BORDERS: TRANSETHNIC DIALOGUES BETWEEN JULIA DE BURGOS AND GLORIA ANZALDÚA AS A THIRD SPACE FEMINIST CONOCIMIENTO PRAXIS FOR COALITION BUILDING

ROBERTA HURTADO

On July 5, 1953, Julia de Burgos was found unconscious on the streets of East Harlem and later died alone, name unknown, in Harlem Hospital. Five decades later, on the 15th of May, 2004, Gloria Anzaldúa died of medical complications alone in her Santa Cruz home. Julia de Burgos, who died homeless and was given an indigent burial by New York City, is lauded by Puerto Rican intellectuals on the mainland as Puerto Rico's best poet. Born three years prior to the Jones Act of 1917, Burgos's life is marked by travesties wrought by the political transitions that rendered Puerto Rico a "commonwealth" (colony) of the United States. Anzaldúa, who died in California though raised in Texas, remains the touchstone of Chicana intellectualism and was similarly marked by an act of U.S. imperialism that stretched across what is now the U.S. Southwest: the Treaty of Guadalupe-Hidalgo signed in 1841. Both women's lives, although distanced by thousands of miles and several decades, bear acute similarities. And yet, despite the significance of their works—works that simultaneously pressure the violent silencing of women of color by hegemonic U.S. structures of inequality as well as resisting acts of domination within their own communities—these women have never had their work placed in direct dialogue with one another for purposes of conceptualizing potential methods for transcending the dehumanization of women of color.

Laura Perez describes in her 2006 book, *Chicana Art*, an imperial practice that had the threefold desire to "conquer, separate, segregate" (147). The power of the masses' potential, as a result of their sheer numbers, to subvert matrices of power is undermined by this dissembling that renders coalition building contentious. Audre Lorde argues in "The Master's Tools Will Never Dismantle the Master's House" that, to subvert the violations made possible by this process, "[d]ifference must be not merely tolerated, but seen as a fund of necessary polarities between which our creativity can spark like a dialectic… Only within that interdependency of different strengths, acknowledged and equal, can the power to seek new ways of being in the world generate, as well as the courage and sustenance to act where there are no charters" (111). As such, I contend that although Burgos and Anzaldúa are rarely discussed, let alone mentioned, in the same conversation, analysis of their works elucidates the importance of dialogue between women of color caught within the grasp of the U.S. empire. It emerges as vital to develop these conversations to demonstrate that, by breaking the borders of ethnicity built within U.S. colonial matrix practices to reduce the power of the masses, it becomes possible to subvert dehumanizing tactics of U.S. imperialism. I argue that constructing a discussion between the works of Julia de Burgos and Gloria Anzaldúa produces a potential for coalition building as part of a third space feminist praxis of conocimiento.

IDENTIFYING POSITIONALITY: THIRD-SPACE FEMINIST VOICES

Both Burgos and Anzaldúa, despite differences in time and ethnic background, articulate an understanding of the psychological struggles inherent to their positions as Latina writers. Julia de Burgos's construction of her poem, "To Julia de Burgos," lends itself to a discussion with the works of Gloria Anzaldúa to create a third space feminist critique regarding the impact of gender oppression on women of color psyches. As the poem begins, the narrator articulates a distinction between herself, as the voice heard in the poem, and "Julia de Burgos" as a woman. The narrative voice identifies the label of "enemy" given to her because she speaks while the other female persona is silent (1). The poet's awareness of the split between her artistic self and that of her "regular" female identity, as well as recognition of how the voice that speaks from a position of oppression is demonized, evinces a deep consciousness regarding systems of control and domination. However, Anzaldúa states in her 1987 publication, *Borderlands/La Frontera*, that "[t]o write, to be a writer, I have to trust and believe in myself as a speaker, as a voice for the images. I have to believe that I can communicate with images and words and that I can do it well" (73). It is vital to have belief in one's own creative process. Despite the temporal and geographical distance between them, both women contend with attempts to silence them.

Further, to label one's own self an enemy—or be aware of how this label is inscribed on the poetic persona by a community—indicates a consciousness regarding how subjugated voices are methodologically silenced. Burgos's narrator acknowledges that she is called this name because "they say in verse I give the world your me" (2). Burgos thereby illustrates that in speaking of her own experiences as a woman, and a specifically Puerto Rican woman, she is accused of baring herself open and making herself available to others. Iris Zavala-Martínez notes in "A Critical Inquiry into the Life and Works of Julia de Burgos" that, in her life, Burgos experienced "the oppressiveness of prevailing social norms, which she later revealed in her poems conveying her assertive unconventional stance" (11). Thus, her poetry functions as an unveiling of how her own society and culture act against her, rendering her traitorous because she refuses to submissively accept her position as a woman. Similarly, Anzaldúa identifies the importance of La Malinche—an indigenous woman given to Hernán Cortés by her own family—as a figure whose definition as "whore, prostitute" in Mexican and Chicana/o culture transforms her into a symbol used to discipline women into submission (44). Questions emerge regarding why women's speech is demonized while the social norms that harm women of color remain unscathed.

Both Burgos and Anzaldúa engage this issue by deconstructing the female body's function as a disciplining tool within matrices of oppression. Burgos writes "Who rises in my verses is not your voice.../because you are the dressing and the essence is me" and later refers to that body as a "cold doll" (4-5, 7). There is a mind/body fracture: the body is physically vulnerable because of its visibility, but the humanity—or essence—is free to move. Mark Mascia contends in "Bodies Politic" that much of Burgos's work exemplifies her social consciousness regarding the "body" as a signifier that enables justification of domination and exploitation (118). The corporeal experience is identified by how it is read within a given society. Anzaldúa contends in "now let us shift" that, as part of this awareness, "[a]fter dismantling the body/self you re-compose it... You turn the established narrative on its head, seeing through, resisting and subverting its assumptions" (560). Women of color must distinguish their "bodies" as an aspect of experience that has been acted upon to condition a social memory that structures the individual's identity, and which must be reconceptualized.

Historically, the positioning of women of color bodies—and, in the cases of Burgos and Anzaldúa, specifically Puertorriqueña and Chicana—as sites of domination and social control is a well-documented U.S. neo-imperial tactic. Iris Lopez describes in *Matters of Choice* the strategic mass sterilization of Puerto Rican women that resulted in over one third of Puertorriqueñas being sterilized by 1982. While sterilization legislation from as early as 1937 was rejected on the island because it directly stated that Puertorriqueñas who were poor should be sterilized, later laws based on the premise of sterilization for health reasons such as Acts 33 and 136 were passed. These acts "condoned sterilization for the majority of the Puerto Rican population because most were poor, malnourished, and in poor health" (Lopez 12). Thus the female body's "health" becomes the premise for this form of genocide rather than a U.S. imperial incentive to control the population. However, what remains striking is the exactness with which the Puerto Rican female body is put under scrutiny as a seemingly *natural* site for U.S. scientific speculation and colonial disciplining. Similarly, as Elena Gutiérrez records in *Fertile Matters*, forced sterilization of Mexican and Mexican-American women in Los Angeles hospitals during the 1970s was a matter of public policies administered by doctors and nurses that was judicially confirmed as a "prerogative" of medical teams.

In this manner, Burgos's poem identifies her colonial status as experienced by a woman and depicts what Gloria Anzaldúa—in conjunction with Cherríe Moraga—will later in the twentieth-century describe as "theory in the flesh." This theory, first officially documented in the groundbreaking anthology *This Bridge Called My Back* of 1981, identifies a new method for understanding women of color's lived experiences within the United States. As indicated in the anthology, "[a] theory in the flesh means one where the physical realities of our lives—our skin color, the land or concrete we grew up on, our sexual longings—all fuse to create a politic born out of necessity. Here, we attempt to bridge the contradictions in our experience" (21). How different people experience the multiple forms of domination and oppression that have been made possible through the meaning inscribed upon the "body" must be illuminated as legitimate testimonies that speak to how these tyrannical systems work. Skin color is given meaning through how it is treated within the community that identifies color as a sign symbol. Constitution of gender as a fixed reality is only knowable through how the flesh is disciplined into accepting it as fact of existence. The physical, lived experiences must be recognized as representing a way of knowing.

This awareness leads towards a unique knowledge: an intuition that cannot deftly be described as scientific or humanistic, but rather an awareness of how different systems of power function and how women of color must interact with and against these systems. Burgos's narrator's dissociation of her poetic persona from the individual and body under discipline enables her to articulate an image of her identity free from the constraints of the colonial gaze, which Anzaldúa similarly depicts several decades later. Burgos states "I am life, strength, woman" (14). She produces an image of self-empowerment rather than succumbing to the despair so available to someone who exists as the abject. Anzaldúa writes in "now let us shift" that "the urgency to know what you're experiencing awakens la facultad, the ability to shift attention and see through the surface of things and situations" (547). The poet's disengagement with the "body" allows a platform from which she can view what has happened to her. Through her awareness and articulation of "theory in the flesh," Burgos enables herself to then depict how the boundaries and borders used to discipline her body and identity can be perceived, deconstructed, and transformed into methods of resistance. Burgos produces a proto-image of what la facultad can look like.

BORDERLESS FEMINISM: DECONSTRUCTING BINARIES AND FOUNDING STRENGTH IN RESISTANCE

Placing the writings of Julia de Burgos and Gloria Anzaldúa into conversation illustrates how both women deploy a third space feminist consciousness to identify the methods of sociosexual racialization that attempt to subjugate them. Burgos's narrator writes of the "husband, your master" (15). In contrast to the woman whom she describes as servile to a husband, the poetic persona articulates a sense of self as an ethereal being. She states, "I belong to nobody, or all, because to all, to all / I give myself in my clean feelings and in my thought." (16-17). Her claim to being unpossessed—or free to choose whom she gives herself to—identifies her own sense of agency. Similarly, as a dimension of the Coatlicue state described in *Borderlands,* Anzaldúa notes that "[t]here is another quality to the mirror and that is the act of seeing. Seeing and being seen. Subject and object, I and she. The eye pins down the object of its gaze, scrutinizes it, judges it, a barrier against the world. But in a glance also lies awareness, knowledge" (64). The act of seeing is of vital importance. Whether one sees an image of the real person or the façade that has been created determines how an individual interprets and understands. Drawing on Anzaldúa's work, it becomes possible to extend Burgos's writing and see how her "self" recognition enables a transcendence that would otherwise be impossible.

The split that Burgos and Anzaldúa identify also requires a contextualization within the multiple methods of domination that they experience within their communities. After noting the importance of family in dominating her, Burgos's narrator turns her attention to "the priest… heaven and hell" (26, 28). Her notation of formal religion—here Christianity—as a form of domination indicates the poet's awareness of its presence in her life as an oppressive force. Her "body" is under threat of not only immediate corporeal harm but also the threat of the afterlife. Anzaldúa notes in "now let us shift" that, "[a]ccording to Christianity and other spiritual traditions, the evil that lies at the root of the human condition is the desire to know—which translates into aspiring to conocimiento (reflective consciousness). Your reflective mind's mirror throws back all your options, making you aware of your freedom to choose" (540). Burgos's *facultad* exposes formal religion as an aspect of society that attempts to discipline her into submission and control her mind and body. In this awareness, both authors distinguish the need to differentiate between religion and spirituality in the move towards conocimiento.

Burgos and Anzaldúa also explore and indict the roles of consumerism, materialism, and capitalism as aspects of U.S. imperialism that impinge on and foster how women of color are categorized and controlled. Burgos's narrator identifies "the dressmaker...the auto, the fine furnishings" as assisting in the violation of her mind and body (26-27). The dressmaker, importantly, constructs the vestments with which femininity is articulated. The "auto" and "fine furnishings" the narrator notes are all items purchased within a capitalist society. Although reflective of how different class statuses are performed, these references in Burgos's poem also indicate the significance of consumer consumption in her time and how Puerto Rican women engage in it. In 1934, Caroline Manning, working on behalf of the U.S. Government's federally funded *Bulletin of the Women's Bureau*, published "The Employment of Women in Puerto Rico" in which she identifies wage earnings and labor conditions in various industries. Interestingly, she documents that "[i]nfants' dressed with fagoting, hemstitching, and an embroidered design on yoke and hem, the type of garment that retailed in the summer of 1933 in some stores for about $1 a piece, are made for $1.50 a dozen. It takes a day to make one of these garments and nets the maker 15 cents, roughly 2 cents an hour" (Manning 6). It would take a Puertorriqueña fifty hours or more to earn one of the dresses she crafted. Similarly, though under different circumstances, Anzaldúa recalls how her own family worked for U.S. dominated farms and corporations: "sometimes we earned less than we owed, but always the corporations fared well...My sisters, mother and I cleaned, weighed and packaged eggs. (For years afterwards I couldn't stomach the sight of an egg)" (*Borderlands* 31). Though the exact experiences of Puertorriqueñas and Chicanas differ, there exist similarities in regards to U.S. economic domination and the positioning of women of color into statuses of automatons from which to extract financial gain.

Thus, by placing these women's writings in dialogue, it emerges as possible to construct a third space feminist discourse for women of color that is founded on a transformative understanding of self-determination. Burgos's narrator claims "only my heart governs, / only my thought; who governs me is me" (29-30). Direct reference to the heart brings connotations of love and emotion. Anzaldúa describes the spiritual practice of conocimiento as one which "enables you to defuse the negative energy of putdowns, complaints, excessive talk, verbal attacks... [it] becomes a port you moor to in all storms" ("now let us shift" 572). As such, movement away from negative emotions that can function as sources of self-destruction begs the question of what is being moved towards. Chela Sandoval's *Methodology of the Oppressed* identifies the importance of love as a hermeneutic within which the "rhetoric of love is identified as a means of social change" (130). Differing, then, from colonial tactics of division and separation is a re-visioning of unity based on respect as a method for subverting structures of domination. Thus, it is Burgos's drawing together and combination of love and active, willful consciousness—as indicated by the word "thought"—that articulates a prototype for the image of love as an emancipatory act for those under domination and political subjugation. Anzaldúa and Burgos construct a language for shedding the denigration of emotion/the flesh.

The shift that Burgos and Anzaldúa articulate thereby transforms into a revolutionary break that must occur in order for new horizons of potential to grow. Burgos writes "we are the duel to death who fatally approaches" (36). There is an overtly masculine connotation to the term "duel." Yet, here, the poetic persona changes the meaning of duel from a battle enacted between two men to a necessary battle of will and determination between the Julia de Burgos who is victim and the Julia de Burgos who is transformed. That together these figures form the duel evinces a recodification of their meaning as being aspects of the same person. Further, the duel itself is humanized and given a personality, depicting a new aspect of the poet's consciousness. As Anzaldúa describes in *Borderlands,* "in our very flesh, (r)evolution works out the clash of cultures" (103). Each individual's flesh contains the avalanches, paradoxes, and contradictions that history represents. Within a colonial matrix structure of power, these contradictory paradoxes are made even more challenging for the oppressed, whose lives have been forced to fit the unnatural meanings ascribed to them. As such, the binaries that Burgos and Anzaldúa illustrate must necessarily collapse and a new consciousness be forged.

Burgos and Anzaldúa advance the significance of this internal change by indicating its emancipatory potential for their different communities. Burgos writes "when the multitudes run rioting, / leaving behind ashes of burned injustices" (37-38). The poet perceives a time of revolution, even if it is not occurring at the present moment in time. Although she does not describe when it will occur, she nevertheless envisions its purpose. Anzaldúa notes that the "work of the *mestiza* consciousness is to break down the subject-object duality that keeps her a prisoner and to show in the flesh and through the images in her work how duality is transcended" (*Borderlands* 102). Burgos's and Anzaldúa's ability to articulate what the revolution will enact and its purpose indicate a social consciousness as well as a political awareness of oppression and subjugation. The vividness of their depictions, in Burgos's case literally describing what the revolution will look like, demonstrates that it is not a foregone conclusion that the masses will continue in their current plights of subjugation. Indeed, there is an indication that those who commit these atrocities will be held accountable for the crimes they have committed.

Significantly, Burgos and Anzaldúa articulate their own active position within the envisioned revolution rather than passively watching it occur. Burgos states that "against you and against everything unjust…I will be in their midst with the torch in my hand" (37, 41-42). The revolution she details is both one of action and one of consciousness. The perception of "multitudes," indicating the various factions within Puerto Rico, is all-inclusive and identifies a new method of understanding the people around her. Anzaldúa states in "Dream of the Double-Faced Woman" that if a woman "changed her relationship to her body and this in turn changed her relationship to another's body then she would change her relationship to the world. And when *that* happened she would *change* the world" (71). The discourses that these women construct, when placed into dialogue within one another, illuminate the desire for transformation and emancipation felt by women of color.

INDICTING EMPIRE: THE BODY'S STATE IN THE CENTER OF THE MACHINE

However, the writings of Burgos and Anzaldúa, when positioned into dialogue, also illuminate the tragedies that drive the birth of conocimiento and how the pain of these tragedies must be addressed. In "Farewell in Welfare Island," Burgos addresses the impact of subjugation and oppression on the psyche and evinces consciousness regarding her position as a Puerto Rican in the United States. Written in New York City in the final months of her life, this poem contains an emotional landscape that displays her despondency and pain. Notable as one of the only poems to specifically detail her location in the United States, the physical locale's name brings forth the connotations historically associated with the Island itself. Welfare Island, previously named "Blackwell Island" until 1921, was home to an infamous penitentiary that, as late as 1914, was documented for its crimes against humanity as reported in such *New York Times* articles as "Blackwell's Island a Prison Terrible; Treatment of Convicts There is Vile and Inhuman, Commissioner Davis Reports." Burgos's stay in this northeastern United States hospital corresponds with a 1953 report entitled "Safety for Hospital Patients," which notes that hospitals in this area were places where "preventable falls" occurred, where patients were given "inadequate protection from X-rays," and where there were "operating room hazards" (465-66). The history of the island, its penitentiaries, and its hospitals emerges as detrimental to the lives of anyone in contact with it, similar to the experiences of Chicanas in the hospitals of Los Angeles in the 1970s.

In their writings, both Anzaldúa and Burgos identify the significance of land as part of their understanding of oppression within colonial structures of power. Burgos's "Welfare Island" begins "it has to be from here" (1). The immediacy and sense of urgency indicated in these words also conveys that it is her very physical location that demands something from her; that her words are somehow interconnected with what is going on around her. Published in the 1956 edition of *Geographical Review,* Robert Novak's "Distribution of Puerto Ricans on Manhattan Island" notes that "[i]n 1950 there were in the continental United States 301,375 persons of Puerto Rican birth or parentage, a number equivalent to more than 10 percent of the total population of Puerto Rico itself" (182). The need to know and document where Puerto Ricans were in the United States, despite their being national citizens, demonstrates Burgos's *facultad* and why she must specify her exact location. Yet, it is vital to ask what it is about physical space that is of such importance. Anzaldúa describes in *Borderlands* how "the U.S.-Mexican border *es una herida abierta* where the Third World grates against the first and bleeds. And before a scab forms it hemorrhages again, the lifeblood of two worlds merging to form a third country—a border culture" (25). Anzaldúa's attention to this component of her existence is thereby illustrated as an aspect of her consciousness in regard to colonial surveillance as it exists and controls her people, similar to Burgos's own awareness.

The creativity in their writing demonstrates specifically attuned methods that these different authors take to make real the experiences of colonial dehumanization in new and humanizing forms. Burgos's phrases such as "my cry into the world" evince an understanding of how her poetry is not insular, or limited specifically to her own experiences, but reverberates out into the public (3). Further, it demonstrates that she is aware of her poetry's power to reach other people outside of her immediate vicinity. Anzaldúa similarly describes how "my 'stories' are acts...the work has an identity; it is 'who' or a 'what' and contains the presences of persons...manifest the same needs as a person, to be 'fed,' *la tengo que bañar y vestir*" (89). Writing transforms into an act of humanization, and contains within it what the Combahee River Collective asserts as a demand "to be recognized as human" (237). This assertion elucidates Burgos's and Anzaldúa's perceptions of having an innate right to make others aware of their lives. Rather than submit to the death of colonizing silence, they build ways to constitute their own vitality in writing.

In combination with this cry, this putting words out into the air, is the pain that is associated with it and from which it originates. Burgos states that "Life was somewhere forgotten/ and sought refuge in depths of tears" (4-5). Yet it is her manner of identifying how objectification interacts with location that indicates a deep understanding of how power works. Her use of the word "somehow" indicates a lack of exact detail or perhaps a mystification of the process through which "life" was lost. However, Burgos emphasizes the *where* rather than the *how*. Imbedded with this could be her dislocation to the United States from Puerto Rico. There could also be a subtext in which the *how* is not of the greatest importance because it is already obvious. Anzaldúa notes in *Borderlands* that "[b]locks (*Coalticue* states) are related to my cultural identity. The painful period of confusion... Gouge out my lame eyes, rout my demon from its nocturnal cave... And in descending to the depths I realize that down is up, and I rise up from and into the deep" (102). The tensions of grappling with the ambiguities wrought by empire renders a sense of sadness, depression. Yet, these moments do not have to be limiting, in and of themselves. Instead, they offer moments and spaces to learn and transform. Thus, the tears that Burgos details can become an actual location and place with heights that can be ascending or descended based on her personal and emotional needs.

Residing in this space enables both writers to describe the dehumanizing effects of empire. Burgos describes "this vast empire of solitude/ and darkness" (8-9). The description of the empire illuminates how she understands the physical act of colonization and its resulting effects. She describes the empire, first, as "vast." At this time, the empire in which she, as well as Anzaldúa, lived was that of the United States. Michael Gonzalez-Cruz notes in his 1998 article "The U.S. Invasion of Puerto Rico: Occupation and Resistance to the Colonial State, 1898 to the Present," that the "U.S. ruling class had occupied the continent from east to west, including the southwestern area once under Mexican rule, and had been developing a colonial agenda since it first took land from the Native Americans" (7-8). The physical terrain that the U.S. Empire stretches across is, indeed, vast. The United States is also notable for the military domination of the Dominican Republic in the first decades of the twentieth-century while simultaneously gaining colonial rights in the Treaty of Paris over Puerto Rico, Cuba, Guam, and the Philippines.[1]

Other aspects of empire depicted in Burgos's poem indicate the poet's awareness of the psychological impact on colonized individuals, similar to Anzaldúa's own portrayals. The poet describes the empire as being one of "solitude." The singularity of this word also connotes a sensation caused by it. There is loneliness, a sense of despondency. Rather than being united with the other individuals caught within the grasp of the colonizer, there are disjunctions and boundaries, borders that cannot be crossed. Similarly, Anzaldúa describes living on the border of the United States and Mexico as "the thin barbed wire" (35). The pain evident in both women's writings, despite their physical and temporal separation, evinces a shared understanding of what it is to be caught within colonial endeavors. The solitude wrought in the barricading of the U.S.

1 See Vedovato, Claudio. *Politics, Foreign Trade and Economic Development: A Study of the Dominican Republic.* London: Croom and Helm, 1986. and *The Treaty of Paris*, 1898.

from Mexico functions as a key component in constructing the tenuousness of life in the borderlands. Burgos's poem similarly illustrates that, despite the differences in her specificity of experiences as a Puertorriqueña from those of Anzaldúa, there exists an understanding among people living in the Third Worlds created in the U.S. mainland.

The envelopment and decimation that Burgos and Anzaldúa associate with empire identifies the impact of imperial mechanics. Burgos describes the empire as "dark," with darkness connoting a lack of light, an inability to see because of that lack, and a despondency that is interconnected with solitude. At the historical time in which Burgos wrote this poem, the "Puerto Rican Government," as chosen by the United States, drafted a new constitution. The various articles of this Constitution bear suspicious similarities to the U.S. constitution, and the first statement made in the document reads "this Constitution for the Commonwealth which, in the exercise of our natural rights, we now create within our union with the United States of America" (153). The phrasing demonstrates the manner in which the U.S. Empire eclipses Puerto Ricans' rights to self-determination and freedom from tyranny and oppression. Further, it is the very language employed in this legal document that also castes them into the shadows of empire, forever living on the margins of their colonizer's society. Belle Boone Beard writes in his 1945 article, "Puerto Rico: The Forty-Ninth State?," that "[t]oday the Puerto Ricans are the Forgotten Men of the Western Hemisphere" (115). Yet, here, Burgos's diction illuminates the various aspects of the empire as it is in the process of blatantly disappearing Puerto Rico's history. Anzaldúa's own text, ***Borderlands,*** attempts to counteract this "disappearing" as it pertains to Chicana history: "She reinterprets history and, using new symbols, she shapes new myths" (104). These women's writings thus transform into acts of subversion, representations of an oppositional consciousness within a hermeneutic of love, as described by Sandoval, and an engagement with their statuses at the margins of society and the pain/potential this space holds.

FIGHTING THE ABYSS: DEMANDS TO BE HEARD DESPITE THE DIN OF OPPRESSION

Awareness of imperial imposition onto the oppressed leads both Burgos and Anzaldúa to question the longevity of its impact. The poet is able to ask questions regarding the impact of colonialism on the colonized object. She writes "Where is the voice of freedom, / freedom to laugh" (19-20). In direct contrast with the solitude and darkness associated with empire, Burgos articulates a desire for liberation. That she seeks to "laugh" demonstrates that she rejects the colonial demand for Puerto Rican submission to dehumanization. She instead seeks freedom, which empire inherently denies. Anzaldúa describes how "[e]very increment of consciousness, every step forward is a *travesía*, a crossing. I am again an alien in new territory. And again, and again. But if I escape conscious awareness, escape 'knowing,' I won't be moving" (70). The idea of remaining stagnant is in opposition to growth and the potential that growth contains. Burgos appears to want the opposite: to not want the obliteration of her existence but instead the ability to physically respond to pleasure; Anzaldúa's writing indicates a similar need to transform.

However, and as examination of both these women's writings illuminates, conocimiento as praxis requires that the oppressed divest themselves of the weight of oppression. Burgos describes wanting to know where the voice of freedom "to move/ without the heavy phantom of despair" is located (11-12). The desire for movement responds to the strict borders and boundaries associated with empire. Anzaldúa continues her depiction in *Borderlands* of the border as a barbed wire by describing how her body was disciplined away from performing her Mexican American culture, with Spanish transformed into a disciplinary infraction in the schools she attended as a small child (75). Thus the mechanics of empire attempt to restrict the oppressed's culture and thereby, as noted in Burgos's previous poem, weigh down the spirits and psyches of the oppressed to methodologically subjugate and dominate them. Yet, both Burgos and Anzaldúa demonstrate a deep and complex consciousness to maneuver and disentangle themselves from the limitations of dehumanization.

Burgos and Anzaldúa are thereby able to use this location of sorrow to articulate a deeper understanding of how there must be a space formed for freedom. Burgos asks, "Where is the form of beauty / unshaken in its veil simple and pure?" (13-14). She seeks something untainted by the sullying of empire and domination. The veil she depicts could indicate W.E.B. DuBois's own theorization of the veil as that which protects the African-American psyche in the United States and enables individuals to function while maintaining a core identity that feeds and nurtures the soul in his 1903 publication, *The Soul of Black Folks* (44-45). As implicit to this knowledge is an understanding on Burgos's behalf that there is necessarily a barrier that the subjugated construct for self-preservation, in which they appear to function one way but maintain something for themselves that enables them to survive, with resiliency, and resist. Anzaldúa describes how "I spent the first half of my life learning to rule myself, to grow a will, and now at midlife I find that autonomy is a boulder on my path that I keep crashing into… I've always been aware that there is a greater power than the conscious I. That power is my inner self" (72). It is from this place of empowerment that organic intellectualism/conocimiento can come to fruition.

Where this conocimiento can lead to is illuminated in the dialogue between Burgos's and Anzaldúa's writings. Burgos asks, "Where is the warmth of heaven / pouring its dreams of love in broken spirits?" (15-16). Here she constructs an image of warmth and soothing spiritually in contrast to the formal religion that she had previously denounced in "To Julia de Burgos." She does not directly assign this warmth to Christianity, but describes it as something that comes from the sky and naturally warms the body. There is a sense that what was lacking in the formal religion is being sought after in other places by those who have not been healed. The source of this potential, however, remains undefined in Burgos's work. In taking up the challenge to find this source, Anzaldúa's articulation of a *nepantla* state appears to find an answer. As described during an interview recorded in *Interviews/Entrevistas, nepantla* is a place where "you're in a liminal, inbetween-space—you can go either way...when I reach these nepantla places I can make choices" (168). Thus, there must be an act of healing that at once soothes the unconscious, or the imagination of the harmed, before it can reach its pinnacle and set to rights that which has been wronged. Upon reaching this new place the individual gains the ability to find new spaces for personal liberty and the agency of making choices.

It is from this new place that Burgos and Anzaldúa can best explore and expose their experiences of empire and its mechanisms. Although third space feminists such as Chela Sandoval in her essay "U.S. Third World Feminism," published in 1991, will later identify their task as giving voice to those women of color who have been historically silenced (4), Burgos, writing in 1953, identifies the pressing need for this action and her desire to enact it in her own time. She states that "My cry that is no more mine, but hers and his forever" (20-21). Burgos thereby understands that now that her cry has gone out into the world, it has reached the ears of others who are also caught within the vices of empire and are joining her in their call. She therefore opens up an invitation for others to join her. Anzaldúa argues in "And When You Leave, Take Your Pictures With You: Racism in the Women's Movement" that the tensions felt between women across racial lines in the feminist movement is something that can be overcome as long as all sides are willing to work together to educate and want freedom for one another (64). Thus, a major component of third space feminisms' conocimiento is to enact processes in which the sentiments of the subjugated masses can be heard, recognized, and respected.

Awareness of this need leads to moments where solidarity can be built. Within her depictions of empire, Burgos also describes that there exist "comrades of my silence," evincing that she is no longer alone in suffering from the ravages of empire (7, 22). The poet constructs an image of resistance to the segregations imposed within imperialism. Anzaldúa describes how "conocimiento shares a sense of affinity with all things and advocates mobilizing, organizing, sharing information, knowledge, insights, and resources with other groups" ("now let us shift" 571). Similar to Anzaldúa, who dedicated years working in collaboration to produce multi-voiced anthologies with other women of color such as *This Bridge We Call Home* and *Making Face, Making Soul*, Burgos's political consciousness can also be witnessed in her own life. While attending the University of Puerto Rico, Burgos "became involved in Nationalist Party agitation and human rights justice" and was later fired from writing "children's radio plays for the Department of Instructions' 'La Escuela del Aire'...for her views on independence" (702, 712). Her voice, one not to be silenced or deterred by attempts at censorship, finds the artistic freedom to explicate the essence of being a colonized subject.

However, and as conocimiento demands, outlining of these experiences of colonialism cannot be the ends but rather must be the means of moving towards transformation. Burgos writes that she is "forgotten but unshaken" (25). Cast away into a hospital on an island removed from both Puerto Rico and the Puerto Rican districts of New York City, she is utterly alone. As evinced by the manner in which she died, within colonialism she becomes the forgotten. However, as the many Puerto Rican communities across the United States show, she has remained as an unshakable symbol of Puerto Rican refusal to be completely conquered by a colonizer. Anzaldúa writes in *Borderlands* of how "[w]e are ashamed that we need your good opinion, that we need your acceptance" in regards to hegemonic imperial culture, but continues by contending that "I search for our essential dignity as a people, a people with a sense of purpose—to belong and contribute to something greater than our *pueblo*. On that day I seek to recover and reshape my spiritual identity. *¡Anímate! Raza, a celebrar el día de la Chicana*" (110). Rather than being silenced by fear, she seeks transformation. Instead of being conquered, these women find and define their individual/community's sacred humanity. Burgos and Anzaldúa thereby illuminate how a third space feminist praxis of conocimiento functions.

Finally, it is within this functioning that mobility away from the devastations of imperialism becomes possible. As Burgos's poem concludes, her depiction of a descent also evinces an awareness and consciousness of despair as a psychological aspect of the empire she depicts. She writes, "deep into Welfare Island, my farewell to the world" (27-28). Although she describes her "farewell," there is nevertheless an appearance of some movement that abrogates stagnancy. Within this movement there is freedom that she had articulated earlier in the poem. There is a new state, similar to that of the nepantla state. However, as Anzaldúa describes in *Borderlands*, there is awareness that "'[k]nowing' is more painful" (70). The pain prevalent in Burgos's poem is illuminated in Anzaldúa's historically later words as an aspect of consciousness that is inevitable for individuals who are oppressed and aware of the mechanics of oppression. And yet, Anzaldúa's writing of surviving and growing elucidates the potential that still exists in the vitality of "a constant changing of forms, *renacimientos de la tierra madre*" (113). The movement concluding Burgos's poem emerges as a realization of how there must be endings to transform into new beginnings. Thus, conocimiento, in all of its pain, offers the depths of true change as well.

CONOCIMIENTO AS PRAXIS: POTENTIAL FOR TRANSFORMATION WITHIN THIRD SPACE FEMINISM

Although Julia de Burgos's poetry is specific to her experiences as a Puerto Rican woman and Anzaldúa's writings to Chicanas, placing these two women into conversation demonstrates the emancipatory potential created by coalition building as part of conocimiento praxis. Burgos's awareness in the mid-twentieth century regarding the impact of colonial gaze renders her words viable prototypes for understanding genderized-racism that is of such great importance to unpack and expose by the end of the twentieth-century. For Anzaldúa, this understanding is coupled with her relentless scrutiny of her culture and community; her writing finds resonance with other women of color writers who also refute the violations rendered possible due to their sociosexual racialized subject positions. Burgos finds comrades in the movement of later decades and it is in this way that her unnamed, homeless body becomes more than a symbol of Puerto Rican identity: it becomes proof that the imagination has the potential to deconstruct the binaries that categorize individuals into vulnerable positions. For Anzaldúa, breaking down these borders was indeed a life commitment. While these women were never able to unite their ideas in life, their dialogues that their works make possible elucidate the strength and power of coalition building, the vitality of literature in pressuring for transformation, and a third space feminist conocimiento that can lead future tactics of subversion.

WORKS CITED

Anzaldúa, Gloria. *Borderlands: La Frontera*. 3rd ed. San Francisco, CA: Aunt Lute Books, 2007. Print.

---. *Interviews Entrevistas*. Ed. AnaLouise Keating. New York: Routledge, 2000. Print.

---. "now let us shift." *This Bridge We Call Home: Radical Visions for Transformation*. Eds. Gloria Anzaldúa and Ana Louise Keating. New York: Routledge, 2002. 540-78. Print.

---. "Dream of the Double Headed Woman." *Gloria Anzaldúa Reader*. Ed. AnaLouise Keating. Durham, NC: Duke UP, 2009. 70-71. Print.

"Blackwell's Island a Prison Terrible; Treatment of Convicts There is Vile and Inhuman, Commissioner Davis Reports." *New York Times,* March 27, 1914. 20. Print.

Blake, Debra. *Chicana Sexuality and Gender*. Durham, NC: Duke UP, 2007. Print.

Burgos, Julia de. "To Julia de Burgos." *Song of the Simple Truth*. Trans. Jack Agüeros. Willmington, CT: Curbstone, 1996. 2-3. Print.

---. "Farewell in Welfare Island." *Song of the Simple Truth*. Trans. Jack Agüeros. Willmington, CT: Curbstone, 1996. 356-57. Print.

Combahee River Collective. "A Black Feminist Statement." *This Bridge Called My Back*. 3rd ed. Eds. Cherríe Moraga and Gloria Anzaldúa. Berkley, CA: Third Women, 234-44. Print.

DuBois, W.E.B. *The Souls of Black Folks*. New York: Penguin, 1995. Print.

Fleming, Jeanne St. Sauveur. "Safety for Hospital Patients." *American Journal for Nursing* 53.4 (1953): 465-67. Print.

Gonzalez-Cruz, Michael. "The U.S. Invasion of Puerto Rico: Occupation and Resistance to the Colonial State, 1898 to the Present." *Latin American Perspectives* 25.5 (1998): 7-26. Print.

Gutiérrez, Elena. *Fertile Matters: The Politics of Mexican-Origin Reproduction*. Austin, TX: U Texas P, 2008. Print.

Lopez, Irís. *Matters of Choice: Puerto Rican Women's Struggle for Reproductive Freedom*. New Brunswick, NJ: Rutgers UP, 2008. Print.

Lorde, Audre. "The Master's Tools Will Never Dismantle the Master's House." *Sister Outsider*. Berkeley, CA: Crossing, 1984.111-13. Print.

Manning, Caroline. "The Employment of Women in Puerto Rico." *Bulletin of the Women's Bureau* 118 (1934): 1-34. Print.

Mascia, Mark. "Bodies Politic: Nature, Nation, and Society As Seen Through the Body in the Poetry of Julia de Burgos." *Unveiling the Body in Hispanic Women's Literature*. Eds. Renée Scott and Arleen Chiclana González. Lewinston, NY: Edwin Mellen, 2006. 117-42. Print.

Moraga, Cherríe, & Gloria Anzaldúa, eds. *This Bridge Called My Back*. Watertown: Persephone Press, 1981. Print.

Novak, Robert. "Distribution of Puerto Ricans on Manhattan Island." *Geographical Review* 46.2 (1956): 182-86. Print.

Perez, Laura. *Chicana Art: The Politics of Spiritual and Aesthetic Alterities.* Durham, NC: Duke UP, 2006. Print.

Sandoval, Chela. *Methodology of the Oppressed.* Minneapolis, MN: U of Minnesota P, 2001. Print.

---. "U.S. Third World Feminism: The Theory and Method of Oppositional Consciousness in the Postmodern World." *Gender* 10 (1991): 1-24. Print.

Springfield, Consuelo. "'I am the Life, the Strength, the Woman': Feminism in Julia de Burgos' Autobiographical Poetry." *Callaloo* 17.3 (1994): 701-14. Print.

Zavala-Martínez, Iris. "A Critical Inquiry into the Life and Work of Julia de Burgos." *The Psychosocial Development of Puerto Rican Women.* Eds. Cynthia T. García Coll and María de Lourdes Marrei. New York: Praeger, 1989. 1-30. Print.

INNER WORK, CREATIVE EXPRESSIONS

POEMS

VERONICA SANDOVAL "LADY MARIPOSA"

AFTER CERVICIDE
POST CARD TO LA GLORIA

April 6, 2012

Today I saw two venaditas on the crest
leading up the entrance ramp of 395
and I thought of you

I wonder if Washington Venadas
are different from Valley Venadas?
Do they like empanadas?
Would they prefer Ruby Reds to Galas?
Do they speak without Caló tongues?

Do Washington Venadas know La Llorona?
Have they grown unafraid of corralling the father?
Would Washington Venadas refuse
to lead La Prieta home,

instead insist they sit and wait
for the warden and his hounds

U.S. Route 395, Washington
C/S

PALMING LIMESTONE
POST CARD TO LA GLORIA
April 20, 2012

El frío de Washington's Spring
plays a humdrum game
of hide and seek

Y como coneja amorosa
he salido from
"My little womb
of a house" & have
sat on the wooden
steps dejando a tú
Julio Cortázar
dentro tomando café

The tall shadows
you clothe
in male garb
do not follow me
to the post office

Estoy sola en
viejitos gringolandia
standing under
the dead pine tree
y mi viejo el sabelo nada
de plants or jardines told me,
echondoles el mower por encima,
that the grape hyacinth flowers

que chuliaba were
nothing but hierbas majaderas
kin to milk weeds & dandelions

Pero ¿qué saben ellos of rasquache-esque
Bell-shaped fragrant flowers
like me? Si aqui la terra is littered
with pine needles and not mesquite pods
¿Qué saben ellos que nunca han visto a Yemayá
con sus cowboy boots
y en BeeKeyKnees besando el sol de la isla?

¿Qué saben ellos de las poetas naufragadas
who palm the limestone tokens of your grave?
de-constructing and reconstructing a borderland
too far away to forget

Lind, Washington
C/S

I WILL BE YOUR BRIDGE
A LITERARY REFLECTION FOR GLORIA & ANALOUISE

I am drawbridge
an island of a woman
Chola rapping sub
whose poems
are connected to
some other America

I am a sandbar &
because you are so young
I will function as your bridge

Where I come from no roads diverge in woods
only rusted fences try to block out ancestry
Where I come from culture and identity
are not interconnected by "English Only"

There is no such thing as
One Nation, One Culture, One Language
My poetry substitutes Shakespearean thous
for barrio howls & sometimes
14 year old girls get knocked up in the hood
And sometimes you throw in a cuss word or two
but caliche roads & mesquite trees do not stop
my poem from being a poem

I am drawbridge
an island of a woman
Academic Chola Sub
whose poems
are connected to
some other America
you don't think your own

I am a sandbar &
because you are so young
I will function as your bridge

Sister hood becomes a "singular utopian fantasy"
when I revolute you with my "Trojan mula swagger"
& selective reality will never patch up racism
I'm American
I have eroded your hyphenation
I'm American
I come from Mexican ancestry
I'm American
I terrorize you un-compartmentalize

And while diversity is sold on billboards
& sitcom-ed out by desperate housewives
as sexy Latina maids cha cha cha-ing
their way into the American dream
I am not as easily crafted into
your restrains as humble day labor
I am not the voice from behind the door

with the patrona's baby on my hip saying
no la senora no esta

my poetry "superceded the pictorial"
my memories demand I tell stories
and these are the realities in my barrio
where my poetry is not for you
only because YOU say so
where babies have babies
and loved ones get lost to addictions
where there is no 401ks or IRAs
far away from your picket white fence
and the privilege of your middle class

I am drawbridge
an island of a woman
and I am tired of "internalizing
and assimilating" your
mestizaless theories
I am drawbridge
an island of a woman
and my existence will continue
to push up "against the boundaries
of the acceptable and the traditional"
I am drawbridge
an island of a woman
And I implore you chavala,
to "hook into a snip of my lived experience"
to look past our cultural differences
to refuse to let language be a barrier
to stop expecting me to assimilate

I am drawbridge
an island of a woman
I am a sandbar &
because you are so young

I will function as your bridge

THE CALMECAC COLLECTIVE, OR, HOW TO SURVIVE THE ACADEMIC INDUSTRIAL COMPLEX THROUGH RADICAL INDIGENOUS PRACTICE

THE CALMECAC COLLECTIVE

STEPHANIE: We're all just a story away from each other.[1]

CATALINA: This is a story about stories. Stories that we are telling, that some want to silence.

AYDÉ: I'm going to stand here and tell you a story.

QWO-LI: The Calmecac in Nahuatl history were educational institutions where people received trainings in the rhetorical traditions and practices of the Mexica Empire. Calmecac provide one of many Indigenous genealogies for higher education in the Americas situated within Indigenous histories and gesture towards what Emma Pérez calls a decolonial imaginary between our colonial present and a postcolonial future.[2]

Drawing on this history, *The Calmecac Collective* (the "CC") emerged as a radical tactic of survival and resistance for graduate students and junior faculty against the backdrop of Texas A&M University by building intentional community within one another, centering our own cultures, families, and ancestors.

Cherokee scholar Daniel Heath Justice talks about the idea of *critical kinship* in the academy and posits these four questions:

1. How do we learn to be human?
2. How do we behave as good relatives?
3. How do we become good ancestors?
4. How do we learn to live together?

Within historically white, male institutions, those from marginalized communities or those pursuing activist scholarship often find themselves further marginalized by increasing corporatization. In the university, like in many other institutions, we are recruited in order to increase "diversity," only to find that our commitments not only remain marginal to the concerns of the academy, but are often actively discouraged and denigrated. As a group of American Indian, Mexican, Chican@/Latin@ and allied scholars whose collective work emerged on the contested and multiply occupied land currently called Texas, the Calmecac Collective remembers and practices Gloria Anzaldúa's maxim, "This land was Mexican once/ was Indian always/ and is/ and will be again" (*Borderlands* 25), as part of imagining multiple decolonizations and honoring strands of stories and memory that weave us together.

VICTOR: El Mundo Zurdo was my first conference ever. In November 2010, I could not begin to describe what that conference was really the beginning of for me. I did not know it then but the Calmecac Collective was the reason why I sat there nervously reading my paper about food next to my brother and my soon to be sisters-from-scratch. Before I ever knew what CC stood for I was already a product of their hard work. Before I would ever find out about what "diversity" really meant at Texas A&M, I was sitting with most of the CC eating dinner and I wondered if this is what grad school was going to be like. If it was, I was excited; everyone was so supportive and friendly—the academy is great!

I often forget I'm spoiled, as I was never forced to read the standard literary canon. I have never not privileged the scholars and nepantleras about whom I wanted to read. Recently in a conversation with some of my sisters-from-scratch, we discussed how we got into English Studies. I was able to answer, "Because of a class on Edwidge Danticiat, Sandra Cisneros, and Toni Morrison." I know it's not like that for most, but I have never known differently.

STEPHANIE/AYDÉ: We're all just a story away from each other.

MARCOS: We learn from those who have come before us, and we build on their work by creating our own theories and practices. Our elders, like Anzaldúa, continue talking to us through their words even though they've passed on. Every time we revisit their work, we arrive with altered subjectivities that create a different understanding. We go to conferences and meetings to listen to elders like Norma Cantú and Norma Alarcón. They are more beautiful and brilliant than ever because years of working in their communities, among their families, and in the academy only make them stronger. I wonder if I will ever have the strength to work and last as long.

CATALINA: I arrived to this east Texas town during an August heat wave. With each passing minute, as we moved my belongings into my new house, our clothes became sweat soaked, the furniture seemed heavier, and everywhere the land was parched and flat. I did not know if I would like this town, but I felt ready for the PhD—giddy, in fact. I had spent all summer with my mom in Albuquerque, mowing her lawn and watering calabasas and tomatoes, rereading Ana Castillo's *So Far From God* and soaking up Sherman Alexie's *The Absolutely True Diary of a Part-Time Indian,* all the while waiting. I'd been offered money and praise, and above all, time to write. I was more than ready for Texas A&M University. I was ecstatic.

AYDÉ: I'm going to stand here and tell you a story. It's a story about my maternal grandfather, Santiago Enriquez who was born and raised in Namiquipa, Chihuahua, Mexico. He lost his mom when he was just a boy; he lost his older brother when he went off to his aventura al otro lado and never returned; he lost his first two children to a bad sobada and to an empache; he lost a brother in the same week he lost his wife.

I'm going to stand here and tell you a story. My grandfather was once a Bracero. He worked the land. He worked with his hands. The Tejas sun burned his skin. He perspired and bled on the land. He did what he had to do to feed his family. He hummed songs under his breath as he worked and remembered his home.

Aquí pararé y te contaré un cuento. Mi abuelo era como mi padre. Padre de mi Madre. Él me encaminaba a la escuela. Él me regaló una pluma azul y me dijo, "Escribe bonito. Aguárdala." Todavía existe. Él me daba pedazos de madera para jugar y construir mis casitas y mis torres. Él me dio su apellido cuando a mi padre no le importé. Él falleció cuando yo tenía dieciséis años en el amanecer de una navidad. Tenía ochenta y cinco años.

CATALINA: I miss my mom y mis abuelas; they are my first community. My mom is gracious; she likes people. She would have welcomed all twelve of the new members of my cohort and learned their names. My grandmothers would have done the same.

I didn't feel welcomed here. That was the first sign that something was wrong. This was followed by more signs until the rancid truth spilled out: this department, this university was poisoned with hatred and that hatred was aimed most vociferously at graduate students, staff, and junior faculty, the most vulnerable. That's how the academic industrial complex works, of course, and Texas A&M is one of its exemplars. It did not take long to understand that this degree would be an exercise in survival, and that the usual survival tactics would not work. I did not understand then how much my voice would wobble under the strain of a conservative, top-down, blatantly-oppressive-and-proud-of-it institution. I did not know that the creative writing dissertation was an afterthought, that the attempts at silencing would be (mostly) transparent but no less brutal. I did not know that there would be the worst displays of racism and sexism, homophobia and ableism, ageism and classism, or that our writing, our stories, our scholarship would be twisted, overridden, undermined.

VICTOR/MARCOS/QWO-LI: We're all just a story away from each other.

AYDÉ: I'm going to stand here and tell you a story.

CASIE: A Recipe from Scratch for Getting Through Graduate School...

1. Learn your place.

    a. Be grateful you are even there. Accept that you don't know anything. Learn the hierarchy. Teach what you are told to teach. Stay quiet in meetings—even the ones about diversity.

    b. Take yourself out: My abuela and I used to make tortillas together when I was a child. If we made flour tortillas, she wiped down the table, an ornate, dark brown table that was too big for the room but never big enough whenever everyone gathered together. The table was second-hand—scratched like a schoolhouse desk, scratched so that the lighter, unpolished wood came out. She made long, strong strokes with her arm, and her shoulder muscles flexed tense and strong. Her knuckles reddened from holding tight to the cleaning rag. Soon, I was in charge of wiping the table down before we started—"Limpiela," she pointed her chin toward the table from the shotgun kitchen and handed me the rag.

c. Cry in a corner. By yourself. Scream in your car on the highway. By yourself. Separate. Yourself.

QWO-LI: [Singing]. Sgwatinisesdi Yihowa eladi gaisvi. Tsiwaniga tliyu ayv, tsalinigidi nihi. Sgisdvlisgi, sgisdvlisgi. Desgigana wadidv.

CATALINA: A woman opened her mouth and out flew mourning doves and hornets, gold-flecked dirt and chokecherries, and stories about the land of red rock and uranium mills, broken families and healing from addiction. There are other stories, and you will hear them. This isn't a story about those who strangle doves, shake hornets' nests; poison the land until it turns gold, drain red ink from chokecherries. This is not their story; we've choked on that narrative. This is a story about stories. Ours, yours, mine, ours.

AYDÉ: As a graduate student I've recognized that the English language is one of the master's tools, and as Audre Lorde reminds us, "the master's tools will never dismantle the master's house" (112). As such, I recognize that my use of the English language must go beyond just pronouncing words correctly. Anzaldúa says, "I am participating in the creation of yet another culture, a new story to explain the world and our participation in it, a new value system with images and symbols that connect us to each other and to the planet" (103). It is within this space of the borderlands that we have the capacity to dismantle the master's house re-utilizing the tools available to us. We might be using the same language, but we are blending it with our other tongues, our bodies, our memories, and our stories. The tools to dismantle the master's house are ours. They are culturally and locally based. They are the discourses of our homes, of our kitchens, of our bodies, of our tongues, of the songs we hear in our sleep, of the movement of our bodies to the beat of a drum, of the land and dirt and smells that make everything okay, of the private, of the "mundane," of our rage, passion, and hate, of the heat in our bodies, and of the loves in our lives and the loves we've lost and never forget: it's the discourse we've always utilized to survive.

CATALINA: Genocide. This word comes to me upon waking, haunts me during the fifteen-minute drive to A&M, clings to me in the classrooms and hallways of Blocker. I smell its stench everywhere. I cannot work in my office or any other room in this building. I attend class, I teach class, I flee. I have cried myself to sleep and with others. We should be dead. We should be dead. We should be dead.

It is the first week of my first semester.

QWO-LI: Memory: I am a PhD student at Michigan State University, taking a class with Indiana Miami scholar Malea Powell. We're talking about universities and colonization, remembering—as Janice Gould writes, "It is obvious that there is not a university in this country that is not built on what was once native land. We should reflect on this over and over, and understand this fact as one fundamental point about the relationship of Indians to academia" (81-82). Malea reminds us that universities are Native places: "Anishinaabe people are relatives of Miamis," she tells us. "We have a long history together. Here. In this place. These are our lands. These are our universities." Malea taught me to remember our protocols as Indigenous people, to *practice* our own ways, to insist on centering our own epistemologies, and to understand that as Indigenous people in the university we are continuing our lifeways. Shawn Wilson writes that "research is ceremony" (Wilson 2009). That's not a metaphor. And so, I incorporate our traditions into the classroom, graduate student exams and dissertation defenses. Our ancestors are watching us.

CASIE/VICTOR/MARCOS/AYDÉ/CATALINA: This land was Mexican once

CASIE/VICTOR/MARCOS/AYDÉ/CATALINA/QWO-LI: was Indian always

CASIE/VICTOR/MARCOS/AYDÉ/CATALINA/QWO-LI/STEPHANIE: and is

CASIE: and will be again

QWO-LI: Put tobacco down. Send smoke up. Tinogi. Halsgi. Speak our languages. Niwi.

VICTOR: For me those in the CC have been my neplantleras; whom Anzaldua defines as, "Artistas/activistas [that] help us mediate these transitions, help us make the crossing, and guide us through the transformation process—a process I call conocimiento" (Keating 310). My conocimiento of the academy has been shaped by their experiences and mentorship.

In the most practical sense they inform me of all those nuances that every graduate student should know yet nobody tells them. All the things they wish somebody would have told them. It sounds simple and I may never know how valuable their advice has been. Things like: apply to conferences, all graduate students are insecure, you don't have to know or read everything...yet. All of these consejos help to navigate the day to day activity of grad school.

CASIE: 2. Learn History—the capital *H* History lineage. Learn Theory—the capital *T* Theory kind. Learn Literature, Rhetoric, Language—capital *L*, *R*, and *L*.

a. Learn George Washington, not George Washington Gomez. Learn Fredric Jameson, not Chela Sandoval. Learn Cormac McCarthy, not Ana Castillo. Learn Kenneth Burke, not Gloria Anzaldúa. Learn Standard American English, not Spanglish or Spanish or Nahuatl.

b. Take yourself out: Sometimes my abuela mixed everything in a bowl—the flour and the lard and the baking soda, the salt and water. Sometimes, the lard was Crisco. Sometimes, it was the fat from leftovers. Other times, the times I remember more, we skipped the bowl completely. She dumped flour straight from a paper bag onto the newly cleaned table. Then, with her fingers, she dug out a small hole in the pile of flour. She used her fingers to dig out the lard from the container and dropped it into the hole. She splashed water from a bowl on to the mixture and added salt. She didn't use measuring cups or spoons. She used her hands to feel the mixture—too wet, too dry, too sticky, too separate.

c. Cry in a corner. By yourself. Scream in your car on the highway. By yourself. Separate. Yourself.

CASIE/CATALINA/AYDÉ: We're all just a story away from each other.

QWO-LI: I am in my first semester as an assistant professor at Texas A&M. I'm sitting in my office when a Mexican American graduate student comes to talk with me. Along with other first year graduate students, she has just been told by a white senior male professor that, "Major scholars write about major authors. Minor scholars write about minor authors." She is in tears because she knows what the professor means. "I don't think I can do this," she sobs as I hand her a box of Kleenex. "I don't want to be here." The truth was, after only a few weeks at the university as one of very few American Indian faculty and after a white colleague constantly says "Hau" to me in the hallway, I wasn't sure if I could do this either. [Singing] Soldier girl, soldier girl hey ya hey ya hey ya hey ya This war is over soldier girl.

We have a long history together. Here. In this place. These are our lands. These are our universities.

AYDÉ/VICTOR: I'm going to stand here and tell you a story.

CATALINA: These are not new to me, these onslaughts. I have lived them and fought them before in different environments, under different guises. But here, I expected that I would be offered an opportunity to do the work I came to do, with others who came to do the same or similar work.

We are doing that work. Just not with the kind of support we should have had. The attacks have been relentless. They still are.

MARCOS: Since last summer, I carried with me the thought of what it means to think and write *meaningfully*, especially in this moment, when Chican@s and other indigenous folks need to create meaningful work to counteract all the hate thrown at us, our traditions, our histories, and our ways of knowing. I feel this daily in an academic setting where undocumented students feel harassed by hyper-conservative student organizations; where graduate students of color get placed on lists as "troublemakers" for defending themselves; and where faculty of color flee the university in alarming numbers. If not for the *Calmecac Collective*, I would be lost. If not for the support and love that serves as a balm against this acidic environment, I would quit.

A frequent remembrance: I sit among esta familia de sobrevivientes wondering whether we are good enough. We even minimize our successes, over-analyzing why we truly did not deserve it. I don't know how many times I've told my friends they are brilliant, wonderful people who are doing great work. I don't know how many times they refuse to listen to those words meaningfully. I'm angry because I mean it from the bottom of my heart, and I love them dearly. But I'm a hypocrite because I react the same way.

Before we can communicate meaningfully, we must learn to listen meaningfully, especially in our closest relationships. Cherríe Moraga teaches me this lesson when she writes about her fallout with Gloria Anzaldúa. She writes, "I wish I had been less afraid and more insistent on resolving the profound ruptures of heart between us, what we could not openly admit or when admitted, could not honor" (127). Moraga takes this lesson earnestly, but understands: "Still, as I age I continue to witness these ruptures, separations from people I once loved in deep and true ways. Loving breaks the heart over and over again. It just does." After I read Moraga's essay, "The Salt that Cures: Remembering Gloria Anzaldúa," I thought about all my relationships and alliances, and those moments of discord when frustrations, fears, and resentments take over, deepening the breach among us. In a system privileging the hyper-individual, solitary scholar, subtle breaches deepen, and we run the risk of losing each other. If we listen with unconditional love, then we seek understanding and heal our mutual wounds. But we must listen and love fiercely.

In our department, I see the deep divisions that the divide and conquer strategy creates. The ugliest parts of people appear in their words and their uses of power. All we merely ask is for listening, and yet that is the most difficult thing to achieve. We thought by voicing our concerns, we would achieve progress. Instead, we receive orders from the top down. I've had it with all this.

I resign from further abuse, disrespect, and trauma.

I resign from false allies who benefit from my oppression.

I resign from accepting piecemeal offerings at the cost of my later subordination.

I resign from allowing this hostile work environment to affect my development as a person, a research scholar, and a teacher.

I refuse to believe that this is what the graduate school experience is supposed to be

Because I have heard, seen, and imagined better.

I deserve much better.

I resign to building communities and networks

Of love and belonging inside me first,

Then among my friends and family.

I resign from allowing hate to infect my relationships,

Even with you.

I resign.

CATALINA: We have a long history together.

CATALINA/QWO-LI: Here. In this place.

CASIE: These are our lands.

CASIE/MARCOS/AYDÉ: These are our universities.

AYDÉ: I vividly remember the cool feel of the cotton aqua-colored Mickey Mouse T-shirt that blistering hot summer of 1988 when we moved to El Paso, Texas. I had worn a dark brown polyester school uniform with a pleated skirt, pressed white blouse, knee-high white socks, and black, rubber-soled shoes all my school days en la Escuela Primaria Ricardo Flores Magón en Ciudad Juarez,

Chihuahua, Mexico. The Mickey T-shirt was my first T-shirt, and I remember I wore it every day until my mom got rid of it. It had Mickey in the front in a Hawaiian button up shirt and black sandals with a palm tree in the background.

We made the move to El Paso when I was in the third grade. My mother had finally started the process of leaving my father; he just didn't know it yet. My two siblings and I were all born on the right side of the border, as they say, so it was a matter of time before we returned to *claim* our citizenship. "Tu eres ciudadana, eh?" My mom always reminded us that we were US citizens and had to tell the customs agent that we were "American" when we crossed the bridge. "American!"—we loudly sounded off every time the brown customs agent peeked into the back seat.

We were the only Mexican kids at the Tree Haven apartment complex in El Paso. I recall one evening in the parking lot two older white boys kept asking me to say "Social Studies." There was a small crowd around us—a bunch of kids whose names and faces I can't even make out in my dreams any more. I don't remember how it started either, but I do recall that they would burst out laughing every time I said "Social Studies." I laughed too. The other kids also laughed. I didn't understand what was so funny about "Social Studies," but I enjoyed being part of the crowd. It was just the title of the book after all, or so I thought, but I laughed along. Years later, I recognized that instead of saying "Social Studies," I was saying "Shosho Studies." My ears could not tell the difference. My mind had not learned the rules. My tongue struggled to sound the word. "Shosho Studies": I kept repeating on demand—laughing with the crowd. That was just the first of my many mispronunciations.

CATALINA: During my first semester, I wrote a total of five new pages in my creative writing class. Before, in my MFA program, I used to write five pages in one night. Now, each week, we spent three hours listening to another adventure in the life of the professor. I was lucky to get the five pages.

CASIE: 3. Learn to Make an Argument.

> a. Write an introduction with a strong, direct thesis statement. Move to a literature review with *major* theorists and critics. Lay out your points in a linear fashion. Write a conclusion.
>
> b. Take yourself out: With the heel of her hands and with her cupped fingers, my abuela pushed the flour up and over to cover the hole with the lard and water, mashed it together with her hard hands. When it became more than just flour and water and lard, when it became dough, she folded it in on

itself. When it was dough, she let me try to work with the ingredients. My hands were smaller, weaker, and so it was a slower process when I folded the dough over itself. Eventually, she would take over again. If she needed more water, she added it. If it was too wet, she added flour. Eventually, she would taste the dough to see if it needed more salt or lard or flour, and I ate pinches of the raw dough until she threatened me with stomachaches.

c. Cry in a corner. Together. Scream in your car on the highway. Scream. Together. Come. Together.

STEPHANIE/CASIE: We're all just a story away from each other.

MARCOS: We need to listen to all our elders, especially those closest to us. And we need to listen to the discord to understand why it exists. We need to understand that when we enter the Academy, we are not only students, but people under attack because we are Atravesados, daring to do the kind of decolonial work our communities need. And we need to understand how the Academy wants us to stop listening to each other and only listen to it.

AYDÉ: Looking back on my first experiences in El Paso is painful. I recognize that the T-shirt was my first taste of American capitalism. Mickey, a worldwide icon, was my way to disguise my foreignness, to show that I belonged, and as a way to embrace the United States. And since the production of Mickey Mouse merchandise is reportedly done with child labor in third world sweatshops, my use of this icon to buy my way in as a child is even more problematic. But my use of Mickey was similar to my projection of "American-ness" as some special gift bestowed upon me: both Mickey and my idealization of American-ness are products sold around the world; both project an idyllic reality hiding the face of the innocent trampled in their very creation. Lastly, my mispronunciation of "Social Studies" and the laughter that ensued speaks volumes about the rhetorical use of "Social Studies" to teach history to elementary school children. At that moment, I learned too that in order to be a part of the laughing-group versus the being-laughed-at-group, I had to learn to use the language efficiently. But I also learned that the dichotomy of the available options presented by these two groups—those who laugh and those who are laughed at—are dangerous and detrimental to communities of color. I didn't want to be a part of either group.

Because my initial immersion into English was difficult and traumatic, it became the language I only spoke at school. In my mother's home, even today, we all still speak Spanish. But my experience learning English led me to recognize the power of language. By speaking the right language in the right way and in the right space, I would not be the butt of the joke. By speaking the right language the right way, I could protect myself from such scenarios by avoiding particular words. And by speaking the right language in the right space, then I could navigate both worlds—English at school and Spanish for my real life. As a child, I recognized that language was a weapon that could be used against me but also one that I could learn to manipulate to defend and protect myself.

CASIE: 4. Relearn that your experiences matter.

> a. Listen to the stories you have heard your whole life. Practice your traditions. Talk to your family, your elders, those who have walked on. Remember that your stories made you. Remember that these stories matter.
>
> b. Keep yourself in: My abuela sectioned off portions of dough into small balls, then rolled the small balls out with a large rolling pin, and she let me roll out my own small balls with a metal can. We stacked them until we had enough for the day. Then I'd stand next to her gas-burner stove, watch her put them straight on the burners and flip them with only her fingers, no tongs—something I still cannot do. I watched brown spots appear and bubbles rise and pop. We made tortillas together.
>
> c. Cry until you laugh together. Scream in the car until you laugh together. Come together until you laugh together. Make familia-from-scratch. Roll out histories, theories, rhetorics, literatures, languages and flatten them out. Roll them out. Flatten them out. Relearn to *practice* them.

AYDÉ: I'm going to stand here and tell you a story. I'm the granddaughter of a Bracero. I'm the granddaughter of a carpenter. Of a man whose vision never failed and hands never stopped. Of a man whose Virgen de Guadalupe tattoo faded with time. Of a man whose songs continue to haunt me, whose words I cannot make out but always remember.

STEPHANIE: We're all just a story away from each other.

VICTOR: What I am most grateful for and what I always keep in mind are the war stories from the front lines. All the racism, sexism, ableism, and homophobia that we encounter and they forget about. All the "diversity" that they talk about and we live. Fortunately and unfortunately I know not to be shocked, afraid, or discouraged in the face of hate. I know that it is more reason why our work matters. I'm living proof of it. So that those after me will know this too and be encouraged as I have been. As Anzaldúa says, "I yearn to pass on to the next generation the spiritual activism I've inherited from my cultures." The culture of the CC encourages me to create conversations between Chakrabarty, Althusser and Anzaldúa. I also know that this work is a constant healing. I know I can't sit comfortably in my corner content that I have the luxury to do what I want. To some extent I can thank the cultural climate of my department; there are constant reminders that we are not safe. So we continue to work and heal.

QWO-LI: This land was Mexican once

CASIE: Was Indian always

EVERYONE: And is

QWO-LI: And will be again.

STEPHANIE: My second semester in grad school, I was assigned as a grader for a linguistics class. I had never been a grader, nor did I have many friends in the program at that time, so I didn't quite know what to do when the lecturer's first correspondence with me was written entirely in emoticons. Or when that first weekend, I received approximately 300 text messages from this woman, saying things like, "How's your heart today?" "I need to wash my hair," and "Want to go to Red Lobster? I've got groupons!" Even more disorienting was how she'd speak about herself in the plural, like, "We need to see the grade book," "Wow, we had SUCH a busy weekend birdwatching, didn't get that quiz written," or "We have an idea about extra credit points!" I really tried to ignore it, until one day she sent me to her office in the middle of class to check on one of those ideas.

"I forgot to ask him, can you run up to my office and double-check how many points we want to add to the exam?" she asked in front of the class. Relieved that she hadn't, in fact, been talking about herself in the plural, I walked up to her office, but found nobody when I opened up the door. Only a single desk pushed against the wall and bits of handmade jewelry strewn across the floor.

I reported that there wasn't anyone in the office, and with a mixture of confusion and exasperation in her voice, she told me to look to the right of the desk, because he would not have left. I walked back in and looked to the right of the desk. There was a wall. And a picture of an alligator.

It was printed from the internet, this picture. On an inkjet printer, to be precise, because one half of the picture was kind of pink and the other half had printer lines all the way through it. And it was a bit worn, with lots of crinkles and water spots. But the picture was clear enough: it was a real-life alligator crawling out of a ditch on the side of the road, looking towards the camera and making the Zoolander face. It was the only thing on the right side of the desk.

I walked back to class, planning to tell her again that there wasn't anyone in the room, but at the last minute decided to blurt out, "Twelve points! He said to add twelve points!"

"Twelve?!" Utter confusion washed over her face. "But that doesn't sound like him...he only works in multiples of fives. Go back and check again."

So I went. But instead of going back to the office, I bought a Dr. Pepper. When I came back into the classroom, she interrupted her lecture to ask what he said.

"Well, he really thinks twelve, but he said to go ahead and do fifteen if that makes you feel better. Said he was trying to break out of the comfort zone."

"Fifteen is still a bit high, but it certainly sounds more like him. We have a comfort zone for a reason."

Have I mentioned yet that this is a true story?

A few weeks later, she called me at 11 P.M. on a Sunday, asking if I'd cover her classes for her. "I'll give you index cards with lesson plans on them. Meet me at the gas station at 8 A.M." *Click.*

I didn't know graders weren't supposed to teach classes, nor did I know where the gas station was. I got up the next morning, took a wild guess, and waited at the gas station next to the English building. Not long after I arrived, an SUV peeled into the parking lot and a passenger-side window rolled down. It was her.

"Get in." I reached for the door handle, but before I could open the door, she stopped me. "Not in front! *He's* sitting there!"

I peeked in. The picture of the alligator was in the front seat, held in place by the seat belt. I climbed into the back of the SUV, and she sped across the street to drop me off. She handed me a stack of fluorescent index cards, only one of which had anything written on it ("linguistics"). As I exited the vehicle, she turned and asked where the Court House was. She had jury duty.

"I'm not sure...maybe down the main road?"

"It's fine. I'll look out one side and he'll look out the other. We'll find it."

It was around that time I convinced myself that if this is what academia was like,

I'd never make it. I didn't have a picture of an alligator making the Zoolander face, let alone an inkjet printer to print it out if I'd ever find one. But somehow I made it to finals week.

"He needs another copy of the grade book," she texted me one day. "Color-coded."

Knowing she was texting on behalf of the alligator, I didn't reply, and instead focused on my final papers. She caught me in the hallway at school and asked where the copies were.

"Could you make copies of the copies I made you?" I asked.

"Well, that would be harder to read."

Frustrated, I made the copies and brought them back to her office. I tossed them on the desk towards her.

"I told you, they're not for me. They're for him," she said without looking up.

"The alligator? Maybe he doesn't like to be handed things. I have no way of knowing if he does or not."

"You're being rude."

"I apologize, I'm just tired."

"Don't apologize to me, apologize to him." She pointed to the crinkled picture to her right.

"The alligator? You want me to apologize to a picture of an alligator?"

Her face flushed a dangerous red and her nostrils flared. "You won't leave until you do."

I clenched my jaw. "I'm sorry."

"To him! Look at him!" she yelled.

I looked at the picture. "I'm sorry. Sir."

Before I could leave, she stopped me. "You know, academia is difficult. We all have our things that get us through. Don't judge someone because what they do is different from what you might do."

She was right. Really, who am I to judge what people do to cope?

My community and I revisit this story frequently. Not because it offers a useful model for coping with academia, but because it's funny. And that helps us cope. It took a full semester after this story took place for me to admit to my friends it was real, and we haven't stopped laughing since.

The alligator story is our story; not because it happened to all of us, or that we even knew each other when it did happen. But the story of the alligator has become embedded in our community about what it means to survive the harsh realities of never thinking you're good enough, that you'll never get it done, or that you'll always be one step behind everyone else. Without my community, I know for a fact that I wouldn't have made it as far as I have today. And for us, part of what keeps us going (in addition to the genuine support, guidance, and friendship that bind us together) is laughter. It's our ability to meet throughout the week and bring our worries and insecurities to the table. And to cry. And then to laugh. It's about your friends finding you near tears for whatever reason and then finding a way to make you smile. Because when we can laugh together, things seem to be more manageable. Life's not as scary, because those shared inside jokes remind me that we're all in this together. And no matter how fundamentally changed we are after the fundamentally ridiculous hoops academia makes us jump through, friends will always be waiting on the other side, ready to start a slow clap in your honor.

We're all just a story away from each other. And we don't need an inkjet printout of everyone making the Zoolander face to know it.

But for the record, talking to an imaginary picture of an alligator is kind of weird.

MARCOS: I'm sitting inside the office of a mentor. At one point, she compliments me on my work, and I say, "You really think so?" She responds with, "Of course, why would you think otherwise?" My reply: "Because I thought you thought I wasn't very good." She tells me that I have to own up to my brilliance because the Academy will take it away from you every chance it gets. "So if I never said it out loud, here it is: you are brilliant." Then I tell her she's brilliant too, and that if she never heard me say it, "Thank you for being a great mentor." We almost break down into tears.

AYDÉ: I am going to stand here and tell you a story.

VICTOR: This land was Mexican once

STEPHANIE: Was Indian always

CASIE: And is

MARCOS: And will be again

CATALINA: We set the timer for twenty-five minutes. No internet, no cell phones, no emails or texts. We write or grade or read. We put earbuds in our ears and listen to music to drown out the loud conversations, which often are fundamentalist Christian prayer groups. By spring semester, two of us will have graduated to full headphones. When the buzzer rings, we take five minutes to check email, return phone calls, write texts. Time passes quickly. Another twenty-five, and we begin again.

This is called a pomodoro, Italian for tomato. I don't know why it's called that, and I didn't know about it before moving here. I only know that this technique has saved my life this year. It helped me concentrate enough to write my papers and grade student papers. My thoughts were clearer, the difficult passages smoothed themselves out, the grading seemed bearable. Before we began, we talked as a group about our experiences, our feelings, our fears, our doubts. We told jokes, traded information. For the first time, I didn't feel alone. More pomodoros followed; and those were followed with dinners, parties, laughing and learning. It got better.

EVERYONE: We're all just a story away from each other.

CATALINA: [QWO-LI sings underneath: "Soldier girl, soldier girl we ha we ha we ha This war is over Soldier Girl. Soldier Boy, soldier boy we ha we ha we ha This war is over Solder Boy."] I am writing this, and I am doubting myself. Is this what I, a member of the *Calmecac Collective,* should be writing? This doubt; this is internalized genocide. This is how they try to kill us. They try to steal our words, make our spirits waver, cause us to question our brilliance. They will not win. Our spirits, our brilliance, our sense of justice, our words, our stories. These will carry us forward.

ENDNOTES

1 This is a script/poem/love letter as well as a vision of transformation and resistance. At the 2012 El Mundo Zurdo conference, some of the members of the Calmecac Collective, (the "CC"), in the spirit of Gloria Anzaldúa's genre-breaking work and in our commitment to collaboration, chose to deliver a multi-voiced performance of stories. We maintain story as both political and theoretical, and intentionally break from traditional academic writing through these stories to simultaneously draw on, and create, what Malea Powell points out is "a much larger, more complicated accumulation of stories" ("Dreaming Charles Eastman" 115). Like all stories, the story we tell here is nonlinear and moves in spirals as our voices converge and diverge. This methodology draws on what Jo-Ann Archibald calls "storywork" (2008) and is informed by Indigenous, Chican@, and Latin@ scholarship that privileges stories/cuentos/testimonios as theory, including Anzaldúa (2007), Marilou Awiakta (1994), Joy Harjo (2012), LeAnne Howe (2002); Thomas King (2008), Lee Maracle (1990; 1996), M. Scott Momaday (1997), Cherríe Moraga (1993; 2000; 2011), Aurora Levins Morales (1999; 2001), Powell (1999; 2002; 2012), Leslie Marmon Silko (2006; 2012) and numerous others.

We would also like to thank those who have cleared a path for radical collective work, including the Combahee River Collective, the Cross-Blood Collective, the Crunk Feminist Collective, and Kitchen Table: Women of Color Press. This is our story, but it is also the story of others who are part of the CC and our extended community.

2 The Calmecac Collective does not take the use of the Mexican word Calmecac lightly, and we understand that without explanation, our use may seem like a paradox since we seek to challenge colonial educational structures within and outside the university. While Calmecac schooling is most often (but not always) noted for its service to the Mexica-Aztec elite, our use of it purposefully serves to challenge dominant European colonial stories (1) that Indigenous peoples across the Americas were uneducated and history-less and (2) that notions of empire/elite travel across time and space in the same fashion (i.e. that "empires" of Indigenous peoples of the Americas functioned the same as colonial empires or that the "elite" necessarily equated to contemporary socio-economic understandings). Among the practices taught in the Calmecac and one of its educational counterparts, the Telpochcalli, were song, dance, poetry, ceremonial practices, military ritual, reading (in its largest, non-exclusive definitions), and writing (again, in its largest, non-exclusive definitions).

In calling on this term/practice through our collective, we bring to the forefront our privileging of epistemologies (particularly those Indigenous-based knowledges of the Americas) that are often not only considered unnecessary in U.S. universities but also belittled. We seek to transform/transgress understandings of the Calmecac, as well as colonial constructions of valid knowledge bases/practices. It is precisely because of this that this group comes together to practice the poetic, the ceremonial, the experiential, and the historical in this piece—as well as in our everyday tactics to survive the U.S. academic complex, an elite colonial institution transgressed by neplanter@s.

WORKS CITED

Anzaldúa, Gloria. *Borderlands/La Frontera: The New Mestiza.* 3rd ed. San Francisco: Aunt Lute Books, 2007. Print.

Archibald, Jo-Anne. *Indigenous Storywork: Educating the Heart, Mind, Body, and Spirit.* Vancouver: UBC Press, 2008. Print.

Awiakta, Marilou. *Selu: Seeking the Corn-Mother's Wisdom.* Golden, CO: Fulcrum Publishing, 1994. Print.

Gould, Janice. "The Problem of Being 'Indian': One Mixed-Blood's Dilemma." *De/Colonizing the Subject: The Politics of Gender in Women's Autobiography.* Minneapolis: University of Minnesota Press, 1992. 81-87. Print.

Harjo, Joy. *Craze Brave: A Memoir.* New York: W.W. Norton, 2012. Print.

Howe, LeAnne. "The Story of America: A Tribalography." *Clearing a Path: Theorizing the Past in Native American Studies.* Ed. Nancy Shoemaker. New York: Routledge, 2002. 29-48. Print.

Justice, Daniel Heath. "Four Questions: Considering Indigenous Sexual Politics." It's Time: A Conference Commemorating 25 Years of LGBT Recognition at Texas A&M University.

Queer of Color Critiques. Texas A&M University. College Station, TX. 31 March 2010. Address.

Keating, Ana Louise, ed. *The Gloria Anzaldua Reader.* Durham: Duke UP, 2009. Print.

King, Thomas. *The Truth About Stories: A Native Narrative.* Minneapolis: Minnesota UP, 2008. Print.

Lorde, Audre. *Sister Outsider: Essays and Speeches.* Berkeley: Crossing Press, 2007. Print.

Maracle, Lee. *I Am Woman: A Native Perspective on Sociology and Feminism.* Vancouver: Press Gang, 1996. Print.

---. *Oratory: Coming to Theory.* Gallerie Publications, 1990. Women Artists' Monographs. Print.

Momaday, M. Scott. *The Man Made of Words: Essays, Stories, Passages.* New York: St. Martin's Griffin, 1998. Print.

Moraga, Cherríe L. *A Xicana Codex of Changing Consciousness.* Durham: Duke UP, 2011. Print.

---. *The Last Generation: Prose and Poetry.* Boston: South End, 1993. Print.

---. *Loving in the War Years: lo que nunca paso por sus labios.* 2nd Expanded Edition. Cambridge: South End, 2000. Print.

Morales, Aurora Levins. *Medicine Stories: History, Culture and the Politics of Integrity.* Cambridge: South End, 1999. Print.

---. *Remedios: Stories of Earth and Iron from the History of Puertorriqueñas.* Cambridge: South End, 2001. Print.

Pérez, Emma. *The Decolonial Imaginary: Writing Chicanas into History.* Bloomington, IN: Indiana UP, 1999. Print.

Powell, Malea. "Blood and Scholarship: One Mixed-Blood's Story." *Race, Rhetoric and Composition.* Ed. Keith Gilyard. Portsmouth, NH: Boynton/Cook-Heinemann, 1999. 1-16. Print.

---. "Dreaming Charles Eastman: Cultural Memory, Autobiography & Geography in Indigenous Rhetorical Histories." *Beyond the Archives: Research as a Lived Process.* Eds. Liz Rohan and Gesa Kirsch. Urbana: Southern Illinois UP, 2008. 115-127. Print.

---. "Listening to Ghosts: an alternative (non)argument." *ALT DIS: Alternatives to Academic Discourse.* Eds. Helen Fox & Christopher Schroeder. Portsmith, NH: Boynton/Cook-Heinemann, 2002. 11-22. Print.

---. "Stories Take Place: A Performance in One Act." 2012 CCCC Chair's Address. *College Composition and Communication.* 64.2. December 2012. 383-406. Print.

Silko, Leslie Marmon. *Ceremony.* Anniversary Edition. New York: Penguin, 2006. Print.

---. *Storyteller.* New York: Penguin, 2012. Print.

Wilson, Shawn. *Research is Ceremony: Indigenous Research Methodologies.* Black Point, NS: Fernwood Publishing, 2009. Print.

CONTRIBUTORS

Norma Alarcón is a noted Chicana theorist and scholar. She is Professor Emeritus of Ethnic Studies, Women and Gender Studies, and Spanish and Portuguese at the University of California, Berkeley. She received her doctorate in Latin American Literature and Culture from Indiana University. Her path breaking essays shaped Chicana Studies and paved the way for contemporary theories of Chicana subjectivity. For over twenty-five years, she owned and ran Third Woman Press (TWP), publishing key writers and texts in Chicana and Latina Studies. Writers such as Sandra Cisneros and Ana Castillo were first published in Third Woman Press; the last published book by TWP was *This Bridge Called My Back*. She resides in San Antonio and is currently working on a collection of her essays.

Stephanie Alvarez is Director of Mexican American Studies and Assistant Professor of Spanish at The University of Texas-Pan American. She is the recipient of the Outstanding Latina/o Faculty in Higher Education Award for Teaching and Service from the American Association of Hispanics in Higher Education (2011), recipient of University of Texas Board of Regents' Outstanding Teaching Award (2009), and co-founder with Tato Laviera and Jose Martinez of Cosecha Voices: Documenting the Lives of Migrant Farmworker Students (www.utpa.edu/cosechavoices). She is also the author of several essays on Latin@ identity, language, culture, and education.

Rusty Barceló is currently President of Northern New Mexico College and a national consultant for diversity and equity in higher education.

Cordelia E. Barrera teaches Latina/o literatures and the literature of the American Southwest at Texas Tech University. Her research interests include U.S. border theory, third space feminist theory, popular culture, and film. She writes movie reviews for the borderlands journal *LareDOS* and has been published in *The Quarterly Review of Film and Video*, *The Journal of Popular Culture*, and *Western American Literature.*

Stephanie Brock is a doctoral student at The University of Arizona majoring in Hispanic Linguistics. She is also currently working as a Graduate Associate in Training with the Spanish Heritage Language Program at The University of Arizona. She graduated in 2012 with an M.A. in Hispanic Linguistics and Literature and a Graduate Certificate in Mexican American Studies from the University of Texas-Pan American. In 2010, she graduated from Miami University at Ohio with a B.A. in Spanish and Latin American Studies. Her research interests include bilingualism in the U.S. and Second Language Acquisition.

The Calmecac Collective is always shifting. The authors of the piece included in this collection are Catalina Bartlett (Texas A&M University), Casie C. Cobos (Illinois State University), Marcos Del Hierro (Texas A&M University), Victor Del Hierro (Texas A&M University), Qwo-Li Driskill (Oregon State University), Aydé Enríquez-Loya (Fayetteville State University), and Stephanie Wheeler (Texas A&M University). The CC also includes Gabriela Raquel Ríos (University of Central Florida).

Tejana born feminist historian **Antonia Castañeda** received her Ph.D. in U.S. History at Stanford University. Now retired, she taught Chicana/o and Women's Studies at the University of California, Santa Barbara, and in the Departments of History at the University of Texas at Austin and St. Mary's University in San Antonio. Castañeda's scholarly publications include the prize-winning essay, "Women of Color and the Re-Writing of Western History." She is co-editor of the Chicana Matters Series, UT Press; a founding member of MALCS; a member of the Scholars Advisory Board of the Recovering the U.S. Hispanic Literary Heritage Project; serves on the Board of the Guadalupe Cultural Arts Center, and is former Chair of the San Antonio Commission on Literacy. In 2007, Castañeda received the National Association of Chicana and Chicano Studies Scholar of the Year Award.

Janie Covarrubias was born in McAllen, Texas and grew up in Reynosa, Tamaulipas, Mexico. She finished high school there and received her B.A. (2010) and M.A. (2010) in Spanish from The University of Texas Pan-American. It was at UTPA that she developed and found her passion for her Chican@ and Indigenous roots. Currently, she is pursuing a Ph.D. in Spanish at Texas Tech University.

Betsy Dahms is an Assistant Professor of Spanish at the University of West Georgia. She received her Ph.D. in Hispanic Studies and a Graduate Certificate in Gender and Women's Studies from the University of Kentucky, where she conducted her doctoral research on the life and work of Gloria Anzaldúa.

Lauren Espinoza is currently a graduate student in the M.F.A. program for poetry at Arizona State University. She is a member of The Trinity, a poetry clica from the Rio Grande Valley, and holds a Graduate Certificate in Mexican American Studies from the University of Texas-PanAmerican.

Kandace Creel Falcón earned her doctorate degree in Feminist Studies from the University of Minnesota. Her work focuses on blurring the boundaries between the creative and academic, with specific attention on the power of storytelling for Chicanas. She is also invested in new media practices, specifically through making, writing about, and presenting digital storytelling and blogging. Falcón is currently Assistant Professor of Women's and Gender Studies at Minnesota State University Moorhead.

Martha Gonzalez, born and raised in East Los Angeles, is a Chicana artivista (artist/activist), musician, feminist, music theorist, and academic. Gonzalez earned a Ph.D. from the Gender, Women, and Sexuality Studies (GWSS) department at the University of Washington in Seattle. Her academic interest in music has been fueled by her own musicianship over the last seventeen years, as a singer and percussionist for East L.A's Grammy award-winning Quetzal. In Fall of 2013, Gonzalez will begin her tenured track position at Scripps College in the Intercollegiate Chicana/o Latina/o Studies Department.

Beth Hernandez-Jason is a doctoral candidate at the University of California, Merced, where she is currently completing her dissertation on the work of John Rechy. Her reviews have appeared in *MELUS, Aztlán, Ventana Abierta,* and *Camino Real,* and her article comparing the work of María Amparo Ruiz de Burton with *Uncle Tom's Cabin* recently appeared in the eighth volume of the Recovering the U.S. Hispanic Literary Heritage series.

Roberta Hurtado is currently a doctoral candidate at the University of Texas at San Antonio. Her dissertation, entitled "Not Flesh of Empire," explores Puerto Rican women's writing as representations of creative subversive tactics made possible within third space feminist navigations of colonial matrices.

Tereza Jiroutová Kynčlová holds M.A.'s in English/American Studies, Political Science, and Gender Studies from Charles University, Prague and is currently a Ph.D. candidate in American literature. Her research focuses on Chicana literature, postcolonial studies, and feminist literary criticism. She is co-editor (with Dagmar Pegues) of *Cesta Amerikou: Antologie povídek regionálních spisovatelek [Across America: An Anthology of Short Stories by American Regional Women Writers]* (Brno: HOST, 2011), for which she translated selected Chicana writings into Czech for the first time. She is also a lecturer at the Department of Gender Studies, School of Humanities, Charles University, Prague.

María del Socorro (Coco) Gutiérrez Magallanes has been a border crosser since childhood, a MeXicana from Guadalajara-Xalisco, Sur Central-Los Angeles, and México, D.F. Coco holds a B.A. from Occidental College and an M.A. from UNAM, where she is currently a Ph.D. candidate. She is a *Nepantlera* de co-razón, a translator, and a poet.

Larissa M. Mercado-López is Assistant Professor of Women's Studies at California State University, Fresno. She received her doctorate in English/Latina Literature in 2011 from the University of Texas at San Antonio. Her research areas include Chicana feminism, maternal studies, and feminist approaches to Latina fitness and health.

Cathryn J. Merla-Watson recently graduated with a Ph.D. in American Studies, with minor certificates in both Critical Sexuality Studies and Geography, from the University of Minnesota. She is a temporary graduate faculty member and adjunct in the English Program at Texas A&M University-San Antonio. Presently she is working on a book, tentatively entitled *Spectral Assemblages: Historical Im/ Materialism and Affective Geographies of Chican@ Cultural Production,* which examines the ways in which Chicana/o cultural production engages "ghostly matters."

Orquidea Morales is currently a Ph.D. student in the Department of American Culture Studies at the University of Michigan. Her research focuses on the intersection between Horror Studies and Latina/o Studies in different cultural productions, specifically films. She received her B.A. in Spanish and Psychology from Texas State University at San Marcos, as well as a Master's in Interdisciplinary Studies with a concentration in Spanish and a Graduate Certificate in Mexican American Studies from the University of Texas-Pan American.

Carolina Núñez-Puente received an M.A. in Women's and Gender Studies (Rutgers University), an M.A. in English (University of Santiago de Compostela, Spain), and a Ph.D. in English (University of A Coruña, Spain). She is currently an Associate Professor in the English Department at the University of A Coruña, Spain. Núñez-Puente is the author of *Feminism and Dialogics: Charlotte Perkins Gilman, Meridel Le Sueur, Mikhail M. Bakhtin* (Valencia: PUV [Javier Coy], 2006). She was recently published in *Aztlán: A Journal of Chicano Studies* and is at present working on a comparative project about multiethnic literatures by women writers living in the U.S.A.

Kamala Platt is a writer, artist, profesora, activist, and independent scholar living in South Texas and at The Meadowlark Center in Kansas. She holds both a Ph.D. and M.F.A, and in her research, creative work, and activism, Platt participates in cultural practicum that engages environmental and social justice in resistancia to walls, militarization/war, environmental racism, and ecological destruction. Her first collection of poetry, *On the Line*, is available from its publisher, Wings Press.

Brenda Romero is an ethnomusicologist who has specialized in teaching New Mexican history and culture by singing, playing, and discussing the songs that span a wide history. Romero holds B.Mus. and M.Mus. degrees in Music Theory and Composition from UNM (1983, 1986), as well as a Ph.D. in Ethnomusicology from UCLA (1993). She conducted fieldwork in Mexico as a Fulbright García-Robles Scholar from 2000-2001 and from January-July 2011 in Colombia as Fulbright Colombia Scholar. In Bogotá, Romero was affiliated with the Pontificia Universidad Javeriana, where she led discussions on issues within the discipline of ethnomusicology. In addition to publishing articles, Romero is active in various musical and cultural organizations, both nationally and internationally.

Veronica Sandoval is Lady Mariposa, the academic chola from Sullivan City, Texas. She is an old school, street style spoken word artist who has been writing and performing for over twelve years. *Hecha en el Valle: (Spoken Word & Borderland Beats)* is her spoken word album. She graduated from the University of Texas Pan-American with a B.A. in English and an M.F.A. in Creative Writing. She currently resides in Pullman and works for Washington State University.

Megan Sibbett is a doctoral candidate in the English Department at the University of Texas at San Antonio. Her work focuses on transnational and queer feminisms and the critique of representations of "terrorism" within U.S. popular culture. She teaches courses within the disciplines of Women's Studies and Queer Studies and is currently the Program Coordinator at UTSA's Women's Studies Institute.

Kelli Zaytoun is Associate Professor of English at Wright State University. Her work focuses on the psychology and narration of self-concept and cognition. Publications on Anzaldúa include "New Pathways to Understanding Self, Relationship, and Cognition: Anzaldúan Re(visions) for Developmental Psychology" in *EntreMundos/Among Worlds: New Perspectives on Gloria E. Anzaldúa*, "Theorizing at the Borders: Considering Social Location in Rethinking Self and Psychological Development" in the *NWSA Journal*, and "Shifting" in

Aunt Lute Books is a multicultural women's press that has been committed to publishing high quality, culturally diverse literature since 1982. In 1990, the Aunt Lute Foundation was formed as a non-profit corporation to publish and distribute books that reflect the complex truths of women's lives and to present voices that are underrepresented in mainstream publishing. We seek work that explores the specificities of the very different histories from which we come, and the possibilities for personal and social change.

Please contact us if you would like a catalog of our books or if you wish to be on our mailing list for news of future titles. You may buy books from our website, by phoning in a credit card order, or by mailing a check with the catalog order form.

Aunt Lute Books
P.O. Box 410687
San Francisco, CA 94141
415.826.1300

www.auntlute.com
books@auntlute.com

This book would not have been possible without the kind contributions of the Aunt Lute Founding Friends:

Anonymous Donor	Diana Harris
Anonymous Donor	Phoebe Robins Hunter
Rusty Barcelo	Diane Mosbacher, M.D., Ph.D.
Marian Bremer	Sara Paretsky
Marta Drury	William Preston, Jr.